Financial Manager's
Manual and Guide

Financial Manager's Manual and Guide

Dr. Sam R. Goodman

Prentice-Hall, Inc. / Englewood Cliffs, N.J.

PRENTICE-HALL INTERNATIONAL, INC., *London*
PRENTICE-HALL OF AUSTRALIA, PTY., LTD., *Sydney*
PRENTICE-HALL OF CANADA, LTD., *Toronto*
PRENTICE-HALL OF INDIA PRIVATE LTD., *New Delhi*
PRENTICE-HALL OF JAPAN, INC., *Tokyo*

Fifth Printing . . . . . October, 1977

Library of Congress Cataloging in Publication Data

Goodman, Sam R (date)
  Financial manager's manual and guide.

  1. Business enterprises--Finance. I. Title.
HF5550.G63   658.1'5   72-14164
ISBN 0-13-315366-5

CONTENTS

1

TAKING THE GUESSWORK
OUT OF LONG RANGE PLANNING

WHAT IS FINANCIAL PLANNING?

The planning process is the manifestation of a company's determination to be the master of its own fate. It is the device by which great corporations have grown and have avoided the reactive type of situation in which they merely responded to external environmental changes. Instead, an organized, integrated planning process has been the vehicle for much of American industry to penetrate the darkness of uncertainty and provide the illumination of probability. When objectives are set, the entire scope of the effort which is made to formulate plans of action, including alternatives for contingencies, gives rise to a concentration of energies within a given period toward the systematic implementation of the corporate goals to be attained.

The term "planning" has found no truly universal definition. To some it simply means a grand design of operations highlighting the development of various aspects of a company's operations and concentrating on the objectives or the work programs for the period under scrutiny. The academicians have given us some very broad definitions of planning in the literature, but they are of little value to the operating executive who does not need a professorial exposition to plan for his future. A definition of planning is important because a true plan contains an immense scope of considerations and, unless the plan is complete on its face, the game plan of the corporation may be imperfect. A short workable definition of planning for our purposes is *that process which makes possible the probable*. In order to appreciate all of the ramifications of this short definition of planning, let us agree that planning is a total analytical process which:

   a. considers probable future occurrences.
   b. constantly measures the actual or probable attainment of performance against the desired goal of attainment.
   c. provides for contingent action which can be placed into being in order to achieve such goals.
   d. highlights various available courses of action.
   e. produces a clear, concise quantitative result.

3

f. considers not only the quantity aspects of money, but also the qualitative effects of various operating policies.

Financial planning is a powerful management tool and is most often subdivided into two general types—short-term planning and long range planning. The span of time covered by long range planning generally varies between three years and can stretch over a period of twenty years. Most often the selection of a time horizon for long range planning is dependent upon the confidence of the planners to anticipate the probable future occurrences and also the nature of the business in which this planning takes place. Most companies generally plan on a three to five year basis because it is a convenient time horizon for most operating managers. Beyond that time period, the temptation is simply too great to forecast the future by merely multiplying by a constant percentage increase or decrease. The end result, therefore, becomes meaningless beyond the fifth year. Some companies, however, especially in the extractive, energy, and precious metal industries do have the innate ability to forecast well into the future. The United Nuclear Corporation, for example, regularly makes long range financial plans up to twenty years ahead. Since long range planning deals with the future, it is essentially a process of information. It is important at this juncture to emphasize that the estimating process must not be merely an estimate based upon intuition but rather an estimate based upon a careful assessment of the *probability* of future occurrences.

THE ESSENTIALS OF A SOUND PLANNING PROGRAM

A successful planning program depends upon the ability and stability of an accounting system. Such an accounting system must be one which is information and decision oriented. An accounting system which is oriented mainly toward custodial reporting responsibilities is not a powerful enough device to produce a meaningful profit plan. Ideally, such a system must be able to create action-impelling data such as profitability by product line, by division, by geographic area and by customer and customer types. It is only in this manner that stipulated company goals which are to be attained can be compared with actual operating results; an unreliable accounting system does not permit a valid comparison of planned estimates or variances with actual results. The planning program also depends upon the existence of an efficient cost accounting system. Ideally, the cost accounting system is based upon standard cost but comprises the components of direct costing. It is important that the elements of manufacturing costs be identifiable by cost center, product type and commodity involved.

Another fundamental requirement for successful planning is a sound company organogram which delineates responsibilities and lines of authority. Planning is only meaningful if someone is held responsible for results. Ideally, there should be no question as to which individual is responsible for various major expenditures and various desired results. More importantly, the people given responsibility for achieving results must have all of the authority they need to accomplish that for which they are being held responsible. In practice, this is an extremely difficult thing for any company to accomplish. A simple example of a paradox in planning is the role of the product manager in profitability planning for the marketing segment. These individuals are often held responsible for profits, yet most often they cannot purchase the raw materials for their assigned products nor can they unilaterally establish the pricing policies for such products. Most often they cannot control manufacturing efficiency and finally, in more modern corporate advertising organizations, they cannot even control the advertising policy for their products. How then, even with the best of plans, can they truly be held responsible for the profits of their products? It follows then, that plans must be directed only at the people who can do something about them.

A profit plan is analogous to off-shore piloting in small boats. The directional chart for a company is the most useful document to enable the company to avoid the shoals and eddies of the forthcoming waters of experience. Before it can decide where it wants to take the company, the management must first find out where the company has been and in what position it now finds itself. This information can only be gleaned from reliable facts and data showing past performance. For example, in order to develop sales and production goals for some future period, management often must have a conception of the past performance of the organizational units concerned. In addition, information regarding past utilization of manufacturing capacity and the potential unused capacity is also necessary in order to assess the impact of higher sales forecasts on profits. The perspective with which to view future sales or production goals for individual products or product lines should be provided by past operating data for those products. This is not to say that past performance is the criteria for future planning goals and objectives. Very frequently what has happened in the past is a very poor assessment of future probabilities. Instead, as will be discussed in subsequent sections, an independent assessment of future courses of action is the essential ingredient for planning. Statistics of the past are only relics which can reenforce a perspective as to the possibility of attainment.

A most important requirement for a successful planning program is the degree to which the highest levels of management within a company endorse the effort and the goals of the planning process. There must be a complete commitment by the management to support the planning effort, and management must see to it that everyone involved in the planning process and its results adheres as closely as possible to plan. It can ensure this commitment by requiring periodic "variation from plan" reports with supporting analyses. A big part of the struggle to make an operating plan successful is the task of educating everyone concerned in the advantages of planning. There is a definite need for a continuing program of planning education which stresses the benefits of a formal comprehensive planning effort to all management levels. It is part of the responsibility of the financial function to demonstrate to managers exactly what can be accomplished by a firmly disciplined planning effort. It is equally important to demonstrate to other operating personnel in the company those things which a planning effort *cannot* accomplish. *Planning can never be a substitute for rational on-the-spot decision making.*

Establishing Corporate Objectives

Corporate planning certainly is not an art; it is more than a philosophy and moreover, it is probably a collection of techniques. These techniques, over a period of time, are modified by the strength and personality of the leader. Thus, a corporation can plan both from the "bottom up" or from the "top down." In other words, the textbook academic approach to corporate planning says that one must plan by first going out into the lowest echelon of corporate executive structure and seeking the probabilities of attainment for next year's performance. At successively higher levels, the same questions are asked until the final compendium is put together and the presentation made to the corporate key executive who will either ratify or invalidate the plan.

The "top down" approach is probably personified by a man like Charles Mortimer, the ex-chairman of General Foods. His strength lay in his ability to say to all his key men, "You will achieve an increase of ten percent in earnings per share each year that I will be holding this office." In effect, he went to his executives and he said, "Create me the plan that will give me this objective." This is not the type of challenge which can be satisfied by drawing a line in the middle between the "bottom up" approach and the "top down" approach. Compromise here is not a virtue. My own view leans toward the "top down" approach especially if the presence of a strong, electric leader is present. It is the strength of his vision and of his persuasion which, in effect, creates the dynamics of corporate performance.

Integral to the establishment of objectives and the need for a strong leader is the question of definition of identity. Without motivation the objectives or goal attainment process is meaningless. It is the rare company that knows how to define itself. Kinney, for example, specifically states that it is a corporation which defines itself as providing services for people, whether those services imply the availability of parking garages or funeral parlors. Mohasco is another example of a company which has defined itself. That company, which is known as a maker of carpets, furniture, and interior furnishings, has stated that it regards itself as a total supplier of home furnishings. In a similar vein, Genesco admits that they are a "total apparel" organization. Other corporations specify their objectives and goals in terms of growth of earnings per share and stipulated returns on investment. The most meaningful objective from an internal operating point of view is the establishment of a corporate goal expressed in terms of *return on investment*. Moreover, that return on investment should be narrowed down to answer the question, to what type of investment is the return being applied? My leaning is toward the concept of *return on funds employed*. That concept essentially includes the result of subtracting current liabilities from total assets. Moreover, the assets included in the base should only be those tangible assets which can be productively employed in the business. Goodwill, for example, is an asset which I would exclude from the calculation. It is the rare company which can smell, touch, see, hear and, further, manipulate goodwill. There are several factors which should be taken into account in establishing profit objectives. They are the components of the return on investment equation:

a. the profit after taxes
b. cash flow
c. retained earnings
d. the reinvestment of earnings
e. the debt-equity ratio
f. the dividend payout to stockholders
g. the capitalization rate (the reciprocal of the price-earnings ratio for a share of stock)

A consideration of the above items can highlight a number of the supply and demand factors upon corporate resources. Desired market share, which may be part of the marketing plan component of a total plan, requires a certain rate of growth of assets to support the supply of products. The growth of assets in turn requires a growth of funding. The growth in funding gives rise to the dichotomy which can see funding taking the shape of equity or debt. Manipulation of the debt-equity ratio in turn produces the degree of leverage employed by the company in its total capitalization. That leverage is often a precursor of the price-earnings ratio. That ratio in turn is one of the elements of satisfaction for the stockholder, the true owner of the business. The other element of satisfaction for the stockholder is the dividend payout rate which is a measure of profitability resulting from the implementation of the plan.

What Planning Can Accomplish

At best, a plan is a scientific estimate, arrived at after a study of a company's past performance. It is predicated upon management's estimate of future conditions within the company, the industry, and in the general economy. What can management possibly hope to gain from such an exercise, which is admittedly little more than "estimating" probable future company performance?

The mere fact of putting firm estimates on paper, thinking seriously about what is likely to take place in this department or that, and of what course overall company fortunes are likely to take, gives management an invaluable insight into the future. A formal planning procedure makes management more alert to conditions that might otherwise go unnoticed. Everyone is affected by the plan, and many people help prepare it. The result is concentrated thought about future plans, and how best to achieve company goals; management has the benefit of ideas and suggestions from personnel throughout the company.

Planning helps define objectives; it also helps develop policies. To properly plan such items as material purchases and expenditures, a company must have definite purchasing policies, inventory control techniques, and expense control techniques. Perhaps the most valuable contribution is in the area of expense control. Expense plans are a constant check on spending. No major outlay not provided for in the plan should be made without special approval.

Planning is a tremendous aid to financial strategies. In coordinating the planning effort, finance must ask and answer many questions. The most crucial question is whether the goals and objectives put forth by top management can be financed with the firm's present resources. And if the company needs additional funds to meet its aims, how can they be raised without jeopardizing the company's long-term financial position? Will the program of activity yield a profit acceptable over both a short term and a long term? Will the foreseeable profit level make it possible to attract other investors? Will there be sufficient debt capital sources if the company follows this plan or that plan? Will one objective conflict with any other company objectives? Only a realistic planning program can answer such questions satisfactorily.

A planning program also influences price-planning. A manufacturer must know how much it costs to produce a given product before it can determine a reasonable price at which to sell the product. Manufacturing companies (and all other business enterprises, for that matter) must price their products in advance of production, on the basis of reliable plans. Without sufficient foreknowledge of costs, the business may either lose money because its products are underpriced, or lose volume because they are overpriced in relation to similar products.

What else can a comprehensive plan program do for a company? Here are a few examples of what the planning process accomplishes:

- It forces management to consider—and evaluate—basic company policies.
- It forces management to look ahead, to predict conditions likely to prevail *outside the company* during the plan period.
- It compels everyone in management positions—from the president down— to take an active part in goal-setting and planning.
- It demands a sound organization, with responsibility for each function specifically assigned.
- It requires each department to lay its plans with a view to complementing plans of other units.
- It means planning for the most effective and economical use of labor, material, facilities, and capital.
- It requires complete accounting data, showing both past and current performance.
- It forces management to put down in cold figures the capital required to achieve satisfactory results.
- It instills in all management levels the habit of giving careful consideration to all factors before reaching a final decision.
- It clears up many questions (particularly in lower management levels) on basic company policies and objectives.
- It helps eliminate inefficiency and waste.
- It promotes general understanding, throughout the company, of the problems faced in each department or unit.
- It serves as a means of checking progress—or noting the lack of progress— toward stated goals; the company always knows where it is as well as where it has been.

Personnel Engaged in the Planning Process

The planning process is complex because it is composed of that aspect of planning which is formal and organized, and that aspect of planning which is largely intuitive and is, in fact, practiced daily. Much of the planning process in manufacturing oriented companies is done by significant individuals in the corporate management, the sales management, and the product management areas. It is less likely that marketing personnel as well as accounting personnel and field salesmen will participate as directly in the process as the managerial personnel first mentioned. In non-manufacturing oriented companies it is far more likely that the higher levels of corporate management and operations personnel will take over the planning process almost to the exclusion of all other types of operating personnel. One recent study found that manufacturing companies with their strong sales orientation include sales managers in their projection of sales twice as often as the non-manufacturing companies which generally are more service oriented. That same study showed that the corporate management group participates directly in the computation and projection of costs in over half of the companies that were surveyed in both the manufacturing and non-manufacturing categories. Department managers and sales and marketing personnel participate more frequently in manufacturing companies, although plant managers participated about equally in the two categories.

This discussion gives rise to the consideration of the role of financial personnel in the planning process. It is not uncommon in today's corporate organization to observe new positions which have been assigned major responsibilities for corporate planning. At this stage in corporate development, this position has been posted at a high level of management and the corporate planner is increasingly reporting directly to the president of the company. His is a unique job with an even more unique assignment. Essentially, the position is that of a coordinator, a motivator who will encourage change and stimulate thought, a teacher of methodology and lastly, a salesman whose function it is to sell the worth of the planning process. His is essentially a service job and in his role he should be helping line and staff to evaluate the plans of their operations, whether they are in decentralized or centralized organizations. In addition to this role, the corporate planner frequently becomes involved in strategic planning. I would differentiate the concept of strategic planning from long range planning only in the sense that major elements of strategy are considered in strategic planning which are not necessarily a part of traditional long range planning. Questions of long-term financing, of diversification, of future avenues of operations for the company, relocation of new physical facilities—these are all considerations for strategic planning. The traditional long range planning is almost mandated to take on the mold of contemporary knowledge within the corporation.

Financial people, per se, have no direct hand in developing many aspects of the long range plan nor, in fact, do they formulate the overall specific budget such as those dealing with production considerations. Finance merely offers technical advice to sales, marketing and production people who draw up various plans. The planner then consolidates the various estimates of operating and staff groups and presents any revisions to a planning committee and to the higher levels of management for study and approval. It is the planner's additional function to prepare and disseminate copies of the final plans to the heads of all departments and divisions.

In all of their dealings with operating personnel, finance people must remember that they have no actual control over operations. Finance must be extremely careful to avoid even giving the impression of trying to assume authority that properly belongs elsewhere. Finance is a staff function; it must not attempt to exercise control over operating or line functions, although it does have an obligation to advise these functions of questionable areas of operation, and in addition, it has a further role of assisting operational areas to optimize their decision making processes.

It follows that finance must never take operating personnel to task for unfavorable budget results. Finance merely designs, directs and coordinates the administration of the planning process. It has no actual responsibility in carrying out budgeted plans and programs. The only way finance can properly influence operations is through timely follow-up reports to the right operating personnel, revealing the progress as evidenced by cost accounting data, general accounting data and other appropriate indicators of performance. Even in a carefully run planning program, knowing what to report and how takes special skills and tact. Further booklets in this series will highlight innovations in financial organization which are permitting finance to depart from the traditional aspect of a purely service and non-control function. The concept, for instance, of a marketing controller runs slightly counter to the emphasis placed just above regarding the non-participatory role of finance in operational performance. Since it is still an innovation in corporate financial organizations, for practical purposes in discussing long range planning, the position taken above is still valid.

The personnel in the financial function who administer the planning program should have a sound background in accounting theory, supported by considerable experience and an even more considerable degree of empathy into the operational problems of various functional areas. They should know the company's general cost accounting system thoroughly, they must have an intimate knowledge of company organization and in addition, they must understand how all the various functions mesh together into an integrated whole. They must also be familiar with a company's "informal" organization. They must possess an above average analytical ability and in addition, must have the ability to write well and to know how to explain complex accounting concepts in simple, straightforward terms.

No one in finance, from the chief financial executive on down should ever be put in the position of having to take action to correct a line department's budget performance. To avoid such occurrences, most finance officers insist that company budget policy and organization be clearly detailed in written instructions for managers. This is one reason why a complete planning manual is of such value in the process.

SOURCES OF INFORMATION USEFUL IN ECONOMIC FORECASTING

The federal government is the greatest collector of basic statistics and the best source of information. Statistics are gathered and dispensed by many departments, bureaus, and commissions, including the Department of Agriculture, Department of Commerce, Bureau of the Census, Department of Labor, Bureau of Labor Statistics, Department of the Interior, Bureau of Mines, Federal Trade Commission, Board of Governors of the Federal Reserve System, Interstate Commerce Commission and many others. The Economic Report to the President by the Council of Economic Advisors contains much useful data, national in scope. This report is usually made twice a year. The assembly, tabulation, and publication of much of the data collected by the government is done by many agencies, trade organizations, and trade publications.

Useful statistical tables of many types are available in the following publications:

Standard and Poor's Corporation, *Industry Surveys*. New York: Standard and Poor's Corporation (Annually).

Federal Reserve Bulletin. Board of Governors of the Federal Reserve System, Washington, D.C. (Monthly).

Survey of Current Business. U.S. Department of Commerce, Office of Business Economics, Washington, D.C. (Monthly).

Bureau of the Census, *Statistical Abstract of the United States*. Washington, D.C.: Government Printing Office (Annually).

Monthly Labor Review. United States Department of Labor, Bureau of Labor Statistics, Washington, D.C.

Current data on population trends, surveys and estimates are found in current bulletins issued in series and in special publications of the Bureau of the Census.

A number of commodity price indexes are available. The best known are the Bureau of Labor Statistics' Wholesale Price Index and Consumer Price Index.

Data on living costs and wage levels are found in the current publications of the Department of Labor.

Current statistical data are usually reported in financial journals, trade papers, and daily newspapers as soon as they are released by the collecting agencies. Indexes of industrial production, living costs, wholesale prices, car loadings, steel production, and other indications of current trends appear regularly in metropolitan dailies. If such data are collected regularly as they appear, they are useful in judging current economic trends up to the latest possible date, before they have been digested by competent economists and appear as full-blown estimates of the current economic level.

The following services discuss business in general and trends from the businessman's viewpoint:

Daily Report for Executives. Washington, D.C.: Bureau of National Affairs, Inc. (Daily).

Kiplinger Agricultural Letter. Washington, D.C.: Kiplinger Washington Agency (Bi-weekly).

Kiplinger Washington Letter. Washington, D.C.: Kiplinger Washington Agency (Weekly).

Prentice-Hall Executive Report. Englewood Cliffs, N.J.: Prentice-Hall, Inc. (Weekly).

Whaley-Eaton American Letter. Washington, D.C.: Whaley-Eaton Service (Weekly).

Whaley-Eaton Foreign Letter. Washington, D.C.: Whaley-Eaton Service (Weekly).

Executive's Tax Report. Englewood Cliffs, N.J.: Prentice-Hall, Inc. (Weekly).

SPECIFIC PLANNING FOR COMPANY OPERATION

Recent study has shown the following among the major items included in long range forecasts by manufacturing and non-manufacturing companies:

Revenues or sales
Cash flow
Capital expenditures
Operating expenses
Net earnings
Rate of return
Source and application of funds
Percent share of market
Balance sheet
Cash dividends

In addition to the above delineated components for long range forecasts, many companies go even further than the above. Some companies include further plans regarding personnel, regarding administrative measures and further, regarding organizational patterns for the future. Behind all of the planning is a formalized system for budgeting, or planning various types of operations.

Systems for planning operations vary from company to company. Some companies prepare only a rough sales forecast and an overall production plan. Such partial planning may serve some organizations, but most firms require more comprehensive programs embracing all company operations and used concurrently for planning, coordinating and controlling. Breaking a fairly typical comprehensive planning program down to reveal its component parts, we might see a result like that shown in Figure 1.

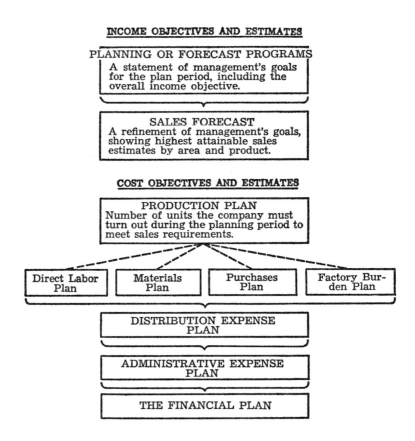

Figure 1
Components of a Comprehensive Planning Program

A comprehensive program such as that illustrated by Figure 1, is perhaps the most dynamic planning and control tool financial management can have at its disposal. Keeping expenses below revenue means setting goals for each activity in advance, then using the proper techniques to control and coordinate efforts to reach these goals, both in individual organizational units and throughout the company. By using a number of specialized plans in an integrated control system, management can establish objectives, coordinate planning and compare actual results with objectives. And all along the line, from the beginning of the period to its end, management can bring about changes as are required to keep operations on course. Generally, such changes are made in operations to bring actual performance up to performance standards. Only occasionally are budgets revised downward—and then as a last resort—unless external conditions prove the forecast upon which the budgets were made was grossly optimistic.

The planning process and the sales forecasting process are estimates of income. The remaining forecasts are estimates of the expense required to attain the planned income; they show the costs involved in manufacturing, distribution and administration and the number of finished products called for in the sales plan. Costs may be related either to time or activity. The costs related to time are often called fixed costs or period costs. Those related to volume or activity are called variable or semi-variable costs depending upon the pattern of their behavior.

- Period Costs—costs or expenses that remain relatively constant and vary more over a period of time than they do with the physical activity of volume turnover. Depreciation, taxes, insurance and administrative costs are fixed costs. These costs are shown in specialized forecasts for manufacturing and administrative activities.
- Variable Costs—these are costs or expenses that vary in direct proportion to increases or decreases in physical output or activity in a given department or work center. Variable costs come about as a result of activity. When there is no activity there is no variable cost. Should activity increase ten times, variable costs would also increase ten times. Since direct labor and material are related to volume and activity, direct labor and material costs are variable. They may be shown in a materials forecast or in a direct labor forecast. These are costs or expenses that have some characteristics of most fixed and variable costs. They fluctuate with volume and activity, but not necessarily proportionately. In fact, they tend more often to vary with capacity. Semi-variable costs are shown primarily in long range production forecasts as well as forecasts for distribution expense and administrative expense.

Each of the above types of expenses are planned for in different forecasts and each fills a definite need. Taken together, the forecasts are a means of determining total costs, the essential factor in any planning effort. Figure 2 shows how the various plans go together to make up a financial forecast.

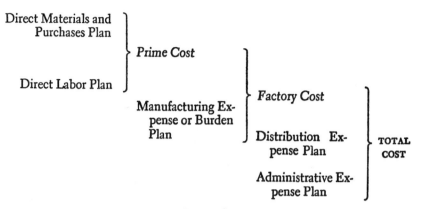

Figure 2
Development of the Financial Plan

Planning for Revenue

The sales forecast is the beginning of the overall planning process. It is a company's best estimate of how much of each of its products it expects to sell during the planning period. It is usually broken down to show anticipated sales volume by months, weeks or even days. Anticipated sales are also classified by product, product line and are often broken down into anticipated sales for geographic or customer classifications. Most sales forecasts show anticipated sales for each product or product line in terms of both dollar volume and product units.

The sales forecast is the foundation of all company planning. The marketing executive and other sales management personnel rely heavily on past sales figures in making the sales forecasts, but they also attempt to gauge the effect of business and economic conditions, competition and other factors on future sales. In making the sales forecasts, sales management must be extremely careful to take all factors into account and come up with the most accurate forecast possible with available facts and figures. Likewise, finance must make as many facts and figures available to marketing as it possibly can. The accuracy of all other plans for profitable activity depends on the accuracy of the sales forecasts. The need for accuracy is so important in the sales forecasting phase of the overall planning process that many companies have developed simulation models to assist them in controlling the variables which enter into the forecasting picture. Sales forecasting, especially in the consumer goods industry, is one of the most complicated of all planning activities. And because forecasts of sales lead to the next evolutionary step—that of inventory management and customer service—completely new sets of variables enter upon the scene and make even more important the recognition that correct sales forecasting can minimize distribution costs. IBM has developed a data processing program called Consumer Goods System (COGS). The system is composed of two parts, one which deals with specific forecasting and the other which deals with allocations. Both of these programs are designed to overcome patterns of consumption which shift constantly, as well as external environmental factors such as seasonality of products. Used properly, the program's capability to simulate can assist the user in predicting in advance the accuracy of given forecast models. It is not the place at this point in a booklet dealing with long range planning to specifically explain mathematical models. Another booklet in the series will go further into variations on these themes. Following is a suggested table of contents for a sales plan. Major programs should be separately described in each case:

1. Projection of sales volume by product line—annually for five years
2. Price and gross margin projection by product line—annually for five years
3. Market share by product line—annually for five years
4. Total market potential by product line—annually for five years
5. Projected changes in capital required for marketing operations—by year of occurrence. (Examples would be new fleet of delivery trucks, purchase of warehouses, or the new plan of dealer financing).
6. Any major changes planned in the marketing operations.
7. Sales projection by new product line—annually for five years.
8. Gross margin projection by new product line—annually for five years.
9. New capital investment in support of new products by product line—annually for five years.

It is important to note that this plan projects the marketing operation only. If new products require new production facilities, then capital spending for such facilities will be shown in a capital program, even though it will then be identified with relevant marketing programs.

Figure 3 shows a completed sales forecast such as some companies might use in planning for revenues. Notice that the first quarter sales are broken down to show anticipated sales in each of the first three months. The forecast, sometimes called a sales plan, reveals estimated sales by product and by sales district. This overall forecast is a consolidation of sales estimates from individual sales territories.

	Totals		Northern District		Southern District		Eastern District		Western District	
Product A—$5.00 per unit	Units	Amount	Units	Amount	Units	Amount	Units	Amount	Units	Amount
January	3,800	$19,000	1,000	$ 5,000	800	$ 4,000	1,400	$ 7,000	600	$ 3,000
February	4,200	21,000	1,200	6,000	900	4,500	1,500	7,500	600	3,000
March	4,850	24,250	1,500	7,500	950	4,750	1,750	8,750	650	3,250
Total First Quarter	12,850	$64,250	3,700	$18,500	2,650	$13,250	4,650	$23,250	1,850	$ 9,250
2nd Quarter	5,450	27,250	2,000	10,000	1,000	5,000	1,750	8,750	700	3,500
3rd Quarter	5,750	28,750	2,200	11,000	1,000	5,000	1,800	9,000	750	3,750
4th Quarter	6,250	$31,250	2,500	$12,500	1,000	5,000	2,000	$10,000	750	$ 3,750
	30,300	$151,500	10,490	$52,000	5,650	$28,250	10,200	$51,000	4,050	$20,250
Product B—$2.00 per unit										
January	5,800	$11,600	2,000	$ 4,000	1,000	$ 2,000	2,000	$ 4,000	800	$ 1,600
February	6,900	11,800	2,500	5,000	1,200	2,400	2,200	4,400	1,000	2,000
March	7,900	15,800	3,000	6,000	1,300	2,600	2,500	5,000	1,100	2,200
Total First Quarter	20,600	$39,200	7,500	$15,000	3,500	7,000	6,700	$13,400	2,900	$ 5,800
2nd Quarter	8,300	16,600	3,000	6,000	1,500	3,000	2,600	5,200	1,200	2,400
3rd Quarter	8,600	17,200	3,200	6,400	1,500	3,000	2,700	5,400	1,200	2,400
4th Quarter	9,200	$18,400	3,000	$ 6,000	1,700	$ 3,400	3,000	$ 6,000	1,500	$ 3,000
	$46,700	$91,400	$16,700	$33,400	$8,200	$16,400	$15,000	$30,000	$6,800	$13,600

Figure 3

Completed Sales Forecast (Sales Plan)

The Production Plan

The major planning tool for production activity is the production plan which is based directly upon the sales forecast. The production plan provides a means of coordinating sales, production and inventories. It is an estimate of production quantities necessary during the planning period to satisfy sales requirements.

The production plan includes estimates for direct labor, for materials, for purchases, and for the overhead attendant to the. activity contained in the forecast. The primary production plan shows only the number of finished products necessary to fill sales requirements. It ordinarily has no cost breakdowns since costs are supplied in other plans which comprise the primary production program.

A table of contents for such a plan would include the following:

1. Replacement plan listing major and minor capital projects to replace existing plant—annually for five years.
2. New plant and equipment for existing production—annually for five years.
3. New plant and equipment for new products (as specified in the marketing sales plan)—annually for five years.
4. Production costs trends by production plant or by product line—annually for five years.
5. New processes and techniques with approximate date of installation and effect on cost.

The new projects detailed in this plan should be coordinated with the new products detailed in the sales plan. The new developments should make reference to engineering feasibility studies where they exist. Care should be taken to avoid rough guesses whenever possible. Projecting five years in the future is understandably difficult, however, the plan loses its value as a management tool if the financial manager resorts to "rough estimates." Since we are dealing with somewhat uncertain forecasts, it is important that the substance of the major programs be described as fully as possible, at least in the supporting text of the report, if quantification is not feasible. Where new facilities are recommended, the justification must be stated in both absolute terms and in terms of alternative courses of action which may be available.

The actual procedures used in formulating production plans vary from company to company. In many small firms, the production executive prepares the plan himself, with little or no help from subordinates. He bases his estimates of production requirements on the sales forecast, and translates sales requirements into a balanced production program. The production plan is then approved, either by the president or by the budget committee.

But in larger companies—particularly those with decentralized production operations—division production managers and even workcenter foremen play a very important part in plan preparation. In these companies, plant accounting departments and production supervisors often work together to prepare cost estimates for each production department or workcenter. In some cases, the central finance office provides each production manager (or the production executive) with cost accounting data on production capabilities and labor and material costs, and the planning director coordinates the data as necessary.

At the same time as plans are being made for the annual operating plan, the company may be planning well beyond the period covered by the plan. In addition to a well-documented plan for the coming year's operations, divisional managers are often asked to submit a three to five year forecast of operations, showing probable volume, new product development plans, research programs, personnel needs, planned organizational changes, and inventory and facility requirements.

The cost estimates for workcenters ultimately become actual operations plans for the workcenters; when collected for all workcenters, they become divisional or departmental plans. Likewise, when these plans are combined, they comprise the overall production plan. Figure 4 is a simplified production plan summary, showing requirements for one product during the plan period.

Production Plan Summary—Product "A"	
Required by sales forecast	$30,300
Desired ending inventory, finished goods	1,000
Total production required	$31,300
Less beginning inventory, finished goods	1,450
Planned production for year	$29,850

Figure 4
Simplified Production Plan Summary

More elaborate production summaries than the one shown in Figure 4 are used in many large production operations; they contain such supplementary information as:

- Number of operating days in each month
- Required daily production rate
- Percentage of capacity at which operations are scheduled through the plan period
- Number of factory workers involved (sometimes stated in terms of direct and indirect hours per week, month, or quarter)

• Machine capacities and machine-hours required by workcenter or production area

With information such as this, every department or unit whose work is related to production activities can plan its activities to complement the manufacturing operation.

Using the production plan summary, production prorates or allocates the required total output throughout the plan period on the basis of such considerations as these:

• Having a sufficient inventory of finished products on hand at all times to meet sales requirements
• Keeping inventory levels of raw material and components within reasonable limits
• Manufacturing the products as economically as possible
• Maintaining a fairly stable production rate
• Attaining maximum utilization of plant capacity

This results in a detailed production plan, with quantities allocated to each month, quarter, etc. Figure 5 illustrates such a plan, broken down to show desired production quantities for two products over a plan period of one year.

Notice that neither the production summary in Figure 4 nor the detailed production plan show costs. Although many companies do include costs in these plans, most companies show cost figures for the first time in the more specialized expense plans that are actually components of the overall production plan. These include the material and purchases plans, the direct labor plan and the factory burden or overhead plan.

The Materials Plan

The materials plan is a statement of estimated quantities of material (both components and raw materials) needed to meet production requirements. The materials plan may or may not include material costs, depending on whether or not the company utilized a purchases plan in addition to the materials plan. Where both plans are used, the materials plan is likely *not* to include costs.

The materials that go into production are classed as either direct or indirect materials. Direct (or productive) materials are generally considered as all materials or parts that become integrated into the finished product and are readily identifiable with the cost of the finished item. Indirect materials are necessary to the manufacturing process, but they are not directly traceable to specific production efforts. Such items as lubricating oils, solvents, and other maintenance supplies are generally classed as indirect materials.

DETAILED PRODUCTION PLAN

PRODUCT A

	Sales Forecast R'qments	Less Finished Goods Inventory	Total Production R'qd.
January	300,000	240,000	60,000
February	225,000	10,000	215,000
March	200,000	50,000	150,000
Total 1st Quarter	725,000	300,000	425,000
2nd Quarter	600,000	200,000	400,000
3rd Quarter	550,000-	100,000	450,000
4th Quarter	400,000	50,000	350,000
Total	2,275,000	650,000	1,625,000

PRODUCT B

	Sales Forecast R'qments	Less Finished Goods Inventory	Total Production R'qd.
January	150,000	75,000	75,000
February	100,000	25,000	75,000
March	90,000	20,000	70,000
Total 1st Quarter	340,000	120,000	220,000
2nd Quarter	300,000	100,000	200,000
3rd Quarter	280,000	140,000	140,000
4th Quarter	320,000	80,000	240,000
Total	1,240,000	440,000	800,000

Figure 5
Detailed Production Plan

The materials plan usually includes only direct materials, leaving maintenance supplies and other indirect materials to be included in the manufacturing expense or burden plan.

Those responsible for formulating the materials plan estimate as closely
as possible the material quantities called for in the production plan, making

Materials Plan—Unit Requirements by Product
and by Time Period

Part or Material #	PRODUCT A		PRODUCT B		TOTAL UNITS MATERIAL R'QD
	Production Planned	Material R'qd	Production Planned	Material R'qd	
Part #47					
January	60,000	60,000	75,000	NONE	60,000
February	215,000	215,000	75,000	NONE	215,000
March	150,000	150,000	70,000	NONE	150,000
Total 1st Qtr	425,000	425,000	220,000	NONE	425,000
2nd Qtr	400,000	400,000	200,000	NONE	400,000
3rd Qtr	450,000	450,000	140,000	NONE	450,000
4th Qtr	350,000	350,000	240,000	NONE	350,000
GRAND TOTAL FOR YEAR	1,625,000	1,625,000	800,000	———	1,625,000
Part #58					
January	60,000	60,000	75,000	75,000	135,000
February	215,000	215,000	75,000	75,000	290,000
March	150,000	150,000	70,000	70,000	220,000
Total 1st Qtr	425,000	425,000	220,000	220,000	645,000
2nd Qtr	400,000	400,000	200,000	200,000	600,000
3rd Qtr	450,000	450,000	140,000	140,000	590,000
4th Qtr	350,000	350,000	240,000	240,000	590,000
GRAND TOTAL FOR YEAR	1,625,000	1,625,000	800,000	800,000	2,425,000
Part #19 (Note: Anticipate approximately 20,000 of this item on hand beginning January)					
January	60,000	40,000	75,000	75,000	115,000
February	215,000	215,000	75,000	75,000	290,000
March	150,000	150,000	70,000	70,000	220,000
Total 1st Qtr	425,000	405,000	220,000	220,000	625,000
2nd Qtr	400,000	400,000	200,000	200,000	600,000
3rd Qtr	450,000	450,000	140,000	140,000	590,000
4th Qtr	350,000	350,000	240,000	240,000	590,000
GRAND TOTAL FOR YEAR	1,625,000	1,605,000	800,000	800,000	2,405,000

Figure 6
Detailed Materials Plan

allowances for normal spoilage, waste, and scrap. Quantities of each direct material or part are shown by month, quarter, or other convenient periods, taking such factors as normal delivery time, economic order quantities, and available storage space into consideration. Figure 6 shows a detailed materials plan, broken down by product and by month and quarter for a plan period of one year.

Purchases Plan—By Product and by Time Period			
Part #47	*Units Required*	*Unit Cost*	*Total Cost*
January	60,000	$3.00	$ 180,000
February	215,000		645,000
March	150,000		450,000
Total 1st Qtr	425,000		$1,275,000
2nd Qtr	400,000		1,200,000
3rd Qtr	450,000		1,350,000
4th Qtr	350,000		1,050,000
GRAND TOTAL FOR YEAR	1,625,000		$4,875,000
Part #58			
January	135,000	.20	$ 27,000
February	290,000		58,000
March	220,000		44,000
Total 1st Qtr	645,000		$ 129,000
2nd Qtr	600,000		120,000
3rd Qtr	590,000		118,000
4th Qtr	590,000		118,000
GRAND TOTAL FOR YEAR	2,425,000		$ 485,000
Part #19			
January	115,000	.40	$ 46,000
February	290,000		116,000
March	220,000		88,000
Total 1st Qtr	625,000		$ 250,000
2nd Qtr	600,000	.45*	270,000
3rd Qtr	590,000		265,000
4th Qtr	590,000		265,500
GRAND TOTAL FOR YEAR	2,405,000		$1,051,000

* Anticipate 5¢ price increase beginning 3rd quarter.

Figure 7
Purchases Plan

The Purchases Plan

If the materials plan is accurate, the company's purchasing section or department can make very accurate predictions of the prices of materials over the plan period. Purchasing submits its estimates in a purchases plan; in addition to quantities, the purchases plan may also show the timing of purchases and estimated material costs. Figure 7 shows a fairly typical purchases plan, revealing estimated costs of materials used in production.

The materials and purchases plans are essential for determining direct material costs. Direct material is one of the two elements of prime cost, which also includes direct labor. The direct labor plan is therefore a necessary step toward determining prime costs.

The Direct Labor Plan

The direct labor plan is an estimate of total direct labor needed to meet planned production requirements. The direct labor plan may show direct labor costs only, or it may indicate both direct labor hours and their cost.

Like material costs, labor costs are classed as either direct or indirect. Direct labor costs are the wages paid to workers engaged directly in specific, identifiable production operations. While labor traceable to a distinct production phase is direct labor, indirect labor *supports* direct productive activity. In a sense, it is incidental to the production effort. Indirect labor costs include all costs other than direct labor, including such costs as supervisory salaries, wages paid to storekeepers, and maintenance labor expense. These charges are generally included (along with indirect materials costs) in the factory burden or overhead plan.

Production prepares the direct labor plan, working closely with personnel and cost accounting. Once complete, the plan becomes part of the overall production plan and is submitted to the plan or finance committee for approval. The direct labor plan provides finance the information it needs in determining cash requirements for direct labor. And by revealing the total cost of direct labor, it also affords a means of controlling direct labor expense.

To pinpoint responsibility for control purposes, direct labor hours are usually shown in the labor plan by product and by workcenter. If the company has a standard hour system, it can compute direct labor costs by multiplying the standard hours required for each unit of production by the total units called for in the production plan, then multiplying this figure by the average wage rate per standard hour. For example, if the production plan calls for 30,000 finished products, and each unit requires two standard hours to complete, there is obviously a direct labor demand of 60,000 standard hours. Multiplying this figure by the average wage rate of, say, $3.00 per standard hour, the company arrives at the direct labor cost to produce the desired number of finished product units—$180,000.

Direct labor costs may also be determined by relating labor cost to some other measure of production activity, such as direct machine hours or direct material costs. For example, historical ratios of direct labor hours to physical output are often used in computing direct labor costs. Many companies simply have workcenter foremen estimate the direct labor hours required to meet

Direct Labor Plan—First Quarter Only					
Product A	Units to be Produced	Standard Hours per Unit	Total Standard Hours	Rate	Total Cost
January					
Workcenter 1	40,000	.5	20,000	$3.00	$ 60,000
Workcenter 2	10,000	.5	5,000	2.00	10,000
Workcenter 3	10,000	.5	5,000	2.00	10,000
February					
Workcenter 1	30,000	.3	9,000	$3.00	$ 27,000
Workcenter 2	42,000	.2	8,400	2.00	16,800
Workcenter 3	15,000	.8	12,000	2.00	24,000
March					
Workcenter 1	12,000	.1	1,200	$3.00	$ 3,600
Workcenter 2	34,000	1.0	34,000	2.00	68,000
Workcenter 3	18,000	2.0	36,000	2.00	72,000
TOTAL	211,000		130,600		$291,400
Product B					
January					
Workcenter 1	8,000	.5	4,000	$3.00	$ 12,000
Workcenter 2	10,000	.2	2,000	2.00	4,000
Workcenter 3	1,500	.6	900	2.00	1,800
February					
Workcenter 1	10,000	.5	5,000	$3.00	$ 15,000
Workcenter 2	8,500	.1	850	2.00	1,700
Workcenter 3	9,000	.2	4,500	2.00	9,000
March					
Workcenter 1	50,000	.3	15,000	$3.00	$ 45,000
Workcenter 2	20,000	.8	16,000	2.00	32,000
Workcenter 3	15,000	.5	7,500	2.00	15,000
TOTAL	132,000		55,750		$132,500

Figure 8
Direct Labor Plan

planned output for each workcenter, then combine workcenter estimates to arrive at a total direct labor figure. Figure 8 shows a direct labor plan broken down to reveal labor costs by product, time period, and workcenter.

The Burden or Overhead Plan

Prime costs (direct material and direct labor) commonly represent only about half of total costs. "Overhead" accounts for the remaining expense. Most overhead charges are fairly constant; they do not vary in direct relation to production activity. Even if the plant remains idle (or nearly so), staff salaries, many sales expenses, advertising charges, indirect labor costs, insurance premiums, taxes, the depreciation burden, and many other expenses continue to accrue.

The manufacturing expense of factory burden figure includes both indirect labor and indirect material expended in production or supporting activities. It includes such items as power, fuel, water, general supervisory expense, tool control expense, building and equipment maintenance charges, depreciation, real and personal property taxes on production facilities, and inspection and engineering costs.

Allocating these costs to specific products and workcenters is sometimes difficult. But in any effective plan and cost control effort, overhead must be charged to the particular department responsible for incurring the expense. Take the cost of power, for example; it is normally an indirect cost and therefore included in the manufacturing expense plan. As difficult as it may appear to accomplish the task, each production department must be held accountable for the power it uses in performing its function in the power (as well as the amount of other indirect items) used in the workcenter in comparison with planned amounts. Planning and cost accounting overlap when it comes to allocating factory burden.

Allocating Expense Burden

Manufacturing expense burden may be allocated in several ways. A common method is to relate burden to direct labor cost. In this method, the burden rate is found by dividing total burden by total direct labor cost for a given accounting period. The resulting rate is then applied to each workcenter according to the number of direct labor hours planned. For example, suppose a company's total direct labor cost is $180,000, with a total manufacturing expense burden of $18,000. The burden rate is 10 percent ($18,000 ÷ $180,000 = .10). Suppose there are nine workcenters, and that each of them has budgeted $20,000 in direct labor charges. By applying the burden rate of 10 percent to the planned direct labor expense, we get the manufacturing expense burden for each workcenter, which is $2,000. It is quite simple to prorate this figure throughout the plan period, or to break it down to show how much overhead should be charged to each product or product line.

The direct labor method is widely used, primarily because of its simplicity. The primary objection to this method of allocating manufacturing burden is that it introduces a variable—the hourly pay-rate—that has little connection with actual productive effort. The cost of direct labor in a given workcenter is ordinarily no indication of that unit's productivity in comparison to the output of similar units. Another method of allocating manufacturing burden—the direct labor-hours method—eliminates the variable and takes effort more into account. To use the direct labor-hours technique, the general factory burden is divided by the total direct labor-hours. The resulting rate is used in allocating burden just as the rate for total labor cost was used in the previous example.

Two other methods are in common use for allocating manufacturing expense burden: the direct materials and labor method, and the machine-hour method. The first of these is similar to the direct labor method just

Partial Manufacturing Expense Plan—First Quarter Only			
	Workcenter 1	Workcenter 2	Workcenter 3
January			
Supervisory salaries	$23,000	$10,000	$ 9,200
Indirect labor	15,000	8,200	3,400
Maintenance	5,000	4,000	4,800
Depreciation	6,500	4,800	3,100
Insurance	2,000	1,400	600
TOTALS	$51,500	$29,200	$21,100
February			
Supervisory salaries	$21,000	$18,000	$11,000
Indirect labor	13,500	6,000	2,100
Maintenance	4,200	3,450	4,700
Depreciation	3,400	800	4,000
Insurance	2,100	900	2,100
TOTALS	$44,200	$29,150	$23,900
March			
Supervisory salaries	$20,800	$12,400	$ 9,400
Indirect labor	6,400	3,300	3,200
Maintenance	4,300	3,100	4,550
Depreciation	800	4,600	3,170
Insurance	700	1,250	1,130
TOTALS	$33,000	$24,650	$21,450

Figure 9
Manufacturing Expense Plan

discussed, except that it combines direct labor and direct material costs. The machine-hour method allocates overhead according to the number of hours various machines are operated. Figure 9 shows a manufacturing expense plan developed under the most commonly used method for allocating burden, the direct labor method.

The Distribution Expense Budget

Distribution expenses include all costs involved in selling, distributing, and delivering products to customers. Distribution expense is overhead, and as such may even be included in the general administrative plan instead of in a separate, specialized plan. Distribution expenses are generally allocated to individual products in much the same way that manufacturing burden is allocated for planning purposes. The allocation is likely to be done in a much more arbitrary manner, however.

While distribution expenses are determined and allocated largely as a help in product pricing, the primary objective in preparing distribution expense plans is to achieve a proper relationship between sales expense and sales volume or income. Distribution expense plans are usually broken down to show planned marketing expenses (including advertising and sales promotion costs) for sales territories and districts. Such a breakdown gives sales managers and salesmen definite expense goals and makes them personally responsible for attaining those goals. The distribution expense plan is a means of controlling sales expenses, of keeping sales costs in line with anticipated results.

Administrative Expense Plan

Administrative expenses include all costs except those incurred in manufacturing and distributing the product. They relate to the general supervision and services performed as a benefit to the total business rather than in connection with any one department or function. Administrative costs are those expenses that cannot be properly classified as either manufacturing or distributing costs.

The administrative expense plan generally includes the salaries and other compensation of officers, directors, and other executives, plus the costs of running their offices or departments; the expense of common services; and miscellaneous expenses such as dues, donations, legal fees and certain tax payments. Obviously, costs such as these are relatively fixed; they show little or no change in relation to changes in production or sales activity. This means that the administrative expense plan is likely to be based almost solely on historical cost figures. Because most administrative costs are not variable, it is fairly simple to estimate future expenditures even for cost items not included in previous plans.

The Manpower Plan

The rapid change of technology requires careful planning of new talents and types of experts required in future years, as well as the normal requirements for more ordinary skills. For example, data processing experts, biochemists or astrophysicists may be needed within five years. Companies often find that a nationwide shortage exists in certain fields and most plan to develop full departments and staff groups from within the firm. The objectives of this plan should be carefully coordinated with the sales and production plans.

The Five Year Financial Plan

As the marketing, production and manpower plans take shape, the major document, the financial plan, will take form along with them. The results of careful planning will be an accurate picture of the future trends and prospects of the company. Three examples of the results of forward financial planning illustrate these benefits:

1. A computer manufacturer found that its marketing plan was so encouraging that its growth over the next five years was limited only by the capital required to match the rapidly growing sales. The financial manager recognized that the company's stock was well received by the public and carried a high price-earnings ratio. Since the sales growth was highly predictable, the risks were considered reasonable in spite of the high growth rate shown in the sales plan. The decision was made to conduct regular stock issues in future years to provide the growth capital required.

2. An airplane engine manufacturer was faced with a declining market as the military converted to missiles and rockets. The financial projection showed large quantities of cash being generated for future years as production facilities were phased out. However, the manpower plan indicated substantial risks. The firm tried to convert rapidly to the new technologies. This technical expertise was becoming obsolete. The decision was made to use the cash to buy small technically oriented firms to help make the transition.

3. A consumer goods manufacturer found that its market would continue to grow at a steady rate. Its production plan showed that the sales increase could be handled readily and that manpower and plan facilities would, in fact, outstrip the sales growth. The financial picture looked stable and secure. The decision was made to make a major effort in new product

development and new market development for existing products. A heavy market research and product planning effort was required, plus the development of an international division for sale of existing products.

PUTTING THE LONG RANGE PLAN INTO WORK

The techniques of developing balance sheets, operating statements and capital budgets are well known to most students of accounting. There is really very little difference in constructing a balance sheet or other similar financial statements specifically for a five year plan as there is for developing one for either a one or two year plan or even for a year's actual results. It should be borne in mind, however, that the five year plan does not contain so much detailed information. Examples of formats for these reports are shown in Figures 10, 11, and 12. In the balance sheet and operating statements, comparative data of recent actual performance are included. A capital plan shows a breakdown into three major groups. The replacement and volume expansion portion which deals with existing product lines and new products are shown in the third category.

Once the plans are put down on paper, they should become a tool; not merely something to file. They are first submitted to the executive committee for suggested alteration. They then go to the board of directors. Once approved, they become the basis for implementation by line department.

The five year financial plan will be developed in less detail than the annual capital budget and profit plan. This does not mean that the two are unrelated, rather that it will be necessary to establish a definite link between the first year of the financial plan and the capital budget and profit plan which is subsequently prepared covering that year. To establish this linkage without at the same time creating an inordinate burden in the planning process is a matter of some skill. However, it is an absolute necessity if we are to be certain that the same general concepts and objectives are present in the two sets of forecasts. Unless the two systems are consistent, there is no basis on which to approve the year's capital budget and profit plan, since there is no certainty that they are consistent with the long range financial plan for the company. In order to avoid the creation of unnecessary detail, it is desirable to have the operating departments comment in an affirmative fashion that their budgets and profit plans are, in fact, consistent with the approved long range financial plan for their activity.

Once the long range planning system has been installed, it is necessary to establish an orderly method of recording actual results against plan. This is desirable to provide a means of revising the company's goals and objectives and to provide insight into better means of forecasting.

	Comparative Data		Projected Years				
	Two Years Ago	Last Year	1st	2nd	3rd	4th	5th

Sales
Product Line I
Product Line II
Product Line III

Direct Costs
Material
Labor
Variable Selling
Variable Overhead

Fixed Overhead
Wages & Salaries
Depreciations
Other

Corporate S & A
Salaries
Other

Profit Before Taxes

Other Income
Other Expenses

Income Taxes

Profit After Tax

Figure 10
Projected Operating Statement

It is also necessary to evaluate the performance of the various managers who are responsible for the forecasts that are built into the plan. Some managers are characteristically "target" forecasters; that is, they make a forecast which does not provide for the possibility of a normal amount of contingencies. Consequently, their forecasts are achievable only under optimum circumstances. At the other extreme, there are managers who retain too much of a "cushion" which will permit them to offset unfavorable performance.

	Comparative Data		*Projected Data (5 years)*				
	Two Years Ago	Last Year	1st	2nd	3rd	4th	5th

Cash
Receivables External
Receivables Internal
Inventories
Other Current Assets

Internal Dept & Equity

Fixed Asset Old
Fixed Assets
Future Purchases
Less Depres. Res.

Other Assets

Payable-External
Payable-Internal
Accruals

L.T. Debt-External
L.T. Debt-Internal

Reserves
Net Worth-Bal. Forward
Plus Earnings
Less Dividends

Plus New Capital
Stock

Figure 11
Projected Balance Sheet

A post-audit will help to expose both types of forecasting. Suffice it to say that all planning should be on the basis of *probable attainment*.

The post-audit must be timed so as to provide a useful measure of actual performance and still be early enough to give information that can be utilized in the preparation of new plans. The post-audit will rarely be of value in correcting deficiencies in the particular project under audit, because the post-audit cannot really be undertaken until some reliable experience has been obtained from the project. By the time this experience is available, the project would generally have been so fully committed as to be irreversible. When dealing with construction projects or the purchase of equipment, the post-audit can usually take place once the facility is operating under so-called normal conditions. When dealing with the introduction of a new product, the post-audit can begin once sales have reached normal commercial levels. This may mean in general that the post-audit might take place at the end of the first third or quarter of the project's estimated life.

	1st. Yr.	2nd Yr.	3rd Yr.	4th Yr.	5th Yr.
Replacement Program					
Machinery					
Land & Building					
Automotive					
Marketing					
Other					
Volume Expansion					
Machinery					
Land & Building					
Automotive					
Marketing					
Other					
New Product					
Machinery					
Land & Building					
Automotive					
Marketing					
Other					

Figure 12
Projected Capital Budget

EXAMPLES OF A MODERN INTEGRATED PLANNING FORMAT

Introducing change and creativity into the planning process requires strong hearts and firm convictions. The example of an integrated planning format, which follows, is a type of format which could be used by a consumer products company finding itself in a highly competitive marketing situation:

a. Annual and Long Range Profit Forecast (Graph) (Figure 13)
b. Growth, Mature, Non-Growth, Development—by Products (Numerical Analysis) (Figure 14)
c. Division Profit and Loss Statement (Figure 15)
d. Division Profit and Loss Statement—Variation Analysis (Figure 16)
e. Statement of Financial Position (Figure 17)
f. Financial Evaluations of Return on Funds Employed (Figure 18)
g. Profit and Loss Statement—Product Groups (Figure 19)
h. Profit and Loss Statement—Grocery Product Groups (Figure 20)
i. Profit and Loss Statements—Individual Product Highlights (Figure 21)
j. Product Marketing Expense Summary (Figure 22)
k. Market Position—by Product (Figure 23)
l. Indirect Expenses (Figure 24)
m. Research Project Expenses (Figure 25)
n. Graphic Analysis of Return on Funds Employed (Figure 26)
o. Forecasted Analysis of Return on Funds Employed (Figure 27)
p. Analysis of Current Assets and Total Cost of Sales (Figure 28)
q. Inventory Forecast (Figure 29)

Wherever it has been deemed important, illustrative numbers have been inserted.

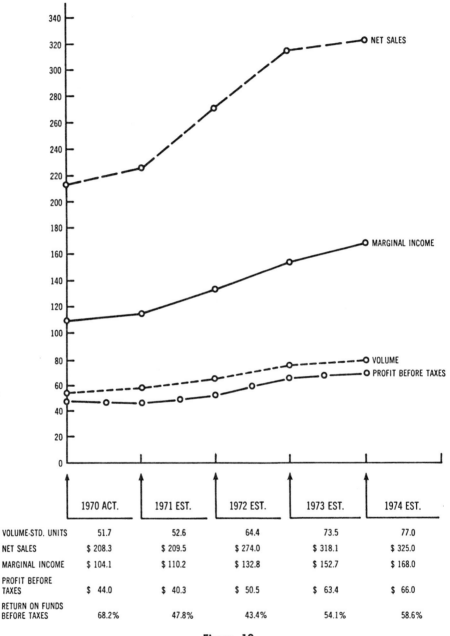

ANNUAL PROFIT FORECAST FISCAL YEAR 1971
(000,000'S)

	1970 ACT.	1971 EST.	1972 EST.	1973 EST.	1974 EST.
VOLUME-STD. UNITS	51.7	52.6	64.4	73.5	77.0
NET SALES	$ 208.3	$ 209.5	$ 274.0	$ 318.1	$ 325.0
MARGINAL INCOME	$ 104.1	$ 110.2	$ 132.8	$ 152.7	$ 168.0
PROFIT BEFORE TAXES	$ 44.0	$ 40.3	$ 50.5	$ 63.4	$ 66.0
RETURN ON FUNDS BEFORE TAXES	68.2%	47.8%	43.4%	54.1%	58.6%

Figure 13
Annual and Long Range Profit Forecast

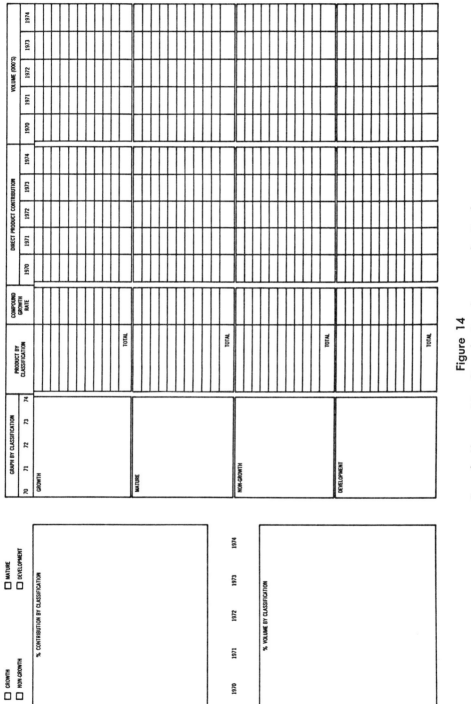

Figure 14

Growth, Mature, Non-Growth, Development—by Products

PROFIT & LOSS STATEMENTS
1971-1974
(000'S)

DIVISION SUMMARY

LONG RANGE PLAN

── 1971 LATEST ESTIMATE ──

── 1971 ──

	MARCH QUARTER	YEAR	FINAL JUNE QUARTER	SEPTEMBER QUARTER	DECEMBER QUARTER	MARCH QUARTER	YEAR	1972	1973	1974
PHYSICAL VOLUME (CUST.)										
GROCERY										
BULK										
TOTAL VOLUME										
GROSS SALES (CUST.)										
ALLOWANCES FX DEALS										
TRANSPORTATION										
WAREHOUSING										
CASH DISCOUNT										
NET SALES (CUST.)										
VARIABLE COST OF GOODS SOLD										
MARGINAL INCOME (CUST.)										
DIRECT COSTS										
MANUFACTURING OVERHEAD										
MARKETING PROMOTIONS										
MARKETING OTHER										
PRODUCT RESEARCH										
TOTAL DIRECT COSTS										
DIRECT PRODUCT CONTRIBUTION										
INDIRECT COSTS										
MANUFACTURING OVERHEAD										
MARKETING										
RESEARCH										
GEN'L & ADMINISTRATIVE										
TOTAL INDIRECT COSTS										
OPERATING PROFIT										
INTER-CO. GROSS PROFIT										
OTHER INCOME (EXPENSE)										
PROFIT BEFORE TAXES										
ADD INTERDIVISION PBT										
TOTAL PROFIT BEFORE TAXES										
TAXES: STATE & PROVINCIAL										
FEDERAL & FOREIGN										
PROFIT AFTER TAXES										
RETURN ON FUNDS EMPLOYED										
CASH FLOW										
CAPITAL EXPENDITURES										

Figure 15
Division Profit and Loss Statement

VARIATION ANALYSIS
1970-1971

DIVISION ——————————

	1970	1971	VARIATION	% CHANGE
PHYSICAL VOLUME (CUST.)				
GROCERY				
BULK				
TOTAL VOLUME				
GROSS SALES (CUST.)				
ALLOWANCES EX-DEALS				
TRANSPORTATION				
WAREHOUSING				
CASH DISCOUNT				
NET SALES (CUST.)				
VARIABLE COST OF GOODS SOLD				
MARGINAL INCOME (CUST.)				
DIRECT COSTS				
MANUFACTURING OVERHEAD				
MARKETING-PROMOTIONS				
MARKETING-OTHER				
PRODUCT RESEARCH				
TOTAL DIRECT COSTS				
DIRECT PRODUCT CONTRIBUTION				
INDIRECT COSTS				
MANUFACTURING OVERHEAD				
MARKETING				
RESEARCH				
GEN'L & ADMINISTRATIVE				
TOTAL INDIRECT COSTS				
OPERATING PROFIT				
INTER-CO. GROSS PROFIT				
OTHER INCOME (EXPENSE)				
PROFIT BEFORE TAXES				
ADD INTERDIVISION PBT				
TOTAL PROFIT BEFORE TAXES				
TAXES: STATE & PROVINCIAL				
FEDERAL & FOREIGN				
PROFIT AFTER TAXES				
RETURN ON FUNDS EMPLOYED				
CASH FLOW				
CAPITAL EXPENDITURES				

Figure 16
Division Profit and Loss Statement—Variation Analysis

STATEMENT OF FINANCIAL POSITION — 1971 TO 1975

DIVISION _____

CLASSIFICATION	MARCH 31, 1971	JUNE 30, 1971	SEPTEMBER 30, 1971	DECEMBER 31, 1971	DECEMBER 31, 1972	DECEMBER 31, 1973	DECEMBER 31, 1974	DECEMBER 31, 1975
CASH								
ACCOUNTS RECEIVABLE								
INVENTORIES:								
RAW MATERIALS								
PACKAGING MATERIALS								
SUPPLIES								
FINISHED GOODS — BULK								
— GROCERY								
TOTAL INVENTORIES								
PREPAID EXPENSES								
CURRENT ASSETS								
ACCOUNTS PAYABLE								
ACCRUED LIABILITIES								
INCOME TAXES								
CURRENT LIABILITIES								
WORKING CAPITAL (CURRENT ASSETS LESS CURRENT LIABILITIES)								
LAND, BUILDINGS, AND EQUIP. — AT COST								
LESS ACCUMULATED DEPRECIATION								
NET FIXED ASSETS								
OTHER ASSETS								
OTHER LIABILITIES								

Figure 17
Statement of Financial Position

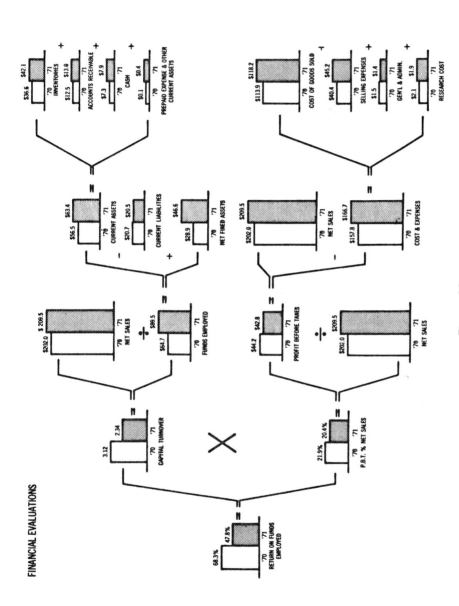

Figure 18

Financial Evaluations of Return on Funds Employed

PROFIT & LOSS STATEMENTS — BY PRODUCT GROUPS

YEARS 1971 THRU 1974

DIVISION

VOLUME (000'S UNITS)
GROSS SALES
NET SALES
Variable Cost of Goods Sold
MARGINAL INCOME
LESS DIRECT COSTS/EXPENSES
Manufacturing Overhead (CGS)
Marketing – Promotional
Marketing – Other
Product Research
TOTAL DIRECT COSTS/EXPENSES
DIRECT PRODUCT CONTRIBUTION
LESS INDIRECT COSTS/EXPENSES
Manufacturing Overhead (CGS)
Marketing
Research
General & Administrative
TOTAL INDIRECT COSTS/EXPENSES
OPERATING PROFIT
INTERCO. GROSS PROFIT
OTHER INCOME/(EXPENSE)
PROFIT BEFORE TAXES
ADD INTERDIVISIONAL PBT
TOTAL PROFIT BEFORE TAXES
PBT SUMMARY BY PRODUCT GROUPS
1971
1972
1973
1974

Product Group columns: PRODUCT GROUP A, PRODUCT GROUP B, PRODUCT GROUP C, PRODUCT GROUP D, OTHER GROCERY — each with 1970 ACTUAL ESTIMATED and ESTIMATED * INDEX OF CHANGE 1971 | 1972 | 1973 | 1974

* 1970 BASE = 100

Figure 19

Profit and Loss Statement—Product Groups

PROFIT & LOSS STATEMENTS
1970-1974

TOTAL GROCERY PRODUCTS

	1970	1971	1972	1973	1974
VOLUME (000'S UNITS)					
GROSS SALES					
NET SALES					
Variable Cost of Goods Sold					
MARGINAL INCOME					
LESS DIRECT COSTS- EXPENSES.					
Manufacturing Overhead					
Marketing — Promotional					
Marketing — Other					
Product Research					
TOTAL DIRECT COSTS- EXPENSES					
DIRECT PRODUCT CONTRIBUTION					
LESS INDIRECT COSTS- EXPENSES					
Manufacturing Overhead					
Marketing — Promotional					
Research					
General & Administrative					
TOTAL INDIRECT COSTS- EXPENSES					
OPERATING PROFIT					
INTERCO GROSS PROFIT					
OTHER INCOME/(EXPENSE)					
PROFIT BEFORE TAXES					
ADD: INTERDIVISIONAL PBT					
TOTAL PROFIT BEFORE TAXES					
TAXES: State & Provincial					
Federal & Foreign					
PROFIT AFTER TAXES					
RETURN ON FUNDS EMPLOYED					
% OF PBT					

TOTAL BULK PRODUCTS

1970	1971	1972	1973	1974

DIVISION

TOTAL DEVELOPMENT PRODUCTS

1970	1971	1972	1973	1974

Figure 20
Profit and Loss Statement—Grocery Product Groups

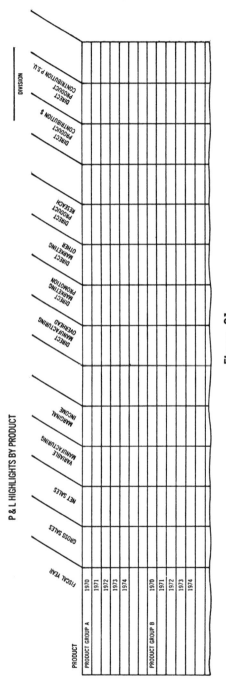

Figure 21

Profit and Loss Statements—Individual Product Highlights

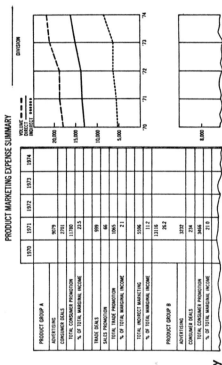

Figure 22

Product Marketing Expense Summary

MARKET POSITION BY PRODUCT

PRODUCT		TOTAL MARKET (UNITS)	% SHARE MARKET	CONSUMER MOVEMENT	DIRECT MARKETING $	
					TOTAL $	PER UNIT CONSUMER MOVEMENT
	70 71 72 73 74					
	70 71 72 73 74					
	70 71 72 73 74					
	70 71 72 73 74					
	70 71 72 73 74					
	70 71 72 73 74					
	70 71 72 73 74					
	70 71 72 73 74					

Figure 23
Market Position—by Product

DIVISION

INDIRECT EXPENSES

CATEGORY	ACTUAL 1970	ESTIMATED 1971	ESTIMATED 1972	ESTIMATED 1973	ESTIMATED 1974
VOLUME					
MANUFACTURING OVERHEAD					
DEPRECIATION					
SUPERVISION					
MAINTENANCE					
UTILITY					
ENGINEERING					
QUALITY CONTROL					
OTHER					
TOTAL					
% M.I.					
MANPOWER					
MARKETING EXPENSES					
KITCHENS					
ADMIN. MARKETING					
SALES FORCE					
SALES ACCOUNTING					
MARKET RESEARCH					
TOTAL					
% M.I.					
MANPOWER					
RESEARCH EXPENSES					
SALARIES					
SUPPLIES					
OTHER					
TOTAL					
% M.I.					
MANPOWER					
GENERAL & ADMINISTRATIVE					
TOTAL					
% M.I.					
MANPOWER					

Figure 24
Indirect Expenses

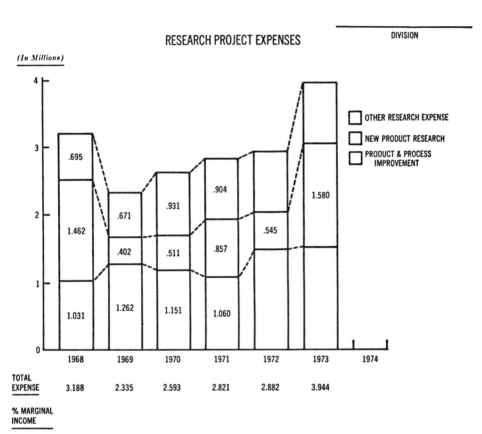

RESEARCH PROJECT EXPENSES

DIVISION

(In Millions)

OTHER RESEARCH EXPENSE

NEW PRODUCT RESEARCH

PRODUCT & PROCESS IMPROVEMENT

	1968	1969	1970	1971	1972	1973	1974
OTHER RESEARCH EXPENSE	.695	.671	.931	.904	.545	1.580	
NEW PRODUCT RESEARCH	1.462	.402	.511	.857			
PRODUCT & PROCESS IMPROVEMENT	1.031	1.262	1.151	1.060			

TOTAL EXPENSE | 3.188 | 2.335 | 2.593 | 2.821 | 2.882 | 3.944 |

% MARGINAL INCOME

HOW SPENT:	EXPENSES 1970 (Act.)	EXPENSES 1971 (Est.)
PRODUCT & PROCESS IMPROVEMENT	1.151	1.060
NEW PRODUCT RESEARCH	.511	.857
OTHER RESEARCH EXPENSE		
INFORMATION — TECHNOLOGY	.429	.390
OTHER (MISCELLANEOUS)	.502	.514
TOTAL	2.593	2.821
WHERE SPENT:		
TECHNICAL CENTER RESEARCH PROJECTS	—	.103
DIVISION LABORATORIES	—	2.718
TOTAL	2.593	2.821

Figure 25
Research Project Expenses

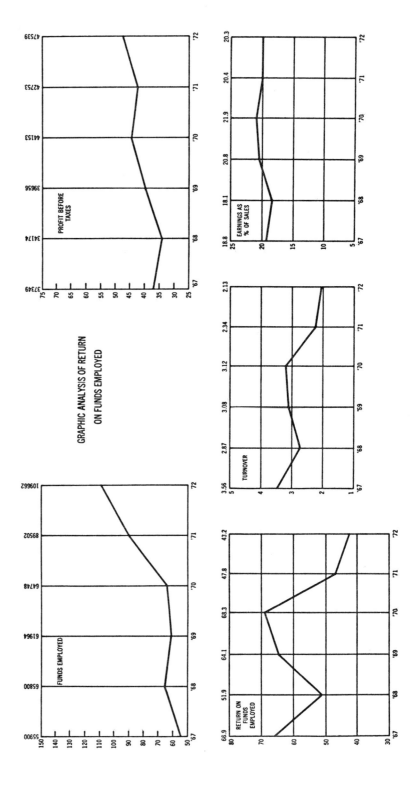

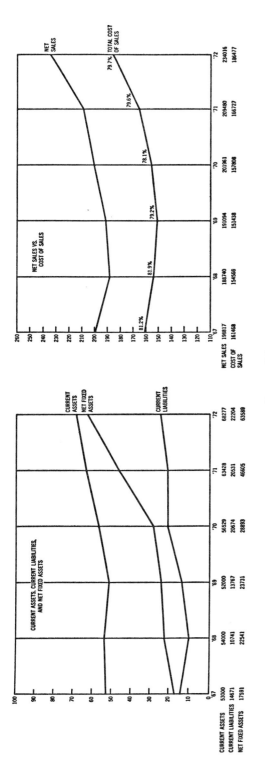

Figure 26

Graphic Analysis of Return on Funds Employed

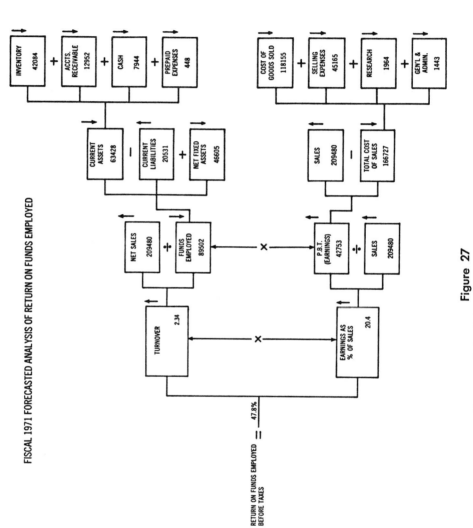

Figure 27

Forecasted Analysis of Return on Funds Employed

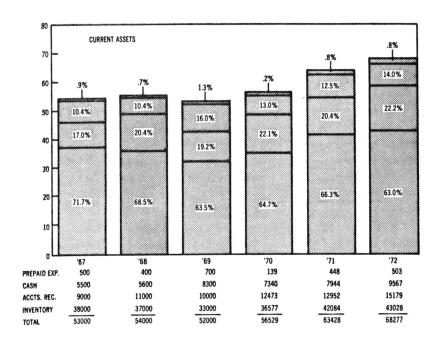

	'67	'68	'69	'70	'71	'72
PREPAID EXP.	500	400	700	139	448	503
CASH	5500	5600	8300	7340	7944	9567
ACCTS. REC.	9000	11000	10000	12473	12952	15179
INVENTORY	38000	37000	33000	36577	42084	43028
TOTAL	53000	54000	52000	56529	63428	68277

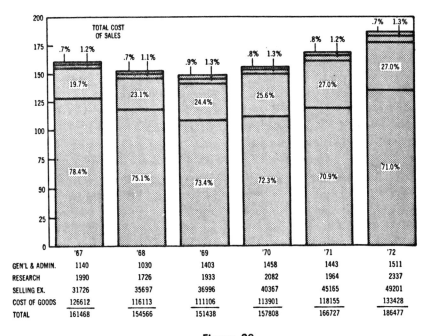

	'67	'68	'69	'70	'71	'72
GEN'L & ADMIN.	1140	1030	1403	1458	1443	1511
RESEARCH	1990	1726	1933	2082	1964	2337
SELLING EX.	31726	35697	36996	40367	45165	49201
COST OF GOODS	126612	116113	111106	113901	118155	133428
TOTAL	161468	154566	151438	157808	166727	186477

Figure 28
Analysis of Current Assets and Total Cost of Sales

INVENTORY FORECAST

____
DIVISION

JUNE QUARTER FINAL						DESCRIPTION	SEPT. 30		DEC. 31		MARCH 31	
APRIL 30 $ AMOUNT	WEEKS SUPPLY	MAY 31 $ AMOUNT	WEEKS SUPPLY	JUNE 30 $ AMOUNT	WEEKS SUPPLY		$ AMOUNT	WEEKS SUPPLY	$ AMOUNT	WEEKS SUPPLY	$ AMOUNT	WEEKS SUPPLY
						GROCERY FINISHED GOODS						
						BULK FINISHED GOODS						
						RAW MATERIALS						
						PACKAGING MATERIAL & SUPPLIES						
						TOTAL INVENTORIES						
						Variations From:						
						FISCAL YEAR 1963						
						FISCAL YEAR 1962						

$ AMT.	WEEKS SUPPLY	VARIATION		$ AMT.	WEEKS SUPPLY	VARIATION		$ AMT.	WEEKS SUPPLY	VARIATION		SELECTED ITEMS	$ AMT.	WEEKS SUPPLY	VARIATION		$ AMT.	WEEKS SUPPLY	VARIATION		$ AMT.	WEEKS SUPPLY	VARIATION	
		'70	'71			'70	'71			'70	'71				'70	'71			'70	'71			'70	'71
												PRODUCT A												
												B												
												C												
												D												
												E												
												F												
												G												
												H												
												I												
												J												
												K												
												L												
												M												
												All Other Grocery												
												TOTAL GROCERY FINISHED GOODS												
												N												

Figure 29
Inventory Forecast

2

ORGANIZING THE
TREASURER-CONTROLLER FUNCTION
FOR EFFECTIVE FINANCIAL MANAGEMENT

THE GROWTH OF A BUSINESS

The discussion which follows is an attempt to critically examine the current role of both the treasurer and the controller. It is the rare corporation which enjoys the professional relationship of tranquility between the two functions. In fact, sweetness and light are rarely found commodities because of the potential conflicts which exist between the two areas. Nevertheless, each serves a vital purpose and each position must be carefully analyzed because changes are currently taking place within the financial sphere which call for a searching reexamination of the role of both the treasurer and the controller. In order to best understand the ramifications of the changes which are taking place, it is best to view them in the light of the total financial organization.

Whether a business is a "one man show" or a large corporation with thousands of owners, its nucleus is money. Finance is the heart of every enterprise—no matter what its size or nature. Every business invests—and reinvests—in plant and equipment, materials, and services. The "dividends" on the investment are whatever the business has left after it meets expenses and sets aside funds for reinvestment. If earnings are high enough, the corporation shares its earnings with the stockholders who have invested in the company. The sole proprietor retains all profits as his personal dividend for risking his time, energy, and capital in the enterprise.

The proprietorship and the giant corporation each have money problems. Both must base their operating plans on financial considerations. Each business defines its goals in financial terms and lays plans according to its financial capabilities. Their problems are alike in principle, different only in scale.

The typical business concern was once owned and run by one man. Perhaps he had a small manufacturing concern, employing a dozen or so people. At first the owner personally handled most financial and accounting duties, as well as the other management activities required by his operation. By

55

tracing the growth of a small business to corporate status, we see the important part finance played in the evolution.

The Crucial First Years

Our hypothetical firm probably had a time getting started. The widely-held American dream—"to be my own boss"—prompts up to 400,000 individuals to establish their own businesses each year. But the word "establish" is misleading. About 335,000 firms cease operating each year. Some 380,000 others change hands.

Not surprisingly, a study by the Small Business Administration shows that a lack of financial acumen is a major cause of business failures. In a carefully selected sample of 81 small enterprises, the SBA found that more than half the firms had an initial capital investment of less than $3,000. The initial investment ranged from $12 to $37,000. According to the SBA report, this wide variation represents two different types of owners:

> . . . there are a smaller number of businessmen, in the traditional sense of the word, who realize that a business needs an adequate capital investment to begin operations. At the other extreme are those with just a few dollars, who decide to go into business either as an alternative to unemployment or in a kind of reckless gambling spirit. These are the people who, knowing nothing about business, open on a shoestring in the blind hope that they will be able to make a go of it.*

Sixty per cent of the total invested by the firms initially was equity capital, mainly cash and savings supplied by the owners themselves.

The SBA observed the sample closely during the first two years after each business began. Four businesses failed within two months of their openings; twenty-eight more closed at some time during the first year. At the end of two years, 40 of the 81 firms were out of business. Only eight of these closed for non-financial reasons. The rest failed either to make money or to manage their financial affairs properly. Bad locations, competition, adverse economic conditions, and other factors kept some of the businesses in the red. Many of the enterprises, however, could have continued with the proper financial management.

The owners made many fatal financial management errors. They overextended themselves in granting credit to customers; they bought in small quantities at high prices; they borrowed too heavily; they began with too little capital; they failed to maintain sufficient working reserves.

---

* Kurt B. Mayer and Sidney Goldstein, *The First Two Years: Problems of Small Firm Growth and Survival*, Small Business Administration, 1961, p. 53.

The Start of Expansion

But the small manufacturing concern that grew into a big corporation survived the first two years. The original owner obviously had better luck— or knew more about financial management—than the 40 who failed in the SBA sample. No doubt the owner knew the operating side of his business equally well.

Suppose the successful firm's growth really began when the owner decided to add a new product to his line. He undoubtedly based his decision to begin producing the product on some form of "market research" (but maybe on nothing more than a hunch that the new product would sell). Unless he went outside for specialized help, he used whatever engineering knowledge he possessed to design the product.

Adding the new product to his line meant hiring more workers, so the owner put on his "personnel director's" hat. He needed new equipment, so he negotiated with a local bank for a loan; he became the firm's "finance officer."

Even after he acquired several "management" employees, the head man very likely held on to nearly all management authority. To promote the new product he became "sales promotion director"; he supervised the training of his new employees. He was both the "sales executive" and the firm's only "sales manager" (and he sold a little, too). In line with his duties as finance officer, he was the "chief accountant," "controller," and "treasurer."

The Developing Need for Management Help

With an expanding business, the owner found it increasingly difficult to find time to really manage his firm. Pressure built up fastest in the finance and accounting area. The new product brought more customers, more sales volume, and more credit problems. Even with the help of a bookkeeper, the "chief accountant" was hard-pressed to keep track of accounts receivable. To get proper sales coverage, the "sales manager" authorized expense accounts for his salesmen, which added to his accounting chores. The new production workers meant more payroll accounting and reporting work, and the additional revenue from sales activities required more attention to tax records. The owner could no longer be "finance officer," "controller," "treasurer," and "chief accountant." To give himself more time to manager, the owner added a credit manager, a payroll clerk or two, and other bookkeepers or accountants.

The Finance Function Grows

The added manpower gave the owner what he wanted—for a while. But after a time he began to feel that he was losing valuable time making routine accounting decisions. The credit manager, the accountants and even the payroll clerks were coming to him constantly for decisions. It was fairly obvious to the owner that the "finance department" was experiencing growing pains. To make certain of his diagnosis, the owner drew a chart of his firm's finance function. He came up with something like the organization shown in Figure 1.

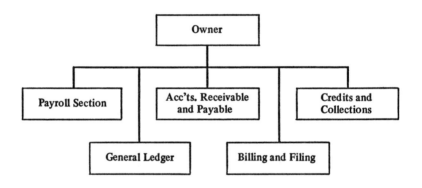

Figure 1

Original Finance Organization

The owner's suspicions were confirmed. The finance function in his small but growing concern was under-organized. *Everyone reported directly to him.* The owner had to do something to free himself from the time-consuming duties his inefficient organization placed on him. After a great deal of study, the owner named an accounting manager or chief accountant and devised the organizational plan shown in Figure 2.

Not a very great change? Not on paper, anyway. But it was a big step to take for a man who had had *all* of the responsibility and authority. More important, the new organizational plan gave the finance function—and the firm—room to grow.

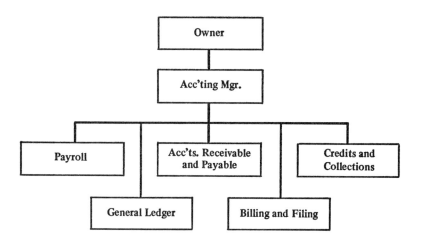

Figure 2

Growing Finance Organization

The implications are clear. The owner continued to handle the most important financial matters, but he leaned heavily on the new chief accountant to take care of more routine matters. Gradually, the accounting and financial duties expanded. New accounting systems were implemented to keep pace with the additional duties. Meanwhile, the business grew larger. Due to the sheer size of his operation, the owner soon found it impossible to make all important financial decisions alone. He began to ask the chief accountant's help in evaluating investment proposals; he gradually learned to rely on the chief accountant's advice. The expanding business was demanding increased attention in other areas, so the owner made the chief accountant his controller. The new controller was responsible for most financial management and planning. For all practical purposes, the controller replaced the owner as "finance officer."

Of course, for the finance function to grow, the business had to grow. As the owner got out of accounting and controllership activities, he also delegated more responsibility to sales and production specialists. To expand sales and production required more capital, and *all* performance is measured in dollars. To pave the way for the firm's overall growth, the finance function first had to take on new responsibilities.

Somewhere along the line, the original owner sold shares of ownership in the business to help finance its expansion. Perhaps it was at this time that he first realized the need for a top-level assistant to advise him on financial matters. But maybe it was after the business was incorporated, *after* the stock offering. Perhaps then the new board of directors, owning a major portion of the newly-issued stock, advised the president to begin building a finance organization. Chances are that one of the directors, or another major shareholder, became treasurer or controller.

At any rate, the president retained a controlling interest; he may be chairman of the board as well as president. Several vice presidents report to him (including a vice president for finance). The board of directors helps establish company goals and policy and advises the president on important problems. The business is financially accountable to its shareholders, to the state that authorized its incorporation, and to the Securities and Exchange Commission.

Finance played a major role in bringing the business to its present status, and the new character of the enterprise puts even heavier demands on the finance function.

WITHIN THE FINANCIAL ORGANIZATION

Small or large business, finance permeates all activities. Production schedules, sales goals, new product research and development—all have financial aspects. In fact, the fundamental nature of *all* business activities is economic. Money is the foundation of all production and marketing efforts. Finance makes it possible for a proprietor—or a corporation—to make and sell goods or services. This is what makes any business a risk—the fact that there is money to be lost or gained. Finance negotiates with lenders and investors to give the enterprise the money it risks. At the same time it attempts to minimize the risk, to insure a profitable return on the investment.

The Functions of the Finance Department

In corporations (which account for some 80 per cent of all business done in this country), the nature of the duties and responsibilities of finance depend largely on the grant of authority given by the board of directors. Under the corporate form of doing business, overall responsibility and authority rest with the board. It delegates this authority to the people charged with managing the day-to-day affairs of the business—the president, treasurer, controller, and other company officers.

Both the board of directors and those associated with the finance activities in a given company are primarily concerned with money. It follows that the finance department generally operates more closely with the board than most other departments. Take the matter of dividend payments to stock-holders, for instance. Obviously, finance is directly concerned. But while the finance executive may recommend the amount and nature of dividend payments, while his department may prepare and disburse dividend checks, the finance executive does not determine the amount of the payment. In this matter—as in many others—he merely advised the board; it makes the ulti-mate decision. Similarly, the board decides what percentage of earnings the company shall retain for reinvestment, the size and composition of stock distributions, and so on. It generally authorizes the sale or purchase of capital assets of more than a specified value. In nearly all companies, the finance executive merely advises the board on such matters, recommends this course of action or that. In many matters, the finance executive has delegated au-thority from the board to act on his own. If a particular problem is outside his area of responsibility, one for the board of directors to handle, the finance executive can only evaluate proposals and make a recommendation to the board. The board than makes the final decision and directs the president, the finance executive, or other company officers to carry it out.

Setting Financial Goals

In most companies, responsibility for financial planning and manage-ment belongs to the chief finance officer, who may have the title of vice presi-dent for finance, controller, or treasurer. In large companies the task may be divided among several officers, but coordinated by the chief financial ex-ecutive.

With the help of all those in the finance department, the finance officer analyzes past and present company programs. He defines trends in sales vol-ume, production cost, administrative expense, earnings, capital outlay, and return on investment. He interprets these trends in light of their probable effect on company operations. He recommends to top management (and to the board of directors) short and long range plans based on his studies. He prepares annual operating budgets as well as long range capital expenditure proposals.

The responsibilities of finance are not confined to analysis of conditions within the company. The company operates within the framework of the general economy. All company financial planning must allow for economic and political events likely to have an impact on company operations. Finan-cial planning includes forecasting the general outlook for the country, the industry, and for the particular company; it takes into account the probable effect of anticipated political events and government policies and programs. To give a complete picture, finance must supply other officers and the board of directors with an analysis that includes forecasts of labor conditions, wage rates, material costs, general marketing conditions, competitive forces, and technological advances.

Evaluating Alternatives

Working within the limits imposed by the board of directors, finance evaluates the countless investment proposals that come to the attention of top management. In deciding whether to invest in new equipment, buy a new building, or select a new supplier for a critical component, a company is faced with an almost infinite variety of alternatives. It generally tries to make the investments that offer the greatest return.

Suppose the problem is whether or not to replace an expensive piece of production equipment. The machine performs satisfactorily, but new models are capable of turning out more work in the same time with less scrap loss. Downtime has increased on the present equipment, with lost production as a result. But the equipment *is* paid for, and the depreciation charged against it over the years does not approach the cost of the new, more advanced models. On the other hand, the new equipment would mean savings in labor and materials, not to mention reduced downtime and lower maintenance costs.

There's no room for intuition or guess here. The suggestion to replace the machine may have come from the production superintendent, who is primarily interested in increased production. From his viewpoint, the proposal looks good. But to properly evaluate the proposal, all the facts must be translated into terms clear to everyone—dollars. What is the total cost to purchase, install, operate and maintain the new equipment? How does this compare with the cost of operating and maintaining the present machine?

Here is where finance enters the picture. The finance executive knows top management's general attitude toward the proposal because he understands the company's financial goals. He converts all aspects of the proposal into their money equivalent and recommends a course of action. In most cases, the choice is clear, because finance makes its decision after studying all possible courses of action. Only then does it make a recommendation. This recommendation takes company policy, available capital, and company objectives into consideration. The recommendation from finance generally answers the all-important question: "Which alternative will yield the best return on the investment?"

Acquiring Capital

Before management gives the go-ahead on an investment proposal, it must be assured that finance can obtain the necessary capital. Where does a company find capital? The answer to this question gives another insight into the broad scope of finance's responsibilities.

Capital generated within the enterprise:

- Income from sales less operating costs, dividend payments, and debt payments.
- Savings in operating expenses (by reducing inventory levels, stepping up production efficiency, or increasing collections).
- Depreciation charged against existing facilities but not used for buying new plant or equipment.
- Revenue obtained by liquidating company-held assets.

Capital obtained from outside sources:

- Short- and long-term borrowing.
- Increasing equity capital by the sale of preferred or common stock.

In fulfilling its most important responsibility—administering the funds used to run the business—finance necessarily gets involved in nearly all company activities. By pinpointing waste in this operation or that, by recommending new methods that result in savings, finance may very well find the funds needed to buy that new machine, start construction on a new plant or warehouse, or expand sales coverage. And if the capital comes from savings in operating costs, the company pays nothing to outsiders for using the funds.

Of course, there are times when a company must go outside for capital. Say the company wants to revamp an entire plant or finance a merger with another firm. It needs immediate capital, and far more than savings in operating costs can produce. Its objective is to obtain the necessary capital at the lowest possible cost. The decision may be left solely to the finance executive, but he is more likely to analyze several sources of funds and present management with alternative plans for acquiring the capital—along with his recommendation.

To make a valid recommendation—or to reach a sound decision on his own—the finance executive must know the prevailing money market, know where to find funds at the lowest cost; he must also know the financial community and understand how it works. Whether he recommends a straight long-term loan or a new stock issue, he must know all the implications— how his recommendation will affect other investment proposals, whether or not it agrees with the firm's tax planning, and what it will do to the existing capital structure.

Financial Control

Once a firm invests in a new machine or process, or acquires a new holding, it must make the investment pay off. In a sense, control is linked to every other finance responsibility. A company can control its expenditures only by planning them in advance; budgeting is a planning measure primarily, but a control and follow-up device as well. Finance "controls" when it questions waste or inefficiency, when it suggests an improved production method. It may turn up needed capital in the process, but its main purpose is to increase the rate of return on the existing investment.

In nearly every company activity, from the planning stages to completion and beyond, financial management records progress, seeking constant assurance that things are progressing according to plan. Repeated over and again in all operations, control and follow-up become an integral part of each company activity. And by controlling continuing activities, finance helps steer the company toward its overall goals. With internal audits and cost accounting techniques, it appraises results; it suggests ways of improving performance. If necessary, it recommends that top management modify company goals, or change plans to cope with changing economic conditions.

THE FUNCTIONS OF THE TREASURER

The treasurer in a business corporation is the financial executive who is essentially responsible for all the functions which are classified under the general heading of "money management." As we have noted, this means that the treasurer serves chiefly as the custodian of a corporation's funds. He retains the corporate funds in trust for the benefit of the corporation and disburses funds only when authorized.

In many companies, the treasurer serves in other corporate capacities, such as a director, or as a vice president of finance. In smaller companies he also serves as a controller. The position of controller exists primarily among larger companies. The two positions are closely related; the treasurer is responsible for money management activities, the controller serves as chief accountant and financial planner.

Duties Assigned to Treasurer by Bylaws

An examination of the bylaws of many corporations shows a wide variety of functions delegated to the treasurer. This is due to the differences in the general organization of many corporations. The following are the duties usually assigned to the treasurer by the bylaws. This list is comprehensive; in many corporations, some of the powers listed here may be delegated to the controller, secretary, or auditor, rather than to the treasurer.

1. Supervising, having custody of, and assuming responsibility for all funds and securities of the corporation.
2. Maintaining bank accounts in designated banks.
3. Making books and records available to any of the directors during business hours.
4. Preparing statements on the company's financial condition for all regular meetings of the directors, and a complete report at the annual meeting of stockholders.
5. Receiving monies due to the corporation.
6. Maintaining records giving a full account of monies personally received and paid for by the corporation.
7. Signing certificates of shares in the capital stock of the company (together with the president or vice president).
8. Signing all checks, bills of exchange, and promissory notes, with such other officer as the board of directors may designate.
9. Advising the corporation on financial matters.
10. Maintaining custody of the stock book, and preparing the dividend payments.
11. Preparing and submitting tax reports.
12. Performing all other duties connected with the office, and any duties that the board of directors may assign.

Duties Assigned to Treasurer by Directors, Committees, and Officers

Bylaw provisions are often brief, and many of the treasurer's duties are delegated to him by special action of the board of directors or of its committees, and by direction of higher executive officers, such as the president and the chairman of the board. These duties are either of a temporary character, usually terminating in a report to the board, or are of a general nature, representing permanently assigned functions.

Typical functions delegated by special authorization and assignment are investigation for the development of pension plans and group insurance plans; examination of companies in which the corporation contemplates purchasing an interest; arranging for listing the company's securities on the stock exchange; and investigation of the feasibility of stock offerings.

The Treasurer's Major Areas of Responsibility

1. *Provision of Capital.* Establishing and executing programs for providing capital need by the business, including procurement of capital and maintaining required financial arrangements.

2. *Investor Relations.* Establishing and maintaining an adequate market for the company's securities and maintaining liaison with investment bankers, financial analysts and shareholders.

3. *Short-Term Financing.* Maintaining adequate sources for the company's current borrowing from commercial banks and other lending institutions.

4. *Banking and Custody.* Maintaining banking arrangments for receiving, holding and disbursing the company's monies and securities, plus responsibility for the financial aspects of real estate transactions.

5. *Credits and Collections.* Directing credit granting and collection of accounts and supervising arrangements for financing sales, as through time payment and leasing plans.

6. *Investments.* Investing the company's funds as required and establishing and coordinating policies to govern investment in pension funds and similar trusts.

7. *Insurance.* Providing coverage as required.

Duties Assigned by Treasurer to Staff

Many treasurers delegate most of the details of their work to members of their staff, giving their attention to the supervision, study, and adoption of procedure consistent with the policies of the corporation.

If a treasurer is in charge of stock books and dividend payments, most of the actual work is performed by the staff. The treasurer, however, ascertains personally whether liquid funds will be available at dividend dates to meet the obligation.

Similarly, when the treasurer is in charge of the interchange of bonds, his staff does the actual work of handling registration and coupon payments. If the treasurer's department is in charge of group insurance plans and employees' saving and profit-sharing funds, the staff, under the direction of the treasurer, keeps the necessary records. And upon the adoption of an employee stock ownership plan, the staff performs the actual detailed work of recording installment payments and stock deliveries.

The extension of credit is usually handled by the credit manager, who has considerable responsibility, but is subject to the authority of the treasurer.

In such cases, only special matters are brought to the treasurer's attention. In regard to receipts and disbursements, the responsibility is often placed on the cashier, who refers special cases to the treasurer. In many instances, the treasurer issues reports prepared by assistants under his direction.

Assistant Treasurer

The assistant treasurer is the officer of a corporation who assists the treasurer in the care, custody, receipt and disbursement of company funds.

The bylaws of large corporations sometimes provide for one or more assistant treasurers authorized to perform, in the order of their rank, all of the duties of the treasurer in the latter's absence or inability to act. Assistant treasurers perform any duties assigned to them by the treasurer or by the board of directors, and assist the treasurer at all times.

Some treasurers' departments follow the policy of assigning as much work as possible to assistants without getting out of touch with the general trend of affairs. This prevents the treasurer from becoming so burdened with detail that he loses sight of more important matters. Assistant treasurers may be delegated nearly all the details of the work of the treasurer's office to enable the treasurer to give most of his attention to outside matters.

If a growing company is financing its expansion through new issues of stocks and bonds, the treasurer's tasks may be confined to the handling of security issues, while the other duties of the office are carried out by an assistant treasurer.

In some cases, specific duties are assigned to the assistant treasurer. For example, the assistant treasurer of a parent company, with subsidiaries in many states, may be required to devote his entire time to tax matters. His full-time job will be to keep constantly informed of the tax status of all subsidiaries and branches and to follow closely all changes in the tax laws of various states. He will also keep a calendar of report dates, and see that taxes are paid within the periods prescribed by law.

In some large corporations, especially where the treasurer performs the function of controller, an assistant treasurer heads up the accounting department.

THE FUNCTIONS OF THE CONTROLLER

The controller is the financial executive of a large or medium-sized corporation who combines the responsibilities for accounting, auditing, budgeting, profit planning, performance reporting, tax control, and other corporate activities.

The control that controllers exert is based on the word "control" in the indirect sense of making decisions and controlling action toward enabling the company to make profits. The purest example of the controllership principle in common practice is in budgetary control, which includes all kinds of appraisal and measurement.

The Office of Controller

Although relatively new in American corporations, the office of controller, so described earlier, continues to increase in importance. Legal statutes recognize the existence of the office of controller. The Securities Act of 1933 provides that the registration statement filed with the Securities and Exchange Commission must be signed by the controller of the issuing corporation or by its principal accounting officer, as well as by its other principal officers.

In some corporations, the office of controller is not an elective one; the controller is employed like any other department head. In other corporations, the board of directors elects the controller, and his duties are outlined in the corporate bylaws. In still other corporations, the office of controller is established by act of the executive committee, and the powers and duties are prescribed by resolution of the committee. Some organizations specify the controller's duties in an order signed by the president.

Duties Assigned to Controller

The controller's duties, as assigned to him by the bylaws, by resolution, or by executive order, usually require him to:

1. Serve as the chief accounting officer in charge of the company's accounting books, accounting records, and forms.
2. Audit all payrolls and vouchers and have them properly certified.
3. Prepare the company's balance sheet, income accounts, and other financial statements and reports, and give the president a complete report covering results of the company's operations during the past quarter and fiscal year to date.
4. Supervise the preparation, compilation, and filing of all reports, statements, statistics, and other data that the law requires or that the company president requests.
5. Receive all reports from agents and company departments that are needed for recording the company's general operations or for directing or supervising its accounts.
6. Maintain general control over the accounting practices of all subsidiary companies.

7. Supervise the enforcement and maintenance of the classification of accounts and any other accounting rules and regulations that any regulatory body prescribes.
8. Endorse for the company any checks or promissory notes for deposit, collector, or transfer.
9. Countersign all checks that the treasurer draws against funds of the company or its subsidiaries, except as otherwise provided by the board.
10. Approve the payment of all vouchers, drafts, and other accounts payable, when required by the president or any other persons he designates.
11. Countersign all warrants that the treasurer draws for the deposit of securities in the company's safe deposit boxes or withdrawal therefrom.
12. Appoint the auditor and his staff and set their salaries.
13. Compose a budget showing the company's future requirements as shown by its accounts and the requisitions of the general manager and other officers.
14. Supervise all records and clerical and office procedures for departments of the company and its subsidiaries.
15. Perform any other duties and have any other powers that the board of directors may occasionally prescribe and that the president may assign.

Other Responsibilities Placed on Controllers

The controller's office is often responsible for tax matters, insurance of corporate property, leases, and office management. In some companies, the controller has charge of all service departments such as telephone, messenger service, janitors, filing, mailing, and similar matters.

The controller frequently serves on various committees, such as the finance committee, investments committee, pension board, budget committee, insurance committee, and special committees of various kinds.

The functions of the controller cover a broad field and relate to the activities of all departments, including the treasurer's department. Primarily the controller wields a check on disbursements and receipts of the treasurer. He may approve vouchers before payment, and frequently prescribes the methods for keeping accounts in the treasurer's office.

The controller performs a quasi-official duty in supplying the president or the treasurer with statistical data drawn from the accounting records and from other sources, as a basis for current or future financing of the corporation. Included also as controllership activities are the application of electronic data processing to accounting systems and procedures, and the installation and coordination of paperwork flow.

The controller sometimes acts in an advisory capacity, with his recommendations carried out by the executives in charge of the departments concerned. The controller may recommend accounting procedures for various branches, with implementation left to each branch manager. He frequently cooperates with the sales manager in compiling data for the production budget. He usually works with the factory superintendent or sales executive, as appropriate, to see that purchases remain as low as possible, consistent with production or sales requirements.

Assistant Controller

The assistant controller is charged with assisting the controller in special areas. His qualifications should supplement those of the controller. If a controller's chief training is in accounting, his assistant should be qualified in cost standards, statistics, budgets, or other areas requiring special experience.

Many companies have more than one assistant controller. A company with two assistant controllers may put one in charge of general accounts and budgetary procedures, and the other in charge of cost accounting. A company with three assistant controllers may delegate accounts and accounting methods to one, standards and statistics to another, and budgeting and forecasting to the third.

An assistant controller, in turn, delegates responsibility to supervisors for a certain amount of the routine work. The aim is to relieve the controller of as much detail as possible by apportioning much of the work among subordinates. This leaves the controller free to concentrate on procedures and policy matters.

NEW DIRECTIONS FOR FINANCIAL MANAGEMENT

During the last ten years, profound changes have taken place which represent a basic switch in management thinking relative to the role of the financial function. Problems are becoming more and more complex and, moreover, the ramifications of these problems are so potentially severe as to tax the imagination of a conventional treasurer and controller. We find, for example, that it is extremely difficult to try any longer to discern a distinct boundary in the jobs of various executives. It is not uncommon today for controllers to participate in data processing or in management information systems design. Because finance is becoming recognized as such a major decision function in business, it is also much more common to see senior officers of companies originate from within the ranks of the financial function. One of the major reasons for this is that the financial officer has developed during his career degrees of judgment which have been tempered by discipline and objectivity. The field of accounting and finance, for example, is no longer the staid, well-defined area which it was once recognized as being. Accounting rules are changing almost daily. Financial instruments used to raise capital are being innovated almost equally as quick. Both the controller and the treasurer are being called upon to render economic judgment as well as custodial financial judgment. As an example, at the present time the Accounting Principles Board of the American Institute of Certified Public Accountants is considering making mandatory the reporting of *imputed* interest in the financial statements of an organization. Imputed interest is a cost which cannot be seen; it cannot be felt; it cannot be touched. Nevertheless, it is an opportunity cost which existed as a result of an alternative which a company has exercised. In this sense, it is not a traditional historical accounting cost. It is an economic concept of cost of funds.

Many more complexities are being generated by changes in current tax laws and these complexities are of such magnitude that it must strain the abilities of the financial officer responsible for tax procedures. Changes in Internal Revenue rulings, for example, in the areas of capitalization versus expense for capital projects, are changing almost daily and what was once an accepted rule of thumb, may no longer be valid in today's changing tax environment. For example, the revenue service is much more stringent about what portion of a capital project may be expensed for tax purposes.

New problems which have been created by the social demands of society upon the corporation can change the nature and motivations of many of our corporate actions. Pollution control, for example, may strain the credulity of a traditional prehistoric financial executive. Nonproductive, capital projects may now be required to be completed and moreover, rather than generating a positive cash flow for a corporation, they may, in fact, serve no other purpose than to satisfy a newly created social goal for corporate behavior. In addition, new forms of social legislation such as Medicare and Medicaid are increasing the complexity of the recording of social obligations of companies. In fact, the traditional profit and loss statement as we know it may someday be relegated to a historical wastebasket. It may be necessary and also desirable in the future to have a profit and loss statement based upon profit oriented operations and a separate profit and loss statement to record the expenses incurred by performing social obligations of the corporation. The two, added together, would comprise the corporate entity.

Other financial problems have been created by the multiplicity of demands on the financial area for statistical data to be reported to various services. Not only does the Federal Trade Commission require data, but the Department of Agriculture, the Department of Commerce and other various governmental functions have gotten in line for data. In addition to these purely governmental functions, quasi-governmental organizations have also assumed an inviolate role of confidant. The voluntary reporting of data to quasi-governmental and industrial agencies is becoming big business. It is not uncommon for organizations such as The National Industrial Conference Board, the Financial Executives Institute, Lionel Edie & Company and other meritorious organizations to often request information from financial executives. Because of the nature of relationships which exist between corporations and these organizations, it is often difficult to ignore requests for information, especially when anonymity is promised.

Another aspect which is changing the future direction of the financial function is the increasing involvement of the function in internal decision making affairs. These affairs may have little to do with finance, per se. They may deal with the complexities of administration of union wage negotiations, the ever present potentials for mergers and acquisitions, the explosion of internal information to various arms of the corporation, and the upset to traditional thinking which has come about as a result of the revolution that the computer and data input have brought to the corporate sphere. The financial executive is being cast more and more in the light of the executive who is to appraise the probabilities of future occurrences. By the same token, he is being required less and less to report the historical objectivity of what has happened. It is becoming increasingly true in the field of finance that yesterday is dead; the challenge is to shape tomorrow.

We are becoming increasingly confronted by esoteric concepts such as financial planning through model building, applications of operations research to aspects of accounting and to portfolio management and moreover, we are being confronted by a younger executive who has been increasingly impatient with the willingness of traditional financial management to tolerate inactivity and to perpetuate custom.

One of the most crucial decisions that is being faced by the financial manager today is the degree to which the financial area should proceed in mechanization and computerization. It is all too easy to state that the computer is a rapid multiplier, or divisor, or adder; it is more than these things. It is a giant, efficient garbage can. The difference, however, is that this particular garbage can can cost an awful lot of money, and it is the rare financial executive who calculates the financial tradeoff in transferring traditional manual functions to the garbage can. Computers, per se, create new layers of overhead. Those new layers of overhead in turn create new peripheral expenses such as the paper supplies which must support the machine operation. One should be patently convinced only after having evaluated the financial tradeoff in computerization that the movement to computer based input is necessary at all. One very large company which was instrumental in developing the entire computer concept a generation ago, has now turned full circle and is beginning to remove some of its financial programs from the computer because they have found that it is faster and in some cases, more accurate to do the job manually as it had been doing prior to the changeover.

Lastly, in the field of new directions, the financial executive is becoming increasingly needed in various other operating areas of the company. The discipline of finance as well as the objectivity form a fine base for adventurers into other decision making functions within a company. It was observed once by Lynn Townsend, the President of the Chrysler Corporation, that no function and no executive was more important than the financial executive. In more recent times, this thought has been echoed by Robert Townsend, the former President of Avis, in his books and in his seminars. The challenge then is to create a well-rounded financial executive who is capable of taking off his blinders, of removing the rubber band from his shirt, and tossing off the green eye shade from his hairline and substituting instead the various dresses and mentalities which accompany the all-around executive required for today's environment.

THE CHANGING ROLE OF THE CONTROLLER

Traditionally, controllership is a type of staff function which in the past has been rather well defined by many organizations. Essentially the function of the position is to maintain some type of system of control and measurement of the historical operations of the business. The word "control," however, does not imply control in the literal sense, because one of the major responsibilities which controllers have in the past shied away from is the very exercise of control in decision making. For the most part they have played shy and permitted various other executive areas in line management to make major decisions. What has been lost upon the traditional controller is the very fact that because of the unique nature of his position within the corporation, he is in a very special niche to observe and moreover to influence the magnitude and direction of profit.

The controller, in exercising his responsibility as it has been traditionally defined, must be familiar with details in all facets of the business. He is the one special individual in the company who probably has, other than the chief executive officer, the best knowledge of products, manufacturing facilities, pricing, and competitive conditions. It has become increasingly important for the controller to accept responsibility in the specialty areas of data processing and communications equipment. More frequently now the controller is finding himself as a major spokesman for corporate policy in representations to governmental agencies, to unions and to interested professional organizations.

Of all individuals within the firm, the controller should be in the unique position to enjoy the mentality of appreciating profit response from various functional areas. In this manner, it is natural for the controller to be the most cost conscious individual within a firm and yet maintain the posture of constructive suggestion. Cost consciousness does not of itself imply miserly, short-term, unconstructive thinking. Cost consciousness can be a dynamic vehicle by which the chief executive officer, with the guidance of the controller, can motivate the balance of the organization to augment the profit planning routine of a company. Cost consciousness and the conservation of resources is not simply a vehicle which should be exercised during times of economic hardship; plans for long range cost reduction are as much a part of daily corporate activity as are profit planning and budgeting and the measurement and achievement for its goals. Long range cost reduction is a subject worthy of special attention and should be considered as an equal and worthy partner of profit planning. In fact, one of the most ideal circumstances would be the concurrent use of both a profit plan and a cost reduction plan for correlative periods of time and the augmentation of each of these plans by a special force appointed by the chief executive officer. Profit planning in a vacuum breeds inefficiency; long range cost reduction in a vacuum breeds negativism. A combination of constructive profit planning and cost reduction programming can bring positive results which can motivate and inspire all areas of the company.

In his new role, the controller is being increasingly cast as an internal quantitative consultant who through his various techniques, his discipline and his objectivity, can assist many other areas of the company to optimize their programs. It is the controller who is in the best position to advise the marketing area of levels of geographic and customer profitability, the efficiency or inefficiency of media and promotion policy. The controller is also in an ideal position to advise the manufacturing area relative to the efficient use of directly applied manufacturing costs as well as the utilization of manufacturing period expenses.

Controllership, in essence, is on the threshold of the next venture into specialization of that function. It is no longer enough to have a single staff controller, or, in fact, even a division controller. Decision making is largely based upon quantitative input and all areas of the company must make decisions in order to insure profitability. It is only a matter of time until we will see the creation of new forms of controllership such as a marketing controller, an advertising controller, a manufacturing controller and a distribution controller. In terms of an analogy, it is not much different from visiting your medical practitioner. It is rare today to be able to enjoy the folksiness of a general medical doctor. Most often as patients we are referred to specialists in certain areas. This same course of events is now evolving for the function of controllership. The controller will, over a period of time, become a specialist who will cross traditional corporate organizational lines and who will participate fully in the decision making function of individual areas.

THE NEW ROLE OF THE TREASURER

The other side of the financial coin is that of treasurership. The position was grounded in pure finance and the basis for the job was the concentration in procuring capital. In addition, the treasurer for the most part has been concerned with cash management and banking relations and sometimes credit and collection and insurance. In more recent times, treasurership has been augmented by increasing attention to pension fund administration.

This has become one of the more marked responsibilities of financial management in many companies. It is true whether companies are uninsured but funded or unfunded with various types of current plans. The dealings with insurance companies has come out of the pure realm of employee welfare expense, and, because of the magnitude and the size of pension plans and investments, drifted toward the sphere of financial management.

Sometimes the responsibility for the investment of the assets of the pension fund has been vested in a trustee arrangement. The trustee in most cases has been a designated lending institution. Under this type of arrangement the actions of the lending institution as trustee are reviewed by the financial executive and his main concern is the evaluation of the efficiency of the investment performance. Sometimes, even though a trustee plan may be in force, individual companies through their financial management retain the right to either advise or cancel investment decisions made by the trustee. In very large companies, it is not uncommon for the investment of pension funds to be handled entirely within the corporate staff area. In those cases company officers serve as trustees for the fund.

In the course of establishing the fund and computing liabilities of the company for invested funds, whether for past service, current or future service, it is the obligation of the financial manager in charge of pension funding to consult with independent actuarial specialists who will assist the company in measuring the degree of risk. The measurement of risk forms the basis of the periodic obligation of the company toward the fund.

In essence, if looked upon in the contrasting shadow of staff vs. line, it may be said that the treasurer is something more of an operating executive and somewhat less than a staff executive if he were to be compared to the controller. The main function of the controller is to report. This is his primary responsibility regardless of whether in the light of the foregoing discussion we agree with this description or not. The treasurer, however, is an operating executive in the sense that his main function is not to report something which happened yesterday. His obligation is day-to-day money management and as such, he is not concerned with whether a debit equals a credit. Instead, as the guardian of all capital activities, he is the designer of the capital structure of a firm and it is his mission to maintain adequate corporate/lending institution relationships which may affect sources of borrowing. One of the major decision areas confronting the treasurer in his recent involvement is the investment of corporate funds whether they be long-term or short-term. This type of investment may take the form not only of excess cash to be invested in a recognized market, but also in the granting of credit to customers. Credit is every bit as much a marketing tool as may be the media or promotion policy which is exercised by the marketing function. Through the treasurer, installment selling, financing through subsidiaries, questions of foreign exchange and possibly lease versus purchase decisions, are all funneled and evaluated.

In the exercise of his duties, it is patently clear that the treasurer is exercising some degree of a public relations function. He needs to deal frequently with the financial fraternity. He must also have immediate access to the senior levels of management of a company and must be in a position whereby he can communicate readily to the board of directors. One of the problems that has arisen to compound and confound the evolution of the position of treasurer is the changing motivation of business and the changing methodology of corporate communications. The sophistication of financial reporting and the increasing penetration into corporate activity of various interested parties also makes mandatory the attendance of the treasurer and/or the chief financial officer at such briefings. It is a reasonable question to ask whether the position of the treasurer as it is traditionally structured is sufficient to achieve all of the objectives of corporate communications and the optimization of operating capital. In the evolving status of financial management, it is also probable that corporations in the future will have two treasurers; one to deal with operating problems and the other to deal with problems of communications with interested parties.

MUTUAL PROBLEMS OF THE TREASURER AND
THE CONTROLLER

If we were to look differently at financial management and examine what part of that function is involved in decision making and what part in the implementation of various decisions, it would become clear that contradictions have entered the picture. Decision making in the area of finance is, for the most part, vested in the chief executive officer of the company and through the chief financial officer and/or the treasurer. Decision implementing activities, however, may be vested in any of the foregoing but also includes the controller. In more recent years the controller is being increasingly called upon to make decisions, also. It is his prerogative, within generally accepted accounting principles, to influence both the magnitude and the direction of profit, within reason. The decision as to corporate policies regarding inventories, expenses versus capitalization, research and development, advertising, and depreciation are all types of decisions which would be within the province of the controller and which may have more of an immediate effect on profit than the overt action of operating line executives.

HOW TO ORGANIZE THE CHANGE

If not properly understood, information technology has the potential of drowning the controller in his own numbers. Change is imminent; change is good, and further, change is sure to come. If the controller will not adapt to new forms of systems control and data technology, he will become remembered over a long period of time as the financial dinosaur. In order to survive, he must, in effect, assume the posture of an internal quantitative consultant who will assume the responsibility for the entire process of gathering, processing, reporting and disseminating all relevant information which is required by the various parties within a corporation. The foregoing is not meant to imply a similarity with the so-called "management information system." I distinguish between the two by the broad scope of executive wisdom and decision making intuition found in the former; whereas I look upon the latter as a more mechanized function, more easily recognizable in the form of computerized data output than as a process of thinking. I am suggesting that in effect, a *corporate command post* be established to act as the headquarters for all relevant quantitative information within a firm. I am further suggesting that the controller is the logical candidate to serve as the chief intelligence officer who will act as the disseminator and creator of information. In effect, what is being suggested is that the controller, in particular, consider his role as that of total corporate data communications. The philosophical essence of the job should be shifted from that of traditional reporting of yesterday to the supplying of pertinent information for estimating tomorrow. In the past, leading financial writers such as Robert Beyer have stated that the controller "is closer to and understands better than perhaps anyone else the entity which is the core of the problems—a system by which information is transmitted to the various management levels." The assignment to the controller of the simple exercise of a management information system is shortchanging the magnitude of the problem. The organizational and conceptual change suggested here goes far beyond the scope of such an assignment. The solution to the reorganization problem would probably require a new approach to corporate organization. In its essence, the controller would have to make clear the fact that his responsibility is manifold. His responsibility for traditional custodial accounting, for cost accounting, for data processing, for budgeting, should all be clearly identified and supplemented by a separate unit which, for want of a better description, might be considered to be *"intelligence gathering and control."*

Rather than accepting the passive historical role which has been traditional with finance, it is suggested that the controller assume a much more vigorous posture in dealing with his fellow executives. If approached in a constructive manner, there is no reason why the controller *cannot impel* improved decisions. His world should include the design and implementation of salesmens' incentive plans, advice and counsel in pricing, timing and strategy as well as optimizing media and promotional programs.

One of the last frontiers for the investigation and improvement of cost control within corporate operation is that of physical distribution. The controller is in a unique position to take advantage and fill the void created by the information vacuum in that area. Methodology which will assist in appraising the efficiency and effectiveness of physical distribution operations will close the gap in corporate standards of performance which has existed ever since physical distribution became common a few decades ago. It is forcing a rethinking of traditional corporate organization. It has already created the position of a product manager. Hopefully, in the future it will include the creation of a specialized position which might be called the marketing controller.

The following four exhibits will illustrate contemporary position descriptions for both treasurers and controllers in well-known large companies.

Position Description for
Treasurer
Diamond Shamrock Company

BASIC FUNCTION

Responsible to the appropriate senior officer for the performance of all the responsibilities of the treasurer as specified in the bylaws of the company; for administering and coordinating financial, credit, and tax policies and procedures of the company; for purchasing and administering property and casualty insurance; and for administering and coordinating shareowner and financial community relations programs.

GENERAL OBJECTIVES AND RESPONSIBILITIES

Responsibility is assigned and authority granted for the specific duties listed below as well as those listed under the section of the Management Guide entitled "Responsibilities, Relationships and Limits of Authority of Every Executive."

1. Formulate and recommend to the appropriate senior officer financial policies and administer approved policies, including the receiving, depositing, disbursing, and managing of all company funds plus investing any surplus funds in securities authorized by the board of directors. Have custody of and account for all company securities. Determine the company's financial requirements and see that sufficient funds are available for operating purposes.

2. Responsible for the formulation and complete administration of all tax policies and procedures, including Federal, state and local taxes.

3. Prepare and distribute all reports to shareowners in collaboration with all other departments of the company with respect to their areas of responsibility.

4. Develop and recommend the program to be followed with respect to shareowner relations and administer such approved programs.

5. Develop and recommend the program with respect to relations with the financial community and administer such approved programs.

6. Administer the necessary program to see that all property and casualty insurance risks are properly insured in accordance with approved company policies.

7. Formulate and recommend credit and collection policies and administer such approved policies.

8. Recommend a program for financing company pension plans and consult with the company trustees concerning investment policies of the pension trusts.

9. Maintain confidential incentive compensation records.

10. Recommend and administer approved programs dealing with governmental relations and political education activities.

11. Responsible for coordinating transactions involving acquisition or disposition of land.

12. Responsible for negotiating loan agreements to be entered into by the company.

RELATIONSHIP WITH OTHER UNITS
IN THE ORGANIZATION

1. Serve as chairman of the contributions committee; as a member of the management advisory council, the thrift plan committee, and the appropriations committee; and as a rotating member of the employee policy committee.

LIMITS OF AUTHORITY

1. General

A. Act in accordance with limits established in the general table "Limits of Authority" and the appropriation procedure manual.

2. Bank Accounts

A. Approval of two appropriate senior officers for opening and closing general accounts in major depositories. No limitation on other accounts.

Figure 3

Position Description for Treasurer Diamond Shamrock Company

Position Description for
Treasurer
Johns-Manville Corporation

Within the geographical limits of his own responsibility, the vice president for finance delegates responsibility to the treasurer as follows:

1. To determine the tax liabilities of the corporation and its subsidiaries.

2. To prepare and to file tax returns.

3. To deal with the appropriate agencies of governments—Federal, state, and local—regarding any problems that arise in respect of the determination of taxes.

4. To study and be familiar with tax laws and regulations, or proposed laws and regulations; to recommend and, as authorized, to take any action that will protect the interests of the enterprises.

5. To pursue such other studies or duties relating to taxes as the vice president may direct.

6. To propose principles and practices to govern receipt, banking, custody and disbursement of money and securities.

7. To receive and have custody of money and securities, except at locations at which, by authorization of the vice president, such duties may be entrusted to others.

8. To propose what banking depositories shall be employed, and the policies to govern such employment, and to conduct relationships with such depositories.

9. To disburse moneys pursuant to the prescribed authorities therefor, except at locations at which, by authorization of the vice president, this duty may be entrusted to others.

10. To recommend where the receipt and disbursement of money can best be performed by the fiscal department, and where best by others.

11. To prescribe policies to govern extension of credit to customers and collection of moneys due the enterprises and upon his initiative or when requested, to consult with and advise others concerning their problems of credits and collections.

12. To authorize extension of credit to and to collect moneys due from customers, except as any of such duties, by authorization of the vice president, may be entrusted to others.

13. To prescribe the form of evidence and the manner of collection of loans to employees.

14. Pursuant to prescribed policies, to collect all moneys due the enterprises from others if collection is the predominant interest.

15. To propose the character and extent of insurance against losses and risks.

16. Within authorized policies, to insure the corporation and its subsidiaries fully against losses and risks.

17. To administer self-insurance funds.

18. To prescribe methods for protection of the company's money and property against loss, except as to methods that have been made the responsibility of another.

19. To prepare the salary payroll and make payment thereof.

20. Where required by law, to withhold from salary payments designated amounts that apply to income taxes of salaried employees, and to pay such amounts to the appropriate government agency.

21. To advise those entrusted with the payment of hourly employees regarding the manner of withholding and the method of payment of income taxes withheld from wages.

22. To compute incentive compensation payable to salaried employees.

23. To interpret the laws and regulations that govern sales or use taxes; and to supply information regarding the invoicing of such taxes to all whose responsibility requires such information.

24. To ascertain the amounts of sales or use taxes billed to customers and to pay such amounts to the appropriate government agency.

25. To maintain the records of the retirement plan.

26. To recommend to their boards of directors the payment of dividends by subsidiary corporations.

27. To provide for loans from one affiliated corporation to another, and for the payment of inter-company accounts, in the best interests of the enterprises.

28. To observe and report upon the manner of performance of fiscal policies and methods by other departments and the divisions.

29. To pursue such other fiscal studies and duties as the vice president may direct.

Figure 4

Position Description for Treasurer Johns-Manville Corporation

Position Description for
Controller
Johns-Manville Corporation

The Vice President for Finance delegates responsibility to the Controller as follows:

ACCOUNTING

Accounts

1. To prepare the accounts of the corporations, except such as the Vice President may entrust to other responsibilities.

2. To recommend what accounting can best be performed by the Accounting Department, and what by other responsibilities.

3. To allocate income and expenditures among classifications and responsibilities.

4. To allocate general expense among operating divisions.

Expenditures

5. To verify the propriety of disbursement to be made at Headquarters.

Statements

6. To prepare financial statements for publication in the form prescribed by the President.

7. To prepare such detailed statements of the transactions and properties of the enterprises as will assist others to improve the earnings of the enterprises.

8. To recommend the nature of the published financial statements of the corporations.

Relations with Others

9. To provide for furnishing information to guide and assist personnel engaged in accounting and cost work throughout the enterprises.

10. To observe generally the manner of performance of accounting by other responsibilities, and to make recommendations for needed improvements.

General

11. To pursue such other accounting studies and duties as the Vice President may direct.

ANALYSIS

Financial Appraisal

12. To appraise proposed expenditures, where required and not otherwise provided for, or at the request of the President, Senior Officer or Senior Operating Vice President; and to advise as to their financial desirability.

13. To appraise the financial results of operations and the benefits received from expenditures made in the enterprises and reported thereon.

Financial Methods

14. To prescribe methods of financial analysis and to maintain such manuals of practice as will be useful.

15. To observe the manner of performance of financial analysis by the operating divisions and to recommend needed improvements.

Profit Planning and Budgets

16. To prescribe the methods and procedures to be followed in profit planning and the budgetary control of expenditures.

17. To appraise proposed profit plans for the President, where not otherwise provided for, and to consolidate corporate profit, action and growth plans.

18. To prepare forecasts of earnings, cash and investment for the corporation, and to determine annually the amount of general expense to be charged to each division during the year.

Services to Others

19. To supply financial service and assistance required by the President, and by vice presidents and department managers who are not in an operating division.

Government Business

20. To develop and recommend policies and procedures that will govern the extent to which J-M divulges cost and price information to contractors or agencies of the Federal Government and to provide general assistance, appropriate to a financial responsibility, when requested by division, research and other personnel dealing with these outside parties.

General

21. In accordance with the principles prescribed by the President, to establish the prices at which one division will sell products to another division, subject to the authority of division general managers to establish such prices by agreement.

22. To pursue such other studies or duties relating to financial analysis, profit planning or budgets as the Vice President may direct.

Figure 5

Position Description for Controller Johns-Manville Corporation

Position Description for
Controller
P. R. Mallory & Co. Inc.

BASIC FUNCTIONS

The duties of the Controller shall be to maintain adequate records of all assets, liabilities and transactions of the Corporation; to see that adequate audits thereof are currently and regularly made; and, in conjunction with other officers and employees, to initiate and enforce measures and procedures whereby the business of the Corporation shall be conducted with the maximum safety, efficiency and economy. His duties and powers shall extend to all subsidiary corporations, and, so far as the President may deem practicable, to all affiliated corporations.

The Controller is the chief accounting officer of the Company. In addition to his responsibility for maintaining all accounting records, the Controller's duties include the development, analysis, and interpretation of statistical and accounting information to appraise operating results in terms of costs, budgets, policies of operations, trends, and increased profit possibilities.

Has those additional responsibilities and authorities normally associated with an officer of the Corporation.

DUTIES AND RESPONSIBILITIES

1. To initiate, prepare, and issue standard practices relating to accounting policies and cost procedures as are necessary to ensure that adequate accounting records are maintained of all assets, liabilities, and transactions of the Company and that suitable systems are followed in compilation of product, manufacturing, distribution, and administrative costs.

2. To ensure that controls are adequate and current so that corrective action can be taken where necessary at the earliest possible moment.

3. To properly record financial transactions covered by minutes of the meetings of the Board of Directors.

4. Share the responsibility to see that properly qualified men occupy the positions of operating unit Controller.

5. To prepare and interpret financial statements, cost data, and management control reports of the Company. In cooperation with the Vice President–Finance, assist other executives in appraising their activities in terms of financial results, pointing out significant trends in operations as indicated by analysis of the reports; and assist the executives in determining future policies based on applying sound business judgment to the conclusions deduced from such facts.

6. To maintain a continuing internal auditing program.

7. To cooperate with public accountants appointed as auditors in the execution of their program of independent auditing.

8. To establish or approve procedures and methods for taking and costing of all inventories.

9. To review and approve procedures for handling cash and property so as to protect the Company from loss through negligence or dishonesty.

10. To maintain adequate records of authorized appropriations, and check against the appropriations the sums expended pursuant thereto.

11. In conjunction with other officers and department heads, to review and approve budgets covering all divisions and activities of the Company.

12. To coordinate clerical and office methods, records, reports, and procedures throughout the Company and its subsidiaries, and arrange for the development of standards for office and clerical activities, forms, equipment, and supplies for use throughout the Company. Develop clerical cost programs to insure that accounting and related records are maintained at lowest possible expense to the Company and its subsidiaries.

13. To supervise the activities of the Corporate Accounting, Internal Audit, Systems and the Budgetary Control departments.

ORGANIZATION RELATIONSHIPS

1. The Controller reports to the Vice President–Finance.

2. Has a functional relationship through the Vice President–Finance and President to the Presidents or General Managers of the divisions and subsidiaries and through them to the Treasurers/Controllers of those divisions and subsidiaries.

3. Maintains such relationships outside of the Company as are necessary to enhance the Company name and reputation.

Figure 6

Position Description for Controller P. R. Mallory & Co. Inc.

3

CASH MANAGEMENT FOR
SMALL AND MEDIUM-SIZED COMPANIES

WHAT IS CASH PLANNING?

Not too long ago, it was a common business practice to keep large amounts of cash on hand at all times. The idea seemed to be to keep as much cash in the till as possible—just in case it was needed in a hurry; budgeting as we know it was practiced by only a handful of companies.

With the advent of scientific management techniques, management learned to avoid most emergencies through careful planning, and to cope with unavoidable emergencies by maintaining only enough ready cash to be safe. It didn't take businessmen long to realize that it was wasteful to keep money idle, that it was just as important to keep money busy as to keep workers busy. This rather apparent advance was only the first step toward what is now an indispensable management technique: cash planning and budgeting.

Today no budgeting effort is complete until management determines the effect its operating plans will have on the company's cash position, and how probable variations in cash position during the budget period will affect operating plans. Using the sales forecast and production and expense budgets as a foundation, most businesses develop sound cash management plans to go with their operating plans, and to insure having sufficient funds to carry out the plans expressed in the operating budget.

Preparing the production budget and related expense budgets is an extension of "cost accounting"; it is a means of determining realistic cost estimates for each of the activities necessary to meet production and sales goals. Preparing projected profit and loss statements, balance sheets, and cash forecasts and budgets is often referred to as "financial accounting"; it is a way of getting an overall picture of a particular company's financial status at a given future time, and of determining the probable financial needs as a result of budgeted operations. In even simpler terms, financial accounting is *cash planning*.

Cash planning is the process of estimating all sources and uses of cash over a definite future period. Cash planning is often characterized by other terms, such as cash projection or cash flow analysis, financial projection or flow analysis, cash or financial budgeting, and cash handling.

Having cash to meet obligations as they fall due is the first requirement for continued business existence. More companies fail for lack of ready cash than for any other reason, and this includes firms earning sound profits. It does a business no good to show handsome profits if all its cash is tied up in inventory, machinery, or other non-cash assets. A certain degree of liquidity is essential in any enterprise. To say that more businesses fail for a lack of cash than for a lack of profits seems at first to be a paradox. But profits and cash are not necessarily similar.

In return for the cash it expends, a business naturally expects to get back *more;* it must take in more than it spends to keep going. But if something goes wrong with the ordinary cash flow so that the firm begins to spend more than it takes in, the financial executive must find additional funds to keep the business going. The very existence of a business often depends directly on the amount of cash the company has and how well this cash is used.

Essentially, cash planning and management help the finance department determine how much liquidity is best; it "calls the signals" for varying the cash position to accommodate changes in requirements, showing when to borrow and when to invest surplus funds. With sound advance cash planning, management can always determine what funds it needs to carry out operating plans, when it will need them, and for how long.

Through advance cash budgeting and day-to-day cash management activities, finance attempts to maintain working capital at appropriate levels; it studies the factors that determine the demand for current assets and plans cash inflows and outflows to meet those needs. The demand for working capital at any given time during the budget period depends primarily on the company's operating plans, as expressed in the sales forecast, production budget, and in the various expense budgets. But the demand also varies in relation to such factors as these:

- General market conditions.
- Sales variations during the budget period.
- Other variations created by seasonal aspects of the business.
- The firm's manufacturing cycle.
- The relative availability of materials and labor.
- The ratio of credit sales to cash sales.
- The seasonal or cyclical distribution of credit sales volume.
- Prevailing terms of sales.
- The company's credit and collection policies.
- Financing measures available to the firm.
- Foreseeable, but unusual, cash needs.

On the basis of its observations and estimates of these conditions, financial management attempts to gauge the minimum amount of working capital necessary to sustain the flow of capital from cash to inventories to receivables and back to cash. It must maintain a constant cash balance sufficient to discount all bills, to purchase the necessary materials and components for production, to carry a stock of finished goods large enough to permit prompt delivery on customers' orders, to finance customers' receivables, and to meet payrolls and other fixed operating expenses.

The problem is determining *how much* working capital a certain company is likely to need at different times during the budget period. Some working capital requirements are relatively stable, while others are highly variable. Regardless of how much direct material is called for in the production budget for some future time, the finance executive must know where to find the necessary working capital to provide additional direct material if the original forecast proves wrong. An error in the sales forecast can have an even greater effect. When sales volume increases, the company must produce more goods. This requires heavier inventories, and the company's receivables may also swell. Finance must provide—in advance—for the possibility of increased working capital requirements; it must supply the cash necessary to process the goods, to store them, and to carry the additional accounts receivable.

In addition to regular working capital, most companies need an additional reserve or cushion to cover contingencies. For example, rising prices often create a need for more cash to finance inventories and receivables. A company also needs a cushion in case of sudden recessions that might create the need for larger amounts of ready cash to carry the firm over to better times. Strikes, fires, and other unforeseeable disasters can eat up cash in a hurry. And what company knows for sure that its competitors will maintain their current level of operations, that it won't have to retaliate against their stepped-up sales or production efforts?

Many so-called "contingencies" are actually foreseeable—with the right advance planning. For example, if a major labor contract expires during a budget period, management should recognize the *possibility* of a strike from the beginning. Although it cannot flatly predict a strike, management should make tentative plans for obtaining short-term funds during that period, or for restricting or deferring major disbursements to generate extra working capital internally. Only by studying past records of cash flow can financial management determine what contingencies are likely to arise and how much working capital they might consume if they do occur.

At the very least, a company must have a sufficient working capital cushion to provide for normal fluctuations of income and disbursements during the budget period, and to cover the cost of such incidentals as banking services in handling deposits and withdrawals.

CASH PLANNING THROUGH CASH BUDGETING

The primary financial or cash planning technique is cash budgeting. Cash budgeting is primarily concerned with planning working capital requirements. In its cash-management function, finance also strives to maintain working capital at levels sufficient to permit flexible operations. Working capital is generally construed as the excess of current assets over current liabilities, including the following items:

Current Assets:

Cash on hand and bank deposits.
Accounts receivable (less reserves for bad debts).
Other short-term notes and acceptances receivable (less reserves).
Most inventories (including raw materials, work in process, finished goods, and supplies).

Current Liabilities:

Accounts payable to creditors and others.
Notes payable.
Accrued expenses.
Bonds and other long-term notes payable within one year.
Cash dividends payable to stockholders.

A balanced working capital position is necessary for many reasons. A liquid current position enables a company to meet its bills for direct material and direct labor regularly, to pay for production and sales activities. This is what keeps a company going—operating steadily. A consistent level of operations increases efficiency, lowers production costs, and raises employee morale. Ready working capital also enables a business to pay its suppliers promptly; it generally means that the firm can buy in bulk quantities and take greater advantage of suppliers' discount terms, adding still more to the firm's earnings. Besides these advantages, a liquid current position enhances the company's reputation as a credit risk and virtually guarantees the availability of credit capital.

In addition to the rather obvious benefit of making available additional funds for investment, and of pointing out impending cash shortages so that finance can provide additional funds through borrowings and other means, cash budgeting provides many less tangible benefits.

Cash Planning Provides Funds for Growth

Growth and expansion generally bring a larger flow of cash into a company. But the initial expenditures that make growth possible (the heavy investment in fixed assets, for example) are likely to restrict a company's cash position for quite some time before it begins to realize increased earnings. By planning its expenditures carefully, a company can operate safely with far less cash, releasing more funds for use in financing expansion.

The value of sound financial planning to an expanding firm is perhaps best explained by an example of what *faulty* cash planning can do to a growing company. This company's owner-managers concentrated primarily on manufacturing activities and paid little attention to their increasing financial problems. At first, profits were sufficient to support the firm's moderate growth rate, but then the owners decided to develop and market several new products. Their production and marketing plans were sound enough, but with little or no advance cash planning the firm's resources proved wholly inadequate to support such an energetic expansion attempt. On paper the business was a "going concern," a real profit-maker. But the profits were tied up in plant and equipment. The business soon ran out of cash and was forced to merge with another company.

At least part of this company's problem was management's failure to use available cash planning techniques to find out how long it would take cash inflows to catch up to outflows once the expansion effort got under way. Management should have budgeted the company's operations to determine how to employ most profitably the funds the company had, how much to allocate to regular operations and how much to expansion efforts. With a clear idea of the minimum funds needed, management might have offered securities or incurred long-term debt to keep the firm alive. But since the owners had virtually no idea of probable cash needs, expansion was practically impossible.

Cash Planning Enhances Temporary Investments

Instead of holding onto idle cash, more and more companies are investing surplus assets in short-term securities and notes. By forecasting its cash requirements well in advance, a company can determine what portion of its cash surplus to invest, and for how long. With this information as a guide, the company can decide how best to invest the surplus. Depending on its probable future cash needs, a company may carry several types of investments. For example, a business might have some investments that it can promptly reconvert to cash if necessary. It may have other investments—perhaps loans—timed to mature at about the same time the cash budget indicates additional funds will be needed; notes on loans might be timed to mature with disbursements for.such major expenditures as tax or dividend payments, for example. Any remaining cash that the firm will not need for a year or more may be invested in regular securities.

Cash Planning Helps Obtain Debt Capital

Reliable cash flow forecasts can often help a firm obtain credit. Such forecasts (or budgets) give the borrowing concern advance notice of the need for credit, allowing finance to seek credit on the most advantageous terms. The company also has time to plan its operations, and to adjust them if necessary to correspond to capital requirements.

Lenders often want evidence of how much a borrowing concern really needs and for how long. They also want some indication of what the borrowing firm intends to do with the loan proceeds, plus a *definite* plan for repaying the indebtedness. A bank or other lender may not require a cash forecast, but the company that provides a detailed cash budget along with its loan application has a far better chance of getting the loan on favorable terms.

Cash Planning Has Other Advantages

To manage its funds effectively, a firm must have timely and reliable information about cash income and expenditures. It must have reliable forecasts of future cash receipts, disbursements, and cash balances to use in planning such disbursements as dividend payments and payments of interest and principle to creditors. Cash planning and budgeting always result in better overall financial control; finance receives regular reports on expenditures and receipts, either from branch finance officers or from operating departments. This is especially necessary in highly decentralized organizations where branch finance managers have authority to act independently. A formal cash budget program in such organizations enables the central finance office to determine the company's overall cash position at any time.

THE CASH BUDGET PERIOD

The cash budget is actually a forecast of receipts and disbursements over the cash budget period. The cash budget or forecast is predicated largely on the sales forecast, the production budget, and the various expense budgets.

It takes into account probable variations in the economy, competitive factors, and other conditions. Because so many different factors can affect a company's working capital position, cash budgets are often limited to periods shorter than that covered by the overall operating budget. Cash projections seldom cover more than two years. Although cash budgeting *can* serve as a general guide in estimating long-term financial requirements, cash budgets are most effective in determining current working capital requirements.

To provide some indication of probable results over a normal budget period, plus more accurate estimates for shorter periods, cash projections are often prepared for a full year (or for the length of the budget period) and broken down to show quarterly and monthly subtotals. But some firms calculate their probable cash position on a weekly basis, and some even project it to show daily totals. Generally speaking, the more decentralized a company's operations, the shorter the intervals covered by its cash budget; and companies with sharply fluctuating levels of income or disbursements often budget their working capital requirements for very short periods as well.

Of course, not every company needs a cash budget broken down to show receipts and disbursements by day or by week. But even those businesses whose budgets show cash flows for longer periods should at least review budget results at fairly short intervals. Company expenditures can be highly predictable, but income is rarely easy to estimate; conditions affecting *both* receipts and disbursements can change dramatically. Finance should reappraise the cash budget at least once each month, no matter what the company's size or line of business.

By estimating cash receipts and disbursements for an entire budget period, then adjusting the forecast each month or week, finance can usually tell when there will be an excess of disbursements over receipts or vice versa. If it appears cash will be in short supply one month, finance can begin planning ahead of time to borrow funds to cover that period. If it appears that excess cash will be available at some future time, finance can begin planning to invest the surplus in appropriate securities or notes.

HOW A CASH BUDGET IS DEVELOPED

Most cash budgets are simply forecasts of how much cash a company will need to finance its operating plans during a specific future period. To develop such a plan, finance must study past company financial statements to determine where the company stands now in relation to past performance levels; it must detect and project trends in past and current financial statements to get an indication of the company's financial position three, six, ten, or twelve months from now. Finance must estimate *all* cash receipts and expenditures over the budget period, based on expected levels of activity, the anticipated rate of accounts turnover, and any seasonal characteristics likely to affect cash flow. The cash forecast may be simple or quite complex, depending on the size of the company, its planning and budget needs, and management's philosophy on budgeting.

Most cash budgets show probable cash excesses or shortages, enabling finance to balance cash flows to protect the firm's working capital position. Figure 1 shows a simple cash budget covering a period of one year. The budget shows estimates of income and expenditures broken down for the first three months and for the last three quarters. As the budget period progresses, finance can develop more detailed estimates showing probable receipts and disbursements for each month in the second quarter, then for each month in the third quarter, and so on.

Notice that the company's cash position is seriously threatened in only one month; the estimates of income and disbursements indicate a probable working capital deficit of $4,000 in March. Since March is relatively near the beginning of the budget period, the estimate is likely to be a highly accurate prediction of the company's cash position in that month. In this case, a short-term loan of $10,000 appears sufficient to offset the deficit and supply a satisfactory working capital cushion. And with a heavy surplus forecast for each of the last three quarters, the firm should have no difficulty repaying the loan at or before maturity. In fact, this business appears to have the enviable problem of determining how to invest its cash surplus most profitably. The cash budget shows how the company plans to invest the surplus it expects in the last three quarters, the amounts it plans to plow back into the business, and the amounts it anticipates investing outside the business.

	Jan.	Feb.	March	2nd Qtr.	3rd Qtr.	4th Qtr.
Cash balance (beginning)	$40,000	$20,000	$12,000	$ 6,000	$14,000	$20,000
Receipts	30,000	60,000	56,000	72,000	81,000	74,000
Less disbursements	50,000	68,000	72,000	44,000	45,000	50,000
Shortage	—	—	—	—	—	—
Bank loan rq'd	—	—	10,000	—	—	—
Ending cash balance	$20,000	$12,000	$ 6,000	$34,000	$50,000	$44,000
Available for outside investment	—	—	—	$20,000	$30,000	$19,000
Retained for operating expenses	$20,000	$12,000	$ 6,000	$14,000	$20,000	$25,000

Figure 1

Simple Cash Budget

Preliminary Questions

Even in a simple cash budget like this, estimating cash flow during the year is not easy. Finance must find the answers to such questions as these before it can even begin to draw up such a budget:

- What are the usual terms of sale? How many days must credit sales be carried as accounts receivable?
- What kind of raw material inventories must be carried and in what quantities? How fast do inventories turn over; what is the time lag from order to delivery?
- How many finished products must be kept in inventory at various times to fill customers' orders promptly?
- How much should be set aside as a reserve for contingencies?
- What bank balance must be maintained at all times in order to discount suppliers' bills and provide a sufficient working capital cushion?
- How much in compensating balances—if any—do the firm's banks require?
- What is the firm's dividend policy? Does management intend to distribute most earnings or retain them in business?

Underlying these considerations, of course, are the estimate of operating costs contained in the production budget and the other expense budgets and the estimate of total sales income found in the sales forecast.

Two Key Items

Since the cash budget describes the cash income estimate and the cash disbursements estimate for a stated period, sharp forecasting is essential. This is critically true in the two areas of collections and material purchases.

Collections

A firm's cash income depends very much on the collection of accounts receivable—one of the most important phases of the business. Establishing a sound method for estimating collections is simple for some firms, complicated for others. In either case, the basic method remains the same because estimates must be based on past sales and collection experience.

To project collections, calculate these four experiences over a three-year period:

1. The average sales figure for each month.
2. The average increase in sales.
3. The collection pattern—the proportion of billings for which payment is received the first month, the second month, and the third month.
4. The proportion of uncollectible accounts.

Sales	Jan.	Feb.	Mar.	Apr.	May	June	July	Aug.	Sept.	Oct.	Nov.	Dec.	Misc.
Jan. $200,000	(Oct.) 15,200	(Nov.) 120,000	60,000	10,000									
Feb. 180,000	(Nov.) 114,000	(Dec.) 19,000	108,000	54,000	9,000								
Mar. 300,000	(Dec.) 239,400	(Dec.) 119,700	(Dec.) 18,850	180,000	90,000	15,000							
Apr. 400,000					240,000	120,000	20,000						
May 350,000						210,000	105,000	17,500					
June 290,000							174,000	87,000	14,500				
July 240,000								144,000	72,000	12,000			
Aug. 220,000									132,000	66,000	11,000		
Sept. 280,000										168,000	84,000	14,000	
Oct. 320,000											192,000	96,000	
Nov. 400,000												240,000	
Dec. 410,000													
Total 3,600,000	368,600	258,700	187,850	244,000	339,000	345,000	299,000	248,550	218,500	246,000	287,000	350,000	108,000

Figure 2

Forecast of Monthly Collections

Figure 2 illustrates a forecast of monthly collections, based on the above four experiences. The sales figures for each month reflect averages for the past three years, after adding five percent for the average annual increase in sales. Collections have formed this pattern: 60 percent of a month's sales if received the first following month, 30 percent the second following month, and 5 percent the third following month. Collections from slow-paying accounts (three percent) appear in the miscellaneous column. The remaining two percent is charged off.

> *Example:* The collections for October, November and December in the current year, which must be carried over to January, February, and March of the following year, reflect the five percent lower sales for the current year.

Some firms sell on discount, others offer 90-day credit, still others sell to prime accounts who almost invariably remit payment within 30 days. Although every business requires a slightly different approach, collections can be forecast with reasonable accuracy, *provided* they are constantly revised to reflect changes as they occur.

Material Purchases

A manager can estimate such items as payroll, taxes, and insurance with a close degree of accuracy. Purchases, however, may pose a nettlesome problem. For a more accurate estimate of material purchases, study your sales forecast in conjunction with the production schedule. Determine material needs on the basis of both production plans and delivery dates. Then, outline projected purchases and due dates for payments, while keeping in mind these variables: (1) revisions in production schedules; (2) failure of suppliers to deliver material; (3) price changes in major items; (4) extra buying because of strikes, unexpected shortages, or announced price increases. The cash outlay for materials must also include an appropriate provision for scrap, damage, or other losses. Be sure to add the amount of these variances to the total standard cost of materials budgeted. Otherwise, the budget will fail to reflect the actual costs you may expect to incur.

The Budget Period and a Common Pitfall

Budget estimates will be most effective if limited to a one-year period. Cash projections become even more useful if you break the annual budget down to show quarterly and monthly subtotals. Some financial managers go a step further and calculate their firm's probable cash position on a weekly basis, or even daily totals. If totals are run monthly, beware of the "tenth of the month phenomena." The practice of mailing checks on the tenth of the month can lead to a cash shortage between the first and the tenth.

Which method of cash budgeting works best? Financial officers use two methods for preparing cash budgets: (1) the receipts and disbursements method, and (2) the adjusted income method.

In using the *receipts and disbursements method,* the first step consists of listing all sources of cash receipts for the budget period—one year, for example. Then, break these amounts down into monthly totals. Follow the

		January	
Cash receipts	*Budget*	*Actual*	*Difference*
Opening balance	$121,400	$121,400	$ 0
Cash sales	36,000	35,600	(400)
Charge sales	160,800	159,000	(1,800)
Sales of fixed assets	20,000	19,000	(1,000)
Interest, dividend income	0	0	0
Bank loans	0	0	0
Total cash available	$338,200	$335,000	($3,200)
Cash disbursements			
Wages	25,600	25,800	(200)
Taxes	7,400	7,500	(100)
Insurance	25,200	25,100	100
Material purchases	48,000	49,700	(1,700)
Operating expenses	120,000	121,000	(1,000)
Rent	1,600	1,560	40
Interest expense	2,700	2,900	(200)
Repayment of bank loans	0	0	0
Capital expenditures	20,000	18,000	2,000
Dividends	4,000	4,000	0
Total cash required	$254,500	$255,560	($1,060)
Cash excess	$ 83,700	$ 79,440	($4,260)
or			
Additional cash needed	0	0	0

Figure 3

Typical Cash Budget for One Month—Receipts and Disbursements Method

same procedure for cash payments. The resulting budget will then indicate the cash income and outlay on a monthly basis, and the cash deficit or surplus.

In using the *adjusted income method,* the income statement is adjusted by taking into account non-cash charges and receipts. This means adding depreciation, other non-cash charges, and estimated earnings to cash on hand at the beginning of the period. Principal cash outlays are for fixed assets, retirement of liabilities, payment of dividends, and the like. The resulting balance gives the amount of cash available for non-operating expenses or for investment. It also gives the cash on hand for the beginning of the next budget period.

August 15, 197___

Balance August 14, 197___	$100,000
Receipts:	
Cash Sales	28,000
Accounts Receivable (collections)	25,000
Other Income	13,000
TOTAL RECEIPTS	$ 66,000
Expenditures:	
Supplies and materials	$ 10,000
Payroll	54,600
Taxes	8,800
Accounts Payable (reduction)	27,000
Other Expenses	4,200
TOTAL EXPENDITURES	$104,600
Balance August 15, 197___	$ 61,400
Balance July 31. 197___	$ 45,300
Forecast Balance for August 15, 197___	60,000
Anticipated Receipts for August 16, 197___	50,000
Anticipated Expenditures for August 16, 197___	100,000

Figure 4

Daily Cash Report

The adjusted income method works well for spotlighting working capital needs, but it doesn't offer as much control over cash as does the receipts and disbursements method, especially in companies with inconsistent sales and earnings. Most financial officers prefer the receipts and disbursements method (Figure 3). This method traces the movement of cash through each item of income and expense, simplifying comparisons of budgeted and actual figures. If cash projections are a particular problem, both methods can be used and the results compared.

Follow-up with Cash Control Reports

During the cash budget period, the company's cash position must be checked against that envisaged in the cash budget. This information is considered so important that many financial officers require cash reports on a daily basis.

Cash budgets are not set up on a daily basis. Cash receipts and disbursements in any one day are rarely very significant. However, daily reports over a period of several days do indicate whether the rate of flow is proceeding as expected. A daily cash report is normally a simple document (see Figure 4). It shows the previous day's cash balance, cash flows for the day, and the day's closing balance.

Despite the importance of cash reports, the finance manager must remember that they give him only a part of the financial picture. For a sound assessment of a firm's cash position at a particular time, he must also know the amounts of accounts receivable and payable, the inventory position, and the accrued payroll. To accomplish this, a Daily Financial Position Report is more meaningful to many financial managers than a simple cash report.

DAILY FINANCIAL POSITION REPORT

This daily report, Figure 5, is a management tool and not an accounting record. Quick comparative data is more important than auditor type precision. The report starts with a computation of cash; next are listed the major cash demands in the next ten days as a reminder and planning guide for the manager. The figures should be a rough estimate based on the number of people on the payroll. The receivables and payables section are similar to the cash section. The figures entered are control totals from bookkeeping runs—either on machine, accounting systems or manual systems. If cash receipts are posted only twice a week, the cash receipts would be subtracted only twice a week. In that case, the comparative data would only be applicable to receivables twice a week when the balances were accurate. The inventory section has two plus quantities—purchases and man-hours. In manufacturing firms, the addition to inventory is the sum of purchases and man-hours times a labor and overhead rate. Cost of sales can be computed as a percentage of invoices sent or actually costed out on an item-for-item basis.

Receivables

Bal. Fwd.		_____ . __
ADD Daily Billing	+	_____ . __
SUBTRACT credits issued	−	_____ . __
SUBTRACT paid via cash rec.	−	_____ . __
ADD Adjustments	+	_____ . __
SUBTRACT Adjustments	−	_____ . __
New Balance		

Payables

Bal Fwd.		_____ . __
ADD Invoices posted	+	_____ . __
SUBTRACT debits issued	−	_____ . __
SUBTRACT bills paid	−	_____ . __
ADD Adjustments	+	_____ . __
SUBTRACT Adjustments	−	_____ . __
New Balance		

Cash

Bal. Fwd.		_____ . __
ADD Cash rec'd	+	_____ . __
SUBTRACT Cash disb'd	−	_____ . __
New Balance		

Figure 5

Daily Financial Position Report

MAJOR PITFALLS OF THE DAILY FINANCIAL
POSITION REPORT

The report can be a useful management tool if properly used as a simple, quick guide. It is not uncommon for one or both of the following faults to show up.

1. The manager may demand more accuracy than is necessary and subordinates will comply by spending large amounts of time generating each day's flash report.
2. Subordinates may be afraid to estimate and will, without informing the manager, spend and go to great lengths to make the report accurate. Left to their own discretion, bookkeepers will try to make the balances on this report equal the general ledger to the penny.

Both situations are to be avoided since they make timely information hard to get and very expensive.

Weekly Cash Meetings Help to Spot Variances

Study each week's activity with top financial personnel and other concerned executives. Seek explanations for variances in the cash budget and probe their influences on future planning. The meeting should result in a decision on the action required to bring results back in line.

Action decisions may be such as these:

1. To change forecasts because of new facts or previous misinterpretations of facts.
2. To change the amount to borrow or pay back next week under your bank loan arrangement.
3. To exert extra effort in a particular area to speed cash flow.
4. To add or remove contingent items.
5. To alter dates for paying major items, when flexibility permits.
6. To determine whether collection trends justify the accounts receivable turnover rate used in calculating income from sales.

Use Monthly Meetings to Appraise Longer Range Developments

At monthly meetings, broader trends and their effects on the monthly, quarterly, semi-annual and annual budgets can be assessed. Items to review at these meetings include financing policies, types of accounts with banks, and timing of new acquisitions and types of funds required. These discussions should include other executives from key areas. The marketing executive can supply data for that all-important area—sales and billings. The purchasing officer can project the receipt of materials based on the orders he has placed. Other division officers can give profitability estimates for their areas of responsibility. These meetings will provide the interchange of information that is so essential for spotlighting slippages in the budget that, if left undetected, could seriously jeopardize anticipated cash flows.

HOW TO MAKE CASH AVAILABLE FASTER

Any company may face occasional cash shortages despite good earnings. They may stem from faulty operating procedures that prolong the interval between the time the firm makes a sale and the time the bank converts the customer's check into usable funds.

This conversion rate directly determines how often a dollar becomes cash during the budget period. The more often a firm turns over its cash supply, the more funds will be available when needed, and the less money will be borrowed. Here are some suggestions for accelerating the availability of funds.

1. *Improve the billing procedures.* A customer will rarely remit payment before he receives a billing. The longer the delay in sending him an invoice, the longer the wait for payment. The objective is to get payment as quickly as possible; you must expedite the transmittal of invoices. A delay of even one day is costly. Example A—If a firm has a daily billing of $60,-000, a delay of one day in converting invoices into usable funds, at five and one-half percent, costs $3,300 on an annual basis.

2. *Centralize the cash functions.* The longer a check is in motion from one processing point to another, the longer it remains unavailable as cash. Centralizing the cash function avoids the "float" that results from a decentralized system.

3. *Step up collection procedures.* Slow payers use cash while they force others to get along without it. The more funds that are tied up in receivables, the more borrowing must be done. A well-managed collection system quickly reconverts goods sold back into cash.

4. *Streamline banking arrangements.* An important method for making cash more readily available consists of shortening the time lag between payments of funds by customers and the deposit of those funds to a firm's bank account. The banking industry offers several ways to do this:

The "Pouch Loose" System

In this procedure, checks from all companies in one city, such as Chicago, drawn on banks in a distant city, such as New York, are sent by air mail to that city in a specially designed and marked pouch. Upon its arrival at the airport, the pouch is taken to the clearing house where messengers at scheduled times deliver the checks to the various banks. This procedure may save anywhere from seven hours to two days, depending on closeness to weekends or holidays that the checks are mailed.

The "Area Concentration" System

Many companies with a great number of distribution centers find it both practical and profitable to regionalize their market areas to speed cash turnover. The company divides its market area into geographic regions, based on the volume of business activity, and selects a depository bank within each region. It then instructs customers to send their checks to a regional company office which deposits the checks in the regional bank.

This arrangement speeds collections because checks received inside a region and deposited with the regional bank have been, in the main, drawn on banks within the region. Arrangements are made with the regional bank to keep funds on deposit to meet regional office expenses, and these funds can be drawn by using wire transfers until the account reaches a prearranged minimum.

The "Lock Box" System

The lock box system is a refinement of the area concentration system. When using the lock box system, a company regionalizes its market areas as with the area concentration system, but asks its customers to send payment to a post office box instead of a regional company office. The regional bank picks up the checks at the post office box and sends them to the banks on which they are drawn for payment.

Concurrently, the regional bank sends the accounting office a list of the checks, and a photographic reproduction of each check. The accounting or billing department processes these lists and photocopies them while the original checks go on their way to be cashed. The checks are often cashed before the accounting process is completed.

The lock box system offers several advantages: it hastens cash availability by one to three or more days; it may eliminate some clerical expenses when volume is heavy; it helps ensure that checks will not be returned for lack of funds.

But it can also be expensive. It costs as much to process a $5.00 check as a $10,000 check. In most cases, the lock box system justifies its cost only when a company has a heavy volume of checks of large amounts. The economics involved, however, frequently differ from company to company. A banker can study each situation to determine if this service warrants the cost. When consulting with your banker to determine cost, have this informa-tion ready: an estimate of how many checks you expect to process annually; an estimate of the average check amount; type of check reproduction re-quired; listings desired, etc.

The "Bank Wire" System

Another technique for improving cash turnover is the bank wire pro-cedure, which provides for a quick transfer of cash to the point where it is needed. Banks that are members of the bank wire system are connected by telegraph or telephone into a wire network. Each bank has its own special code word, and prefaces its messages with this code word to authenticate a transaction. Within minutes a money transfer of any size is completed. Any bank that is not a member of a wire network can take advantage of these services through a member bank with which it corresponds.

OTHER WAYS TO MAKE FULL USE OF CASH

Take advantage of cash discounts. Cash discounts may be viewed as bonuses offered to customers for advance payment. Cash discounts are typi-cally stated as:

(1) 2/10, net 30
(2) 3/10, E.O.M.

The first set of terms means that the seller will reduce the customer's bill by two percent for submitting payment within 10 days. Otherwise, he pays the full amount in 30 days. The second set of terms permits the pur-chaser to deduct three percent for payment by the 10th of the month follow-ing the invoice date, with the full amount payable by the end of the month.

These discounts offer significant savings. On a $1,000 order, terms of "2/10, net 30" permit a savings of $20. Another way of recognizing the value of this arrangement is to consider the loss incurred by *not* taking the discount. By paying the full amount in 30 days, the buyer pays two percent interest for using $1,000 for only 20 days. In this example, he would pay $1 interest per day for holding onto his money. In terms of yearly interest rates—the only true basis for measuring money costs—this equals $365 a year, or 36.5 percent on $1,000. As a corollary of the rule to take advantage of cash discounts, there is also the rule that where no discount is available, the payment should be made at the last possible date, consistent with the maintenance of good credit standing. Thus, with a net 30 day account, pay-ment should be made at the end of the 30 days.

Manufacturers and wholesalers offer a variety of credit terms free of interest charge. In many industries, payment terms up to 90 days are common, and even longer in seasonal lines. Taking advantage of these terms can help stretch your cash supply.

Lease Instead of Buy

Numerous industries now make available a wide variety of leasing plans that avoid the large initial cash outlay required in making a purchase. Tax-deductibility is an added fillip. Each finance officer must review his own case in detail. Short range advantages may not always outweigh long range drawbacks, but as an immediate means of preserving working capital, leasing has great appeal.

WORK IDLE CASH HARDER

Almost every company occasionally has more cash than it needs for the immediate future—the next four to six months or longer. When cash is available to meet near-term obligations and when no benefit, such as a discount, can be gained by making advance payment, that idle cash can be put to work in income-producing investments.

Of paramount concern is the safety of the investment, because surplus funds are not intended for investment purposes, but are merely in excess supply for a short period. They will soon be needed to meet upcoming obligations. Fortunately, there are ways for idle cash to earn income and incur virtually no risk.

Bank Time Deposits

Many companies transfer surplus funds from their checking accounts (demand deposit) to savings accounts, or time deposits. The investment manager restricts time deposits to those banks that are insured by the Federal Deposit Insurance Corporation. This government agency insures accounts up to $15,000 in all insured banks. Firms wanting to deposit more than this amount must open accounts with additional banks.

Interest rates on time deposits are regulated either by the Federal Reserve System or by the Federal Deposit Insurance Corporation. Both of these federal agencies set their rates at the same levels. This rate varies, depending on economic conditions. Typical rates are 3.5 percent per annum on deposits of less than a year, and 4 percent on deposits of a year or longer.

Savings and Loan Associations

These associations acquire funds by selling shares for the purpose of lending the proceeds for the construction, repair, and purchase of residential property. They are chartered by both federal and state governments, and deposits of most associations are insured up to $25,000 by the Federal Savings and Loan Insurance Corporation.

An advantage of buying shares in a savings and loan association is that dividends on shares generally amount to more than interest on a time deposit in a commercial bank. A disadvantage is that savings and loan associations are not required to meet withdrawal demands if money is not available. However, they must use substantial proportions of amounts collected on loans to meet outstanding withdrawal requests. In practice, investments are as accessible and safe in insured savings and loan associations as they are in commercial banks.

Treasury Bills

Treasury bills are short-term obligations of the United States government. The maturity period does not exceed one year, and is generally for three to six months. The Treasury Department issues these bills in denominations of $1,000, $5,000, $10,000, $100,000, $500,000 and $1,000,000. Two batches of bills are sold every week on a discount basis in the open market. Income from a Treasury bill is represented by the difference between the purchase price and the maturity value. This return varies, but it has been above 3.5 percent on an annual basis.

Business corporations comprise the largest group of Treasury bill holders, with total corporate holdings estimated at more than $25 billion. Since an issue matures every week, Treasury bills offer an ideal media for investing idle funds that will not be needed for three to six months.

Treasury Certificates

Treasury certificates have maturities ranging from six months to one year. They are issued as the government's need for cash arises, and not weekly, as are bills. It is generally possible, however, to buy any amount of outstanding certificates through banks and other brokers in government securities. The certificates have a coupon attached providing for the payment of principal and interest at maturity.

Negotiable Time Certificates of Deposit

Banks introduced negotiable time certificates of deposit in 1960 to lure back corporate funds that had been disappearing into other short-term securities that we describe in this section. The "CDs," as they are called, have become phenomenally popular. They now represent the second most important money-market instrument, surpassed in volume only by Treasury bills. Corporate holdings now amount to over $11 billion.

What Is a CD?

A CD is a bank time deposit, but unlike other time deposits the CD draws interest and is negotiable. Under the provisions of the CD, the bank provides as evidence of the time deposit a negotiable certificate of deposit, payable to the order of the named depositor or to the bearer. The corporate treasurer can select any maturity ranging from three months to one year.

Interest

The interest rate on CDs is calculated on a 360-day basis and depends on conditions in the money market, but it has invariably been above the Treasury bill rate by amounts ranging from 0.15 percent to 0.40 percent, depending on fluctuations in the bill rate. However, CDs with a popular maturity date (as just before a tax date) often trade at a spread as low as 10 basis points (1/10 of 1 percent) above the rate on similarly dated Treasury bills. Although CDs compete with all short-term instruments for corporate funds, financial officers see them competing most directly with commercial finance paper. When the rates of these two instruments differ by as much as 1/8 of 1 percent, there is a noticeable flow of funds from the lower to the higher paying investment.

The CD gives the corporate investor the benefits of the time deposit (interest) while avoiding the time deposit's disadvantage (poor liquidity). Banks generally require a notice of 30 days before releasing time deposit funds, but the negotiable form of the CD gives it high liquidity, since the principal and interest are guaranteed by the depository bank.

Bankers' Acceptances

Bankers' acceptances, sometimes called "time drafts," are time bills of exchange, drawn on and accepted by a bank or trust company. Companies use bankers' acceptance to finance the sale of manufactured goods or raw goods in large quantity, either through export-import channels or in domestic transactions.

How They Originate

Suppose that Walters, in New York, wants to purchase a large shipment of goods from LeBlanc, in Paris. To finance the purchase, Walters asks his bank to issue a commercial letter of credit in favor of LeBlanc. This letter permits LeBlanc to draw a time draft on Walters' American bank, which LeBlanc discounts with his local bank in Paris so as to have immediate use of the funds. The Paris bank then forwards the draft with the appropriate documents to the American bank, which, if everything is in order, "accepts" the draft, and thereby substitutes its credit for that of Walters'.

There is a broad market for the purchase and sale of bankers' acceptances, with about $4 billion worth outstanding. They offer liquidity, safety, and usually a higher rate of return than Treasury bills and commercial paper. A local bank, or its correspondent, has probably created a number of acceptances. If a bank cannot offer an acceptance from its own supply, it can enter the market and bid for a prime acceptance on a customer's behalf.

Commercial Paper

Commercial paper is unsecured promissory notes issued by industrial and finance companies with excellent credit ratings to raise short-term funds. These notes are usually sold payable to bearer on a discount basis, although interest-bearing notes are also available. Some companies issue 3-day paper, but for the most part, maturities range from 5 to 270 days for prime finance paper (notes issued by leading finance companies), and from 30 to 120 days for prime industrial paper (notes issued by leading industrial firms). Denominations range from $1,000 to $5,000,000. An investor in commercial paper can usually select the day the note is to be issued and select the maturity date. This gives the advantage of having funds become available on a predetermined date to match specific commitments.

Federal Agency Issues

Securities issued by various U.S. government agencies enjoy wide acceptance by corporate finance officers because of their investment merits and favorable yields. Their popularity in the public market is reflected by a growing similarity in yields between them and Treasury obligations, but securities of government agencies still offer a higher yield. The agency is solely responsible for its obligation. The federal government assumes no liability, but it does maintain an interest in these obligations through supervision and, in many cases, through capital ownership.

There are six federal agencies whose securities make excellent short-term investments:

1. *Federal Home Loan Bank.* The Federal Home Loan Bank System consists of 11 government-supervised banks, organized to stabilize the home financing field. These banks issue consolidated notes and bonds, having maturities up to one year, backed by all 11 banks.

2. *Federal Land Banks.* There are 12 Federal Land Banks that offer long-term mortgage credit to farmers. Loans may not exceed 65 percent of the appraised value of the property offered as security. Their consolidated bonds, with maturities up to one year, are secured joint-and-several obligations of the 12 banks.

3. *Federal Intermediate Credit Bank.* There are 12 of these banks, established to provide seasonal credits for the production and marketing needs of farmers and stockmen. The banks raise their lending funds chiefly by selling short-term consolidated collateral trust debentures, having a maturity of nine months or less.

4. *Federal National Mortgage Association (Fannie Mae).* This association buys and sells mortgages insured by the Federal Housing Administration or guaranteed by the Veterans Administration. Its borrowings from the public provide it with funds to repay the Treasury for previous advances.

5. *Banks for Cooperatives.* A Central Bank for Cooperatives and 12 District Banks were created by the Farm Credit Act of 1933 to make credit available to eligible cooperative associations owned or controlled by farmers. Banks for Cooperatives sell to the public collateral trust debentures, with maturities up to one year, that are the joint-and-several obligations of the 13 banks.

6. *Tennessee Valley Authority.* TVA is a corporate agency of the Federal government, established to develop the Tennessee River and other resources of the Tennessee Valley. TVA sells bonds and notes, with maturities up to one year, to finance its power program and to refund such bonds.

Five of the six federal agency issues have the same tax status as Treasury obligations—interest earned is subject to federal taxes, but exempt from state and local taxes. Securities of the Federal National Mortgage Association are taxed by all three levels of government: federal, state and local. To avoid sacrificing income for unneeded liquidity, consider investing some of excess cash in high-grade, short-term, tax-free securities.

Tax-Free Securities

The first step is to segregate surplus cash into two categories: a reserve for unpredictable needs, and money set aside to meet planned disbursements, such as tax or dividend payments, progress money on contracts, and the like. The excess cash set apart for unpredictable needs to securities must have the greatest liquidity, such as Treasury obligations and federal agency issues. Less than maximum liquidity is needed for planned disbursements so why pay for maximum liquidity? An investor gets an extra ⅛ to ½ or 1 percent in tax-free basis points by holding the following securities to maturity.

1. *Public Housing Authority temporary notes.* Local agencies of the Public Housing Authority, organized under local state laws, develop and administer low-rent housing projects. Obligations issued by these agencies prior to permanent bond financing are called "temporary notes." These notes are unconditionally secured by the Public Housing Administration.

2. *Housing and Home Finance Agency preliminary loan notes.* Local public housing and development agencies issue "preliminary loan notes" to finance slum clearance and urban redevelopment projects. These notes are secured by the local agency and the United States of America acting by and through the administrator of the Housing and Home Finance Agency.

3. *State and local housing obligations.* These either are direct obligations of the state concerned or are guaranteed by it, and are treated as "full faith and credit" instruments. Major issuers of this type are Connecticut, Massachusetts and New York State.

4. *Other notes of states and municipalities.* Another broad category of short-term securities arises from borrowing by states and municipalities, either in anticipation of taxes or other revenue, or in anticipation of longer-term bond financing.

A word of warning is appropriate with respect to the use of tax-free securities when the corporation has debt outstanding. For many years there has been a rule that for federal income tax purposes, the interest deduction would be disallowed with respect to interest on money borrowed to carry tax-exempt securities. The courts seem now to be accepting the interpretation that the funds need not be traced specifically to the tax-exempt security. Thus, if a corporation purchases a tax-exempt security, rather than paying off the interest-bearing debt, interest on an equivalent amount of interest-bearing debt may be disallowed. As a result of these rulings, some corporate treasurers consider it safest to avoid the use of exempt securities altogether.

Select the Maturity That Fits the Investment Planning

Corporations don't have to hold tax-exempt securities to maturity, but it's to their advantage to do so. The originators of these securities try to make it easy to find a security that meets each investment schedule by tailoring maturities to the requirements of most corporate investors. For example,

	Obligation	Marketability	Maturities	Denominations	Basis
United States Treasury bills	U.S. Government obligation. U.S. Treasury auctions 3- and 6-mos. bills weekly. Also offers, through special auctions, one-year maturities and tax anticipation bills.	Excellent secondary market.	Up to 1 year.	1M to 1MM	Discounted. Actual days on a 360-day year.
Prime sales finance paper	Promissory notes of finance companies placed directly with the investor.	No secondary market. Companies under certain conditions will usually buy back paper prior to maturity. Most companies will adjust rate.	Issued to mature on any day from 30 to 270 days.	1M to 5MM	Discounted or interest bearing. Actual days on a 360-day year.
Dealer paper I. Finance	Promissory notes of finance companies sold through commercial paper dealers.	No secondary market. Buy-back arrangement can usually be negotiated through the dealer	Issued to mature on any day from 30 to 270 days.	5M to 5MM	Discounted or interest bearing. Actual days on a 360-day year.
Dealer paper II. Industrial	Promissory notes of leading industrial firms sold through commercial paper dealers.	No secondary market.	Usually available on certain dates between 60 & 180 days.	5M to 5MM	Discounted. Actual days on a 360-day year.
Prime bankers' acceptances	Time draft drawn on and accepted by a banking institution, which in effect substitutes its credit for that of the importer or holder of merchandise.	Good secondary market. Bid usually 1/8th of 1% higher than offered side of market.	Up to 6 months.	25M to 1MM	Discounted. Actual days on a 360-day year.
Negotiable time certificates of deposit	Certificate of a time deposit at a commercial bank.	Good secondary market.	Unlimited.	500M to 1MM	Yield basis. Actual days on a 360-day year. Interest at maturity.
Short-term tax-exempts I. Temporary & preliminary notes of local public housing agencies	Notes of local agencies secured by a contract with Federal agencies. Also pledge of "full faith & credit" of U.S.	Good secondary market.	Up to 1 year.	1M to 1MM	Yield basis. Thirty-day month on a 360-day year. Interest at maturity.
Short-term tax-exempts II. Tax & bond anticipation notes	Notes of States, municipalities or political subdivisions.	Good secondary market.	Various, usually 3 mos. to 1 year from issue.	1MM to 1MM	Yield basis. Usually 30 days on a 360-day year. Interest at maturity.

Figure 6

Guide to Money-Market Investments

the largest obligor—the Public Housing Authority—schedules most of its short-term financing to mature on quarterly tax and dividend dates. Securities that mature on quarterly dates are of greater value to most corporations than securities that mature on intermediate dates and command a better price. If the exact maturity cannot be found, it will usually be advantageous to take a nearby shorter date and fill in the unexpired investment period with other short-term obligations.

A REFERENCE TABLE FOR CASH INVESTMENT

The use of the table in Figure 6 is a quick reference guide for help in selecting the best investment for your surplus cash.

BE SURE TO MAINTAIN A MINIMUM CASH BALANCE

The finance manager must maintain adequate working capital to maintain the flow of capital from cash to inventories to receivables and back to cash. This means that it is important not only to maintain an adequate margin of current assets over current liabilities, but that it is also important to see that cash represents an appropriate proportion of the total current assets. Both trade creditors and banks give first attention to a corporation's cash account.

Trade Suppliers' View of Cash Holdings

Suppliers do not sell on account to every company that asks for this service. They base their decision on an assessment of whether the prospective buyer will be able to pay within the credit period. This means that they concentrate their attention on the buyer's cash holdings, along with his entire working capital position. Consider the different cash positions of these two corporations having identical total current assets (Figure 7).

At first glance, it appears that both corporations offer a supplier equal security for a credit sale, but a closer look reveals marked differences. Although the dollar amounts of their working capital are equal ($96,000), a credit manager would notice that Corporation X has only about one-fifth as much cash as Corporation Y. Corporation X could pay off less than 8 percent of its current liabilities out of its cash holdings, whereas Corporation Y could pay off almost 40 percent of its current liabilities.

If some of the inventory became difficult to sell, or if many of the accounts receivable became uncollectible, Corporation X would be hurt much more than Corporation Y. Though a credit manager might not reject Corporation X's credit application, he would grant Corporation Y's application much more readily, all other considerations being equal.

Financial managers must never succumb to the temptation to lower their standards for minimum cash balances when money is in short supply. It is at these times that trade suppliers can be particularly selective, causing a firm to exhaust its cash balance and to find no one willing to lend it—the very situation that the minimum cash balance is designed to prevent.

A bank may require a compensating balance. The lending capacity of commercial banks stems largely from deposits left with them by their customers, rather than from the proceeds of the sale of stock to stockholders. Therefore, when considering an application for a loan, bankers give preference to those who strengthen this lending capacity by leaving substantial balances with them. This is especially true during times of tight money— when loan applications exceed money supply. During such times, bankers may not be willing to make even a small loan to a firm that doesn't have a qualifying minimum balance.

In addition, commercial banks often stipulate that borrowers must maintain a balance equal to a stated percentage of the loan, usually about 10 or

CORPORATION X

Current Assets		Current Liabilities	
Cash	$6,000	Accounts payable	$48,000
Accounts receivable	72,000	Accrued wages	6,000
Inventories	90,000	Notes payable	18,000
Total Current Assets	$168,000	Total Current Liabilities	$72,000

CORPORATION Y

Current Assets		Current Liabilities	
Cash	$28,000	Accounts payable	$48,000
Accounts receivable	48,000	Accrued wages	6,000
Inventories	92,000	Notes payable	18,000
Total Current Assets	$168,000	Total Current Liabilities	$72,000

Figure 7

Current Assets versus Current Liabilities

15 percent. These are called compensating balances; they not only expand the bank's lending capacity, they also give it a higher rate of interest than that stated in the loan contract. This arrangement places a certain burden on the borrowing firm, but partially offsetting this disadvantage are the reduced service charges that most banks offer their best customers, such as the free processing of checks drawn on the account, and notes taken for collection.

Counteract the Compensating Balance with Link Financing

From the borrower's viewpoint, a compensating balance has the drawback of raising the interest rate on his bank loan. For example: The Smith Company borrows $2,000,000 from its bank at 5 percent interest or $100,-000 a year. But if the company must keep a 20 percent compensating balance with the bank, its effective interest cost rises to 6.25 percent, since it is paying $100,000 for the use of $1,600,000.

How Link Financing Works

Under link financing, a firm can make full use of a bank loan by having an insurance company (or mutual or pension fund) replace the compensating balance at prevailing interest rates. Here's how the arrangement works.

1. After first getting the bank's approval for a substitution deposit, the insurance company is given the requirements and other information.
2. The insurance company deposits with the bank an amount equal to the required compensating balance, usually in the form of a Certificate of Deposit that carries a specified maturity date.
3. If the deposit must be made for longer than one year—the normal maximum period—the firm can ordinarily renew the deposit without renegotiation.
4. Upon retirement of the bank loan, the substitute deposit is returned to the insurance company, along with interest, usually at the rate of 5 percent.

Chief Advantages of Link Financing

Two chief advantages accrue from using link financing to replace compensating balances.

1. *The total interest rate declines.* As noted earlier, 5 percent on a $2,000,000 loan is nominally $100,000 but the effective rate is 6.25 percent, only $1,600,000 is actually available. When paying 5 percent for link financing $400,000 for a year, the total interest for the bank loan plus the substitution deposit comes to $120,000, or 6 percent. Thus, .25 percent less interest is paid when a firm maintains its own compensating balance.

2. *The compensating balance is not available for full use.* If the freed capital generally brings a return of 10 percent, the gain is 4 percent, or a dollar-profit increase of $16,000 (4 percent $\times$ $400,000).

These advantages apply to companies that need all the money that they can get—a situation typical of firms that must build up inventories to deliver products during seasonal peaks. But the value of these advantages diminishes to the extent that a borrower needs a day-to-day working balance that approaches the required compensating balance.

Fees as a Substitute for Compensating Balances

Historically, banks have insisted on compensating balances, not only in connection with certain loans, but also in connection with a number of other services which the bank performed. As banks have become more sophisticated and competition among them has become more intense, there has has been a willingness to negotiate with important customers as to the value of the services performed. It is then possible to pay a cash fee to the bank in lieu of maintaining an additional compensating balance. This sort of negotiation merely recognizes that the funds may have a greater value to the customer than to the bank, so that a cash fee can provide the bank with the profit it had hoped for, without depriving the customer of an equivalent value.

LESSONS TO BE LEARNED FROM BIG COMPANY CASH MANAGEMENT TECHNIQUES

Speeding Up Cash Inflow

Large companies are continuing to make a great deal of progress in improving the rate of speed of cash inflow. Treasurers of large companies have been quick to recognize that there are significant opportunities for profit improvement in the manner in which they handle company cash. In this sense, many cash conscious companies have established the treasurer's function as a profit center. One of the opportunities to exercise profit improvement options is in the area of cash receipts from customers. *Depository transfer checks* is a device which is most useful to companies who have collections from a diversity of sources and from a widespread geographic area. The use of this technique involves "no signature" transfer checks which are made out by region or district sales managers who act as collectors of customer invoices. In each instance when a region or district manager might make a deposit, he also completes a "no signature" transfer check and mails it to a region or collection bank. When this is done, it has the effect of reducing cash held in local banks to a much lower level of equivalent days receipts. In fact, it is quite possible to reduce the equivalent days receipts to about one-third of the total under a conventional system. Quite often the lower level of receipts is still adequate enough to compensate banks for the activity and services which may be performed by them on behalf of the company.

Canadian Investment for Corporate Funds

Small and medium-sized companies should also be aware that Canadian issues will frequently yield a higher rate of return than will the equivalent American short-term money market paper. Money market paper, of course, can vary in terms of time horizon anywhere from just a few days to over 180 days. The gap between higher Canadian rates versus the American rates does not really show up in the time span for short-term notes until one begins to look at 60 to 180 day paper. The differentials between Canadian rates and American rates widen as the length of maturity of the paper becomes longer. For instance, at one point in time, late last year, the average quoted rate for commercial paper in the United States was 8¼ percent; in Canada it was 8½ percent. As the length of maturity grew longer, that spread widened to ¾ of a point for six month paper.

These notes can be bought in denominations of $25,000 or more through an American bank or its correspondent in New York. One business advisory service cautions that an investor, whether he be an individual or a company, should try to get a paper that's guaranteed by a Canadian company's U.S. parent. It then provides an increased assurance that the money is safe. Two points to be kept in mind in this type of investment are that there is a 15 percent Canadian withholding tax on interest and in addition, there is no secondary market for this type of paper. In effect it means that you should not invest in this type of paper unless you are fairly certain you will not need the money before the maturity of the note purchased. In the event that the money is needed before the maturity date of the note, the rate would then become subject to negotiation between the investor and the company whose paper is held.

Another vehicle for investment is that of short-term dollar deposits. This is a device whereby one places on deposit with the American agency of a Canadian bank at least one million dollars of investible funds. Since the money remains in the confines of the United States, it is not subject to Canadian withholding taxes or any U.S. balance of payments restrictions. As with other short-term Canadian investments, there is no secondary market but maturities can be negotiated in advance. Generally speaking, the differential between Canadian and American paper of this type varies between ½ and ¾ of a point higher than that available in the United States.

Investment Services

Many banks will provide businessmen with all types of free services which might range from the placement of short-term funds to actual investment advice. It is quite possible that smaller, more consumer-oriented local banks will give a customer such free service, provided that he keeps a sufficient amount of compensating balance in his checking account. Compensating balance requirements vary widely from bank to bank and since there are no hard and fast regulations, the rate of compensating balance is usually negotiable. Within the investment sphere, companies will find that their options are fairly constrained if they have only $100,000 to invest. However, even that amount is quite sufficient to purchase commercial paper, treasury bills and agency notes. There is, of course, no shame to ask your banker to invest idle funds even for a fee. He may charge a small fee each time he buys an instrument for your account, but the magnitude of the charge should not be more than $10 or $15 for each placement.

Bank Loans

Although it may be hard for many businessmen to accept as truth, it is probably true that bankers don't mind lending to smaller companies when money is tight; provided, of course, that the smaller company is willing to pay a rate higher than prime. It is important, of course, for any company to attempt to get the most favorable interest rate from his banker and there are some positive steps which can be taken by companies to get favorable interest rates. One of the most important aspects of borrowing is that of maintaining a consistency of banking relationships. A company should not switch banks unless it is absolutely necessary. In addition, it is probably a smart thing for a company to keep a fairly sizeable balance in the checking account. Although this is an anathema to most corporate treasurers because it means a sacrificing of interest income, it is, nevertheless extremely important because frequently a company can borrow up to four times its balance for operational needs. Another idea worth considering is to deliberately purchase interest in your local bank's certificate of deposit. This can be a fine demonstration of loyalty to a bank and its services without an appreciable sacrifice in income. Lastly, obtaining a line of credit can be an important device for displaying a good credit game plan. A smart thing for a company to do is to deliberately establish a line of credit even though it may not need any funds. Monies are deliberately borrowed on that line of credit and repaid punctually when due. This type of strategy can be employed whenever the bank may not be aware of the fact that funds are not actually required for operational uses. The timely payback for borrowed funds can be of immeasurable help when larger amounts of borrowing may be needed.

Eight Routes to a More Efficient Money Management Program

1. Have your suppliers bill you on the day of the month that follows your monthly peak of receipts from your customers. You will be paying bills out of cash just received and this releases your bill paying reserve for action.
2. Don't pay bills ahead of the discount date just because your accounting staff may favor some routine "bill paying day." Bills should be paid only when due—not earlier.
3. Refinance heavy mortgage payments to reduce the size of your immediate cash outlays and spread them into the future. This also has the effect of enabling a company to pay back mortgage payments in more worthless dollars under the refinance mortgage than under the present mortgage. The worthless dollars follow as inflation continues.
4. On major purchases, see if your suppliers will allow you to apportion payments over a period of months.
5. Make every day a billing day. Bill as you ship. Clear your paper work routes so that invoices will not be held up waiting for shipping papers, discount information or extra billing help.
6. Don't leave customers loopholes for holding up payment. Explain credit adjustments, unusual charges, debit memos—even small items—*written on the invoice.*
7. Spot accounts as they are going bad. Keep a running record of what each customer owes. Follow up when the account passes a set time or dollar limit.
8. Weigh what each of your slow payers is worth against what it is costing you, because goods you ship him could have been turned into bank deposits by this time, had he been a normal customer. Determine which accounts are not worth carrying and only service them on a COD basis. Don't let them run their business on money which they owe to you.

MEANINGFUL APPROACHES
TO PRODUCTION PLANNING
AND COST ACCOUNTING

WHAT COST ACCOUNTING DOES

Financial accounting provides facts and analyses of overall conditions. It seldom shows how one product's profitability compares with another's, or how much more efficient one process or plant is than another. The average stockholder or investment analyst cares more about a company's overall showing than about details. But management must take a different view.

To maintain—and improve—the overall profit showing, management must know specific short-term cost and profit figures on a per-product, per-plant, per-department basis. Cost accounting supplies this information, showing the cost of producing one automobile, a dozen shirts, or a single major appliance. It helps determine the cost of single activities as well, such as the cost of drilling holes of a certain diameter into a given material, or of forging metal of a certain size and quality.

What Can You Expect from Cost Accounting?

Financial accounting determines total results after-the-fact, at the end of regular accounting periods. Financial accounting evaluates performance and reveals the current financial status of the business and the amount of profit or loss incurred during the period in question. Cost accounting is more concerned with estimating financial results within accounting periods, evaluating performance as the accounting period progresses. Cost accounting continually evaluates the approximate position of costs and profits, enabling management to take corrective action *before* the time comes to report to stockholders on overall profits.

Cost accounting also helps control expenditures, giving a measure of production efficiency. Having decided that a product can be made for a certain cost—or within a certain cost range—production management must keep costs within that range. Checking costs each week or month gives management a picture of the efficiency of operation; it shows management where to apply pressure to get costs in line.

The primary advantage of cost accounting, of course, is that it shows precisely where costs are incurred, giving a realistic basis for cost-cutting. The traditional method of cutting costs across the board only penalizes efficient organizational segments and establishes permanently the real causes of loss: inefficiency and waste. Cost accounting does more—it enables management to attribute cost to those units responsible for incurring them.

Recording material, labor, and overhead costs by job enables cost accounting to observe cost build-ups and to let management know where they exist. To give management the cost information it needs, cost accounting supplies periodic accounting summaries, including studies of costs by production order, cost trends, and inefficient production operations. Such complete cost reports allow management to compare *actual* production costs with budget estimates and standards as a guide to sales and pricing strategy, and an aid in cost control.

Why is it necessary to know how much it costs to turn out a given product? To sell their goods at a profit, manufacturers must know what their products cost to make, how much materials, labor, and overhead cost to add to the price of each product. When a manufacturing concern prices its goods on the basis of an inadequate cost accounting system, its price to consumers may be drastically high or low. If too low, the manufacturer makes insufficient profits. What's more, other companies within the industry must meet the low prices or lose sales volume. If its price is too high compared with other companies', the manufacturer gives up sales volume to its competitors.

Of course, some products cannot be produced profitably. Cost accounting determines the profitability of products being made and sold. Many companies run cost analyses on their best-sellers and find out they are best-sellers only because they are priced like "loss-leaders." Many companies drop these products after finding out that sales prices are lower than production costs—and likely to remain that way.

Cost accounting contributes to these management objectives:

- Reducing costs by comparing actual and budgeted costs
- Increasing production by comparing records of output per man and per unit with predetermined standards
- Locating appropriate operations for automation or mechanization
- Balancing production between departments, keeping materials flowing evenly throughout
- Developing sales and pricing strategies
- Providing fair, accurate performance records
- Creating a competitive spirit between organizational units

- Establishing quality standards
- Distributing overhead or burden charges
- Determining anticipated profit from varying production levels

The Limitations of Cost Accounting

Cost accounting is a practical necessity in all but the smallest manufacturing concerns, but it has limitations. One is that cost accounting costs. No system is any good unless it pays for itself by reducing other costs. Cost accounting involves accounting procedures and record-keeping chores far more detailed and intricate than those required in ordinary financial accounting.

At best, maintaining an efficient cost accounting system is difficult. Errors in attributing costs to the proper source are compounded in a cost accounting system. If product A is considered to bear a $1,000 overhead cost when the cost should properly be attributed to product B, both A and B's profit picture will be misleading, with a total error of $2,000.

Cost accounting does not control costs. It only gives management information with which to control costs. To provide management with this information, those engaged in cost accounting activities must be thoroughly familiar with the processes, materials, and equipment used in the business as well as with cost accounting techniques, report writing methods, and record-keeping. The cost accounting function is usually kept separate from general accounting for the simple reason that those with backgrounds in general accounting are not often familiar with production processes and distribution methods. (A complete cost accounting system includes accurate costing of distribution and sales activities. The techniques of cost accounting for distribution are very similar to those described in this booklet.)

Of course, production and distribution costs alone don't always determine the sales price for a given product. To meet competition, a manufacturer may sell certain items at less than their actual cost, counting the resulting loss as an advertising or sales cost. For this reason, cost accounting activities might be wasted in some production operations, since the manufacturer may use some basis other than *actual cost* for pricing his products.

An effective cost accounting system comprises an integrated group of basic cost records and control devices. The system's precise character depends upon the nature of the business, the type and volume of transactions with customers, and requirements of the manufacturing process. Quite different cost accounting systems are necessary in the two basic manufacturing operations—continuous and intermittent (job-order) production. Accounting in continuous production (called process cost accounting) is by far the less complex of the two accounting systems.

THE PRODUCTION BUDGET PREPARES THE WAY FOR MANUFACTURING

Once there is agreement on the sales forecast, you are able to devise a production budget by determining the amount of goods that must be manufactured (or purchased) to meet sales goals. The quantity of goods produced will equal the sales forecast less on-hand inventory for each product, as Figure 1 illustrates.

To formulate a reliable production budget, management must (1) consider length of production period, (2) ensure coordination of activities, and (3) decide on inventory policies.

Consider the Length of the Production Period

The production period rarely matches the sales period, because the time lag between initial production activity and the completion of the first products may take weeks or months. This situation requires additional schedules describing the timing of the units to be started. If processing requires two months, then the starting of units must be moved two months ahead of the production budget date for units to be completed.

When production consists of many parts, it may be necessary to prepare a separate *parts production budget* showing the dates for parts to be started and parts to be completed. Copies of supplementary production budgets and schedules must go to the purchasing division well ahead of start-up dates if this division is to provide a timely supply of production materials.

Ensure Coordination of Activities

Translating sales demands into production effort can be exceedingly complex. The task requires, in addition to production plans, detailed planning for material and labor requirements, plant capacity, capital additions, and inventory policies. Though the production manager is primarily responsible for drafting and executing the production budget, the finance officer must help coordinate activities among production, finance, personnel, research and development, and sales.

Coordination between sales and production, for example, is indispensable for keeping these two divisions fully aware of each other's problems. It may be necessary to adjust the sales forecast to capitalize on those products that can be produced most efficiently. When revising the sales estimate for any product, selling and promotional expenses must also be revised.

PRODUCT A

	Sales Forecast R'qments	Less Finished Goods Inventory	Total Production Req.
January	300,000	240,000	60,000
February	225,000	10,000	215,000
March	200,000	50,000	150,000
Total 1st Quarter	725,000	300,000	425,000
2nd Quarter	600,000	200,000	400,000
3rd Quarter	550,000	100,000	450,000
4th Quarter	400,000	50,000	350,000
Total	2,275,000	650,000	1,625,000

PRODUCT B

	Sales Forecast R'qments	Less Finished Goods Inventory	Total Production Req.
January	150,000	75,000	75,000
February	100,000	25,000	75,000
March	90,000	20,000	70,000
Total 1st Quarter	340,000	120,000	220,000
2nd Quarter	300,000	100,000	200,000
3rd Quarter	280,000	140,000	140,000
4th Quarter	320,000	80,000	240,000
Total	1,240,000	440,000	800,000

Figure 1
Detailed Production Budget

Decide on Inventory Policies

A satisfactory production program rests on definite inventory policies. One of the main advantages of production budgeting is that it forces a consideration of inventory problems in advance. Inventory standards are often fixed in terms of (1) months' supply or (2) minimum and maximum inventory limits.

Months' supply: The months' supply method of determining standard inventory is usually budgeted sales requirements.

> EXAMPLE: Sales forecast for X Manufacturing Company calls for 10,-000 units of Product A, a figure that anticipates a monthly sale of 833 units. If production requires a two months' supply of this item, then the standard materials inventory level for single components of Product A becomes 1,666.

Minimum and Maximum Limits

The minimum inventory limit is determined first, based on how fast the item moves and the time required to replenish it. This is the safety level below which the inventory should not be permitted to go for any item. The maximum limit is then set to prevent excessive accumulation of goods.

Standard Inventory Turnover

The restocking rate is regulated by setting a ratio for the size of the inventory to the number of units that will be withdrawn (sold).

> EXAMPLE: If 300,000 units will be sold during the year and sales require an in-stock inventory of 50,000, the materials inventory turnover ratio for single components of each product will be set at 6.

$$\frac{300,000}{50,000} = 6 \text{ turnovers a year}$$

> NOTE: In establishing inventory standards be sure to consider (1) perishability of products, (2) storage facilities, (3) extra capital to finance inventory, (4) protection against material and labor shortages and price increases, and (5) a reporting system for keeping inventory information current.

GUARANTEE THE RIGHT QUANTITY OF MATERIALS

The quantities of materials (both components and raw materials) needed to meet production requirements are specified in the materials budget. Quantities of direct materials or parts are shown by month, quarter, or other convenient periods, taking such factors as normal delivery time, economic order quantities, and available storage space into consideration.

The materials budget may include material costs, but this information is usually reserved for the purchases budget. The sample budget in Figure 2 gives total quantities required, broken down by product, part, and period.

Estimating Material Quantities

Estimating material quantity requirements poses no problem when you know how many units of each kind of raw material you need for each manufactured unit. These unit rates are often developed during the initial engineering and development of the product. But quantity requirements can be a critical matter when unit consumption rates are unknown. In such a case, you can often devise reliable estimates based on historical ratios:

1. Ratio of raw material used to some measure of production, such as direct machine hours or direct labor hours.
2. Ratio of material cost to some measure of productive output, such as machine hours or direct labor hours.
3. Ratio of material cost to direct labor cost.

It is advisable to test estimates by comparing them with results of past years. If standard costs are not used as the basis for the estimate, they should, at least, be taken into account. If standard costs appear stringent, it may be necessary to budget a material usage rate that varies from the standard.

ACCOUNTING FOR MATERIAL COSTS

Cost accounting works with production to exercise control over material costs through periodic reports and records on both direct and indirect materials. These records show the quantity and cost of materials received, stored, and subsequently issued. Cost accounting's material control arrangement must include systems for accomplishing these objectives:

• Accounting for materials received
• Accounting for materials used
• Costing materials used

Material Budget-Unit Requirements by Product and by Time Period

| | PRODUCT A | | PRODUCT B | | |
	Production Planned	*Material R'qd.*	*Production Planned*	*Material R'qd.*	*Total Units Material R'qd.*
Part #47					
January	60,000	60,000	75,000	NONE	60,000
February	215,000	215,000	75,000	NONE	215,000
March	150,000	150,000	70,000	NONE	150,000
Total 1st Qtr.	425,000	425,000	220,000	NONE	425,000
2nd Qtr.	400,000	400,000	200,000	NONE	400,000
3rd Qtr.	450,000	450,000	140,000	NONE	450,000
4th Qtr.	350,000	350,000	240,000	NONE	350,000
Grand Total for Year	1,625,000	1,625,000	800,000	–	1,625,000
Part #58					
January	60,000	60,000	75,000	75,000	135,000
February	215,000	215,000	75,000	75,000	290,000
March	150,000	150,000	70,000	70,000	220,000
Total 1st Qtr.	425,000	425,000	220,000	220,000	645,000
2nd Qtr.	400,000	400,000	200,000	200,000	600,000
3rd Qtr.	450,000	450,000	140,000	140,000	590,000
4th Qtr.	350,000	350,000	240,000	240,000	590,000
Grand Total For Year	1,625,000	1,625,000	800,000	800,000	2,425,000

(Note: Anticipate approximately 20,000 of this item on hand beginning January)

Part #19					
January	60,000	40,000	75,000	75,000	115,000
February	215,000	215,000	75,000	75,000	290,000
March	150,000	150,000	70,000	70,000	220,000
Total 1st Qtr.	425,000	405,000	220,000	220,000	625,000
2nd Qtr.	400,000	400,000	200,000	200,000	600,000
3rd Qtr.	450,000	450,000	140,000	140,000	590,000
4th Qtr.	350,000	350,000	240,000	240,000	590,000
Grand Total For Year	1,625,000	1,605,000	800,000	800,000	2,405,000

Figure 2
Detailed Materials Budget

Accounting for Materials Received

In job-order operations, production determines material requirements only upon receiving customer orders. Then it prepares a list of materials and parts needed to do the job. This list includes a manufacturing schedule, showing where and when each part or material item is needed to turn out the product by the scheduled completion date.

After determining the quantity and timing of material purchases, production (through the purchasing department) schedules orders to take advantage of availability, prices, and quality. Purchasing sees that materials meet quality requirements and that the company gets the most favorable price and delivery terms available.

The purchasing department sends copies of purchase orders to cost accounting as a basis for preliminary charges against work or job orders or against cost centers.

Certain employees unpack all incoming material shipments in most plants, checking to see that goods meet quality and quantity specifications. Receiving prepares a report for cost accounting, which compares the receiving report with the supplier's invoice and the purchase requisition to see that quantities, prices, and materials specifications agree on all three forms. It checks extensions and footings on the supplier's invoice, and investigates discrepancies and makes corrections or adjustments promptly if needed.

Once cost accounting is satisfied with the goods as delivered, it stamps the vendor's invoice with its approval, authorizing entry of the goods in inventory stock records. When this is done, purchasing can prepare a payment voucher, posting the data on the approved invoice to a stock ledger sheet or card.

Cost accounting keeps stock ledger cards in vertical files, in multi-ring binders with visible edge tabs, or in drawer card index files. It maintains a separate card for each material or part stocked in inventory. Once suppliers' invoices are verified, cost accounting enters the invoice number, the number of units received, the unit price, and the total cost in the "received" section on the appropriate stock ledger card, then adjusts the quantity on hand figure in the "balance" section of the card.

If practical, cost accounting should record the cost of material and parts of the net cash price plus transportation costs, at least if shipments include similar items. If shipments generally include mixed items, the task of apportioning transportation charges and computing cash discounts for each unit may make it more reasonable to use gross costs and charge transportation costs to production overhead. If transportation costs on incoming shipments are a substantial portion of total inventory cost, cost accounting may assign them to production orders or producing departments periodically without entering the cost on stock ledger cards.

Accounting for Materials Used

For effective cost accounting, a firm must maintain a running inventory of all materials and parts on hand. A requisition system makes this possible. In a job-order system, material requisition forms should indicate the job for which each type of item is to be used. Under a process system, the form can be changed slightly to indicate the process for which withdrawals are being made.

Production supervisors prepare material requisitions, which are presented at the appropriate stock room to obtain the specified materials. The stock-room attendant uses the requisition as authority to enter the withdrawal on the appropriate stock ledger card. If the materials withdrawn do not apply to specific jobs, but are for the benefit of overall production, they are "indirect materials," and their costs are not entered on cost sheets. If a stock attendant handles a great many "direct" and "indirect" materials, it is convenient to have requisitions for "direct materials" and for "indirect materials" in different colors or shapes. A stock clerk makes frequent entries on stock ledger cards to keep balances and totals current. At the end of each month, cost accounting totals requisitions for direct and indirect materials separately. It then debits the material-in-process account with the direct materials, and debits the overhead account with the indirect materials. Finally, it credits the materials account with the grand total of all requisitions.

Accounting for materials inventory is the job of the stock clerk, or stores ledger clerk, who maintains perpetual inventory records by noting receipts, issuances, and balances of each inventory item on a regular basis.

Most modern cost-accounting systems use letters, numbers, or a combination of the two to identify inventory accounts. Cost accounting records usually contain a great many material accounts. A firm may have more than one hundred different items in its storeroom; it might assign the code numbers to identify certain groups of items. It might even use code numbers to indicate specific materials.

Using location numbers in a code system expedites locating material for issuance and placing material in proper bins and storerooms on receipt. Cost accounting records and refers to various material accounts constantly. Using code numbers instead of account titles saves a great deal of time, and time-savings reduce cost-accounting costs.

The material requisition is the basic accounting cost record for withdrawing materials from stock and placing them in production. It authorizes storekeepers or stock clerks to release a specified quantity of a given material or component for manufacturing. Production foremen or department heads usually authorize the requisition; cost accounting may approve it to maintain tight control. Cost accounting always receives a copy of the form as the basis for charges against the specified production order or against the using department.

As shown in Figure 3, the material requisition generally includes the cost of the item requested for use in production. This enables cost accounting to figure material costs and record its figures on cost records for the appropriate production order. The person who releases the material to production changes the stock ledger card to show the new balance-on-hand figure after issuing the goods.

MATERIAL REQUISITION					
DATE_____		REQUISITION NO._____			
DEPARTMENT_____		PRODUCTION ORDER NO.____			
REQUESTED BY_____					
INVENTORY NO.	QUANTITY REQUESTED	DESCRIPTION	QUANTITY ISSUED	UNIT COST	TOTAL COST
RECEIVED BY_____			DATE_____		

Figure 3
Material Requisition

Costing Materials Used

Once a storekeeper accepts and fills a material requisition, he must determine the unit cost of the items he issues in order to price the materials and charge the work center or job order for the items.

When purchasing buys a definite quantity of a particular item for use at one time, it may easily identify and record the item's cost in production.

But more often, production uses accumulated purchases on many different jobs over a protracted period, obscuring their individual costs in production. So cost accounting must establish a definite procedure for determining prices and for costing material requisitions. Most manufacturers use a first-in first-out valuation method, or an average cost method.

If cost accounting uses the first-in first-out method, storekeepers enter on each material requisition the unit price of items on hand the longest, as determined from stock ledger cards. This method requires that cost accounting show each unit price represented in the inventory on stock ledger cards. A company that buys goods with shifting prices at frequent intervals can find this method rather awkward and expensive to maintain.

Cost accounting may also use either a running average or an end-of-month-average for costing materials issued to production. The end-of-month-average method is naturally easier to use and maintain because it requires calculating unit costs just once a month. But it does not permit posting up-to-date costs to jobs within the month.

In the running average method, cost accounting determines unit costs of materials following each new purchase; it divides the total cost of items on hand by the total number of units remaining in stock. It then costs successive issues at the resulting unit cost until the next batch of items enters stock.

Using the end-of-month-average method, cost accounting allows material requisitions to accumulate for one month. Then at the end of the month, it divides the total inventory value at the beginning of the month plus the cost of items purchased during the month by the total number of units on hand during the month. Cost accounting then applies the resulting unit costs to all requisitions filled during the month just ended.

CALCULATE LABOR NEEDS

The direct labor budget describes estimates of direct labor requirements for carrying out budgeted production. The finance officer works closely with the production and personnel officers in planning the labor required to meet production goals. The direct labor budget gives him the information he needs for determining cash requirements for direct labor. And by revealing the total cost of direct labor, it affords him a means of controlling direct labor expenses.

The two chief ways for developing a direct labor budget are (1) to multiply standard hours for each unit by total number of units, and (2) to base labor costs on historical ratios.

Standard Hour Method

By using a standard hour system, you can compute direct labor costs by multiplying the standard hours required for each unit of production by the total units called for in the production budget, then multiplying this figure by the average wage rate per standard hour. For example, if the production budget calls for 30,000 finished products, and each unit requires two standard hours to complete, you clearly have a direct labor demand of 60,000 standard hours. Multiplying this figure by the average wage rate of, say, $3.00 per standard hour, you get the direct labor cost to produce the desired number of finished product units—$180,000.

Standard hours for some companies are always loose, in others they are always tight. Such a situation requires budget planners to decide on the variations from standard hours that must be incorporated in the budget to meet annual goals.

Figure 4 shows a direct labor budget based on standard hours per unit, and broken down to reveal labor costs by product, time period, and workcenter. This arrangement helps to pinpoint responsibility for control purposes.

Labor Cost Ratio Method

Direct labor costs may also be determined by relating labor costs to some other measure of production activity, such as direct machine hours or direct material costs. Some companies simply have workcenter foremen estimate the direct labor hours required to meet the budgeted output for each workcenter, then combine the workcenter estimates to arrive at a total direct labor figure. In the case of new products, a rough estimate may be necessary.

ACCOUNTING FOR LABOR COSTS

Labor costs often comprise the largest single business expense. In accounting for labor costs, cost accounting fulfills its objectives by (1) relating labor costs to specific jobs, and (2) segregating labor costs in payrolls.

Relating Labor Costs to Specific Jobs

In most jobbing plants, someone keeps time records of the number of hours—and minutes—each worker spends on each production order. Usually, the worker enters the time he begins or ends work on specific production orders. The worker may punch a card, or a timekeeper or department fore-

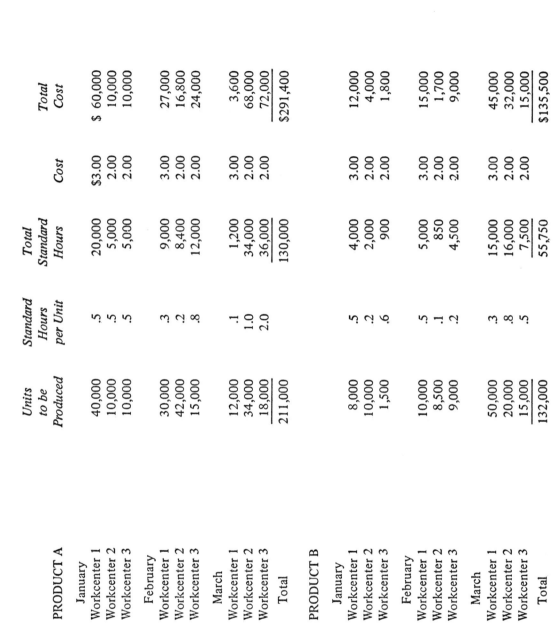

	Units to be Produced	Standard Hours per Unit	Total Standard Hours	Cost	Total Cost
PRODUCT A					
January					
Workcenter 1	40,000	.5	20,000	$3.00	$ 60,000
Workcenter 2	10,000	.5	5,000	2.00	10,000
Workcenter 3	10,000	.5	5,000	2.00	10,000
February					
Workcenter 1	30,000	.3	9,000	3.00	27,000
Workcenter 2	42,000	.2	8,400	2.00	16,800
Workcenter 3	15,000	.8	12,000	2.00	24,000
March					
Workcenter 1	12,000	.1	1,200	3.00	3,600
Workcenter 2	34,000	1.0	34,000	2.00	68,000
Workcenter 3	18,000	2.0	36,000	2.00	72,000
Total	211,000		130,000		$291,400
PRODUCT B					
January					
Workcenter 1	8,000	.5	4,000	3.00	12,000
Workcenter 2	10,000	.2	2,000	2.00	4,000
Workcenter 3	1,500	.6	900	2.00	1,800
February					
Workcenter 1	10,000	.5	5,000	3.00	15,000
Workcenter 2	8,500	.1	850	2.00	1,700
Workcenter 3	9,000	.2	4,500	2.00	9,000
March					
Workcenter 1	50,000	.3	15,000	3.00	45,000
Workcenter 2	20,000	.8	16,000	2.00	32,000
Workcenter 3	15,000	.5	7,500	2.00	15,000
Total	132,000		55,750		$135,500

Figure 4
Direct Labor Budget—First Quarter Only

man may keep separate time records. At the end of each day—or perhaps once a week—all workers' cards are sorted by production order number (and perhaps by department). Cost accounting then computes the total direct labor costs for each production order, and charges the cost to the appropriate cost records.

In process type industries, the same operations are performed in each department on a continuing basis. Time cards form the basis for charges against *all* work done in a particular department or unit. But in job type manufacturing, cost accounting keeps separate records on an individual job basis, not on a department basis, distinguishing between direct and indirect labor. From time records, cost accounting determines the number of direct labor hours expended on any product or order. Cost accounting must charge direct labor costs to specific jobs, and charge indirect labor costs to overhead. Direct labor costs are those charges for employees who work on the product with tools, or who operate machines in the production process. Indirect labor costs comprise wages and salaries of foremen and supervisors, and for other employees whose services are incidental to production.

Segregating Labor Costs in Payrolls

Cost accounting prepares payrolls from time clock records or other time records. Its special task in payroll preparation for intermittent production is to separate direct labor and indirect labor, and to compile separate payrolls for the two classes of employees. It also distinguishes regular and overtime wages; in some instances overtime for direct labor is charged to overhead. Each payroll gives a complete breakdown of each worker's earnings in terms of hours worked or pieces produced, hourly wage rate or piece rate, gross earnings, itemized deductions, and net amount paid. Most companies prepare payrolls weekly. By ending the work week on Thursday, workers can collect their wages at the close of work Friday.

ACCOUNTING FOR OVERHEAD

"Overhead" refers to the many manufacturing, sales, and administrative costs not readily associated with specific processes or products. It includes such items as indirect labor, supplies, depreciation, insurance, taxes, fuel, sales costs, and office costs. Obviously, overhead costs fall into two categories: those involving production activities, and those involving sales and administrative activities.

Usually, cost accounting enumerates factory overhead costs in a special ledger. Most manufacturers maintain a factory overhead ledger with 10 to 20 account classifications. Cost accounting posts overhead charges to a special ledger from the voucher register, the general journal, and from other books of original entry, all of which have columns for overhead charges. Cost accounting posts to the special ledger by totaling the columns in these subsidiary journals and ledgers at the end of each week or month, entering these totals to the special ledger.

Manufacturing overhead is a real cost; it must become a part of the cost of goods manufactured. But manufacturing overhead, by definition, cannot be assigned directly to individual processes or products. The cost accounting system must provide some method for calculating overhead costs, then apportioning these costs among products or production departments.

To indicate true manufacturing overhead—and to provide complete cost information to production management—cost accounting may use predetermined rates for assigning overhead charges. For example, it might assign overhead on the basis of direct labor hours, direct labor costs, or machine-hours. The basis for measuring overhead depends upon the circumstances. Suppose, for example, that all direct laborers in Department A operate machines. Machine-hours would then provide perhaps the most satisfactory means of measuring overhead and applying overhead costs in Department A. If there were no wide range between the lowest and highest wages paid in the department, direct labor costs might provide a good basis for apportioning overhead charges. This index of overhead allocation has an advantage in that labor costs are always available from payroll records, while machine-hours might not be readily available. Using direct labor hours, or machine-hours, cost accounting establishes overhead rates in term of dollars and cents per hour. If direct labor is the basis, the overhead rate is expressed in terms of a percentage.

Allocating overhead costs to individual products or organizational segments poses a real problem in most manufacturing operations. Cost accounting has a total overhead figure, perhaps for a month's operations. Part of the total was expended to maintain plant and equipment, part to provide clerical and administrative help for *all* departments and products, and part spent in connection with individual products. How much of the total should cost accounting charge to each product turned out during the period in question?

Theoretically, cost accounting should allocate overhead costs to individual products on the basis of each product's responsibility for costs. Practically speaking, however, this is neither possible nor economical to do. Both continuous production and intermittent production use roughly the same methods for applying overhead charges to product units. Cost accounting may work from a prepared overhead budget, including predetermined overhead rates, based on direct labor hours, machine-hours, or direct labor cost.

After deciding on an appropriate basis for allocating overhead, cost accounting applies the rate directly to individual operations. If cost accounting applies overhead on a machine-hour basis, job costs records should contain a column for the number of machine-hours put in on each job. Then cost accounting simply takes the number of hours from workers' time cards or daily production reports, enters the figures in these columns, applies the overhead rate and makes extensions on the job cost records to show the amount of overhead expended on each job.

ESTIMATING DISTRIBUTION COSTS

The distribution expense budget (also called selling expense budget) includes all costs involved in selling, distributing, and delivering products to customers. The primary objective of the distribution expense budget is to achieve a proper relationship between sales expense and sales volume or income. If sales estimates are revised because of production schedules, selling expenses may have to be changed. These costs should bear a close relationship to sales volume rather than production volume.

Selling costs involve consideration of (1) the sales potential in each territory, (2) the number of salesmen's calls expected, and (3) the need for additional salesmen to sell additional units of a product. Salesmen's salaries might be budgeted on this basis:

Annual Sales Volume	Salesmen's Salaries Required
480,000 units	$192,000
510,000 units	204,000
540,000 units	216,000

In this schedule, it was determined that the present sales force could sell 480,000 units. Adding a new salesman would produce 30,000 units (the difference between 480,000 and 510,000) at an additional cost of $12,000 (the difference between $192,000 and $204,000). To add still another sales-man would produce 30,000 units at a cost of $12,000, and so on.

IDENTIFYING AND CONTROLLING DISTRIBUTION COSTS

The stage of development of distribution cost accounting is still quite primitive and based upon my observations as well as many other studies, it is probable that very few companies really know the extent of their distri-bution costs. Often such costs are charged as overhead and almost ignored in the analysis process. At other times the distribution cost may be considered as a reduction of sales in order to arrive at a net sales figure, and therefore, for purposes of observing the behavior of such costs, they are often lost in the maze of sales analysis. This type of handling for distribution costs not only conceals the dimension of this cost, but in addition, obscures the recogni-tion that such costs are fully controllable and moreover, are perhaps the last frontier within the corporate accounting and systems housing to achieve meaningful cost reductions.

Drake Sheahan-Stewart Dougall, Inc., well-known expert consultants in the field of physical distribution and marketing, have cited some examples in recent surveys which they have undertaken. In one example, the jobbing arm of a major U.S. corporation took pride in having achieved major trans-portation economies by exploiting carload and truckload incentive rates whenever they shipped to any of their distribution points. Their market was so bad that their distribution points numbered well over two hundred. The method of accounting which they employed, however, did not reveal that the attempt at pursuing increased volume in corporate sales was having an opposite effect on profitability. The increased volume did have the effect of lowering aggregate shipping costs because of the truckload savings. How-ever, in order to accomplish the volume, additional period costs were created which negated the transportation savings and in fact, overall caused a net deficit as a result of higher warehousing and inventory costs which were created. The company, of course, failed to recognize completely that the trade-off involved in physical distribution is not merely a trade-off between volume and the shipping rate per unit.

It was necessary in the final analysis for the company to completely restructure its cost accounting system and orient costs away from considering distribution costs as period costs which were to be applied equally to a $20 emergency order as well as a $600 regular order. It was structured instead to optimize distribution costs to be able to raise red flags and warn sales managers when excesses were creeping into the order procurement system. There is an implied recognition that not all customers should be sought after. It may not pay if the manufacturing facilities are located on the east coast to ship to a customer on the west coast. It may rather be more important profitability-wise to limit your customers to a certain radius of the manufacturing facility.

Another example cited by the consultants had to do with a firm in the chemical industry which developed a distribution costing system which associated distribution costs with specific types of customers. On the basis of that type of segmentation, it felt that it was able to identify the profit contribution made by each class of trade. The study revealed that many of the firm's smaller customers were, at best, marginal, because they ordered less and more frequently than the larger customers. The specific process of identifying these customers assisted the firm to selectively reduce the number of sales calls made on the customers and also to develop a volume pricing arrangement which recognized the contribution to profit made by different classes of customers.

A proper analysis of distribution cost can be a tremendous help to increase profitability, either through a reduction in costs of the function itself, or by means of shrinking out weaknesses in the marketing program.

COST ACCOUNTING AND STANDARD COSTS

We hear a great deal about "standard costs" in connection with cost accounting activities. A sound cost accounting system is essential in most manufacturing organizations of any size, but a standard cost system is not. A cost accounting system can function without standard costs.

Standard costs are predetermined unit costs for each product produced. To determine standard costs, a company calculates in advance the quantity and cost of direct material, direct labor, and overhead borne by each product-unit. Of course, where standard costs form a part of the cost accounting system, the overall effect is usually infinitely better. With a standard cost system in operation, management can establish *predetermined costs* for each product (using the standard cost system), determine the *actual cost* of producing individual units (through cost accounting techniques), and compare actual costs with standard costs and historical costs to find out where costs are running too high.

Many plants conduct their cost accounting activities on the basis of historical costs, but more and more production organizations are using standard costs. Standard costs are estimates of what various cost elements *should be.* They are prepared only after a great deal of study, and are actually based to some degree on historical costs. They are changed constantly to meet changing conditions. With standard costs, cost accounting can compare actual current costs with standard costs and previous actual costs to find cost trends and to learn where cost reduction efforts would be most effective.

The following illustration shows a manufacturing company's actual costs for a five-month period after it set up standard costs. These costs apply to four operations in manufacturing a single product.

Actual Costs

Operation	April	March	February	January	December	Standard Cost
Cutting	$2.10	$2.15	$2.18	$2.24	$2.30	$2.00
Shaping	3.73	3.71	3.68	3.70	3.65	3.50
Welding	4.55	4.60	4.58	4.65	4.68	4.50
Painting	1.20	1.19	1.21	1.21	1.20	1.20

Cost accounting obtained these per-unit costs by dividing the total monthly cost of each operation by the number of times performed. By setting unit costs for the current period against previous periods and the standard cost, cost accounting finds a revealing profile of the cost-trend for each operation, and compares actual costs with standard costs. The facts show that the cost of the cutting operation is declining steadily, dropping from $2.30 per operation in December to $2.10 in April. The cost of performing the shaping operation, on the other hand, is rising steadily. Welding costs have dipped slightly, while painting remains stable.

Comparison of actual costs with standard costs reveals that costs are running too high for all operations except painting; the comparisons show how far actual costs fall short of standard cost goals for each operation. Management must take steps to bring actual costs in line with its standard cost goals. If this is not possible, it then must devise more realistic cost goals.

Realistic standard costs permit cost accounting to determine the probable cost of producing an item—or of an entire production run—before production begins. This enables a company to bid on special jobs with some assurance of making a profit. Cost accounting observes variations between actual and standard costs once production begins. By keeping standard costs in line with actual costs—and vice versa—cost accounting uses the standard cost system to control operations and appraise overall results.

UNCOVER VARIANCES WITH A STANDARD COST SYSTEM

A standard cost is the expected cost of a product produced at a specified volume under a given set of circumstances. Variances above or below the standard are the profit or loss of internal operations. Standard costs help to strengthen the budget program by controlling current activities directly, whereas the budget serves as a yardstick against which to measure actual costs incurred. The standard costs themselves are based on the same data used in preparing the budget.

Using Standard Costs

There are many ways to use cost standards, but they all have these common objectives:

1. To obtain the cost of production in standard dollars.
2. To compare the standard cost data with actual costs.
3. To determine the variances between 1 and 2, and the reasons for such variances.

This can be accomplished in a variety of ways; the two chief methods use the Work in Process account. With both methods, standard costs are credited to this account when products are transferred to Finished Goods. One method, however, debits the account with *actual costs,* the other method debits the account with *standard costs.*

Charging Work in Process with Actual Costs

With this method, the accountant records all expenses (direct material, direct labor, and overhead) at their actual costs and transfers them to the Work in Process account at actual costs:

		DR.	CR.
STEP 1	OVERHEAD	18,200	
	Indirect labor		6,000
	Depreciation		5,000
	Electricity		5,200
	Rent		2,000
	To transfer factory expenses incurred		
STEP 2	WORK IN PROCESS	74,200	
	Materials		32,000
	Labor		24,000
	Overhead		18,200
	To transfer actual costs to Work in Process		

Standard costs become part of the accounts under this system when completed units are transferred to Finished Goods at standard cost. To complete the operation and determine the variances, a physical count is made of the work in process inventory. Accounting then converts this count to equivalent completed units and multiplies this number by the standard cost per unit. The result is subtracted from the balance in the Work in Process account and any balance remaining in this account is the variance—the difference between actual and standard costs. Finally, the variance is closed to the Cost of Sales account. The variance can be subdivided into Labor, Material and Overhead by maintaining separate accounts for each department.

Charging Work in Process with Standard Costs

With this method, the accountant debits Work in Process with standard costs of the goods worked on during the period, and he credits this account with the standard costs of units transferred to finished goods. The accounts for direct labor, materials, and the summary account for factory overhead are charged with actual costs, but transfers from them to Work in Process are made at standard costs. Thus, the variances are developed in the materials, labor, and overhead accounts. Any debit balances remaining in these accounts at the close of a period are unfavorable, and credit balances indicate favorable variances. These balances are closed to variance accounts, which, in turn, are closed to Cost of Sales.

NOTE: If desired, charge these variances directly to variance accounts when incurred. Suppose the standard cost of an item is $2.00 and you purchase 1,000 at $2.20. The entry could be:

	DR.	CR.
Raw materials	$2,000	
Raw materials price variance	200	
Vouchers payable		$2,200

Computing Equivalent Production

If your company produces a large number of physical units, not physically identifiable one from the other, you undoubtedly use a process cost system of accounting which, in effect, averages costs over all units produced in a given time period—week, month, quarter. To gain the benefits of a standard cost system under these circumstances, your production departments must convert partially completed units to an equivalent number of completed units, a computation that gives you *equivalent production.*

Finding equivalent production is sometimes quite simple. This is the case when the materials, labor, and overhead involved in producing 100 units that are 50 percent complete is the same as for 50 units that are 100 percent complete:

Completed units transferred to next department	17,200
1,800 units in ending inventory (50 percent complete)	+900
	18,100
1,200 units in beginning inventory (40 percent complete)	−480
Equivalent production for period	17,620

Making Separate Computations

The computation above, however, applies only when materials, labor, and overhead go into the units uniformly throughout the production process. If, for example, materials are issued only at the beginning of the process, the following computation must be made for applying material costs to units:

Completed units transferred to next department	17,200
1,800 units in ending inventory (50 percent complete, 100 percent as to materials)	+1,800
	19,000
1,200 units in beginning inventory (40 percent complete, 100 percent as to materials)	−1,200
Equivalent production per period	17,800

If materials costs in this department are $32,000 for the period, and labor and overhead are $38,000, unit costs are determined as follows:

Direct Materials—
$32,000 + 17,800 units = $1.798
Labor and Overhead—
$38,000 + 17,620 units = 2.157

Cost per unit $3.955

The $3.955 unit cost is used to value the ending inventory and the units transferred to the next process where, starting from the $3.955 base, another computation of equivalent production determines unit costs in that process.

For a precise calculation of costs of equivalent production units, be sure to apply costs for any waste or shrinkage that takes place during a production process.

Pinpointing Variances with Budget Reports

Budget reports may be prepared for a section, a department, or an operating division. Although their complexity varies, all budget reports serve a common purpose: to indicate budgeted and actual costs and to explain any budget variances.

See that line management prepares budget reports as often as is necessary. You may need weekly reports for critical cost items, while monthly or quarterly reports may be adequate for evaluating overall performance. You will also want to set standards for explaining variances. For example, it may be unnecessary to require explanation for variances from the budget of 5 percent or less. Benefits derived from the explanation might not justify the cost of the investigation. In the following example, however, variances are substantial enough to require explanation.

Departmental Budget Performance Report
Production Department "A," Quarter Ending 6/31

	Budget	Actual	Variance	Percent
Wages	$240,000	$288,000	$48,000	+ 20
Material	120,000	144,000	24,000	+ 20
Supplies	10,000	12,000	2,000	+ 20

EXPLANATION: Variances in all areas caused by increases in production schedule to meet shipping department requisitions.

If the basic budget estimates are sound, the use of reporting techniques forces personnel to be alert and efficient. Budget reports perform the inspection function of showing management the weak areas, and they are helpful in evaluating the administration capabilities of personnel. Budget control and its accompanying standards are instrumental in implementing a standard cost system.

An effective budget control system depends on honest reporting. Don't let department heads feel that reporting an overrun cost is necessarily a reflection on their personal efficiency. In many cases, it may be out of their control entirely. The budget control serves to improve operating efficiency, not to find scapegoats.

Regardless of how well managers understand the management information system, there will always be a certain amount of complaints if a manager consistently receives reports showing variances over which he has no control. This will be particularly so if the amount of these variances is significant. Much of this difficulty can be avoided by structuring the reports in such a fashion that certain of the costs which are controllable only at a higher level of management are reported in a separate section of the cost analysis. Thus, for example, certain interdepartmental charges may be accumulated in a separate section which is added to the manager's costs, but for which he is not specifically accountable. Continuing this system at the next higher level of management, a larger proportion of the total costs will become controllable, and therefore subject to that manager's accountability.

STATISTICAL METHODS FOR ESTIMATING COSTS

The traditional approach, which was explained earlier, does have alternatives which are available which may also produce estimated costs developed from historical performances. The means by which to develop the costs depend upon a mathematical linear relationship which can be compiled by the cost accountant and used by him to arrive at costs for particular segments of an operation and assist him to understand better the cost relationships which are inherent within a given number of variables.

Using the statistical approach has the virtue of removing much of the work from the realm of various forms used in cost control and also eliminates the need for understanding many of the complexities of statistical programming. The approach can be a very effective assist to the judgment and intuition of the various cost operators. In essence, the statistical approach involves the least squares equation which can be found explained in simple form in most basic texts on statistics. The essence of the equation is the formula for a straight line. In other words, we are dealing here with attempting to discern among cost variables the straight-line relationships of costs to another basis for comparison. For example, we might compare total manufacturing costs with total units produced, or we might compare direct labor hours with total salaries and benefits. By plotting each of these relationships, either on a scattergram or computing them with the least squares formula, we should be able to determine the linear relationship which exists between the two variables.

Much of this approach of cost estimating is based upon the foundation that the cost of any manufactured item is largely a function of its characteristics. In this sense, we are saying that the cost of an item largely flows through the sequence of manufacturing cost, the characteristics of types of labor employed to make the product, and the cost of the materials which go into making the product. Certain relationships exist between each of these product characteristics, and the job of the cost accountant in using the statistical method is to isolate what portion of the relationship will exist regardless of whether any units are produced. In other words, we are seeking a breakout of fixed and variable costs, and moreover, within the variable costing plan, to determine the nature of the variable relationship that exists.

Scattergram

A scatter diagram is merely a form of a graph with many different points plotted, the points representing different numerical values along the relationship of two variables. The vertical axis in the scatter diagram may represent one variable and the horizontal axis may represent an additional variable. For any given value on either axis, the point is plotted on the diagram. The nature of the pattern of these points is the key to answering the question of cost variability. If the points fall largely in the pattern of a straight line, the relationship may be developed subjectively by drawing a line which would pass through the most number of points. In lieu of using this subjective judgment, the least squares formula may be used. That formula will mathematically compute the line which will pass between most of the points or statistically have the most equal distance from any of the points.

The Least Squares Formula

This formula seeks to find the line of relationship in which the computed pattern goes through plotted points in such a way that the sum of the squares of the deviations from the line to the points is a minimum. In addition, deviations are always measured against the vertical scale on the graph. The statistical formula for a straight line is generally stated as $y = a + bx$. The least squares method uses that formula and in addition, one other, and creates a simultaneous equation in which values of a and b will be solved. The two equations are as follows:

Sum col. 2 = Na + bx Sum col. 1
Sum col. 3 = ax Sum col. 1 + b Sum col. 4

in which Sum equals the total of value shown in the column. N equals the number of units produced or data under consideration.

The following table was created with linear values and has been prepared with all of the data arranged in order of hierarchy. Transcribing data from the table into the equation yields the following values:

In Millions

Manufacturing Costs	Total Labor Costs	Computations	
		Col. 1 × Col. 2	Col. 1 × Col. 1
Column 1	Column 2	Column 3	Column 4
$ 5.48	$ 5.24	$ 28.72	$ 30.03
6.16	6.08	37.45	37.95
6.76	6.49	43.87	45.70
7.64	7.01	55.56	58.37
8.03	7.58	60.87	64.48
$34.07	$32.40	$224.47	$236.53

The Sum of column 1 equals 34.07; the Sum of column 2 equals 32.40; the Sum of column 3 equals 224.47; the Sum of column 4 equals 236.53; N equals 5. Using the columnar data in the equation shows that the equations become as follows:

$$32.40 = 5a + 34.07b$$
$$224.47 = 34.07a + 236.53b$$

The method of solving a simultaneous equation entails a multiplication of one or the other of the equations by a number that will neutralize one of the unknowns in both equations. Then, subtracting one of the equations from the other eliminates the unknown and enables us to solve for the value of the remaining unknown. In the present example, if the first equation is multiplied by 6.814, then a can be made to equal b as follows:

$$220.774 = 34.07a + 232.153b$$

The first equation can then be subtracted from the second equation. This would then yield us $3.696 = 4.377b$; b would then be equal to 0.84441. The tables are then reversed and b is substituted and either one of the equations can solve for a. On that basis, the solution to a is found to be a $= .72619$. Since these numbers have been rounded, replacing them to the full value yields an answer that $a = \$726,200$. This answer yields the level of fixed cost for that relationship of cost. In addition, it tells us that variable labor costs are equal to .84441 percent of manufacturing cost.

USE BREAK-EVEN ANALYSIS IN ADAPTING TO CHANGES

No matter how carefully you calculate the many elements that go into profit planning, changes beyond your control are likely to occur that drastically affect anticipated profits. During the budget year it may be necessary to expand the sales territory, to meet union demands for more wages, to buy new machinery, or to put unused plant capacity into production. In each instance, break-even analysis will indicate the effects of the new situation on profits. It does this in much the same way as it finds the profit-making level of any business operation.

Computing the Break-Even Point

The break-even point refers to that level of business activity where a firm neither makes a profit nor incurs a loss, where income is just enough to cover expenses. To make a profit, the firm must have sales volume higher than the break-even point; to avoid a loss, it must not sell below the break-even point.

To compute the break-even point, take the following steps:

Step 1. Separate all costs into fixed and variable categories.

Step 2. Express the variable expenses as a percentage of sales, and subtract that percentage from 100 percent. The difference represents the percentage of each sales dollar available for fixed expenses and profit.

Step 3. Take that last percentage and divide it into the total fixed cost. The resulting figure is the total sales required to absorb the fixed cost. This is the break-even point.

EXAMPLE: The Acme Corporation forecasts sales of $5,000,000, variable costs of $3,300,000, and fixed costs of $1,200,000. Sales at break-even point = variable expenses as a percentage of selling price + total fixed expenses.

Variable expenses $= \dfrac{\$3,300,000}{5,500,000} = 66$ percent of sales

100 percent — 66 percent = 34 percent = sales required for absorbing fixed expenses.

Fixed expenses $= \dfrac{\$1,200,000}{34 \text{ percent}} = \$3,530,000 =$ break-even point

Proof of computation:

Sales at break-even point $3,530,000

Less:	1,200,000
Variable cost at break-even point	
(66 percent of $3,530,000)	2,330,000
Total costs	$3,530,000
Profit or loss	None

Loss per sales dollar if sales fall below break-even point = $1.00 —
66 percent = 34 cents.

Applying the Break-Even Analysis

The Acme Corporation's sales forecast is $1,470,000 above its break-even point ($5,000,000 — $3,530,000). The fixed and variable expenses of $4,-500,000 on sales of $5,000,000 will permit a net profit before taxes of $500,000 or 10 percent. But suppose that the cost of materials suddenly rises 10 percent and that management considers it necessary to maintain the current selling price. How much will sales have to be increased to maintain the present dollar profit? Break-even analysis supplies the answer:

Current Data:		
Fixed costs		$1,200,000
Variable costs as percent of sales		66%
Profit		500,000
Sales		5,000,000
Additional Cost Burden:		
Increase of 10% in variable costs (materials)		
Analysis:		
New ratio of variable costs to sales (66% + 6.6%)		.726
Sales dollar available for fixed costs and profit		.274
Total		1.000
Required Sales:		
($1,200,000 + $500,000) + 27.4% = required sales		
$1,700,000 + 27.4% = $6,204,375		
Proof:		
Sales		$6,204,375
Costs:		
Fixed	1,200,000	
Variable (72.6%)	4,504,375	5,704,375
Profit		500,000

To maintain the same profit of $500,000 while incurring a 10 percent increase in material costs, sales must advance from $5,000,000 to $6,204,-375. If management considers this goal feasible, it can absorb the increase in variable costs; otherwise, it will have to adjust the selling price. Break-even analysis assumes these conditions: (1) a change in sales volume will not affect the per-unit selling price, (2) fixed costs remain fixed regardless of volume, and (3) variable costs vary directly with production. Since these conditions never exist in actuality, the analyst should frequently determine whether the degree of error is significant.

He should also recognize that some expenses, instead of falling neatly into a pattern of variable and fixed costs, contain elements of both. Though these "semi-variable expenses" fluctuate with volume, they do not do so in direct proportion to changes in business activity. Examples include expenses for advertising and utilities.

5

EFFECTIVE CONTROL OF
ADMINISTRATIVE COSTS

INTRODUCTION

Cost reduction programs which are to be meaningful are serious business and they should not be entered into unless the full cooperation of the entire management of the company is also present. There are probably five basic truisms which are attendant to any efforts at reducing costs:

1. Over the short term, a crash program may have a very temporary benefit; however, over the intermediate term or a long term, a crash program may accomplish as much harm as it does good.
2. A scanning of financial statements and a picking out of likely targets for cost reduction is a careless and improperly planned approach to a cost reduction program. It will likely meet only with mediocre success.
3. Cost reduction programs may carry with them the obligation to increase certain levels of expenditures while decreasing expense levels in likely areas.
4. Cost reduction programs without meaningful stipulated objectives for accomplishment are doomed to failure. A command from on high to simply reduce costs provides no leadership or guidance for the operating executive.
5. Cost reduction programs are every bit as much a part of corporate planning as are profit plans. As such, cost reduction on a planned basis should be given equal weight and equal status with a profit plan. They should be constructed and carried out concurrently and each should be under the guidance of a task force which will see to it that the objectives of each of the plans are met. Such plans are most likely to be successful if they are drawn up and pursued even in times of rising profits.

Robert Pudder indicated that a plan for getting the best results should include the following elements:

a. The leaks in cost control, the erosion of profits, and the lags in needed innovation in production and marketing must be identified.
b. A program must be devised to plug those leaks, to restore those profits, and to get the company back on the road to progress.
c. The program must be vigorously carried out at all company levels.
d. Constant surveillance must guard again costs that soar and profits that dip. Similarly, there needs to be vigilance against flaccid company reaction to dynamic change.

CONTROLLABLE COSTS

Controllable costs are costs which are subject to management control over the short-term time horizon. At least one writer has said that this type of cost really can be separated into two specific identifiable patterns:

a. *Policy costs*—This is the type of cost which is dependent upon the evaluation, intuition and insight of the highest levels of management. It might include costs associated with advertising, development and research work for new products, methods and procedures which are innovative, etc. This type of cost is not variable with sales volume and may be associated with the traditional cost accountant's description of overhead.

b. *Operating costs*—Operating costs are those items which are needed to carry on the daily affairs of the business. These costs nevertheless are subject to a great deal of judgment on the part of managers and are most closely associated with staff service elements. The purchasing function for a company is an excellent example of such a cost as are the traditional service areas of finance, physical distribution and industrial relations.

Corporate profits in the recent years of the late 1960s and the early 1970s are suffering from a lack of dynamic growth. The lack of dynamic growth centers mainly on the conflict between labor costs per unit of production and productivity per worker. This conflict, which is causing the increased inflation pattern of more recent years, has made even more important the emphasis placed on cost reduction programs. I think that certain generalizations regarding controllable costs and the implications regarding cost reduction programs during the decade of the seventies can be made. I believe that the likelihood for staff service departments continuing at the expansionary growth rate which has been pursued up to the decade of the seventies is likely to begin to recede in popularity.

Outside Service Companies

It is probable that the flexibility that outside service companies can offer in the way of pricing and services will have a tendency to cut down on the need to maintain large staff overhead services within companies. A current example of this is the evolution in the field of advertising toward creative venture groups which sell their services to independent clients. These creative workshop groups are independent of the large established advertising agencies. This type of program will most likely have its application in the area of public relations and computer services.

Likewise, the high fringe benefit costs associated with hiring permanent workers will accelerate the use of temporary help agencies. These types of services can often provide similar skills to that possessed by long-term staff employees, but yet offer cost savings as the result of reduced requirements for fringe benefits. It is not uncommon, in today's corporate environments, for fringe benefits to approximate thirty to thirty-five percent of salaries. I would suspect also that another area which is likely to be hit is college recruiting on the snob level. Many companies have gone out of their way to give the impression that their new college recruits are taken only from the best of the ivy league colleges and possess the proper bloodline. This type of individual, regretfully, has in the past inflated the economic worth of his hiring by commanding much higher levels of salary than his counterparts in lesser-known educational institutions. It is probable that hiring programs for college recruits may be tempered to the extent that the well-known "name" educational institutions will no longer be sought after as a prestige symbol.

Management Consulting Firms

Another area of significant growth leading to reductions in costs will be an accelerated use of management consulting firms that specialize in specific functional expertise. Many consulting firms are widely known in specialized areas of decision making. Arthur D. Little, for example, is well known in the field of engineering problems. Drake Sheahan/Stewart Dougall are well known for their expertise in the area of physical distribution. McKinsey & Company specialize in problems of financial profitability. Booz Allen & Hamilton and Paul Mulligan have specialized and pioneered in the areas of clerical work measurement. There is a golden opportunity for companies to selectively choose that consultant who is best able to provide assistance in specialized areas.

HOW TO ORGANIZE FOR ACCOMPLISHING COST REDUCTIONS

The most pressing need for accomplishing cost reductions is that of reliable information. Such information must not only be quantitatively oriented but relevant to the problem being looked at, reliable and timely. The ideal vehicles are performance reports for individuals, efficiency reports for labor, usage reports for physical materials used in production and manufacturing variance reports for factory operations. Special "flag" reports should be established which will enable key management personnel to constantly track progress against the predetermined cost reduction objective. Profit improvement responsibility should include the types of assistance which are needed for all affected personnel to examine the essential information about the company's performance and, in addition, its outside customers, suppliers and competitive environment.

Committees of Key People

The next key move is to establish a task force to head the operational aspects of the program. This may consist of setting up committees of key people from important departments in order to parcel out specific assignments. Such a committee should see to it that its recommendations are carried out and it should regularly report to the task force heading the operation. During the course of a cost reduction program, there are many other avenues for creative suggestions which should not be overlooked. The line employee who is not in the management level often feels left out of the program because he feels that he has no direct line of communication to the levels of management making decisions about cost reductions. Two specific methods of helping that level of employee contribute their thoughts to an overall cost reduction program have proved effective in the past:

1. *Set up a hot line.* One Chicago chemical company has said that, "All an employee has to do is to dial C-O-S-T and one of the girls in the secretarial pool will take down his idea." The result of that type of procedure has been a report by the company president that he is getting about five times as many suggestions now as he did when the ideas had to be written out.

2. *Set up a raffle.* A key executive in a St. Louis construction company has said that, "Each month we pick one suggestion from all of those entered, and award the lucky person a prize. It doesn't matter whether the employee's idea will actually be used or not. The important thing is that every person who turns in an idea has a chance to win." The result of this type of technique has been that the company has tripled the number of suggestions it formerly received. The executive cited above indicated that, "Putting at least one suggestion in the box each month seems to have become a habit for just about everybody in the company."

CUTTING YOUR INVESTMENT IN COMPANY
TRANSPORTATION

If employees use automobiles in your business, you may be able to make substantial savings by either (a) finding a more efficient plan than your present one or (b) making better use of the cars you now operate.

You have three alternatives:

a. Use employee-owned cars
b. Use company-owned cars
c. Use leased cars

What is best for you depends on such things as:

—The number of cars you will need to operate
—The number of miles they will travel in a year
—Auto insurance rates in your area
—The stability of the used car market in your locality
—The make and size of the cars you will operate

Your decision should be based upon a careful study of all of your present car expenses compared with your possible future costs under other plans. Figure 1 will help you to analyze your costs. List the costs which you incur under your present system, then compute operating costs per mile for your cars. It would be helpful if the same approach were used with other possible car operations plans. Car leasing concerns usually will supply you with approximate costs for any method you are considering. If there are several such firms in your area, get separate cost estimates from each of them. You will find it wise before you decide to compare their estimates with the experience of firms like yours in your community.

There is no one best way to solve your company car problem. In fact, there is no one best way for a particular size or type of company. You will want to carefully examine each possible plan and what it can mean to your business. The company car problem for the most part concerns sales personnel, but the discussion here applies as well to cars for service representatives or executives.

Employee and Company-Owned Cars

Employee-owned cars are the simplest and most widely used means of providing transportation on the job. Usually companies will pay a mileage allowance which may vary between 10¢ and 14¢ per mile, but makes no addi-

COMPARISON GUIDE – COMPANY CAR OPERATION COSTS

Direct Costs	Company Owned	Salesman Owned	Finance Lease	Full Maint. Lease	Net Lease
Leasing Fee					
Depreciation					
Gasoline					
Lubrication					
Insurance					
Interest					
License Fees					
Property Tax					
Tires					
Maintenance					
Average Repair					
Miscellaneous					
Total Direct Costs					
Indirect Costs:					
Administrative					
* Other Indirect					
Total Costs					
Per Mile Costs					
Per Salesman Cost					

* INCLUDE ESTIMATE OF TIME YOUR REPRESENTATIVES SPEND IN BUYING & SELLING CARS, LOST TIME ON REPAIRS TO CARS, AND ANY OTHER EXPENSES FOR WHICH YOU RECEIVE NO BENEFIT.

Figure 1

tional investment in the car or its operation. If the salesmen cover local territories and drive on the average of less than 1,000 miles a month, this is probably the least expensive way to provide company transportation, but there are certain problems which result from this type of operation:

1. Mileage payments to salesmen who cover different distances in a year will vary. The result is that some make a profit; others take a "loss" on operating their automobile. The employee with a "loss" is likely to become dissatisfied with his job and let his selling efforts suffer. The man with a "profit" is likely to consider that extra income and slacken his sales drive.
2. Most top-notch salesmen would rather work for a firm that gives them the prestige of driving a company car.
3. The impact of your company on prospective customers will suffer as your salesmen keep their cars longer to get a satisfactory return on their investment in them. The result may be that salesmen will drive a rapidly aging and dissimilar collection of automobiles.

Company ownership of cars hinges on (1) cash available to invest in cars and (2) the ability to operate them economically. This last factor can take a huge bite out of profits—it's often overlooked. Over a three-year period, company-owned car operating costs can equal twenty percent of the original purchase outlay. Car ownership costs climb higher unless you can get a substantial discount from the new car dealer and can couple this with a high price when the car is put out on the used car market. The president of a Chicago car leasing concern estimates that operators of company-owned cars could get almost $60.00 more resale value per car through careful study of the used car market, a flexible plan of car replacement, and better contact with dealers. The hidden expenses of running company-owned cars can be the biggest factor which one must consider in deciding whether to buy or lease.

Car Leasing Plans

Before you decide to have your company lease cars for business use, the responsible officer should personally investigate each major type of lease plan and its impact upon operations.

1. *Full maintenance leasing* is generally used by small and medium-sized companies. It is the most expensive method of auto leasing, however, it permits the company to avoid being caught in two highly variable cost factors:
   (a) As soon as the lease is signed, the company knows exactly how much the car is going to cost to operate on an annual basis. This information is provided with the exception of information for gas, oil and insurance usage.
   (b) The company is protected when the car is sold. Many companies which operate cars under this plan successfully handle gas and oil

payments through the medium of credit cards. Bills are sent directly to the company for payment, eliminating cash payments to employees. The plan, however, does not give the company the benefits of any possible savings it can make in car operations costs. In addition, the company is responsible for any damages to the cars resulting from negligence. Rates under the full maintenance plan can vary. For example, rates are lower if the plan includes limitations on tires or mileage.

2. *Finance leasing* assures the company of a car's fixed cost, but does not include operating expenses in the plan. Under such a plan, the company avoids tying up capital in cars, but it pays for this privilege and it assumes all the responsibilities of car ownership. The plan works by having the company pay the concern from which the car is leased a monthly sum to cover interest on its investment in the car, depreciation, administrative expenses and the cost of buying and selling the car. Each month a portion of the payment is set aside against the eventual sale of the car. If the car sells for less than the amount in this fund, then the company pays the difference to the lessor. If the car sells for more, the company receives the excess as a refund. Under this plan, cars may be sold after twelve months but can be kept longer. Under other plans, the minimum lease period may be eighteen months or longer. Under the finance lease plan, the company gets the full benefit of any cuts which can be accomplished in operational costs for the cars. Any improvements in operating efficiencies are, of course, incremental dollars in the bank.

3. *Net leasing* is the same in all respects as finance leasing except that the company is protected against loss when the cars which the company has been using are sold. The leasing firm collects an additional payment each month. If the cars are sold at a loss, the company is not charged with extra expenses. If the cars are sold at a profit, the leasing company keeps it. This type of leasing is not really necessary when the car operation is well managed. When cars are kept in good condition with frequent preventive maintenance, the added expense of a net lease is not generally considered to be worth the protection offered.

Savings on Car Operations

No matter what sytsem of ownership or leasing is employed, cost cutting for car operations is possible. Many firms have successfully managed their car operations by employing any one of the following devices:

—One large leasing firm found that annual savings from discontinuing tire rotation on cars every 5,000 miles *averaged $17.00 per car.*

—One company found that using oil one price below top grade makes no difference in the condition of a car and *saves 10¢ on each quart.*

—Another firm stopped using compact cars for two reasons: (1) it found that the smaller cars do not hold up as well as larger cars to 40,000 miles of travel a year and; (2) company salesmen did not take care of the cars because they felt the smaller cars created a poorer image of their company.

—This same company set up a special fund as self-insurance for collision and comprehensive coverage on its financed leased cars. It had previously carried a $50.00 deductible policy with an outside insurer. The fund receives $5.00 per car each month. After eighteen months of operation under its own insurance, the firm has reduced its insurance expenses and has earned a surplus of $6,000 in the fund.

—Another leasing company says that some company officers do not take full advantage of discounts available for such items as replacement tires and small parts. Some firms pay as much as $13.50 more per car on such equipment than the operators of large fleets and the difference is not due in most cases to large purchase discounts usually given to leasing companies.

—Many firms are neglecting to make full use of manufacturer's warranties on new cars. Out-of-pocket costs on a company car average around $20.00 a year more than what a leasing company pays for replacement parts.

Smaller companies now are increasing the usage of leased automobiles for salesmen and top executives. The obvious advantage to the company is that it is an attractive motivator for a key employee and in addition, payments under the lease are tax deductible to the company. The employee, of course, to whom the car is given must be able to justify it on a business basis. Basically, monthly leasing payments average slightly less than the same costs for owned cars. This is especially true over the initial years of a car's life when the heaviest portion of depreciation takes place. The double benefit of a lease payment also is that it foregoes the necessity of a large initial cash outlay with its attendant interest costs. One of the largest factors in the auto leasing business, Kinney Rent-A-Car, has estimated, according to a leading business service, that by the end of the decade, based upon present growth rates, small fleets and individuals will account for about sixty-five percent of cars leased compared with the current rate of forty-five percent.

Contract periods are generally running between twenty-four and twenty-six months and the payments are stable over the length of the lease. Two types of leases are emerging in practice. A *closed-end lease* is effective when the leasing company takes full responsibility for disposal of the car when the lease has terminated. Individual customers, however, have tended to prefer the less expensive *open-end lease*. That type of lease has provisions in it which will permit the customer to pay the difference between the depreciated value of the car and the actual selling price realized by the leasing company.

It should stand as a truism that when leasing a fleet of cars, any company should get several bids. Financial considerations, however, should not be the sole vehicle for determining which bid to accept. It is equally important to consider the length of time that the leasing company has been in service, the reliability of the company's insurance carrier and whether the tires provided by the company under the terms of the lease are those which are products of reputable tire makers. Speed of service is equally important and the amount of allowance for replacement of defective parts is additionally of extreme importance. The following are checkpoints to help cut the cost of operating business cars. Most companies are able to trim expenses somewhere along the line by reviewing these points and comparing them with company practices. In all but a few instances, a negative answer calls for investigation.

Yes	No	
___	___	Do we have a preventive maintenance program, and are our drivers following it?
___	___	Do we follow manufacturers' maintenance suggestions?
___	___	Are we using premium where regular gas will do?
___	___	Have we considered gasoline credit cards as a cost control procedure?
___	___	Do we audit dealer repair orders?
___	___	Do our cars favorably reflect our corporate image?
___	___	Have we looked at floor mats and seat covers as a way to increase our resale value?
___	___	Have we determined whether there is a pattern of failure?
___	___	Are we using the lowest cost suitable oil?
___	___	Do we rotate tires regularly?
___	___	Have tire lease and rental programs been investigated?
___	___	Do we have a safety program and is it up to date?
___	___	Have we compared our car cost with other companies like ours?
___	___	Do we ask manufacturers' representatives to help us specify the right equipment and options?
___	___	Is our mileage-rate payment to employees fair?
___	___	Have we investigated automobile leasing programs completely and without bias?
___	___	Do we know the best time of year to trade cars for best resale value?
___	___	Have we investigated the cost savings of compacts?
___	___	Do we buy cars of a color and trim that help resale?

Yes No

___ ___ Do we encourage automobile dealers' cooperation through prompt payment of invoices?

___ ___ Can small automobile dealers understand our forms, such as invoices, purchase orders, and so forth?

___ ___ Have we looked at our trade-in program recently?

___ ___ Do we consider the driver, the terrain, and the driving conditions when we specify make, model, and optional equipment?

___ ___ Are we buying optional equipment that gives the best resale value?

___ ___ Do we consider total cost—what we'll have to pay for operation, service and repairs—when deciding the make and model to be purchased, or do we buy the make on which we get the lowest bid?

___ ___ Is an engine governor practical for our cars?

___ ___ Have we considered ways of reducing our insurance cost, license fees, and taxes through the purchase of different models or makes?

___ ___ Have we analyzed cost of outside dealer maintenance vs. our own shop maintenance?

___ ___ Would we be money ahead to keep our cars longer, or replace them sooner?

___ ___ Should we operate various segments of our fleet under different plans, or is one plan best for the whole fleet?

MINIMIZING WAGE-HOUR COSTS

It is quite possible to arrange the workweek so that employees can work more hours, produce more and yet the company incur savings by cutting overtime costs. One of the ways in which this can be accomplished is through a change in the workweek. When one California company closes down each July for its two-week vacation, it loses only about a week of production. There is no overtime to be paid for any extra work necessary.

The "Nonstandard" Workweek

The way that is it accomplished by the firm is as follows: Even though the employees generally work a Monday through Friday schedule, the company workweek begins on Wednesday. The company, therefore, can have employees work more than forty hours in the calendar workweek before vacation without having to pay overtime. (A union contract may, of course, affect this policy.)

The plan is accomplished by having the employees work eight hours a day on Monday and Tuesday. They work thirteen hours a day on Wednesday, Thursday and Friday. That's a total of fifty-five hours in five consecutive days. But, there is no overtime involved because the work is done in two different workweeks. The workweek schedule is illustrated in Chart 1.

S	M	T	W	T	F	S
0	8	8	13	13	13	V
V	V	V	V	V	V	V
V	V	V	V	V	V	V
V	13	13	8	8	8	0

Chart 1

In addition, after vacation, employees work thirteen hours on Monday and Tuesday and eight hours on each of the following days—without overtime. The reason that no overtime is incurred is because the last three days are in a different workweek. The result of the above is that the company gets twenty-five hours extra work and has to pay for it. It pays for it, however, on a straight-time basis, not on a time-and-a-half basis.

A treasurer in North Dakota uses the "nonstandard" workweek for still a different purpose. His special operation requires several employees to work ten consecutive days between days off. Using a regular calendar workweek, he would have to pay for fifty-six hours some weeks and twenty-four hours other weeks. Instead, he switched his workweek making it begin on Saturday while the workers begin the ten-day work period two days later (see Chart 2).

S	M	T	W	T	F	S
0	8	8	8	8	8	8
8	8	8	8	0	0	0
0	8	8	8	8	8	8
8	8	8	8	0	0	0

Chart 2

Labor law violations occur regularly in company operations. At one time, the Labor Department reported that almost 270 thousand workers are due over $55 million in back wages as a result of such violations. The complexity of the law is complicated further by the rapid turnover of company personnel and an economy which frequently encourages vast changes in staffing and manning of corporate operations. In addition to that, higher minimum wages and new salary requirements frequently compound the problem. It is almost mandatory that any company thoroughly review its wage-hour policy. It can provide an unexpected dividend in savings on payroll costs.

Avoid Unnecessary Overtime Costs

Many companies are paying employees for activities which are job-oriented but which are not necessarily related to "working time" under the law. Other companies incur unnecessary costs because they are not sufficiently versed with existing options available under the rules for determining overtime work. One of the first steps in insuring proper wage-hour compensation policy is that any overtime work by employees who are classified as nonexempt are reported and paid for. Methods of checking will vary between companies. However, one method is to *compare time and payroll records* of departments which do similar work or branches of the company which are comparable. Another technique is to *interview a sampling of employees*. It would also be profitable for the appropriate executives to *tour plants and offices* shortly after closing time to observe who is working overtime and determine the reasons for the work.

It should be remembered that the law does allow a variety of pay plans which are specifically designed to hold overtime costs within predictable limits and which have a tendency to level the peaks and valleys in employee earnings.

If the type of work performed is such that production is not level and tends to peak from week to week within some defined limits, a "time off" plan can assist in holding down overtime costs. In effect, this plan says that for every hour of overtime worked, an employee will enjoy one and one-half hours of time off during the same pay period. If this type of situation does not apply for your company, the same type of principle may still be enjoyed in the form of a "prepayment" plan. In effect, under this arrangement, the employee is prepaid for overtime work which he has not yet performed. The money is advanced to him by the company and the advance is carried forward from pay period to pay period until it has been absorbed by subsequent overtime work or a direct repayment by the employee.

Other types of plans are in existence, but since these are of a highly technical nature, it is most prudent to seek advice from competent experts in the area. An excellent manual for the guidance of company employee relations officers can be found in a publication by the Research Institute of America, Inc., called "Everything You Need to Know About the Wage-Hour Rules."

TRIMMING POSTAL EXPENSES

Stanley Fenvessy wrote an interesting piece recently which outlined his views on methods to curtail costs and speed operations in the corporate mail room. Essentially, he spoke about six distinct techniques which will enable the operations manager to cut costs and improve service.

His first thought is to *thoroughly analyze the mail room function*. It is Mr. Fenvessy's contention that the best way to accomplish this task is to assign a systems man or office manager responsibility for studying the flow of the mail room and its basic policies. He advocates using either the office manager, if it is a smaller company, or the controller. In his experience, he has noted that there is a marked need for new equipment to replace time-consuming and obvious manual efforts which can be better accomplished by a machine. He has also observed that there is a great deal of idle time between mail-handling peaks that could be used for other tasks in the interim. In addition, he has noted that in many cases there isn't enough space to perform an adequate job and in many respects the improper decisions which pertain to mail classification and postage are due to a misunderstanding of company policy directives because the directives themselves are not sufficiently clear-cut.

Training Mail Room Personnel

It is probably not known to many, but the postal service conducts free classes to train mail room personnel. The sessions are called "Postal Information and Orientation" and are devoted to assisting mail room personnel in understanding rules and regulations of the postal system and how the two organizations can best work together to achieve maximum efficiency. The service will also offer free assistance by correcting mailing lists, by zip coding the lists and also by loaning electronic data processing zip code conversion tapes and furnishing copies of mail sorting instructions used by postal employees. Mr. Fenvessy indicates that for companies which are generators of large quantities of mail, the postal service will arrange for acceptance of mail at the plants and offices of the company. He notes in his article also the more commonplace understanding that one should be careful in addressing mail, that mail should be separated into major categories and that it should be banded and sacked according to zip code sectional centers.

An interesting point made in the article relates to the automation and refurbishing of the mail room. It is Mr. Fenvessy's contention that the average mail room has been a stepchild too often and too long. His rule of thumb for determining what automation is needed is as follows:

- If your weekly volume exceeds one hundred pieces, he advocates having a hand envelope opener, a postage scale and a postage meter.

- If your weekly volume exceeds one thousand pieces, consider an automated mail opener and an automatic postage meter.

- If your weekly volume exceeds two thousand pieces, consider postage meters with sealing and stacking attachments.

- If your weekly volume exceeds ten thousand pieces, consider an automatic mail weighing and sorting machine and an envelope candler that will determine whether the contents have been removed from discarded envelopes.

- He also speaks of folders and collators and advocates that if more than eight hours a week are spent on any of these functions, automatic folding or collating equipment may be warranted.

The foregoing discussion has been more in the nature of a generalized overview of mail room operations. There are specific plans of action and specific techniques which can be placed into practice immediately by companies to achieve rapid cost savings. These are outlined in the following.

Hints on Reducing Mailing Costs

1. *Lighter paper can bring your mailing costs down.* You can use lightweight paper to cut your mailing costs. Even a company that mails in limited volume can achieve savings as a result of this technique.

    a. *Office stationery*—Many lightweight papers on the market are about as durable as the heaviest stock, but they get through the mails at less cost. For example, Waylite, put out by the Olin Mathieson Company.
    b. *Office copying machine paper*—The forty percent heavier paper used by many copiers can send postage bills climbing. Copy documents can cost twice as much to mail as the originals. At least two companies have done something about it. The Xerox machine makes copies on ordinary paper. Thermofax goes even further in terms of postage costs; it uses lightweight paper.

2. *Start a corporate drive on mailing costs.* Simple checks will show many companies that they are paying a much higher postage bill than is necessary.

One of the reasons for this is a policy in the mail room quite often which can be characterized as a "better be safe than sorry."

3. *Rate information.* Postal shipping rates are too complicated and changeable to be remembered. Post a break even chart which shows the cheapest shipping for all weights and distances and see that it is continually updated and used. One of the methods which can be employed is to send yourself a package weighing just under a rate weight break and see if the correct rather than the "safe" amount of postage is used.

4. *Insurance.* Postal insurance rates are intended mainly to apply to one-time mailing. If you mail in quantity over the course of the year, commercial parcel post insurance might save a considerable amount of money. One of the ways in which to spot this potential savings is to compare last year's post office insurance charges with the annual commercial insurance premium which may be available from a commercial insurer. If the annual losses of your company are small, you may even wish to assume the risk yourself or to establish a reserve.

5. *How to cut postage bills.* Looking for a fastest mail delivery at the lowest cost can often be wasteful in terms of expense. When fast mail delivery is necessary, however, in order to get it, the company should prepare and give the person who handles the mail in the office two lists of cities. One list should carry the cities where first class mail can reasonably be expected to be delivered overnight. Make it crystal clear that the letters to these cities are *not* to be sent airmail. The other list names the cities where next day deliveries require airmail. It should be easily recognizable that a company will not gain time by using airmail on Fridays. It is rare that key mail will be delivered in over a three-day period.

6. *Spreading the work.* Don't let a flood of incoming mail tie up your office help for hours every Monday while other work has to be neglected. Priorities should be established and you'll want to open first class and airmail upon its arrival, of course—you can reserve much of the remainder for the next day. This idea can often be more efficient. Many companies find Monday the heavy day for incoming mail with Tuesday a much lighter one. General practice in industries is to process Monday's incoming mail the same day. A large confectioner reports that it has cut clerical costs by dividing the load and handling an equal amount on Monday and Tuesday.

7. *Use airmail at first class rates.* Surprisingly enough, more and more first class mail is being sent by air. It goes right along with letters carrying air mail postage—but at a forty percent lower cost. This use of air service for first class letters is going to increase. The post office is using fewer and fewer trains to carry mail. Any company which has been mailing an average of 100 airmail letters a day can save approximately $1,000 a year by using first

class instead of airmail. One smart maneuver is to check with the local post-master. He is in the best position to know which destinations get automatic air lift from the area. When that is ascertained, the mail room management should make certain that employees never use airmail to these cities.

8. *Use certified instead of registered mail whenever possible.* Certified mail costs much less, yet can still provide a receipt to the sender and a notice of delivery.

9. *Use third and fourth class mail, not first class, for supplies and forms.* Supplies and forms and the like sent to salesmen, distributor to representatives, should be sent out well before they will be needed. One eight-ounce pad of forms will cost 80¢ airmail, 48¢ first class and only 18¢ third class. Even with a little advance preparation, it is evident that the cost of this item can be slashed by seventy-eight percent.

10. *Use lightweight material for large mailings.* Check the weight of paper and envelopes that are being used. If your mail is just breaking the next highest rate barrier, you can save plenty with lighter materials.

11. *Use regular postage to post office box addresses.* Don't send mail with a post office box address at special delivery rates. Regular mail will get there just as fast.

12. *Have one person in one place control postage used.* Eliminate separate stamp stocks and set controls on use of company postage for personal mailings. You might want to consider a postal meter which prevents stamp waste and keeps an accurate record of stamp use.

13. *Mail early.* If you can get your mail to the post office before 4 P.M. it may be delivered as much as one day sooner.

14. *Be sure large envelopes are clearly marked as "first class" or "airmail."* This prevents confusion with slower third class mail and speeds up delivery.

15. *Use an accurate scale.* An inaccurate scale can cost you money, especially when weighing mail that's on the borderline between two rates: (1) you may pay too much, (2) if you use insufficient postage, you get your mail returned for additional fees, or it's presented to your customer with "postage due." Either way, there is a loss of time and certainly a dissatisfied customer.

16. *Split up large parcels.* Third and fourth class mail covers the same types of material. It's the weight of a single parcel that makes the difference. If it weighs under a pound, it mails third class at 8¢ for the first two ounces and 2¢ for each extra ounce. If it's one pound or more, it must go fourth class at rates based on zones with a minimum charge of 50¢. One of the ways to determine whether you can achieve savings is by splitting up any package weighing more than a pound into two or more weighing less than a pound each. The treasurer of a New York company indicated that by using this

technique they have achieved a substantial savings on mailing costs. He indicated that "we used to pay parcel post zone rates on 18 ounces of material going to Miami. At the new rates, we pay 90¢ postage. Instead, we now split the material into two 9 ounce packages and send it third class at a total cost of 44¢." That same individual indicated that he also told his people to use book rates whenever possible. A minimum of twenty-four printed pages is all that is required to qualify for a book rate. The payoff is that book rate costs about one-fourth of the cost of third class mail.

EFFICIENT HANDLING OF INTERNAL COMMUNICATIONS

When you or any employer leave the desk to get or give information that can be transmitted over an intercom system or telephone, you could be setting off a chain reaction that eats into profits. You may be able to erase dissolution of profits through an internal communication system.

An obvious question is whether an intercom system is needed at all. The first step is determining the answers to various questions which must be raised about the nature of internal communications and customer needs. The checklist which follows will help you to find out:

—Do you and other executives have to leave your desk very often to locate each other or other employees?

—Do administrative employees spend much of their time going to the file room, the purchasing and shipping departments, and other areas?

—Is there a rash of call backs made on incoming, local or long distance calls? Work post absenteeism is a major reason why thirty percent of monthly business phone bills are for call backs.

—Do customers complain that it takes too long for them to get information when they call in? Are they kept waiting because the person they want to speak to is using his phone for an internal call or is out of his office?

—Is production ever held up longer than necessary because information on a breakdown or jam-up takes too long to reach the party who could resolve the difficulty?

—Do employees complain of too many people on the same extension?

—Are employees who must be in constant contact continually calling one another back because of busy signals?

—Does your business regularly require fast transfers of papers, records, etc., among widely scattered departments?

Choice of Basic Systems

The ultimate question of what sort of system is needed must be resolved among a number of basic systems to choose from. The ultimate choice will depend upon the type and size of your company. In many instances, the simple, less expensive system will serve your purpose.

1. *Intercom system.* This is most effective when the phones are distributed over a large area. Some companies use their public telephones internally— the local phone company makes the necessary adaptations. The main drawback of using regular phones is that internal calls often block external calls.

An alternative is the Private Automatic Exchange (PAX). The phones in this system are for internal use only. PAX systems have many desirable features. For example, when one line is busy, an automatic device hunts for and rings a free phone in the department. An automatic device also prevents a third person from breaking in on a call. Another device holds a call to a busy station while the caller hangs up. When the station is no longer busy, the call is put through automatically.

2. *Paging system.* This is a simple way of conveying messages to one individual only, usually via coded messages. Its prime effect is to reduce the use of the telephone and does largely eliminate the ensuing evils listed above. Coded messages can be sent automatically or manually to an individual without disturbing anyone else. Available are pocket-sized receivers with a miniature microphone that can carried on the person.

3. *Amplifier-speaker system.* This intercom consists of a master station (or stations) which is connected to substations by cables or your electrical circuit. Messages ordinarily are delivered through the speaker. However, the speaker can be cut out by a handset (generally optional) to allow private conversation. It has other available features:

—If someone is not at his desk, a light over the nameplate of the caller remains lit until the call is answered.

—Intercoms can be plugged in at various spots and messages transmitted to central stations.

—Personnel can be paged and can answer from the substation.

—An executive can break into a conversation instantly or a light signal will inform the speakers that someone wants to break in.

If you are contemplating a new plant, consider installation of the two following systems:

4. *Conveyor system.* This old-time yet highly effective means of sending material uses a pneumatic tube or power belt. Pneumatic tubes are best used for long distances or confined spaces. They take up little space since

the tubes can run through ceilings and floors with only sending and receiving ends exposed. Belt systems are simpler to install and operate. They can be arranged in a single flat belt or multi-lane. An outstanding feature is their ability to make a 90 degree turn, a difficult feat for other types of conveyors.

5. *Facsimile system.* Any writing, drawing or typing can be transmitted in duplicate between two points by a scanner and electronic longhand machine. The scanner picks up light and dark areas, converts them into similar impulses and sends them to a receiver which records the image on paper. The recorded image is ready for instant use. Longhand transmitters consist of a pen at the transmitting end and another at the receiving end. Electrical impulses pick up the sender's handwriting and the pen at the receiving end records an almost exact duplicate. Usually, these transmitters are operated over leased wires at a flat rate. This restricts them to high volume users.

Examples of What These Systems Can Do for You

a. An Oregon meat packing company found that seventy-five percent of its calls were internal. The switchboard was almost always jammed and customers were continually receiving busy signals. When the customer did get through, he often had to "hold" or leave a message which necessitated a call back. The president had an independent intercommunication system installed. It gives incoming calls a clear track to the wanted party and has increased orders handled in the sales department by seventeen percent. With the old system, if a customer requested information that wasn't at hand, he had to hold a "dead line" while the called party got it for him and he was told that he would be called back when the information was available. With separate internal communications, the party calling gets the information while the caller is still on the outside line.

b. The president of another company had an intercommunications system installed because he found that he had to meet with two or more of his top men five or six times a day. Instead of being short and to the point, the meetings lingered on and became full-fledged conferences. The new system allowed the president to talk to his associates without any of them leaving their desks. It also meant that they were available for incoming calls. The result was that the company president has dropped plans to hire a special assistant to help him with his workload.

c. One soap company president found that an intercom system helped him keep his extensive conveyor line rolling at peak efficiency. During a breakdown, men on the line use an internal communications system to call for help and to notify maintenance men where to go and what to look for. The conveyor now gets back into operation in one-third the time it took before the system was installed.

d. Other presidents of companies have installed systems to make fast and accurate inventory checks and to track the route of messages and materials.

e. A president discovered that it was taking too long to reach his supervisors. If the line was busy, he had to leave a message or call back. He installed an internal communications system that visually notifies the called party that he is wanted and by whom. This allows the party to cut his conversation short and pick up the president's call. The visual unit also reminds the supervisor of the president's call if the supervisor is away when called.

f. The New Jersey Warm Air Heating Company is not a large company. It has a small permanent staff. The company was able to cut costs when it installed an Executone Paging and Intercom system. Prior to installing this system, the company was paying $48.50 every month for the dial intercom equipment it rented from the telephone company. The telephone equipment is now eliminated which saves almost $600 a year. In thirty-two months alone, this will pay for their intercom system.

Prior to the installation of the new equipment, if a man couldn't be reached at his usual post, the receptionist had to phone in various places or run around until she found him. Any outside caller had to wait on a dead line. If the person couldn't be located, the caller's phone number was taken down and a call back made later. Every call back, of course, meant extra costs. Now, the receptionist pages the man she wants over the intercom system. She can locate him anywhere in the office or shop in a matter of seconds. She simply asks him to pick up his call at the nearest phone. She saves her time plus the caller's time, and a costly call back doesn't have to be made. In other areas, inter-office matters kept telephones jumping with calls to (1) the shipping department to find out when an order was shipped or scheduled to be shipped; (2) the shop to check on the progress of an order; (3) the stockroom to learn whether a certain item was in stock and in what quantities; (4) the bookkeeper to check credit or payment records. Now, such calls as these are carried over the separate intercom system. It's faster, and more likely to get through the first time and leaves telephones free for important outside calls. The determination of need for an intercom system begins with the switchboard.

Check Your Switchboard

In checking your company's communications system, begin with the switchboard. The switchboard operator will be able to estimate what percent of the total calls made during the day are within the company. In addition, she can supply the following information:

1. At what hours during the day the switchboard is operating at capacity.

You may be able simply to get a couple of persons to concentrate calls at other times without getting more equipment.

2. Who uses the switchboard most often for within-the-company calls.

3. How many call backs have to be made during the day because the people wanted are busy with internal calls.

4. How long people phoning the company were kept waiting because internal calls were tying up the lines. Even five or six such incidents a day mean trouble. The switchboard operator should keep a record each day for a week or more and that record should be kept on several different days scattered over a period of several weeks. If your telephone traffic is heavy, the suggestion here is that someone sit with the operator and mark the chart as calls are placed. A good rule of thumb is that when more than fifty percent of the switchboard load is in internal calls, a separate intercom system is needed.

It might also be a good idea for the top echelons of management to fill out a telephone usage report. (Figure 2.) This report shows the number of calls within the company each man makes. Have them fill the chart out on the same day the switchboard operator is keeping her telephone communications survey report. The two records will give you a quick picture of your call load.

I think we suffer from a syndrome in this country and that is that there is a symbol of a bell all over and that if you have a telephone somewhere it has to go through the Bell system. Really, it doesn't. You can save up to thirty percent, in fact, if you don't, and in addition, still get similar or better service. Contel Communications Corp., RCA, Phillips, and International Telephone and Telegraph Corporation all compete in the telephone leasing business. Phillips Broadcast Equipment Corp. and International Telephone and Telegraph sell systems outright. In fact, their customer list so far numbers approximately thirty-five companies. Large companies, namely Mobil Oil and Continental Can, have already leased telephone systems from Contel and that particular company has underbid Bell Telephone by about thirty percent so far. Their contracts run for ten years and include maintenance. RCA so far has leased a dozen systems. Phillips has sold about sixteen, mainly in New York City and Los Angeles and that's the main area where they have their maintenance technicians. Whether these systems are sold or leased, they still are required by the Federal Communications Commission to lease AT&T made devices to connect the phones to AT&T's trunklines. This is not a question of having your place ripped up and new telephone lines installed. The phones go on existing equipment just the same as cable television can go through phone lines. It is possible in the future that one would not be required to lease AT&T's interfacing devices in order to lease or purchase these telephone systems. Contel, for example, has a device made for them by a Japanese company and they claim that the specifications of the device are equal to or greater than the specifications that Bell requires of Western Electric. Further, they have even instructed their people not to pay

TELEPHONE USAGE REPORT

PLEASE LIST THE PEOPLE YOU CONTACT BY PHONE REGULARLY, AND THE ESTIMATED NUMBER OF TIMES PER DAY YOU CALL THESE POINTS. USE THE IN COLUMN FOR INTER-OFFICE CALLS – THE OUT COLUMN FOR OUTSIDE CALLS,

PERSON CALLED	DEPT. OR COMPANY	DAILY IN	CALLS OUT

NAME _____

DEPT. _____

DATE _____

TOTAL INSIDE CALLS

TOTAL OUTSIDE CALLS

Figure 2

a maintenance charge if they are billed by Bell Telephone systems if the fault belongs to Bell.

An extremely interesting article dealing with the management of communications costs was recently written by Jack Epstein from the accounting firm of Lybrand, Ross Bros. & Montgomery. In the article he observes some specific types of techniques and systems options which may be employed in order to effectively manage costs. One point made by Mr. Epstein is that *long distance charges* often represent fifty to sixty percent of the total communications costs. He noted that this type of stratification of costs frequently leads to an impulsive decision to reduce long distance calling. The interesting point he makes is that experience has shown repeatedly that the typical business letter generally costs about $3.00 plus filing costs and that it may be far less expensive to accept the fact that calls must and should be made; given the acceptance of that fact, the question becomes how to best accomplish these communications.

Wide Area Telephone Service

As Mr. Epstein observes, there are different types of options available. The first of the options is the Wide Area Telephone Service (WATS). WATS is a system which is offered by Bell Telephone and is often used to reduce long distance costs. It provides calling to selected geographic areas over special physically separate circuits. He notes that the rate for a minute of calling on measured-time WATS closely parallels the long distance cost to the same area. He observes then, that the best application for measured-time WATS is to make many short calls and realize meaningful savings by avoiding the three-minute minimum. An interesting point made by Mr. Epstein is that misuse of a measured-time WATS can result in a higher cost per call to a nearby part of the WATS area than if it were placed by directly dialed long distance. He concludes then, that only in special circumstances will measured-time WATS be the answer. In addition to the measured-time WATS, full-time WATS is billed at a flat monthly rate and is available 24 hours a day, 7 days a week. If the distance calling volume which is carried over the line is sufficiently dense and has the proper geographic distribution, he observes that significant economies may be obtained by using full-time WATS. Mr. Epstein's article is of such great interest that I would commend it to the attention of readers. It appeared in the *Management Adviser,* July–August 1971. It contains a great deal of information, some of it slightly complicated in nature, but always illuminating. It provides the detailed means by which the questioning executive can determine what type of communications system may be best used within the company.

HOW TO SAVE MONEY ON THE THINGS YOU BUY

Stop the dollar loss on small orders. The small order problem plagues many companies. The hundreds of thousands of miscellaneous items required for maintenance, repair, and operations generate an avalanche of paperwork from one end of your company to the other and use up valuable time of employees. Included in these well-hidden losses is the higher price you pay for not ordering in large quantities.

What Is a Small Order?

The National Association of Purchasing Agents points out that the four most common criteria are: dollar value of the order, quantity ordered, importance of the item, and complexity of the negotiations involved in the purchase. The simplest of these to determine is dollar value (in terms of the total rather than unit cost). The NAPA indicates that the dividing line for a majority of firms is generally for orders under $100. You may wish to establish a lower or higher basis, but remember that the monetary value of the item being purchased is your most reliable standard; mainly because the costs of processing each order can be reflected as a percentage of its total cost.

For example, consider the labor costs on each order you place—requisitioning, ordering, receiving, inspecting, handling, and accounting. Whether an order is for $25, $50, or $75, your costs of processing are virtually constant. For small orders, the costs generally increase only in relation to the number rather than the value of purchases.

Immediate Improvements

You can get substantial discounts from some suppliers by ordering fewer items in larger quantities. Moreover, curtailing the number of different supply items to be stored and handled can produce considerable savings. How many varieties of similar office equipment and supplies are taking up storage space? One firm reduced the types of file folders from twenty-three to six without forfeiting efficiency or convenience.

Under this method, sometimes called Family Buying, some firms establish a calendar schedule for placing orders with suppliers. On a certain day of the week or month, all items are reviewed to determine if adequate stocks exist for the next period. Consolidating orders in this way will substantially reduce paperwork and virtually guarantee adequate supplies of materials.

Using a Traveling Requisition

The TR is a formal record of the purchases and withdrawals of any inventory item in your company. The TR moves back and forth between the storeroom and the purchasing section. This form becomes your Inventory Record, a Re-Order Point Notice, and a Purchase Record all in one. The primary advantage of the form is to reduce the time needed by warehouse personnel to write requisitions and by the purchasing section to check on previous orders. The TR moves from the warehouse to purchasing when an order point is reached—purchasing makes an entry for the placement of an order and returns the TR to the warehouse—when the material arrives, a receipt is noted on the TR which is then filed. Withdrawals of the material are recorded on the TR and the cycle continues. If the number of materials in your storeroom is substantial, the savings with this method of recordkeeping would be large.

Capitalize on Discretionary Pricing Practices

Many suppliers mark up (or discount) their blanket orders on what they think the market will bear. A fifty percent spread between the maximum and the minimum price a supplier charges for the same item is not unheard of. Often these variations in price have little or no relation to the size of the customer or the size of his order. Moreover, if you deal with a supplier's salesman for your small orders, remember this: in many cases, the salesman is informed of the wholesale price of each item, and anything he can charge above this price is divided between him and the vendor. Hold out for the lowest possible price consistent with the amount of service you expect and the business you afford to the supplier.

Take Advantage of All Cash Discounts

If you are losing these savings on material which arrives after the due date on the invoice, include the following on your purchase orders: "All cash discounts allowed are taken with the date starting as of receipt of invoice or material, whichever is later." When money is tight and interest is high, it may pay you to bypass the discount. You would do this, of course, only when the cost of borrowing were less than the savings you realize on taking the discount.

Let Your Suppliers Help You Cut Costs

Your suppliers can be more than order fillers; they can be made important members of your cost-cutting team. Get them thinking about *your needs,* and often they'll be able to give you more for your dollar.

Astro-Star Co. cut its cost and boosted profits by cashing in on a number of supplier-suggested savings. The company did this by giving suppliers a checklist that it had originally made up and used itself. Astro-Star makes a photocopy of each parts invoice it receives, and sends it with the checklist to the supplier's sales manager. (He's sure to give it his full attention. He wants to keep the customer.) The checklist forces each supplier to ask himself:

—Can we improve the type of shipping container, or packaging?
    Yes—No—How?

—Can we improve the tools, jobs, fixtures to save production costs?
    Yes—No—How?

—Can we alter or redesign any part, or parts, to save on costs or to improve appearance ?
    Yes—No—How?

—Can we change the finish to improve appearance or reduce costs?
    Yes—No—How?

—Are we using the right material? Can we substitute a less expensive material?
    Yes—No—How?

—Does each feature that adds to cost also fill an essential function?
    Yes—No—How?

—Can we provide split shipments on a blanket order and still give bulk price on individual shipments?
    Yes—No—How?

Use a profit checklist of this kind to get cost-cutting help from your suppliers. And make sure it's used throughout your own company, in every operation.

One Supplier Rather Than Competing Bids?

You may be able to get big savings by dealing with just one or two suppliers. One small company reported that shopping around to find the lowest bidder was costing it more money than it was worth. It stopped being only a price-buyer, and began looking at other considerations, too. Among the advantages it lists for buying from one supplier:

—Inventories don't have to be segregated.

—A single supplier can be persuaded to carry more inventory for you.

—Deliveries are smoother, and lead time is reduced. There's less paperwork.

—Substantial quantity price discounts may be available.

CAPTIVE INSURANCE COMPANIES—SELF-INSURANCE

Captive insurance companies, as they are so called, are very misunderstood vehicles when looked at as a cost-savings device. One of the greatest reasons for this is that they have acquired a reputation for being "tax gimmicks" and having their domiciles primarily in tax avoidance havens. There are many reasons why one should consider a captive insurance company as a cost-savings vehicle. However, tax considerations should always be secondary. If one is going to establish a subsidiary company, tax advantages are not the most solid foundation upon which to build a subsidiary relationship. That relationship must be justified by other reasons. As financial investments, insurance companies are eminently worthy of attention. It was only recently that IT&T purchased the Hartford Insurance Company for investment purposes. Thus, it is easy to see an increasing acceptance of an insurance company as a subsidiary operation for whatever purpose the relationship is established. William Hare, writing in the *Financial Executive,* once estimated that there are probably 300 to 350 captive insurance companies in existence world-wide today. Mr. Hare distinguishes between deductibles and self-insurance. He relates that alert insurance buyers usually investigate self-insurance of normal losses while continuing to insure against a catastrophic type of loss by investigating deductibles. The distinction between the two is not always very clearly defined. Self-insurance of risks where there is little possibility of catastrophe is quite commonplace now, but rarely involves a large percentage of the total insurance cost for a company. On the other hand, deductibles receive credit proportionate to their size. Credits for deductibles of $100 thousand or more per loss can be quite attractive. Unfortunately, Mr. Hare states, reserves against the individual deductibles or their cumulative effect cannot be expensed. As a result, the answer in many instances seems to be the use of an internal insurance company which has now become known as the "captive insurance company." For the most part, the establishment of these types of companies involves internal loss adjustments. The captive insurance companies have been used extensively to insure the parent company's property involving fire, profit losses, marine cargo, money and securities, and other types of extended coverages. For the most part, liability or other types of exposure requiring widespread service and dealings with the public, are and should be avoided, as should coverage for workmen's compensation and employee benefits.

Within the framework of captive insurance companies, there are two basic types. The first provides coverage backed by reinsurance; the second provides coverage which is funded. In essence, the former insures liabilities for coverage which can be obtained in the insurance market. The latter covers insurance normally unavailable either because of the type of loss or the amount of liability. Marianne Burge who is the Manager of International Taxes for Price Waterhouse & Company wrote recently about the subject in the Price Waterhouse Review. She cited the following as the tax advantages of a foreign captive insurance company and further, the financial and commercial advantages of a captive insurance company.

Tax Advantages of a Foreign Captive Insurance Company

These are the principal tax advantages of paying premiums for the insurance of *non-U.S. risks* to a controlled foreign captive insurance company incorporated in a "tax haven," such as Bermuda.

1. The premiums are deductible for U.S. tax purposes, and in most foreign countries even when paid to an "offshore" affiliate.
2. Since the cash funds are paid to a company within the group, operating companies would cover more risks with the captive and the excess of premiums paid over the captive's reinsurance expense represents the additional tax deduction resulting from the use of a captive insurance company as opposed to informal self-insurance.
3. There is no U.S. withholding tax on premiums except for an excise tax on U.S. risk premiums. The same is true in many other countries, although some impose a tax on premiums, for example, Canada.
4. There is no U.S. Interest Equalization Tax on insurance premiums.
5. The captive can invest in foreign securities without payment of Interest Equalization Tax.
6. Premiums paid do not constitute a transfer of capital under the U.S. Foreign Direct Investment regulations.
7. The captive's income from investments in "unrelated" entities is not subject to U.S. corporate tax under the "Subpart F" rules. Dividends and interest on U.S. securities would be subject to thirty percent withholding tax but capital gains would be tax free.
8. Since a "related" person is one more than fifty percent controlled, the captive could make loans or equity investments in up to fifty percent owned joint ventures.
9. Investment income on investments in related entities could amount to up to thirty percent of gross income without being subject to U.S. tax under Subpart F.
10. If the captive insurance company operates for at least ten years, it could be liquidated in whole or in part at capital gains rates.

Financial and Commercial Advantages

The following nontax reasons are often given by insurance specialists for using a captive insurance company to centralize and formalize a group's insurance coverage:

1. The advantages of centralizing world-wide insurance policy for an international group include uniformity of procedures and faster service in loss adjustments.
2. Management regards the captive as a profit-center rather than as a pure expense.
3. Self-insurance can be increased in times of high premiums without loss of tax deduction. The captive uses the premiums to invest and hopes to earn at least as much as the outside insurer would. The cost of the outside insurer's overhead and profits are saved.
4. Reinsurance is said to be cheaper than insurance and claims with reinsurers can be settled more quickly than with direct insurers.
5. Risks otherwise virtually uninsurable can be covered by the captive, e.g., strikes, acts of war, foreign losses on confiscation, devaluation, loss of trade secrets, goodwill, loss on loans to foreign borrowers.
6. The cash flow advantages of paying premiums, say, monthly rather than one year or more in advance as is required by outside insurers, can be worthwhile.
7. In countries where there are currency restrictions, a loss of equipment from dollar areas might result in a long wait for replacement if a company is self-insured. Quick payment of insurance dollars would speed replacement.
8. In countries where profit repatriation is restricted, additional insurance premiums to a captive could be useful.
9. Foreign employee insurance benefits could be provided through a captive.

COST SAVINGS THROUGH FORMS CONTROL

Many top executives are plagued by the costly problems of filing old records. You may be among them holding onto thousands of pieces of paper which are useless and costing you a lot of money. These papers, forms, records, etc. take up valuable space. One recent estimate set these costs at $7 a cubic foot. These antique records choke your files. They make it almost impossible to find a paper that's needed in a hurry.

The following is a plan of action for cleaning out your files safely:

1. *Set up a record-retention schedule.* Know exactly how long you're going to keep each type of information that comes into your company. Some

records are essential because they can protect you in the event of a lawsuit, but after a certain period you're protected even against the danger of lawsuits. How long you keep various types of records isn't something you can decide on a whim. Federal and state laws spell out just how long you must retain a particular record, and state laws vary widely on this point. But failure to comply with both federal and state laws can lead to costly fines. Check your retention plan with your lawyer and accountant. They can tell you what special requirements, if any, must be met in your state.

2. *Go through your files.* Or have your secretary do it. Weed out the material you don't need anymore.

3. *Store inactive but important records.* Use lightweight storage cartons for records you have to keep but will rarely use. Mark them clearly—what they are and the period they cover. Then store them away in an unused corner of your warehouse or in a rented storage area.

4. *File current correspondence separately.* Keep it right at hand for a month before putting it in a general file. This way you'll have the facts handy to answer any request for information.

Suggested Schedule for No-Waste Records Retention

To set up practical guidelines, over 200 companies were surveyed on their record-keeping practices. The results, tabulated below, follow most state requirements. They'll make a good starting point in developing your own records retention schedule.

2 to 3 years
Acknowledgements
Bank statements
Bond paid-interest coupons
Correspondence, general
Delivery receipts
Payroll checks, cancelled
Tabulating machine cards
Time cards

3 to 4 years
Claims, closed, by company
Customer account records, closed
Deposit slips
Finished goods, inventory records
Insurance policies, expired (all types)
Proxies
Purchase orders
Requisitions
Tariffs

4 to 5 years
Bills of lading
Correspondence with applicants
Employees' application (after termination)
Employees' tax withholding statements

5 to 6 years
Correspondence, license
Correspondence, purchase
Correspondence, traffic
Complaint reports
Credit memos

4 to 5 years
Express receipts
Freight bills
Freight claims (after expiration)
Freight drafts
Labor contracts (after expiration)
Manifests
Remittance statements
Receiving reports
Sales slips
Salesmen's expense accounts
Service reports
Shipping tickets

6 to 7 years
Bond registers
Bonds, cancelled
Claims, closed, against company
Contracts and agreements (expired)
Correspondence, war bonds
Credit files
Employee records (terminated)
Expense reports
Federal income tax returns
Insurance, group disability
Inventory, recaps
Invoices, copy of order
Invoices, paid
Patent assignments
Payroll, bonus
Payroll, general
Payroll, part time
Payroll, temporary
Price and policy bulletins (superseded)
Real estate records (after disposal of
    land and buildings)
Stock dividend checks, cancelled
Stockholder lists

9 to 10 years
Vouchers, A–Z copy
Voucher register

5 to 6 years
Employees' daily time reports
Equipment inventory records
Insurance, fire inspection reports
Internal audit reports
Monthly trial balances
Payroll, overtime
Photographs of installations, etc.
Price exceptions and adjustments
Safety reports
War contracts and all papers pertain-
    ing thereto

7 to 8 years
Checks, payroll
Commission statements
Correspondence, production
Cost statements
Employees' earning records
Employees' salary & wage rate changes
Insurance, pensions (after expiration)
Purchase orders for capital expenditure
Sales sheets
Specification sheets

8 to 9 years
Accident reports (after settlement)
Agreements, leases (after expiration)
Checks, dividend
Checks, general
Checks, petty cash
Compensation cases (after closing)
Engineering problems (killed)
Vouchers, cash
Vouchers, numeric copy

Permanent
Agreements, deeds
Applications filed with regulatory agen-
    cies

10 years
Insurance claims (after settlement)
Vouchers, capital expenditure

17 years
Agreements, licenses

Permanent
Engineering and research project records
Ledgers and journals, cash
Ledgers and journals, customer
Ledgers and journals, general
Ledgers and journals, payroll
Ledgers and journals, plant
Ledgers and journals, royalty
Ledgers and journals, stock
Minutes, executive
Minutes, stockholder
Patents
Plant surveys
Property papers
Reports, annual
Reports, audit
Securities registration documents
Stock certificates
Stock transfers
Taxes, federal
Taxes, property
Taxes, sales and use
Taxes, state
Time-study reports
Unsolicited outside suggestions

MANUFACTURERS' REPRESENTATIVES—COST-SAVINGS POSSIBILITIES

In a recent article, Marvin Gandelman, Board Chairman of Sales Development Bureau, Inc., participated in a question and answer session regarding the subject of manufacturers' representatives. The interview directly addressed itself to the problems which are confronting companies each day. In essence, the problem revolves around the situation in which a bright young man is located for the sales force. He is interviewed, hired and thousands of dollars are spent training him before he writes a single dollar's worth of business. After a few months of calling on customers, he decides he doesn't like that kind of work and resigns. This cycle then begins all over again. It's an almost universal problem among businessmen who use their own company's sales forces. An estimated fifty percent or more of the salesmen hired this year will quit within eighteen months. While different companies are using different methods of combating this dollar drain, a significant number of them are turning to manufacturers' representatives. Many others are considering the switch. The question and answer session then addresses itself mainly to the points of the effectiveness of a manufacturer's representative: do they really do the job, and if so, how? The interview is reproduced below:

Some Questions and Answers

Q. Manufacturers' reps have been around a long time, what makes them such a hot item right now?

A. Speedy results, flexibility, and, most important, the bottom line of the P&L. A rep can turn merchandise into dollars fast. He knows his market, so he can go right to the decision maker—the fellow who can say yes or no —and get the order. Cash flow improves and inventory costs go down. A manufacturer must move his merchandise fast today if he wants to stay in the ballgame. And that's particularly true with a new product. A smaller business-man has to get into the market and get wide distribution before the competi-tion moves in. He can do it with reps. Bigger companies have different problems, long-range forecasting and budgets, for example. Reps can balance out sales departments and provide predictable sales costs. *Remember, reps are paid only on a commission basis.*

Q. What's the story on costs?

A. Let's start at the beginning. For example, it might cost anywhere between $15,000–$20,000 to recruit and train a salesman. And after the money is spent there's still no guarantee it will pay off for you. (As a matter of fact, with turnover running as high as it is, there's every chance that you won't even break even on the new salesman.) A lot of young fellows go into selling as a steppingstone to another job. And this is especially true today with the job market being what it is. On the average, only one salesman in ten stays with a company more than three years.

The rep, on the other hand, is a career salesman. He is selling because he's chosen that as his life's work—and he likes it. He's a pro and chances are he's been selling for some fifteen or twenty years. What's more, he's going to stay with your product as long as he's making money with it.

Q. Okay, that takes care of starting-up costs. But how about actual on-the-job costs?

A. Reps have a big advantage here, too. Let's say you're the top man in an established company and you have an experienced salesman earning $18,000 a year. There's a new territory you want to open up. If you send that salesman to the new area, he has to learn it and he has to prospect for customers. That takes time. Meanwhile, you have to pay him—some $1,500 a month—while he's putting in that time. And, of course, you have to foot the bill for travel, lodging, and entertainment costs, *plus* social security and other payroll taxes, *plus* employee benefits that could easily amount to twenty-five percent or more of his salary.

Put a rep in the same territory, supply him with the necessary literature, catalogues, and so on, and he's off and selling. Chances are he's already calling on people who are prospects for your product. All you shell out is his commission—period.

Does a rep pay off? You figure it. Remember the $15,000-plus we said it would cost you to recruit and train a new salesman—even before he wrote a single sale. If you were selling industrial chemicals, for example, through a rep, you'd pay about 4.1% commission. So that same $15,000 would bring you some $365,000 in sales.

Q. But isn't a rep, since he handles other products too, really a part-time salesman for my product?

A. That's absolutely true. For example, a rep might be handling five lines. So it's possible that he's spending only twenty percent of his time on any one of them. But—and this is an important but—the rep might well be putting in as much face-to-face selling time for your product as a full-time salesman would. Remember, he has a lot less prospecting to do. He's already selling these customers, so he gets in a lot more *real selling time* than the average salesman.

Q. What kind of a job can a rep do for me if I'm trying to introduce a new product?

A. Here again, because he has a loyal following, the rep has a big advantage over the company salesman. He knows the buyers well. And, of course, purchasing agents know him well and rely on him. So while he's selling a customer your unknown product, he's also selling a known quantity —himself—along with it. A company salesman just doesn't have this "extra" going for him.

Q. If I use reps, can I use my own salesmen as well?

A. Sure. A lot of companies use both. The usual idea is to use the company salesman near home and the reps elsewhere.

Q. What's the single most compelling reason for me to use a rep?

A. You can always afford a piece of something you don't have. In other words, what I'm saying is that with a rep you really can't lose money. You don't pay until, and unless, he produces for you. At the same time, you know he's going to be out selling because if a rep doesn't sell, he doesn't eat.

Q. How do I find the right rep?

A. You could advertise for him or ask around through friends and business acquaintances. But I would like to think that our company has the best answer to that question. For example, if you ask us to find a rep for you, we do the following: (1) We make a preliminary search of our extensive files and select a group of reps who meet your specifications and we offer them your line. (2) Reps who are interested sign contract forms. (3) We present these to you along with a profile of each rep, his background, qualifications, and other info that may be important to you. You make the final decision.

Q. What if the rep doesn't work out?

A. Our business is making sure that we supply you with reps that do work out. So if a rep doesn't satisfy you *for any reason whatsoever,* we'll replace him without any additional charge. And the same guarantee applies to the new rep. This free replacement feature is effective only where you have tried the rep for at last ninety days before asking for a change. And you must request the change within one year after signing the agreement.

SAVINGS IN THE PLANT

In a recent paper, John Heath made the point that many companies overlook optimizing their cash flow and tax planning because they do not segregate properly the various components of a facility. The key, of course, in plant construction is to segregate expense and capital components of construction, and furthermore to segregate what part of the construction is related to the process and what part of the construction is related to the building. All of these assignments and segregations are related to either Section 1250 (building) or Section 1245 (property).

Procedures which permit you to carefully segregate and analyze costs can substantially increase cash flow by optimizing the depreciation available. Depreciation, you must remember, is a tax subsidy. The Tax Reform Act of 1969 limits depreciation on buildings to not more than 150 percent of the declining balance method, but still permits a double-declining balance method for depreciation of equipment. The disparity then is a potential boon to careful planners who can segregate those facilities used in the process and those facilities which are related to a building. To properly obtain the benefits of careful planning, Mr. Heath suggests the following four questions be asked:

1. What are the component parts of the construction?
2. How do you segregate their costs from the total contractual cost?
3. How do you establish the useful life to the taxpayer of each component?
4. How can you separate Section 1245 property from the rest of the building?

In sequence, the next step, according to Mr. Heath, is to inventory the property to determine what components exist, the identification and actual costs of these components, where available and the analysis of each subcontract in order to allocate costs to the components. Following that, the useful life of each component is determined and in a large measure, should not be done by guesstimating useful lives. This procedure calls for a great deal of experience and expertise and the units which are being examined should be individually reviewed by a qualified appraisal engineer. And after all careful consideration has been made by interested parties, the following factors should be evaluated:

1. The quality and type of construction.
2. Anticipated operating conditions affecting the property.
3. Potential obsolescence, both functional and economic.
4. Management's capitalization policy.

Because the Section 1245 property is not very explicit as written in the law, many financial people tend to rely on lawyer-specialists or in-house engineers to identify that property applicable to the section. Some of the problems encountered in attempting to identify material to Section 1245 are examined by Mr. Heath and one example in particular is pertinent. A detailed analysis of the cost information, the plans, and specifications for construction are not sufficient to establish a carefully planned case, capable of being defended if challenged by the Internal Revenue Service. Mr. Heath cites the example of floors which are not generally considered Section 1245 property. However, a wood block floor in a machine shop or a quarry tile floor in a food processing plant may be eligible property for Section 1245 depreciation. In other words, the manufacturing process may be so unique by itself that it could not be conducted without special kinds of floors and therefore, the nature of the floor construction attaches itself more to the process than to the physical construction of the building itself. Such analogies may be extended to electrical property and to plumbing property. However, the complete analysis of the entire building contract can result in substantial differences in allowable depreciation.

How to Control Maintenance Costs

Observe these four main essentials of a controlled maintenance program:

1. Centralized maintenance control.
2. An efficient inspection staff.
3. Reliable maintenance and repair cost records.
4. First-rate property records.

What Management Needs to Know

Assuming that you have the four essentials just mentioned, a procedure should be set up to show:

—What the maintenance needs are.
—How many of these needs are absolutely essential.
—How many are deferrable.
—How costs, after authorization, can be controlled.

The following steps constitute the procedure for answering the above questions.

Preparation of a basic maintenance estimate, covering only the productive assets that are necessary to the operation of the plant. The maintenance and repair cost records will show the cost history of each machine. From this record, the costs for the fiscal period under consideration must be projected. The maintenance staff can inform the maintenance supervisor which of the machines are subject to extraordinary repair. Allowances must be made for fluctuation in material costs, and any unusual cost or saving must be calculated. If cost records do not give adequate experience data, an engineering department or manufacturer's estimate must be included.

To these direct costs must be added the cost of maintaining adequate inspection of these assets to insure that the equipment is maintained at an efficient point and will not be subject to unforeseen and costly breakdowns.

When all of the items have been assembled, they should be individually tested for economy between self and contract servicing. Obtain estimates of the cost of contracting for the work if repair services are inadequate, if trained personnel are not available, or if repair work will be concentrated within a short period.

Also, methods of maintaining and servicing equipment should be examined. More frequent inspection, improved efficiency of spare parts, or better familiarity with operation may have improved the performance of a machine and deferred the major overhaul period. An increased or decreased rate of production can also greatly affect the cost of maintenance and the production estimate must be consulted to cover this contingency.

When all of these factors have been taken into consideration, the maintenance supervisor has the basic cost of maintaining the plant's operating assets. This is the irreducible minimum below which the plant cannot attain the scheduled production.

Examination of all of the remaining plant assets, such as buildings, auxiliary equipment, and nonoperated assets. A careful inspection should be made of each item shown in the property records to determine the amount of maintenance necessary. The cost of this maintenance should then be carefully estimated and classified as urgent, deferrable within the fiscal period, and deferrable beyond the fiscal period.

Presentation of maintenance cost program to management. When the entire maintenance cost program of the plant has been assembled, it is presented to top management for its consideration. After management has selected the nonproductive assets that are to be scheduled for maintenance and has indicated the extent of its authorization for maintenance costs, the program is ready for budgeting and scheduling.

Budgeting and scheduling. In budgeting and scheduling the authorized portions of the program, attention must be given to the following important points:

—The authorized tasks should be converted into time units in order to schedule an even flow of work.

—Production department heads should be consulted before scheduling major repair work.

—All routine work should be done by the same individual or crew, wherever possible.

—Schedule sheets should be made up for each machine or group of machines to aid in controlling the amount of work planned and completed.

—The items of deferrable maintenance should be evenly spread over the entire schedule so that, when the inevitable variations occur, the slack or overload can be adjusted.

—If a peak repair period is to be scheduled during an anticipated shutdown, services of competent personnel should be secured well in advance to insure no delay in starting operations again.

—Material requisitions should be scheduled to cause no delay in any portion of the program.

—Correct accounting and cost distribution must be assured to evaluate properly the progress of the program and to furnish dependable figures for future programs.

When the scheduling is completed, it may be translated into work orders, limiting to the scheduled amount the labor and material costs budgeted. In this way, the maintenance supervisor is able to follow the development of the program and to watch closely the variation from the planned schedule. At stated periods he must then report to top management how the work that was authorized is being completed, both in respect to maintenance tasks completed and budgeted funds disbursed.

Value Engineering

Value engineering has become a systematic, widely effective technique for cutting product costs. Many companies claim startling results. For example, the Carrier Corporation of Syracuse, New York, applied value engineering in altering the design of a float valve and slashed its cost from $35 to $6.

Value engineering, sometimes called value analysis or value control, finds new ways to produce a product of equal or superior performance at lower cost. The underlying principle of value engineering is that it is easier to boost profits by reducing costs than by increasing sales. These principles work as well for the small businessman as for the large corporation. Value engineering needs no elaborate organization, involves little expenditure, and requires minimum training. It does demand, however, the application of common sense, observation, investigation, and imagination.

Where to begin? Value engineering might begin with products that have been in full-scale production for some time and may be improved with new technology. A list of these items, ranking them from high to low according to annual purchase or production costs is a good starting point. From this list items for which costs are out of line with prices of approximately similar items should be selected.

The Seven Basic Steps

The value engineering method involves seven basic steps. These steps, however, are not always distinct and separate; they often merge or overlap. Completing them answers these questions about a product: What is it? What does it do? What does it cost? What is it worth? What other product or products might do the job? Which is the least expensive? What is needed to implement?

The seven steps are:

1. *Product selection.* Select the product to which value engineering efforts are to be applied.
2. *Determine function.* Analyze and define the functions that the product must perform.

3. *Gather facts.* Learn the specifications, development, and inventory of the product. What are the costs of its operation?
4. *Make comparisons.* Find out whether other products can do the same job, and if so, how much each one costs to make or buy.
5. *Refine the idea.* What new concept emerges after all functions, methods, and alternatives have been studied?
6. *Overcome obstacles.* Prove that the alternatives will not jeopardize the fulfillment of performance (functional) requirements and effect a change-over.
7. *Review results.* Compare actual with expected results to determine merits of changeover. Was the original information accurate and applicable? Were savings effected where expected? What was learned from the execution of the plan that can be used again?

Savings often result when a switch is made (1) from a heavy metal to a light one, or vice versa, when weight is not a factor, (2) from machining to casting of a metal item, (3) from casting to stamping, (4) from various metals to lighter-weight or more resistant plastics.

What Value Engineering Means to Defense Contractors

Value engineering is a must for defense contractors. It is needed both to increase their profits and to improve their chances for contracts. The Secretary of Defense places contractors' value engineering proposals under direct surveillance. To help contractors with value engineering efforts, the government formed a top-level Value Engineering Evaluation Group. This Group is expected to bring about annual savings of $500,000,000 in defense procurement. The Defense Department estimates that $1 of value engineering should produce $10 of savings.

It is up to the financial manager to get a good value engineering program underway or to find ways to improve an existing program. To find out about value engineering, write for these two booklets: "Value Engineering—a Challenge to Management," single copies are obtainable free from the American Ordance Association, Transportation Building, Washington, D.C., 20006; "Organizing and Operating Value Engineering Programs," Defense Department publication H-111, 40¢ per copy, from the GPO, Washington, D.C. 20402.

The Control of Plant and Equipment Costs

If some, or all, of the equipment in your office is covered by a maintenance contract, you may be able to cut the cost of maintenance by cancelling some (or possibly all) of these contracts and placing the care of the machines on an on-call basis. Companies report that this switch can result in savings of from twenty-five percent to ninety-five percent in the cost of maintenance.

Most office equipment makers feel that they have a strong stake in keeping the machines they sell operating at top efficiency. Yet, the service facilities they operate must be self-supporting. Thus, salesmen are under heavy pressure to sell the contract and get the customer to prepay for it. Some companies offer special commissions to employees who sell maintenance contracts. In other instances, salesmen are permitted to reduce the cost of the contract if the customer signs for at least three years.

It's true that contract maintenance provides you with service and parts of consistent quality. (Generally, overall quality is higher when you deal with a factory branch service operation, rather than with a dealer or an independent maintenance firm.) Yet, the contract ties up important operating cash—costing you the return you'd get if your outlay were invested. And you often end up paying for something you don't need or use.

But when you put maintenance on a *per-call* basis, you pay only for the care and repair your machines actually need—you don't tie up cash. On the other hand, the quality of labor and parts may vary widely.

Per-Call Maintenance

For over twenty years one company has kept comprehensive maintenance records of all its office machines. The purchasing agent records the nature of each repair, the date it was made, and its cost on a form that also lists purchase date and price of the machine. (A form to do this for your own office equipment is illustrated in Figure 3.)

Initially, maintenance costs on a number of typewriters were compared by placing some on a per-call basis and keeping the rest on contract. Though age of the machines and their use were about the same, the per-call machines cost sixty percent *less* to maintain over a five-year period. The company decided to drop all office equipment maintenance contracts. Since then, large yearly savings have occurred every year. Every piece of equipment has outlasted manufacturers' estimates of life expectancy. (Machines on per-call maintenance have regularly outlasted those under contract.)

Periodically the company runs similar tests on other pieces of equipment. Results consistently favor per-call maintenance. Over the years the company has also found that:

> —*Some machines simply don't need maintenance.* For example, one particular machine has been in use during the entire period of over 20 years. It was 12 years old when the first small amount was spent for repairs. There hasn't been any need since then to spend an additional cent on this machine.

—*Periodic cleaning and adjustment can do more harm than good.* Records showed that minor repair calls often followed shortly after regular cleaning and adjustment by the repairman. Disturbance of operating adjustments by the repairman contributed to later breakdowns and downtime.

DESCRIPTION	SERIAL #
LOCATION	
DATE OF PURCHASE	PRICE

REPAIRS		
DATE	ITEM	COST

Figure 3

—*Regular maintenance doesn't increase turn-in allowances.* Turn-in prices are based on the condition—not the age—of the machine. All maintenance costs represent a supplemental equity in the machine that cannot be recovered when the equipment is disposed of. Per-call maintenance keeps this equity at the lowest figure possible.

Added benefits of a per-call system. Under its maintenance control program the company has also:

1. *Used the repair records to spot "lemons" early.* Machines with heavy repairs can be disposed of early while the turn-in price is still high.
2. *Eliminated duplicate costs.* When the records show that a repair was made or a part replaced recently, the company refuses to pay for the repair job and the maintenance firm stands the extra expense.
3. *Switched older machines from high-use areas to low-use areas to extend equipment life.* For example, typewriters used for several years in high-volume order preparation may be shifted for a couple of years of extra use to preparing bills of lading on the shipping dock.
4. *Batched repair calls.* Every effort is made to have the maintenance man handle several machines on a single call. Savings in labor time have cut repair costs per machine by over one-third.

Leased Building Maintenance

If you go about it properly, the chances are you can make substantial savings in building maintenance if you use a contract cleaning concern. Companies report savings up to twenty percent, and no responsibility. In a word, you are letting someone else pay your janitor's salary, carry the insurance, buy materials and supplies, and take over your headaches.

What a Contract Cleaner Will Do

Cleaning contractors offer to do your maintenance job *better* for the same amount of money or for less than it's now costing you. They offer both experienced full- or part-time cleaners and constant, trained supervision. There are many savings:

—You are freed from the time you would otherwise devote to bookkeeping, scheduling, taxes, etc. and after-hours time which you'd spend on the premises in order to talk to your own maintenance people on the progress of the job, technical problems which develop, etc.
—You get savings on supplies because the cleaning contractor buys materials in bulk and passes the savings on to you.
—You save on operating capital because it's not tied up in equipment you'd need if your own personnel did the work.

—You eliminate the cost of the retirement, insurance, and other benefit programs your own labor force might require.

—You make out one check once a month to cover all the costs.

EXPENSE ITEM	FULL TIME		PART TIME	
	COST MONTHLY	COST YEARLY	COST MONTHLY	COST YEARLY
JANITORS' SALARIES	$	$	$	$
JANITRESSES' SALARIES				
MATRONS' SALARIES				
ELEVATOR OPERATORS' SALARIES				
WATCHMEN'S SALARIES				
JANITORS' VACATIONS				
WINDOW CLEANING				
COMPENSATION INSURANCE				
LIABILITY INSURANCE				
STATE UNEMPLOYMENT INS. TAX				
FEDERAL O.A.B. TAX				
JANITORIAL SUPPLIES				
TOILET PAPER				
PAPER TOWELS				
TOILET SEAT COVERS				
LIQUID SOAP				
DEODORIZING CAKES & PERFUMES				
VACUUM CLEANERS & EQUIPMENT				
AMORTIZATION OF EQUIPMENT				
MAINTENANCE OF EQUIPMENT				
DRIP MACHINES				
TOTAL	$	$	$	$
EXTRA MEN TO RELIEVE SICK OR ABSENT MEN	$		$	
EXTRA HELP TO HIGH DUST AND CLEAN CHANDELIERS				
VALUE OF SUPERVISOR'S TIME				
COST OF BOOKKEEPER'S TIME FOR TAX AND PAYROLL PURPOSES.				
TOTAL	$		$	

Figure 4

In addition to general cleaning nightly, here are some other services contract maintenance firms offer:

- window cleaning
- elevator cleaning
- day porters
- fluorescent light maintenance
- carpet and upholstery shampooing
- leather dressing
- venetian-blind reconditioning

- security
- floor waxing
- furniture polishing
- exterior cleaning
- gardening
- wall washing
- exterminating
- dry-cleaning drapes

What Will It Cost?

There are many "hidden costs" in your building maintenance bill. For instance, if you're now paying your part-time janitor $70.00 a month, you're probably spending an additional $17.50 per month fringe benefits and overhead costs to keep him working. Your total outlay may be higher than you think. You can use the chart shown in Figure 4 to figure your actual costs. Then call in a contract cleaner from your community to estimate what he would charge to do the job. Contracts run from $5.00 a month for floor waxing jobs to million dollar-plus contracts. Most agreements are on a yearly basis with thirty, sixty, or ninety-day cancellation clauses.

To set a fixed price on the cost of maintaining your building, contract cleaners consider several factors:

1. Concentration of desks, cabinets, files, etc. will increase the price of dusting and sweeping.
2. Floor coverings differ as to type of equipment and cleaning methods used, e.g., ordinary vinyl tile will not hold up well under heavy equipment; wood floors need special care; carpeting requires vacuuming and shampooing.
3. The charge for window washing depends on types of windows—double hung, frosted, laminated, etc.
4. Prices for services also vary according to the location of your building. In many cases buildings in rural areas are less expensive to maintain than those in major cities.

How to Get Your Money's Worth

As a final check you'll want to inspect carefully the quality of work the contract maintenance firm has been doing for another company in your community. Ask the firm you're dealing with to give you the name and address of one or two of their customers. Also, check the quality of housekeeping work your own people are doing for you now. Here are nine basic things to look for:

Sweeping and Dusting:
1. Floors must be cleaned so that there are no remaining dirt streaks. See that no dirt or dust remains under radiators, in corners, behind doors, hanging from ceilings or corners of rooms, etc.
2. Gum, tar, or any other sticky substance must be removed where possible.
3. Dust on or around grilles, woodwork or radiators must be removed.

Polishing and Wall Spotting:
4. Doorknobs, railings, doors, lightswitch plates, etc. must be cleaned and polished.
5. Spots or smudges on painted surfaces that have been caused by the touch of a treated dustcloth must be removed.
6. Walls must be free of water streaks and marks—especially around water fountains and in lavatories. Woodwork must be free from streaks caused by splashing of cleaning solutions and rinse water.
7. All surfaces must be dry and crevices and corners clean after wet mopping.

Equipment and Materials:
8. All equipment must be clean, in proper repair, and placed in an orderly manner in an assigned storage location.
9. Soaps, furniture and metal polishes, and other cleaning materials be returned to their assigned storage locations.

Check Your Maintenance Contract

Before signing a maintenance contract, do these things:

- Request the names of maintenance company customers and talk directly in each case to the man who deals with the maintenance company.

- Check the maintenance company's credit rating.

- Check the security measures the maintenance company uses when they hire a janitor. What screening methods do they use?

- Require proof of bonding and secure a certificate of public liability and property damage from the maintenance company.

- Be sure the company has a record of good union relations, if unions are a factor in your city.

- Spell out the duties and specifications you want in a contract.

- Visit the maintenance company office and see how effectively they control and supervise their employees and each job.

- Make sure you can reach the maintenance company's night telephone number, in case of emergency.

CUTTING THE COST OF EQUIPMENT

Following are some simple purchasing procedures used by leading companies that can cut your buying bills by thousands per year. Some of these procedures are overall approaches that can lead to savings on many purchases. Others cover specific, widely used items of supplies and equipment. The examples chosen illustrate a basic principle: concentrate your cost-cutting efforts on large-quantity, high value, purchases.

Savings on Big-Dollar Buying

Here are some ideas on your large-amount purchases:

1. *Buy new year-old models.* This is particularly effective with standard equipment items, such as: typewriters ($50 less per typewriter), vehicles, and even certain types of industrial machinery. Obviously, where drastic improvements in efficiency show up in new models, you may want to take advantage of the improvement, even at added cost.

2. *Don't stop at one saving.* Many companies may make a big saving, but fail to follow through for other savings. Persistence pays off. For example, a New England maker of laboratory equipment cut costs of a glass funnel from $111,000 to $80,000 by switching vendors. Because the item was bought in such large quantities, the company continued to press for further ways to cut its price. An engineer came up with a proposal to change from glass to plastics and costs were cut again from $80,000 to $30,000, a little more than a quarter of the starting total.

3. *Consider only qualities needed.* In considering competitive bids, there is no need to pay for features not essential to your operations. For example, a large mail order house was testing two types of calculators, an item used in quantity around the clock. One cost $200 more than another, and had many desirable features lacking in the other. The only difference *essential* to the company's operation was speed, and the company wasn't willing to pay that much for this one difference. After consultation with the company's buyers, the maker of the lower-priced machine proposed to speed up his motor at a relatively small cost. Tests proved the new machine operated satisfactorily.

Specific Hints on Individual Items

Here are some money-saving ideas on individual purchases:

1. *Get your tires retreaded.* The retreading industry has grown, and small manufacturers and dealers are providing quality work. The cost: one-

fourth to one-half the cost of a new tire. One company got 100,000 miles out of a tire retreaded seven times.

2. *Get one style desk.* You can buy one style of desk and adapt it to various needs. Some companies buy two or more types.

3. *Crash-print multi-part forms.* The usual way to produce a multi-copy form is to print the form, then interleave with carbons. You can, however, assemble blank sheets with carbon, and then print the form. One impression will print the full set of sheets, and save fifty percent on the printing bill. Naturally, the last copy will not be as clear as the first one, but you will usually find it legible enough for internal use.

Three Easy Steps that Reduce Production Costs

Cut costs the way the giants do—use value analysis. Don't let its rather forbidding name scare you. This is today's easiest, fastest-spreading and most effective technique for cutting costs. Ask these three key questions about everything you make, buy, or sell: (1) What does it do? (2) What does it cost? (3) What would do the job cheaper?

How does value analysis differ from ordinary cost-cutting? This approach goes much deeper. It doesn't just look for ways of doing the same thing cheaper. It looks for *different* procedures to follow *different* things to use.

A Pennsylvania firm was making cutting rods used to burn the rough edges from steel castings. Looking for a way to get a jump on competition, this company focused on wastage. After two-thirds of a rod had been consumed in the trimming process, the rest had to be thrown away. At this point the company applied the three critical questions: What does the product do? What does it cost? What could do the job cheaper? As a result of value analysis, someone came up with the idea of making the rod in two pieces, one serving as a reusable handle. And also as the result of value analysis, someone else worked out the idea of an unthreaded tapered joint. This allowed the cutting portion to be plugged into the handle. As a result, the company had a superior product and drastically reduced wastage. Over the long run, customers saved fifteen to twenty-five percent on cutting rod costs.

Your suppliers can be of tremendous help in cutting costs. Make a practice of telling them the *purpose* of what you're buying. Let them suggest alternative parts or materials. Prompt them to come up with cheaper ways of carrying out the function of a given part or material already in use. One company had been in the habit of buying special bolts costing $1 each. At the suggestion of a steel jobber who was selling other things to the company, a drawing of the bolt was submitted to him. The jobber came up with a quotation of 52¢ each. Total annual savings amounted to $1,400.

Look Before You Leap and Buy Equipment

Question whether you are paying through the nose for tailor-made equipment when you could be using standard, off-the-rack units. The U.S. Defense Service Agency was buying custom-made 250-foot hose lengths to transport petroleum products. Cost: $2,781 each. Someone discovered that five standard 50-foot hose lengths worked just as well and saved $1,225. Things to do: use standard sizes, shapes, and quantities wherever possible. Don't OK any custom-made units unless there's absolute proof that standard equipment can't do the job.

Is this machine really necessary? Question routine machine replacement and repairs. You may frequently find you can do without machines you've been sinking money into and nail down top-dollar savings. For example, Pesco Products Division of Borg-Warner put a fast $8,000 on the profit side of its ledger by *not* doing a planned overhaul job on an automatic screw machine. Instead of routinely putting an O.L. on the repair order, Pesco officials shopped around the plant and found that other machines had time to take on the whole work load the automatic had been handling. Pesco gained the $8,000 it would have spent on overhaul, plus the income from sale of the machine. Also on the profit side: the added floor space the removal of the machine provided.

An added cost-cutter is to check and determine whether you are producing parts on machines whose upkeep and replacement "nickels and dimes you to death." Don't keep making these parts yourself just because it was once the right thing to do. See if you can eliminate this drain by purchasing the needed parts. Since you last checked, they may have become a lot cheaper to buy.

CASH IN ON ZERO DEFECTS

Now is the time for your company to cash in on "Zero Defects." It can work for every business—small, medium, or large. Zero Defects is just what the name says: a system to get every employee to do the job right the *first time*. Sounds simple and it is simple. The hard part is to get every single employee to believe he can hit 100 percent—time after time after time. But, as many companies are proving right now, it can be done. A Zero Defects program is based on the idea that in some things a person is willing to accept imperfection; in other things, which he considers more important, he demands perfection. Get your workers to put their jobs on the "most-important" list.

Remember though, you must convince yourself that your people can do the job right the first time—every time. You must shoot for 100%—not 98%, 97%, or 95%.

How to Set It Up

1. Meet with all your supervisors. Get them in on this program early in the game. They must be enthusiastic about it. Passive acceptance of Zero Defects by supervisors won't sell the program to employees.

2. Stress that the program includes everybody in the company. This is not a quality control system aimed only at your technical staff. It includes everybody from the president on down. A mistake in typing an invoice or specification can do as much damage to your business as a badly soldered circuit.

3. Hold a meeting to explain Zero Defects to all your employees. Do it with as much ballyhoo as possible.

4. Get your enthusiasm for the program across to your workers in every possible way—you can be serious or humorous. Use your imagination, but make sure that every message you use transmits the excitement of Zero Defects to your workers. The Albion Malleable Iron Company of Albion, Michigan, gives employees who work twenty consecutive error-free days a free dinner for two—at a good restaurant. Workers who rack up one week of 100% work get Zero Defects lighters.

5. Try using ideas like these:

Wallet-size pledge cards	ZD lapel pins
Brochure supporting ZD	ZD banners
Stickers for car windows	ZD memo pads
Cardboard pennants	ZD suggestion boxes
Kick-off posters	ZD bulletin boards

6. Use every possible way to publicize ZD accomplishments and individual achievements.

7. Indoctrinate all new employees on ZD goals.

8. Provide a method of displaying the record of every group in your operation, so that each employee can see just where he stands.

The Cost-Cutting By-Products You Get from ZD

Once they're in the swing of a Zero Defects program, employees look for ways to do their jobs better. Examples:

- Secretaries at one company designed an operating manual for themselves.
- An assembler pointed out that metal staples used in sealing could and did

get into bearings accidentally. Another sealing method was worked out.

- Lighting was improved in an inspection area at the request of one quality control man. Efficiency immediately shot up.
- A special Zero Defects effort in a finance section produced the most accurate inventory count in the department's history.
- A clerk recommended changes in a benefit program paperwork system, eliminating a number of common administrative errors.

Techniques to Keep Enthusiasm High

1. A Zero Defects card is displayed in front of each operator, typist or what have you. For each day of defect-free work, the card is stamped "Zero Defects." Each defect is also entered on the card. These cards are updated in the first half-hour of each shift. When this was first tried in one company, workers resented the card. However, they quickly learned that when a discrepancy was found they could find out what was wrong, discuss it with their supervisor and change methods.

2. Zero Defects workers at another plant receive a special ZD stamp along with a Certificate of Merit. They use the stamp to identify their work when they have completed a job. The Certificate of Merit may be hung over a work station.

3. Zero Defects pledge cards signed by employees dedicating themselves to trying for Zero Defects in everything they do.

4. Keep emphasizing competition between groups, units, or whatever.

5. Get all suppliers to use ZD.

ZD Can Be a Powerful Tool—But Know How to Use It!

ZD can be a vital element in your profit picture. But you must know how to use it. Pushing ZD too hard and in the wrong direction may antagonize workers into resisting the whole idea. Follow these rules in planning. You'll avoid making serious mistakes that could backfire and wreck your Zero Defects program.

Don't cultivate enthusiasm in the wrong direction. Your employees could get the idea that simply by hiding errors, they can get an award. You should constantly play up the sense of achievement and pride they feel from a craftsmanlike job.

Don't overstress the application of Zero Defects to management decisions, especially on the junior executive level. An executive who is under pressure to "get it right the first time" will soon start playing it safe—he'll avoid decisions which involve a risk.

Don't make your workers overcautious. This can lead to slowdowns from a sincere desire to do things right the first time. This kind of caution can sometimes lead to even more errors from "trying too hard."

Seven Ways to Stop Inefficiency

Built-in profit corrosion may be eating away your profits. You may be losing these profits to employees—including key men—who look out for themselves at *your expense*. Spot and stop the workers who are running up your costs and running down your profits. Employees who use their jobs to promote their own interests ahead of the company's can be found at all levels, taking advantage of every loophole. You might begin by checking your supervisors for:

1. *The Overtime Dispenser.* Even if this supervisor doesn't get overtime pay himself, his workers are always there to remind him that *they* make more money with overtime. And he's the friendly sort. So he finds some way to make sure they get it. You're the only one who loses.

Even worse are cases where he, himself, is eligible for time-and-a-half. He sees to it that there's more and more late work and Saturday work. In either case, you can probably find the culprit by identifying the area that's running up constant overtime. To eliminate this situation, take him *off* the overtime basis. Let him know that from now on, if there's any overtime work, he'll be the one to do it—and on his own time. Watch the overtime drop in a hurry.

2. *The Indispensable Man.* This fellow has been around awhile and is making sure he stays around. He knows the ropes. But he sees to it that no one else does. Information and decisions must be funneled through him since he's the man with the know-how. (He should be; he's kept it all to himself.) The thing to do: (1) Have a heart-to-heart talk with "Mr. Indispensable." Explain that his failure to train a back-up man is holding *him* back. (2) Switch him with someone on another job as part of his "development."

3. *The "Second" Market.* You may be keeping a number of your workers in business—*for themselves*. Many companies give "seconds" or "rejects" to employees. Others sell them to the workers at a fraction of cost. The employees often conduct a brisk business on the side; selling these "seconds" at bargain prices. As a result, the reject rate keeps going up. *Your* profits may suffer, but the employees are doing a booming business. This happens most often where there's a ready market for the "reject," i.e., dented cans of food, improperly packaged toiletries, substandard builders supplies, and so on. If there aren't enough "seconds" to meet the demand, your worker-businessmen will make "seconds" out of "firsts." What to do—check up on distribution of these items to employees, both through records and plant exit inspection.

If there's even a hint that this "fringe benefit" is being abused, cut it out entirely—and immediately.

4. *The Scrap Disposal Specialist.* Here's an operator who can point to an excellent quality record. Inspectors never turn down any of his work. Why? Because he inspects it first. And he does his own rejecting first, too—before any inspector sees it. If a piece is off-dimension, he turns it into innocent shavings on his lathe. If he's working on small parts, he sends any imperfect work down a drain. He's even adept at concealing whole ruined assemblies. To eliminate this profit-killer, set up a close comparison count for your various operations. Check unfinished material going to each worker vs. finished material coming from him. Don't allow scrap barrels to be carted out and dumped routinely. Have them checked.

5. *The "Sure It's OK" Bully.* This profit-killer is characterized by a loud voice and terrible temper. He browbeats work inspectors into okaying substandard output. This operator or supervisor can boast of a production record which shows few blemishes. You must lay down this law and make it stick: (1) pressure on inspectors from either production operators or supervisors is OUT. (2) Inspectors—and only inspectors—are responsible if substandard material gets into customers' hands.

6. *The Safety Device Defuser.* This man is out to set production records and has his own way of doing it. He views safety devices as being there to "slow him down." He's an expert at deactivating the most sturdily constructed safety devices and machinery guards. As a result, you wind up paying top insurance rates because of high accident rates. What's more, these accidents often happen to the next man who uses the machine. Things to do: Penalize any employee who interferes with the function of a safety device. In fact, go a step further: have all your operations checked by an expert to see that they incorporate adequate accident guards. Your insurance company can often be a big help here.

7. *The "Think Bigger" Administrator.* This manager believes "the bigger the payroll, the bigger the boss." His area will be a beehive of activity—buzzing with unnecessary paychecks. When activity slows down to the point where it might be noticed, he promptly:

   (a) creates some more;
   (b) spreads what there is around to make it look like more; or
   (c) issues a fresh flood of memos, reports and analyses.

What he will not do is voluntarily reduce the size of his work force. The way to find him is to look for the man who's always asking for more employees. Don't let any one key man ruin your profit picture.

Nine Ways to Increase Profits

Your company can't afford to accept this profit-killing phrase: ". . . but that's the way it's always been done." In itself, this just isn't a good enough reason to keep doing things the same old way, especially when one simple change might put you on the road to *big* savings. Take a look at the small changes nine cost-minded companies have made to rack up big savings. Each company set out to cut costs by thoroughly questioning every aspect of its operations.

1. One manufacturing company always required three inspection steps to check the strength of a welded joint in its product. A brief study revealed that the welded joint had never, in the entire history of the product, failed to hold. One of the three inspection steps was abandoned and as a result, a quick saving of over $20,000 in wages and inspection equipment was achieved—with no sacrifice of quality.

2. A small hardware company manufactured a complicated assembly for use in commerical aircraft. The cost of making the item was $83.25. Then a hard-eyed look at the assembly showed that it was doing the job "much too well." Two pinion gears and four ball bearings were eliminated, along with associated machining operations. A savings resulted whereby the item now costs $57.40 to manufacture—a cost reduction of thirty-one percent.

3. Another company had its machinists driving for perfection where it wasn't called for. A simple change in tolerance requirements resulted in the elimination of a complete manufacturing step.

4. Thompson Ramo Woolridge, Inc., of Cleveland, Ohio, was using expensive special-purpose containers for in-plant parts handling. The company found that common wash tubs, purchased from a local discount house, did the job just as well. When necessary, the tubs could easily be lined with plastic foam inserts for protection of machined parts and resulted in savings of $4,550 in materials handling costs.

5. An aircraft parts supplier "always" used high grade steel for major structural components. A switch to lower-grade steel (just as suitable for the job) turned up savings in both cost and weight.

6. Another company used stainless steel mounting blocks, costing $1.80 each, in its product. It switched to aluminum, and gained easier machining and fewer production delays. The aluminum blocks cost 40¢ each—an eighty percent saving per block.

7. A consistent checking for material improvement paid off big for another company. A tube insulator was originally produced using a cylinder of glass soldered onto sheet metal. The cost: $13.50 per insulator. After checking with glass manufacturers, the company found that a one-piece

molded glass design would do as well and cost one-half as much ($6.50 per insulator). But there were still more savings to come. A later investigation revealed that a nylon part could be made to replace the glass. The cost this time was $1.25 each. This was a total saving of $12.25 per insulator—an item that the company used in big quantities.

8. Working on a government contract, General Precision, Inc. was using special high-pressure hoses, built to military specifications. The cost—$15,735 in a year. Commercial grade high-pressure hydraulic hoses filled the bill. The cost: $4,110 in a year—an annual savings of $11,625.

9. A classic cost-cutting example. One company checked into its choice of materials and found a not-so-simple washer washing away profits. It was a special-material, highly polished, a beauty of a washer—costing $2.54 each. Washers now are standard material with a plated finished. They cost 24¢ each—a cost reduction of 90.5 percent.

SMOOTH OUT SEASONAL RUSHES WITH A DRIVER DEPOSITORY

By installing a depository safe, and passing off part of the counting and verification of cash to the bank, a bottling company smoothed out the daily reporting of cash by some sixty drivers. According to Chris A. Fuerisch, Branch Treasurer of the Pepsi-Cola Metropolitan Bottling Co., Teterboro, N.J., this was the situation: cash, checks, and miscellaneous papers were turned in daily by the drivers; in summer the seasonal nature of the business increased the load; the work required a full-time cashier and comptometer operator; cash was exposed for long periods of time.

As a first step, the company discussed the problem with the bank, which agreed to take over the function of counting and verifying the driver deposits. Next, they received satisfactory specifications from a major safe-builder for a depository. Lastly, they designed new forms (such as a three-part snapout deposit form acceptable to the bank). The safe depository was built into the wall, accessible in a check-in area for the drivers, and in the main office. It consists of a deposit hopper and safe.

The new system works like this:

1. The driver inserts his key and turns the receiving hopper until it stops; he pulls it out, deposits the cash, and then turns the hopper back. The key cannot be removed until the hopper stops; this prevents it being left open, and insures that the deposit goes into the safe. Deposits are made in a canvas bag or heavy-duty extension envelope.
2. After receiving hours, the cashier unlocks the safe and removes the deposits in the presence of another person. The deposit purses are

counted and placed in a large canvas bag for pickup by armored car. At the bank, the canvas bag is emptied and each deposit is verified by the bank teller on the deposit slip submitted with the funds. The original deposit slip is retained by the bank; the duplicate is returned to the cashier. Minor discrepancies are posted to the settlement sheet during the course of the day and settled with the driver at the end of the same day. The deposit dropped in the safe contains bills and coins only. The triplicate deposit slip, customer checks, charge tickets, and other papers are stapled to a settlement sheet by the driver and deposited in a special depository. The cashier removes the attachments the following morning and prepares sales recapitulation and the bank deposit from the data available. He audits all settlement sheets turned in by the drivers and corrects mathematical errors.

The system:

—Eliminates the need of the full-time comptometer operator.
—Eliminates the slow-downs at the cashier's cage.
—Eliminates the exposure to robbery of large amounts of cash lying around the cashier's cage.

REDUCING OFFICE EXPENSES

The old saying that, a penny here and a penny there can easily become dollars here and dollars there, is especially applicable to office expenses. Wasted time in writing needless memos and using up needless thousands of single sheets of paper have put a sizable dent in the profits of many a company. They have found, to their chagrin, that they could have accomplished the same things at a fraction of the cost if they had paid more attention to the "pennies" being spent.

The basic idea in cutting office costs is to find the cheapest way you can do things without sacrificing accuracy or speed and still turn out the work at top efficiency.

Are You Wasting Money on Correspondence?

In almost any business, you can come up with important cost-cutting ideas in the office. A good place to start is with your correspondence.

Some experts say it costs more than $2.00 to produce a dictated letter. This makes correspondence, or the writing of letters, one of the most costly of all office activities. Here are some tips on cutting down this cost:

—Use guide or form letters wherever possible. A guide letter costs less than half; a form letter costs a fraction of $2. You can personalize a guide letter,

of course, by having the bulk of the letter uniform, with one or two person-
alized paragraphs.

—Try replying by longhand at the bottom of the incoming letter. This may
not work in all cases, but will be effective in a surprising number of situations.

—If you anticipate a follow-up in certain classes of correspondence, this device works for some: use a carbon or second sheet on which the words
"We're Looking for Your Answer to the Letter Below" are printed at the
top in bright red.

—If you have no objection to breaking with tradition, the National Office
Management Association has devised and recommends a streamlined format
(no salutation, no complimentary close, and so on) that reduces the average letter by eleven percent.

—You can undertake special training for your employees to write compactly
and to the point. The effort here can pay off. One firm reduced its average
cost per letter by more than fifty percent.

—You can reduce the time you waste giving instructions on each letter if you
have a procedures manual which gives rules for salutations, closings, indenta-
tions, spacings and punctuation.

—You'll get better cooperation from your clerical help if you have them write
the manual. In a small office you can appoint each girl to be responsible
for a different section. Have all your office personnel review the sections
as they're completed and add their suggestions.

A Los Angeles appliance manufacturer with 120 employees—an office
force of eight—asked his clerical help to work on a procedures manual at
a weekly luncheon he paid for. In one month the final draft was approved by
management with very few corrections, and the thirty-page manual was typed
and duplicated in the office within six weeks after the idea was first proposed
to the girls. The manual covered grammar rules, telephone procedures, and
methods of handling and filing correspondence. And it gave samples of each
form used in the company with detailed explanations of the number of copies
required, approvals needed, and distribution.

Consider Secretarial Pool Ideas

It is practically impossible for some executives to keep a "secretary"
fully occupied—and in most cases, the employee is not a true secretary. In
many cases secretaries exist (at least for supervisors and lower echelon executives) purely as a status symbol.

Solutions: Some companies centralize steno work. One company eliminated all private secretaries by having its executives answer their own phones
and by equipping them with dictating machines. Another solution, a major

bank had its executives dial a code number and "talk" their letters to a dictating machine. Unseen secretaries transcribe the letters and send them for signature by conveyor belt. As a result, fewer female employees are required, office equipment is more fully used, space is conserved, letters are produced more uniformly, and work standards can be more readily installed.

How to Keep Filing at a Minimum

A filed item is worth the space you give it only if it is essential for the smooth and profitable operation of your business. Here is what one company did to (a) cut down the length of time items were filed, and (b) eliminate the filing of unnecessary items:

Here's how you can keep your file drawers free of dead records:

1. Screen the types of information you now file. Decide how long you need to keep each one.
2. Make up a list of the number of days or weeks, possibly months, each kind of record should be kept. Then stamp on each copy you keep the date it should be destroyed.
3. As your employees file a new piece of material, coded with its expiration date, have them check the folders to pull out old records.

In order to cut down on the number of copies of various documents typed and filed, one company did these three things:

—*Acknowledgements have been discontinued.* If deliveries are made within a few days, acknowledgements are unnecessary. The company found that eliminating them saved from $10 to $20 a day.

—*No orders are written for low-cost single items.* As a supplier of penny items, the company receives many orders of less than $10. An order of this type is returned with a notation that it would be more economical for the customer to order a larger quantity. On orders of $10 to $100, a postcard tells the customer that orders totaling more than $100 are shipped freight prepaid.

—*Forms have been improved.* The company, working with its forms supplier, devised an invoice which cut typing time and increased clarity of data reported. In the old system, "dittoed" forms were used. Carbons had to be inserted each time copies were needed. In the simpler version in use now, all copies needed are produced at one time by using a set of multi-color carbon snap-outs.

Eliminate Unnecessary Reports

According to the *Records Management Institute,* twelve percent of the reports prepared by industrial concerns are useless. Of the remaining number, the contents of two out of three could be improved. One West Coast company discovered that thirty-five percent of its reports were valueless. The solution was to test the usefulness of reports numerous companies discontinue without notice; those reports which seem to be questionable or marginal in value. One company posted all of its reports in a special room. Its executives reviewed each one and signed only those they felt should be kept. Some firms reduce reports by "pricing" or costing them and billing each department that insists on receiving a copy. As a result, each of the above methods not only brought savings in paper, printing and distribution costs, but it eliminated the waste of time spent in reading the reports.

Don't Let Your Forms Control You

For every dollar spent on forms, up to $20 may be spent in processing them. Most companies initiate new forms only after comparing the cost of the form, and the time spent in gathering information, with the anticipated benefits. The same companies, however, continue to use forms long after their usefulness has ended. The following have proven to be successful:

1. Keep forms to a minimum. It has been estimated that it takes only about eleven new forms to add a clerk to the payroll.
2. Design forms to avoid superfluous information and waste of typing because of poor spacing and alignment.
3. Save money by cutting down on size, grade of paper, and use of multi-colors. A Chicago company that reduced a factory production from 57.8 square inches to 46.7 was able to obtain 10,000 units from 625 mill sheets instead of 1,112—a saving on paper of forty-four percent.

In another company, study and watchfulness resulted in using two documents instead of eight, and one large firm reduced its number of forms from 1,501 to 807.

A Look at Round-Dollar Accounting

An increasing number of companies of all sizes are using round-dollar (or even-dollar) accounting to decrease clerical expense, and make reports more readable and simple. What is round-dollar accounting? Here's the background:

How Round-Dollar Accounting Works

Here are the basic principles:

1. All amounts ending in 50 to 99 cents are *raised* by adding one dollar and dropping the pennies. For all amounts ending in one cent to 49 cents, the pennies are simply dropped.

2. Entries directly reflecting transactions with other companies, individuals outside the company, and salaries of employees are recorded exactly to the penny.
3. All cross-classifications of these original transactions (sales, purchases, expenses and labor payments), as well as all summary accounts and financial reporting, are rounded to the nearest dollar.
4. Differences between summaries of the exact penny entries and the rounded entries are accumulated in an exchange account, and the net differences, which should be very small, are written off periodically.

The following are some advantages of dropping pennies:

—A fairly substantial reduction of clerical work and its resulting savings.

—Dealing with fewer digits reduces the chances for clerical errors, and the time spent in tracing and correcting them.

—Reports are read more easily.

Disadvantages of dropping pennies:

—The mechanics of rounding off and posting the clearance account take time and require training of the employees involved. While this will reduce the advantages somewhat, a significant gain will almost always result.

—There could be a loss of control. A trial balance which comes out to the penny is fairly reliable evidence that there were no serious errors in arithmetic and posting. The dollar-rounding differences in the clearance account could conceal unrecognized accounting errors.

—A bias can affect the figures significantly. For example, a great many amounts might end in 98 cents, or there may be an inherent bias if the 50-cent breaks are not properly handled.

How to deal with the problem: If you add up a column of all of the possible penny endings ($.00 to $.99), the total is exactly $49.50. If you round each figure in the column to the nearest dollar (which is either $1 or zero dollars), the total is exactly $50.00. Other things being equal, over a period of time, the number of 100 possible penny endings will be about equal (about the same proportion as the list which added up to $49.50). This is inherent rounding bias.

Since the $.50 error resulted from 100 roundings, the average error to be expected is ½ cent per item rounded. This bias occurs because the penny endings from $.01 to $.49, which are rounded *down,* are exactly offset by the items from $.51 to $.99, which are rounded *up.* If most accounts range from $1 to $999, this bias is so small as to be safely ignored. However, if most of the amounts rounded range from $1 to $9, or thereabouts, you will probably wish to add one simple step to correct this bias.

Ideally, each 50 cents should be alternately rounded, the first one up, the next one down, etc. But since on an average, only one 50-cent item will be found per 100 items rounded, it has been found more practical for a clerk to round each 50-cent item either up or down in the same way as the last item which she rounded either up or down. Since the number of items rounded up should be about equal to the number of those rounded down, the alternate rounding of 50-cent items will maintain the proper balance.

The Sensible Use of Dollar-Rounding

Clearly, round-dollar accounting makes sense only when:

1. The minor differences which it creates will not affect the usefulness of the summary information produced.
2. The differences produced will be at a minimum.
3. The savings produced are worthwhile.
   —If many clerks spend most of their day posting, summarizing, or otherwise using figures which can be rounded, the potential savings should be well worthwhile.
   —If only a relatively small portion of the clerk's time is so used, net savings are likely to be too small to warrant round-dollar accounting on the basis of savings alone. However, it still might be worthwhile because of the simplification of records and reports.

Faster Ways to Handle Checks

You can have one of your employees sort up to 1,000 checks an hour or better, without buying expensive sorting equipment of any kind.

Assume that a girl has to sort a number of checks running from numbers 7,277 to 8,651. Ordinarily she would sort from left to right, putting the checks numbered in the 7,000's in one pile, and the 8,000's in another. Then she would break the piles down by hundreds, tens, and so on. But the speedier method is to start sorting from the other end—reading the numbers from the right to the left. It's done in five steps:

Step 1—Your sorter puts the checks in ten piles, each according to the last number to the right. Numbers ending in "0" go in one pile, those ending in "1" in the next pile and so on.

Step 2—She picks up the piles in an order determined by whether the number of digits in the check numbers are odd or even. In our example, the digits in checks 7,277 to 8,651, add up to four—an even number. Referring to the chart below, she knows to put the "9's" on top, the "8's" below, etc., with the "0's" on the bottom. If the number of digits is odd, by checking the chart again she picks up a reverse sequence, with the "0's" on top.

Step 3—She makes 10 stacks according to the second digit from the right—the 10's digit.

Step 4—She reverses the order of pickup, placing the "0's" on top, the "1's" next, etc., and the "9's" on the bottom (see chart). As a result, in this case, the checks fall into exact numerical sequence on the fourth pickup.

How to use the speedy "reverse sort" check-handling method:

	Even number of digits	*Odd number of digits*
First Pickup (units)	"9's" stack on top	"9's" stack on bottom
Second Pickup (tens)	"9's" go on bottom	"9's" go on top
Third Pickup (hundreds)	"9's" go on top	"9's" go on bottom
Fourth Pickup (thousands)	"9's" go on bottom	"9's" go on top

6

PRACTICAL USE OF THE
COST OF CAPITAL METHOD

217

THE COST OF CAPITAL

The cost of capital is an important tool used in financial decision making. It provides guidelines for the management of a company to allocate the firm's financial resources to the activity that promises the most value and to select the needed resources at the least cost. It is the procedure used to estimate the cost of providing the needed funds and it is the standard of comparison in representing the minimum level of acceptability for projects the firm will accept.

A number of myths have grown up about the concept of the cost of capital, and unfortunately, it has caused confusion in the mind of the practicing businessman. The confusion that has arisen has generated a great deal of controversy and has often prevented business from making the correct and natural decision. The blame for the creation of the confusion can be laid largely at the doorstep of theoretical academicians. They have seen fit to expand the argument about the cost of capital into a situation analogous to the wise men who considered the number of angels who can dance on the head of a pin. The cost of capital is a difficult concept, there is no question about that and even today, in our sophisticated financial organizations, there is sometimes disagreement about how one should effect its use. The determination of a firm's cost of capital is one of the most complex and challenging problems in business. It is indeed a concept relevant not only to the overall management of the business, but also to each of the individual functional areas.

The cost of capital refers to that amount of money which a company, as a result of accepting a proposal, is expected to pay to and/or reinvest for the suppliers of funds during the life of the proposal, over and above the amount of funds required to initially finance the proposal. Essentially, we are talking about an idea which is akin to an *economic profit*. Some businessmen consider cost of capital to be merely the interest rate at which their company may borrow money or they may think of it as actual interest plus financing costs incurred. The apparent assumption in such views is that the owner's investment, including retained earnings, is cost free. Such a conclusion is erroneous since it ignores the earning possibilities from alternative investments of such retained earnings. *In a word, the cost of capital is not the cost of borrowed money.* In fact, the cost of capital may be many things.

Just as the definition of cost depends upon the uses to which the answer may be put, so too, the definition of cost of capital may depend upon the purpose for which it may be used.

Dispelling the Myths

One of the myths surrounding cost of capital is that it is the weighted average of the sources of the given corporation's funds—that it is a composite weight of average of common stock, preferred stock, short- and long-term debt, etc. While this is not necessarily completely false, it is only one part of the entire spectrum of the cost of capital. There may be many other methods of measuring the cost of capital, and they may differ appreciably in amount depending upon the use for which they are to be put.

Another myth surrounding the cost of capital is that it is simply an academic concept which is most useful for viewing the academic aspect of capital budgeting. Nothing can be further from the truth.

In terms of pragmatic business decisions, the cost of capital has applications far beyond capital budgeting. Indeed, if the expression "capital rationing" were substituted for the term "capital budgeting," it may be far more appropriate for its use. In fact, the cost of capital is inherently and directly involved in different aspects of investment decision making such as:

> mergers and acquisitions
> expansion of operating aspects of a business
> repurchase of equity
> optimizing debt ratios
> optimizing dividend policies
> lease financing
> captive finance companies

A further myth which should be attacked is the myth which says that the cost of capital is really undefinable, and in any event, it is an historically real number. The actuality of the case is that cost of capital need not necessarily be a real number. It may take the form of an opportunity cost, a number which does not yet exist, cannot be seen or touched, but nevertheless is the cost of the next available alternative or the benefit to be derived from an alternative use of funds. In many ways that is one of the most important aspects of cost of capital. For most decision-making situations, it is the *opportunity* calculated cost of capital which is far more important for a given decision than an actual calculated cost of capital based upon something which happened yesterday. In essence, the analogy may be made that the sources of funds, varied as they may have been, which a corporation used to secure capital in the past, may have little relevance to the sources which it will have to use in the future for a new project not yet in existence.

An additional myth to be dispelled is that myth which holds that the cost of capital is stable irrespective of the risk involved in a given project. All practicing businessmen know that different projects bear different risks and in our capitalistically oriented society, the nature of capital demands a return commensurate with risk. In essence, the greater the risk, the greater the demanded return. In that sense, the cost of capital may be a graduated cost of capital for any one firm depending upon the types of projects or decisions it must undertake.

Definitions

A precise definition of cost of capital can best be served by considering it relative to the function which it plays. Ezra Solomon has defined the cost of capital as:

a. The minimum required rate of return on proposals using capital funds.
b. The cutoff rate for capital expenditures.
c. The "hurdle" or "target" rate of return which must be surpassed if capital-use is to be justified.
d. The financial standard.

In Professor Solomon's estimation, the conceptual difficulty which has been encountered in measuring the cost of capital is based upon two fundamental business factors. The first factor is that of uncertainty; funds for a business generally are of a varied nature and rarely offer secure, finite returns. The second of the factors of which he speaks is almost an outgrowth of the first factor. He states that business funds are derived through a variety of financial instruments. At one end of the spectrum is pure capital stock; at the other end are debt instruments which in turn are subsidized partly through tax benefits. The various instruments which lay in between the two extremes comprise the world of capital structure. The manner in which these instruments will be apportioned in the total capital mix can profoundly affect both the calculation of the cost of capital and the benefit of leverage to be granted to stockholders/owners of the company.

In the view of Joel Stern, the cost of capital to a firm's stockholders can be viewed as:

1. The minimum acceptable rate of return of investment in order to compensate the stockholders for the business risk they undertake by investing

in the firm, because the stockholders have alternative opportunities available upon which they can earn the firm's cutoff rate for investment.

2. It is this market return, in the form of dividends and capital appreciation (or depreciation), that the stockholders seek over time, for an unlevered company.

3. Since a firm can be viewed as the sum of many plants, the capitalization or discount rate of the expected net operating profits is also the cost of capital.

There is really not very much difference between the views held by Messrs. Solomon and Stern, even though the semantics make it appear as if there is a diversity of opinion on the subject. In subsequent portions of this text, we will examine each of these definitions in order to determine the applicability of each for varying financial decisions.

Calculations

When one speaks of the cost of capital, presumably the thought in mind is expressed in terms of a future investment opportunity. Hence, we are necessarily speaking of a medium for financing a new investment. In that vein, the cost of capital rate depends upon the financial structure of the company. Whether the financing will be done through a fresh equity issue, whether internal funds will be utilized or newly borrowed capital required, is the essence of the problem. If financing is accomplished through a fresh *equity issue* and the price-earnings ratio is used as the present determinant for the cost of capital, consideration has to be given as to how the price-earnings ratio will be affected by the new investment. Will the value of the stock be diluted, or will the value of the equity appreciate? Also, if the stock does appreciate, how substantial will the increase be? Will it be substantial enough for investors to forego other investment possibilities? In this respect, the investment is an opportunity cost to investors. If existing stock is diluted by the new investment, the investor would rather purchase the outstanding stock rather than fresh equity. In addition, the alternative cost by financing through retained earnings or debt must be considered. The question must be asked whether a company is gaining or losing by financing through an equity issue as opposed to the other two alternatives.

If financing is accomplished through *retained earnings,* other factors become apparent. By keeping the capital within the company, presumably the company is holding back funds that would normally be paid out in the form of dividends to investors. In one way, this benefits both the company and the investor. As opposed to financing through debt, retaining funds allows the company to forego interest charges, possibly lowering the cost of capital. Also, by not paying out dividends, the investors are not subject to the extra personal tax they would experience by receiving the dividends. Taking this into consideration, the cost of capital may be lower as a result of this type of financing. However, we must also consider the return on the new investment. We cannot forget that the investors are giving up monies that could possibly be invested elsewhere, perhaps even at a higher rate than implied in the investment proposal of the company. Again, this is an opportunity cost in that sense to the investor. Another possibility is that the majority of the investors are in low tax brackets and the dividends they will receive will not appreciably affect the amount of tax they pay. Perhaps there is a definite need for the money they receive in dividends. All of these factors must be considered in the cost of capital for they are all opportunity costs to both the company and the public.

An alternative financing route would be to *acquire debt*. The cost of borrowed money seems rather simple if we merely consider the interest rate involved. But, for a true cost of capital, other factors have to be considered. The alternative financing paths must consider retained earnings (as above) and the issuing of fresh equity. By surpassing acceptable debt limits, risk and interest rates climb as market stability declines. This may tend to raise the cost of capital, and it was, in fact, this primary question which led, almost fifteen years ago, to the beginnings of the academic confrontations dealing with the behavior of the cost of capital over varying levels of debt equity ratios. If debt and equity are in total imbalance as a result of newly acquired debt, alternative means of financing will have to be found.

In substance then, there are three distinct methods of financing investments, each with its own factor for determining the cost of capital. Distinct as they are, however, they must be integrated in order to determine the company's true cost of capital. One cannot be used in the context of ignoring the others if a true rate is determined. In addition to considering each one individually, they must also be considered as an entity in order to arrive at a valid answer. As it is seen now, a company must be considered in its totality. There are three distinct yet integrated alternatives, and alternatives even within those which must be considered in calculating the cost of capital. Only through scrutinizing and then integrating the others, can the true cost of capital be determined. Accomplishing this will also assist the financial decision maker in determining the most efficient balance within the financial structure in order to reach optimum efficiency by attaining the optimum capital mix.

Cost of Capital Equity

If a firm had no debt in the capital structure, the cost of capital to stockholders of the firm would become an opportunity cost. In other words, the cost of capital of any given stock would be that return which stockholders could earn for an alternative investment. In order to generalize, however, the cost of capital can be considered as a market rate of return. Joel Stern holds that the formula for computing cost of capital for a debt-free firm considers the relationship between dividends and capital appreciation (or depreciation). The presence of debt, however, which is common in the capital structure of most firms, can change the variables included in Stern's concept of the cost of capital for a debt-free firm. In effect, the market return on equity, the dividends and capital appreciation (or depreciation), become what he calls the "Cost of Capital Equity" and the effective rate of interest on the debt therefore becomes the cost of debt capital.

A cost of capital is computed separately for equity, for debt and for other types of capitalization. A *weighted average* is the traditional fashion for measuring the cost of capital. However, it has the shortcoming of measuring the capital structure of the firm as it existed at some historical point in time. It is not necessarily the guide which will provide the minimum criteria for a *future* project.

THE TRADITIONAL WEIGHTED AVERAGE
COMPONENT METHOD

It is important in measuring the cost of each segment under the weighted average method that the same tax basis is used which was used for calculating the expected return under the investment. In other words, rates of return must be comparable to the after-tax cost of capital.

Cost of Debt Capital

The cost of capital of debt is calculated similar to preferred stock with added considerations for premiums for discounts. In essence, the calculation is made by dividing annual cost (interest plus discount or minus premium) by the average of net proceeds and par value. The formula becomes more complex as present values of money are employed, but for this immediate purpose, the cost of debt capital is calculated as shown in the following example:

Total amount of debenture	$5,000,000.00
Term stated interest rate	10 years/8.40%
Price to public	$5,100,000.00
Flotation costs	$ (155,000.00)
Direct cost to company	$ (95,000.00)
Net proceeds	$4,950,000.00
Discount	2.0%

Cost of capital = Interest + Discount/Average of net proceeds and par value
Cost of capital = ($5,000,000/8.40% + 2.0%)/$4,950,000
Cost of capital = $520,000/$4,950,000
Cost of capital = 10.5%

Because interest is tax deductible, the after-tax cost is approximately half of that amount of 5.25%. The above is almost a capsule of the final technique for computing the cost of capital for debt. In between the beginning and the end of the technique are many considerations. For example, short-term debt is considered in the computation of the cost of debt capital when short-term borrowing will later be financed through the issuance of long-term debt.

The true interest rate on short-term debt is determined not only by the stated interest rate used by a lending institution, but also by the proceeds which are made available to the borrower and the length of time the borrower has full use of the funds. Such common practices of lending institutions as discounting loans, requiring compensating balances, and installment loans will cause the cost of short-term debt to be higher than the stated interest rate because they make available to the borrower fewer funds for the stipulated period of time. Also in considering the character of short-term debt, trade accounts payable should not be considered unless discount terms are missed since the cost of interest is included in the price of the material purchased.

Long-term debt, whether privately placed or otherwise should be looked at much in the same manner as the short-term debt explained above. In most cases it is true that the interest rate is approximately equivalent to the stated, nominal rate. There may be differences, however, when measuring the effective rate of interest for a debt issue which is traded on an exchange. The wrong way to measure the interest rate on publicly held debt issues is to consider the relationship between the current interest rate and the current market price of the security. The actual interest rate of long-term debt is best determined by the net proceeds made available to the firm. Consequently, a bond premium will cause the actual interest rate to be lower than the stated rate while a bond discount will cause the actual rate to be higher than the stated rate. The actual interest rate on long-term debt is that interest rate which equates to the present value of all interest payments over the term of the loan and the present value of the principle paid at maturity. Accordingly, it is equivalent to the amount of the net proceeds made available to the borrower at the beginning of the term of the loan. In financial circles the calculation is known as calculating the "yield to maturity."

In order to use this method, present value tables are employed which will fit the pattern of interest payments. Since most interest payments are made semiannually, it is not enough to merely use pencil gymnastics. Mr. Stern indicates that an approximation of the present value technique can be obtained with a formula which reads as follows:

$$\frac{\text{Annual Interest Expense} + \dfrac{\text{Par Value} - \text{Current Price}}{\text{Number Years to Maturity}}}{\dfrac{\text{Current Price} + \text{Par Value}}{2}}$$

Cost of Capital for Preferred Stock

The cost of capital for preferred stock is computed by dividing the dividends or dividend rate by the net proceeds of preferred stock issued. Unless a firm is unable to attract investors by means of another financing source, preferred stock would be the least desirable and possibly the most expensive method of obtaining capital. For example, the dividends, which are in essence a fixed cost, are an annual cost for which the firm receives no tax subsidy. In addition, the fact that preferred stockholders have a dividend preference over common stockholders can possibly cause the common shares to decline in price on the market because there is a potential dilution of equity position for the common stockholder. Should such a decline occur, this could cause an increase in the firm's overall cost of capital.

The computation itself is a relatively simple calculation which involves dividing the annual preferred dividend by the net proceeds from the offering. Net proceeds are generally calculated as a public offering price, less flotation cost, less other direct cost to the company. For example, see the tabulation following:

Total number of preferred shares	20,000
Par value and price to public (per share)	$ 100.00
Total par value and price to public	$2,000,000.00
Less flotation costs	$ 65,000.00
Less direct costs to company	$ 33,000.00
Net proceeds	$1,902,000.00
Net proceeds per share	$ 95.10
Dividend per share	$ 6.80

Cost of capital preferred stock = $6.80/$95.10 = 7.15%

Retained Earnings

Internal financing through *retained earnings* is never cost free; it always involves an imputed cost. This occurs because funds that may otherwise be distributed to stockholders have been retained in the company. The cost of such funds is the amount of money the shareholder could have made if the funds, after taxes, had been in his possession. Since tax rates vary so significantly with the demography of stockholders, a more logical method of establishing a cost of capital for retained earnings is to assume that if all earnings had been paid out in dividends, the company would obtain capital by equity financing. Under this type of assumption, the cost of capital for retained earnings may be given the same rate as the cost of equity capital.

Cost of Capital for Common Stock

In a word, *the cost of capital for common stock is the reciprocal of the price-earnings ratio,* the capitalization rate. As simple as the foregoing sounds, a multitude of problems arise as well as a proliferation of academic arguments. For example, the variables to be considered in calculating the cost of capital for common stock may range from the extremes of measuring the degree of growth of a company to the consideration of whether the price-earnings ratio is a reflection of dividend policy or earnings per share. In a sense, there is a great similarity between the cost of capital for equity issues and the cost of capital for debt and for preferred stock. This is said in the sense that in the computation described earlier, regarding these two types of capitalization, mention was made that streams of future types of income are discounted to the present value in order to obtain some measure of present worth (in the case of debt, it was described as the yield to maturity calculation). In that same sense, the current market price of equity generally represents some type of present value for an expected amount of payments in the future which are discounted to the present. In considering this aspect of the problem, questions first arise as to whether the nature of the future payments are in the form of earnings, dividends, or a stream of future cash flow.

The other question arises when the problem of establishing a discount rate for the future stream is considered. For example, what is the effect of growth on the discount rate in terms of stockholders' expectations affected by the debt-equity ratio of a firm?

There is some disagreement with respect to the computation of the cost of common stock equity capital as mentioned earlier. Some financial theorists (as opposed to practicing businessmen) believe that anticipated earnings should be the basis of the computation of the cost of common stock equity capital. Others believe that dividends plus an anticipated profitability growth rate should serve as such a basis.

The rationale behind the use of *anticipated earnings as a basis* for computing the cost of equity is that common stock investors wish to maintain the present value of their investment; that is, they do not want any dilution of their position. Therefore, a new product or a product line whose creation and marketing program are being financed through the issuance of common stock must earn a return for the firm which will permit the present common stockholders to maintain their position. In short, marketing projects financed through new common stock issues must earn a rate of return which will permit the investor's earnings per share to be at least equal to that which was enjoyed before the issuance of the new stock.

Some financial theorists believe that a *dividend basis* would be more appropriate for the computation of the cost of equity capital than an anticipated earnings basis because the market price of a growth stock would be unrealistically high when compared to its relative earnings per share. Since investors will pay a high price in anticipation of high earnings which have not yet materialized, the computation of the cost of equity, based on earnings, will yield a cost of equity capital which will be lower than it really should be.

The *dividend basis* calculation assumes a constant growth rate in dividends into perpetuity. It also assumes that investors place their values on anticipated streams of dividends and constant dividend payout rates. Since these assumptions may be unwarranted in many situations, a dividend approach to computing the cost of equity capital must bear some relationship to earnings. Joel Stern mentions that, in fact, at least two authors have shown that using either dividends or earnings yield almost identical results. The reason for this is that dividend policy is reactive to earnings anticipation. Therefore, there tends to be a somewhat correlative relationship between dividends and earnings so that whether it is the stream of dividends that is discounted or the stream of earnings that is discounted, the result is immaterial to the final result.

Earlier in this section, it was mentioned that in essence, the cost of capital for common stock is the reciprocal of the price-earnings ratio, or as it is sometimes called, the "capitalization rate." Although this is generally true, it poses particular problems for those companies which have a significantly higher growth rate than most and which consequently have very high price-earnings multiple. For example, if one were to assume that a growth company sells at forty times earnings, the cost of capital in effect would be calculated at approximately 2½%. Obviously, such a company could not continue the implied rate of growth if it accepted projects or made financial decisions based upon an acceptability criterion of 2½%. The missing link was supplied by Myron Gordon when he developed his growth model which included a factor representing the premium that the investor is willing to pay for a firm's ability to make investments in projects where the return significantly exceeds the nominal cost of capital. The Gordon model contains a mathematical formula as follows:

$$k = D/P + g$$

In this formula, k = cost of capital of common stock funds
                D = current cash dividend per share
                P = current market price per share
                g = the anticipated rate of increase for future dividends
                    expressed as a decimal fraction

The common example which is frequently shown in the literature is that of IBM as its performance existed between 1954 and 1964. During that period, a capitalization rate for the stock implied an average dividend yield of 1.5%. Obviously, IBM could not and did not afford that low percentage criterion for acceptability. To that factor is added the compound growth rate of world-wide consolidated earnings for that time period. Accordingly, that calculation showed the rate to be approximately 15%. Adding the 15% growth rate to the 1½% nominal cost of capital rate yielded a total cost of equity capital of approximately 16.5% for IBM.

It should be obvious that the components technique for measuring the cost of capital can be affected significantly by the numbers used for purposes of weighing. In all of the foregoing discussion, it has been assumed that market values of the components of capitalization would be used in the calculation as opposed to book values. An example of the effect of using either of the two techniques can be shown in the example below which is based upon Mr. Stern's work. Book values for purposes of cost of capital calculations are accounting oriented and based upon historical, irrelevant costs which may have absolutely no significance to a stockholder in the contemporary market. It is only market value which has significance when considered in the light of the earlier definitions of cost of capital given at the beginning of the discussion.

Following is a tabulation (Figure 1) showing differing results from both the book value and market value method of calculation.

THE EFFECT OF LEVERAGE

Increasing the mix of capitalization in favor of debt can exercise a great deal of beneficial leverage for the stockholder because of the tax subsidy involved. In a riskless world, the optimum capital structure would be the complete maximization of debt usage. Obviously in our practical times, the higher amount of debt which is used to finance operations leads to a decreasing preference on the part of the investor and the lender because of higher attendant risks in capitalizing a firm through larger uses of debt. Nevertheless, there is a point at which optimum capital structures can be achieved and through the use of financial models they are largely a calculable measure.

It is doubtful if any long range beneficial effects for a stockholder would accrue if the management of the company increased the firm's financial leverage through increasing the amounts of preferred stock whether convertible or unconvertible. This type of financing can never provide a long-term increase in the valuation of a firm because the dividend payment which

	(1)	(2)	(3)	(4)
		Book Value Weights		
		% of	After Tax Cost of Each	
	Amounts	Total	Segment [2]	(2) × (3)
Short-Term Interest Bearing Debt	$ 250	6.0%	3.83%	.23%
Bonds (par minus flotation costs and discount)	960	22.9	3.84	.88
Preferred Stock (10 shares, stated value)	290	6.9	6.00	.41
Common Stock ($1 par, 200 shares)	200	4.7	12.50 [3]	.58
Capital Surplus (shares sold at $10)	1,800	42.9	12.50	5.36
Retained Earnings [1]	700	16.6	12.50 *	2.08
Total	$4,200	100.0%		9.54%
		Market Value Weights		
Short-Term Debt	$ 250	3.4%	3.83%	.13%
Bonds (current price = $94)	940	12.6	3.93	.50
Preferred (current price = $25)	250	3.4	6.67	.23
Common Stock (current price = $30)	6,000	80.6	11.00 [4]	8.87
Total	$7,440	100.0%		9.73%

Figure 1

---

[1] Current Earnings = $400 or $2 per share.

[2] Tax rate is 48%.

[3] Earnings-to-Price Ratio.

[4] Assumed as the discount rate which makes the present value of the firm's expected net profits equal to the current market price of the common equity.

* A "cost" of 12½% is also assigned to retained earnings because, although these funds appear free, they are available for repayment to stockholders in the form of dividends or repurchase of equity. Thus, these funds are, in effect, a compulsory, pre-emptive rights offering, bearing an opportunity cost.

is mandated through the use of that vehicle is not tax subsidized. Debt financing, however, can increase a firm's total value because of the very fact of the tax subsidy. It may, however, cause the price-earnings ratio of common stock to fall but at the same time, it may maximize the price of an individual share. An illustration of the effect of increasing leverage on the cost of capital is shown in Figure 2.

A Mathematical Formula

Mathematically, the effect of leverage upon cost of capital can be expressed in a formula. The formula, after Stern, says that the total stockholder return (dividends plus capital appreciation) is equal to the weighted average or the overall cost of capital plus the difference between the cost of capital and the cost of borrowed capital, multiplied by the debt-equity ratio. It may be easier to visualize it through the formula which expresses itself as:

$$Y = c + (c - b) \times D/E$$

Where Y = cost of equity capital
     c = cost of capital
     b = cost of borrowed capital
     D = debt
     E = equity

It should be emphasized that in all of the above calculations, the formulas expressed are compatible with the use of the term "net operating profits after taxes." Stern abbreviates this as NOPAT. The essential difference between the expression "net profit" and "NOPAT" is the interest expense for interest-bearing debt. Thus, in all of the calculations for cost of capital, NOPAT should be used and can be accomplished by adding back the after-tax effect of interest to net profits. This procedure additionally holds true for all calculations involving a return on investment for given financial decisions.

AN ALTERNATIVE PRESENT VALUE APPROACH— THE ENTITY METHOD

There is yet another method of computing the cost of capital for an entire firm without resorting to the arithmetic of isolating each of the components of the capital structure. Essentially, the procedure involves finding an interest rate which will equate future cash flows to the present value (market value) of the firm's capitalization. The one caveat which I must

Stage	Market Value of Bonds	Pre-Tax Marginal Interest Rate on Bonds	After-Tax Marginal Cost of Debt Capital	Pre-Tax Average Cost of Debt Capital	After-Tax Average Cost of Debt Capital	Average Cost of Equity Capital	Market Value of Common Stock	Total Market Value of Bonds and Stocks	Leverage	After-Tax Combined Cost of Capital
0	$ 0	—	—	—	—	11.0%	$60	$ 60	0	11.0%
1	20	4%	4.0	4.00%	2.00%	11.5	55	75	.27	8.9
2	40	4	4.0	4.00	2.00	12.0	50	90	.44	7.6
3	60	4	4.0	4.00	2.00	12.5	54	114	.53	7.6
4	80	5	5.0	4.25	2.13	13.0	58	138	.58	6.7
5	100	6	6.0	4.60	2.30	14.0	60	160	.63	6.6
6	120	7	7.0	5.00	2.50	15.5	65	185	.65	7.1
7	140	8	8.0	5.43	2.71	18.0	63	203	.69	7.5

Figure 2

render to the reader if he is to use this technique, which is by far simpler than taking the components approach, is that the accuracy of this technique rests with the reliability of forecast future cash flows.

If, as in the normal business world, it is often true that the calculation of cash flow need not be precisely accurate but simply give a rendition of the "ball park" in which the firm's cost of capital is found, then the entity approach may easily be substituted for the components approach. Assume the situation exists as is shown in Figure 3.

Historical Results

Note in the example that we are looking at a ten-year time span between the years 1965 and 1974. This does not necessarily mean that we are projecting backwards in terms of operating results; rather, assume in that example that we are in the year 1972, and that we are showing the actual results from the year 1965 and the forecast results through the year 1974. The historical results are shown so that when equating the present value of the future cash flows, we will also be considering the growth rate of cash flow of the firm as it may have affected the present value of the firm's capitalization. Note also in the example that what we have done is to take the profit after taxes and add back to that number the after-tax effect of interest expense on debt. Summarizing then, our interest is on line 6 on that statement and, more specifically, in the following year-by-year operating cash profit after taxes.

	(000's dollars)
1965	8782
1966	7570
1967	9441
1968	6895
1969	3291
1970	8251
1971	8487
1972	3914
1973	3889
1974	11534

The other part of the calculation deals with a rather simplified approach to the current market value of the firm's capitalization and can be expressed in a mathematical formula which summarizes the thought that valuation equals the sum of the market value of equity, plus the sum of the market value of debt, plus the sum of the market of preferred stock. This amount

NET OPERATING CASH PROFIT AFTER TAXES

Capitalizing to Approximate Cost of Capital (in 000's dollars)

	1965	1966	1967	1968	1969	1970	1971	1972	1973	1974
1) Net Profit After Taxes	8,811	11,153	11,192	12,741	4,925	12,237	8,425	6,050	8,616	14,138
2) Add: After-Tax Effect of Interest	525	480	440	422	363	307	296	210	184	122
3) Net Operating Profit After Taxes (1) + (2)	9,336	11,633	11,632	13,163	5,288	12,544	8,721	6,260	8,800	14,260
4) Capital Expenditures	7,127	9,685	10,798	6,850	5,125	7,862	8,974	9,781	10,900	11,400
Less: Depreciation	7,600	8,212	7,922	7,604	5,918	7,207	7,650	8,120	8,560	9,752
	(473)	1,473	2,876	(754)	(793)	655	1,324	1,661	2,340	1,648
5) Increase in Working Capital	1,027	2,590	(685)	7,022	2,790	3,638	(1,090)	685	2,571	1,078
6) Net Operating Cash Profit After Taxes (3) − (4) − (5)	8,782	7,570	9,441	6,895	3,291	8,251	8,487	3,914	3,889	11,534

Figure 3

is then arithmetically calculated and becomes the dollar constraint for the present value calculation. In essence then, what we are trying to do is to find an interest rate which will equate the cash flows expressed in Figure 3 with the market value for capitalization calculated as shown below.

Market Value	
Debt	$ 30,000
Preferred Stock	$ 10,000
Equity	$ 60,000
Total Capitalization	$100,000

Figure 4 shows the actual calculation of cost of capital under this present value approach utilizing cash flows for the company. Note that the cash flows are set forth in the example year by year and that the market value of capitalization is considered almost as an investment might be considered in a discounted cash flow calculation. It is the constraint to be met—the interest rate must equate the cash flow with that constraint.

HOW TO CALCULATE AN ACQUISITION PURCHASE PRICE

One of the most difficult arts in the realm of finance is the selection of the proper method by which a potential acquisition can be priced. Unfortunately, many of the techniques which are used today involve a great deal of subjective judgment. Too often a financial man is willing to wet his finger, hold it up in the air and say that he will pay fifteen times earnings or eleven times earnings or twelve times earnings for an acquisition. This type of method for calculating a purchase price tends to rely too much on the subjective judgment of the individual and his estimation of the current tenor of the stock market. The problem lies in the fact that, were the same set of data given to three different individuals, each with his own perspective on the behavior of the stock market, a probability exists that three separate and different purchase prices would be calculated for the same company. Another method for pricing acquisitions is the technique whereby financial men will agree to pay a stipulated premium over the book value of assets purchased. This, of course, strains the credulity of the financial statements since book values are based upon costs less any accumulated depreciation. This latter "valuation" is hardly the vehicle for determining the current purchase price of a company because the assets involved may be worth far more or even far less than the stated numbers on conventional financial statements. Cost in the past is a poor guide to valuing the future, especially considering the changes in the value of the purchasing value of the dollar.

What is suggested is that, instead of using subjective techniques or techniques which rely on pure accounting historical data, that a method be employed which will take into consideration both the time value of money and an objective approach to establishing the value of an acquisition. In

The Capitalization of Net Operating (Cash) Profit Approach
($ Thousands)

Year	Net Operating Cash Profit After Taxes	Present Value Factors 10%	11%	Present Values 10%	11%
1 (1965)	8,782	.9091	.9009	7,984	7,912
2	7,570	.8264	.8116	6,256	6,144
3	9,441	.7513	.7312	7,093	6,903
4	6,895	.6830	.6587	4,709	4,541
5	3,291	.6209	.5935	2,043	1,953
6	8,251	.5645	.5346	4,658	4,411
7	8,487	.5132	.4817	4,356	4,088
8	3,914	.4665	.4339	1,826	1,698
9	3,889	.4241	.3909	1,649	1,520
10	11,534	.3855	.3522	4,446	4,062
				45,020	43,232
		10.0000	9.0909		
11	14,260	6.1445	5.8892	54,980	45,656
		3.8555	3.2017		

Total Present Value   100,000   88,888

Market Value of Capitalization:

Common Stock (share outstanding)	$ 60,000
Debt	30,000
Preferred Stock	10,000
	$100,000

Figure 4

Figures 5 and 6 an example is shown whereby the Trace Company is a candidate for purchase by an acquiror. The first step in determining the purchase price under the technique which is suggested is for the acquiring company to estimate on a pro forma basis the operating results of the Trace Company as it would appear here under the umbrella of the acquiring company. In actuality these projections need not be overly precise since what we are attempting to establish in the technique is a "ball park" area of purchase price which will reveal to the acquiring company *the worth* of the Trace Company to the acquiror. The worth will be expressed in terms of a dollar amount which represents the highest price that the acquiror can pay for the Trace Company and still not exceed the acceptable limits for the acquiror by violating its cost of capital constraint. In the example, it is assumed that the minimum acceptable criterion for cost of capital by the acquiring company is 14%.

Pro Forma Statement

The first step is to establish the pro forma profit and loss statement for *future* periods. The object of the pro forma statement is to establish what is called the net cash flow. In all acquisition as well as capital program models, cash flow is far more important than is the accounting concept of net profit. Once the cash flow is established, incremental working capital requirements are estimated based upon the amounts of new working capital which would have to be injected into the Trace Company by the acquiring company. The new working capital is not money which is irrevocably given to the company; rather it is money temporarily injected into the Trace Company until such time as the accounts receivable may be collected and the inventories may be sold. In accordance with the type of calculation shown, that is, the discounted cash flow method, it is assumed that the Trace Company will have a ten-year life span. At the end of this time, the working capital injections by the acquiring company into the Trace Company will be recovered. The importance of this factor is that the recovery of the working capital will be ten years hence and therefore subject to measurement on a time value basis. Note in Figure 6 that the net cash flow (the last line on Figure 5) is shown in the second column and represents the net cash flow through all years with the exception that in the year 1976 the accumulated *incremental* working capital which has temporarily been plowed into the Trace Company will be recovered by the acquiring company. The cost of capital factor at 14% is applied to the net cash flow. On a discounted present value basis therefore the calculation shows a value to the acquiring company *now* of slightly over $12 million. This represents the highest price that the acquiror can pay for

Trace Company—Acquisition, Estimating Net Cash Flow
(Thousands of Dollars)

	1967	1968	1969	1970	1971	1972	1973	1974	1975	1976
Net sales—10% average growth	$37,000	$40,700	$44,800	$49,300	$54,200	$59,600	$65,600	$72,200	$79,400	$87,300
Profit after taxes—6%	2,220	2,442	2,688	2,958	3,252	3,576	3,936	4,332	4,764	5,238
Depreciation	162	197	140	120	110	105	100	95	90	80
Cash flow	2,382	2,639	2,828	3,078	3,362	3,681	4,036	4,427	4,854	5,318
Less: Incremental working capital (16.7% of incremental sales)	6,179	618	685	752	818	902	1,002	1,102	1,202	1,319
Net cash flow	$(3,797)	$ 2,021	$ 2,143	$ 2,326	$ 2,544	$ 2,779	$ 3,034	$ 3,325	$ 3,652	$ 3,999

Figure 5

239

Figure 6

Trace Company—Acquisition, Calculation of Purchase Price
(Thousands of Dollars)

	Net Cash Flow	Cost of Capital Factor at 14%	Discounted Value	
1967	$(3,797)	0.9332	$(3,543)	
1968	2,021	0.8112	1,639	
1969	2,143	0.7053	1,511	
1970	2,326	0.6131	1,426	
1971	2,544	0.5330	1,356	
1972	2,779	0.4634	1,288	
1973	3,034	0.4029	1,222	
1974	3,325	0.3502	1,164	
1975	3,652	0.3045	1,112	
1976	3,999	0.2647	1,059	
1976	14,579	0.2647	3,859	Return of '67–'76
Discounted purchase price at 14% ROI			$12,093	working capital

the Trace Company and still not dilute the minimum acceptable criterion
of 14%.

USING THE COST OF CAPITAL AS AN
ACCEPTABILITY CRITERION IN A CAPITAL PROGRAM

The most commonly used perspective for the cost of capital is its use in
implementing the capital evaluation program for a company. Indeed, this use
is quite consistent with the definitions given earlier citing as reference the
works of Ezra Solomon and Joel Stern. Figures 7 through 11 demonstrate
a discounted cash flow application using the cost of capital as a constraint in
evaluating a common business problem, that of a new product being considered for manufacture. In Figure 7, it is seen that the Ace Company computed
its cost of capital based upon the traditional weighted components method.
Using that method, the cost of capital *was* 8.6%. They, however, recognized
that different capital projects entail different degrees of risk. As a result,
their corporate policy states that for the moderate risk entailed in this project,
the minimum acceptable criteria will be at least 14%, representing a 65%
premium over the cost of capital. As in the previous example, pro forma
operating statements are constructed for the product as it would appear on

Figure 7

Ace Company, Capital Project Analysis

Assume:

Product Gamma, a new product, is being considered for manufacture and distribution. Risk is moderate and corporate policy requires a premium over cost of capital of at least 65%. P&L data is as shown:

Estimated cost of plant	$0.2 million	1965
Estimated cost of machinery and equipment	0.8 million	1966
Estimated cost of machinery and equipment	0.3 million	1969

Target return: 14%
Capital data:

	Market Value	Rate after Tax	Dollar Cost
Notes payable	$ 100,000	4%	$ 4,000
Debentures	400,000	3%	12,000
Preferred Stock	300,000	5%	15,000
Net worth (capital stock)	2,700,000	10% [a]	270,000
	$3,500,000		$301,000

Cost of capital $301,000/$3,500,000 = 8.6%

[a] Earnings/Price.

an "in-business" basis. Utilizing that statement shows that cash flow ranges from a loss of $500 thousand in the first year to an ultimate profit level of $1.2 million in the year 1979 and continuing onward. The important item to note in Figure 8 is that all of the numbers which appear are numbers incremental to the product.

That is, if the product were not in existence, no numbers would appear on Figure 8. This is another way of saying that all of the numbers shown in Figure 8 are created as a result of the product's existence. No period expenses which were in existence prior to the creation of the product and the marketing of the product should be allocated in this example. Figure 9 demonstrates a method for computing the working capital for the product. It assumes that ordinary sales terms for the product are based upon terms of 2/10, net 30. Not all of the customers of Ace take advantage of the offer of 2% if they pay within a ten-day period. However, on an average, all receivables are collected by the fifteenth day. Since there are twenty-four 15-day periods in a 360 day year, it is equivalent to dividing annual sales by 24 to establish

Product Gamma, Profit and Loss (Millions of Dollars)

Year	Sales	Direct Profit	New Plant Period Cost	Depreciation [a]	Profit Before Taxes	Profit After Taxes	Add Depreciation	Cash Flow	7% Credit	Total
1965	$ 4.5	$(0.8)	$0.4	$ —	$(1.2)	$(0.6)	$ —	$(0.6)	$0.1	$(0.5)
1966	5.7	(0.3)	0.4	0.1	(0.8)	(0.4)	0.1	(0.3)		(0.3)
1967	6.5	0.1	0.4	0.1	(0.4)	(0.2)	0.1	(0.1)		(0.1)
1968	7.4	1.1	0.4	0.1	0.6	0.3	0.1	0.4		0.4
1969	8.0	1.5	0.4	0.1	1.0	0.5	0.1	0.6		0.6
1970	8.7	1.5	0.4	0.1	1.0	0.5	0.1	0.6		0.6
1971	9.0	2.1	0.4	0.1	1.6	0.8	0.1	0.9		0.9
1972	9.3	2.2	0.4	0.1	1.7	0.8	0.1	0.9		0.9
1973	9.7	2.2	0.4	0.1	1.7	0.8	0.1	0.9		0.9
1974	10.1	2.3	0.4	0.1	1.8	0.9	0.1	1.0		1.0
1975	10.4	2.4	0.4	0.1	1.9	0.9	0.1	1.0		1.0
1976	10.8	2.4	0.4	—	2.0	1.0	—	1.0		1.0
1977	11.2	2.6	0.4	—	2.2	1.1	—	1.1		1.1
1978	11.5	2.6	0.4	—	2.2	1.1	—	1.1		1.1
1979	11.9	2.8	0.4	—	2.4	1.2	—	1.2		1.2
1980	12.3	2.8	0.4	—	2.4	1.2	—	1.2		1.2

[a] Does not add because of rounding.

Figure 8

Product Gamma, Computation of Working Capital (Millions of Dollars)

Year	Accounts Receivable		Inventories	Total Working Capital	Increment
	Sales	Divided by 24			
1965	$ 4.5	$0.2	$0.9	$1.1	$1.1
1966	5.7	0.2	1.1	1.3	0.2
1967	6.5	0.3	1.2	1.5	0.2
1968	7.4	0.3	1.4	1.7	0.2
1969	8.0	0.3	1.5	1.8	0.1
1970	8.7	0.4	1.6	2.0	0.2
1971	9.0	0.4	1.6	2.0	—
1972	9.3	0.4	1.6	2.0	—
1973	9.7	0.4	1.7	2.1	0.1
1974	10.1	0.4	1.7	2.1	—
1975	10.4	0.4	1.8	2.2	0.1
1976	10.8	0.5	1.9	2.4	0.2
1977	11.2	0.5	1.9	2.4	—
1978	11.5	0.5	2.0	2.5	0.1
1979	11.9	0.5	2.1	2.6	0.1
1980	12.3	0.5	2.2	2.7	0.1
					2.7

Figure 9

the amount of accounts receivable which are outstanding at any one point in time. Inventories used in the calculation of working capital are easily calculated by observing the physical volume of product manufactured and sold. As a result, the total working capital requirements are set forth in Figure 9. However, it is only the *increments* of working capital which will be used in the calculation. It is assumed that as the product grows and is successful, it will be self-supporting to a degree with the exception of its additional growth over a period of years. This working capital, as in the last example, will be recoverable in the year 1980, the last year in the time horizon for this calculation. Figures 10 and 11 show the attempt to determine the discounted cash flow correct rate which will equate both the total investment and receipts. It is apparent under the trial at 10% that the investment is discounted to a present value of $2.9 million whereas the receipts under the 10% trial are calculated at $4.2 million at the present value. Observe further that the trial at 15% produces a different result. There the investment is calculated at a present value of $2.5 million and receipts also are calculated at $2.5 million. Under the technique of discounted cash flow which is used, this is the ultimate solution to the calculation. An interest rate (15%) has been found which will equate both the investment and the receipts. Therefore, the return on investment for this project is 15%. That result must be measured against the minimum acceptable criterion which was previously established at 14%. On that basis then, the project is acceptable.

Perspectives

When reading this monograph, the reader should not expect to gain instant wisdom about the subject of cost of capital. It is so intensely complex in all its aspects that it would be unfair both for the reader to expect such wisdom and the writer to anticipate that he has the ability to dispense such wisdom in such a small dose. At best, the desirable result from reading this text should be an appreciation for the utility of the cost of capital concept and awareness that this is *not* a highly theoretical idea; further, that it does have merit and practical application in the business world. It is most important to bear in mind that decision making is an art and that art should be fed by the knowledge that most decisions are finally made on a "what if" basis. In that context, opportunity costs should never be overlooked since it may truly represent the minimum acceptable rate for accepting a proposal. An excellent short presentation on the subject of the cost of capital entitled "A Quantitative Approach to Financial Planning" by Joel Stern appeared in the *Banker's Magazine* in the spring of 1969 issue. It is recommended for any reader who wishes to pursue the subject further.

Product Gamma, Discounted Cash Flow (Investment) (Millions of Dollars)

Investment	Capital	Incremental Working Capital	Total	Trial 10%		Trial 15%	
1965	$0.2	$1.1	$1.3	0.9516	$1.2	0.9286	$1.2
1966	0.8	0.2	1.0	0.8611	0.9	0.7993	0.8
1967		0.2	0.2	0.7791	0.2	0.6879	0.1
1968		0.2	0.2	0.7050	0.1	0.5921	0.1
1969	0.3	0.1	0.4	0.6379	0.3	0.5096	0.2
1970		0.2	0.2	0.5772	0.1	0.4386	0.1
1971			—	0.5223	—	0.3775	—
1972			—	0.4726	—	0.3250	—
1973		0.1	0.1	0.4276	—	0.2797	—
1974			—	0.3869	—	0.2407	—
1975		0.1	0.1	0.3501	0.1	0.2072	—
1976		0.2	0.2	0.3168	0.1	0.1783	0.1
1977			—	0.2866	—	0.1535	—
1978		0.1	0.1	0.2593	0.1	0.1321	—
1979		0.1	0.1	0.2347	0.1	0.1137	—
1980		0.1	0.1	0.2124	0.1	0.0979	—
	$1.3	$2.7	$4.0		$2.9		$2.5

Figure 10

245

Product Gamma, Discounted Cash Flow (Receipts) (Millions of Dollars)

Receipts	Total	Trial 10%	Total	Trial 15%	Total
1965	$(0.5)	0.9516	$(0.5)	0.9286	$(0.5)
1966	(0.3)	0.8611	(0.3)	0.7993	(0.2)
1967	(0.1)	0.7791	(0.1)	0.6879	(0.1)
1968	0.4	0.7050	0.3	0.5921	0.2
1969	0.6	0.6379	0.4	0.5096	0.3
1970	0.6	0.5772	0.3	0.4386	0.3
1971	0.9	0.5223	0.5	0.3775	0.3
1972	0.9	0.4726	0.4	0.3250	0.3
1973	0.9	0.4276	0.4	0.2797	0.3
1974	1.0	0.3869	0.4	0.2407	0.2
1975	1.0	0.3501	0.4	0.2072	0.2
1976	1.0	0.3168	0.3	0.1783	0.2
1977	1.1	0.2866	0.3	0.1535	0.2
1978	1.1	0.2593	0.3	0.1321	0.1
1979	1.2	0.2347	0.3	0.1137	0.1
1980	3.9 a	0.2124	0.8	0.0979	0.6
			$ 4.2		$ 2.5

a Includes recovery of working capital.
Difference + 1.3 = 0.
Answer: Return on investment = 15%.

Figure 11

246

7

SIMPLIFIED USE OF THE DISCOUNTED CASH FLOW METHOD OF EVALUATION

DISCOUNTED CASH FLOW TECHNIQUES

To the uninitiated, the subject of discounted cash flow theory and techniques can strike fear into the hearts of ordinary men. I indicated in *Practical Use of the Cost of Capital Method,* another booklet which deals with cost of capital, that the academicians and the theoreticians have done a great disservice to the practicing business executive, because they have succeeded in muddying the waters of an otherwise rather simple to apply, financial evaluation technique. One of the problems that has grown around the mystique of the discounted cash flow technique is the fact that in more recent years it has been very heavily identified with capital budgeting. In actuality, the financial technique has uses which go far beyond the scope of capital budgeting. In fact, its inception and original use antedate capital budgeting by many years. The technique itself was first used before the turn of the twentieth century in evaluating the profitability of real estate transactions. In subsequent years, it became heavily used in financial circles to calculate "yield to maturity" calculations for bonds and mortgages. The technique itself is sometimes called the *financial method* or the *investors method*. It remained in that tight compartmentalization for use until the decade of the fifties when Joel Dean first referred to it in his works on managerial economics. He popularized the use of the term for capital budgeting and to a large degree, its applications have largely concentrated in that specific area. Indeed, in order to illustrate the theory and the technique of discounted cash flow, this presentation also will begin with the capital expenditure area.

The discounted cash flow rate of return is also known in financial literature as the *internal rate of return* because the rate of return which is determined by the solution to the problem is a rate which is generated from the input to the problem itself. In other words, it is not affected by external rates of return such as cost of capital, costs of borrowing money, etc. The essence of the technique involves a determination of *finding* an interest rate. When using another present value technique which is also called the *present value method,* an external interest rate is applied to differing cash flows. The distinction then, between the two methods, is that under the discounted cash flow method no interest rate from outside factors is applied. Instead, an interest rate is generated based upon the cash inflows and outflows. This interest rate is then to be compared to some external criterion for evaluation. The essence of the technique says that a discount rate will be generated which will bring all of the cash flows, both inflows and outflows, back to a present value of zero. Normally the discount rate must be found by trial and error process; however, after the analyst has made a small number of elementary computations this should not be a great hurdle to overcome.

UNDERSTANDING THE INTENT
AND MEANING OF TERMS

Notice that in the above simplified definition of the technique, a number of terms were used such as, *discount rate, inflow and outflow,* and *present value.* It would be well at this point and before proceeding further in the discussion to make certain that the intent and meaning of each of these terms is completely and simply understood. The *discount rate* is exactly what the name implies. It is an interest rate which is less than 1.0. It is a rate which will bring a future amount back to a present value. The expression "time is money" has a great deal of validity. One is not often faced with the practical reality of that type of problem. However, if one were to be given a choice as to the receipt of $1.00 now or $1.04 a year from now, either of two options obviously are available. One option is to take $1.00 now and (a) spend it, (b) invest it. The other basic option is not to take $1.00 now but to take $1.04 a year from now. The financial evaluation to determine the correct option rests largely on the perception by the receiver of his alternative investment opportunities. If one were to be able to accept the dollar now and place it in the bank in order to earn 5%, then a year from now he would not have $1.04 but instead, $1.05. In that case, obviously the acceptance of $1.00 now would be the better alternative. If, however, he had no options for reinvesting the money, then receipt of the $1.04 a year from now would be the better choice. In any case, we can say by means of this type of logic that if the available alternative were investment in a bank at 5%, then $1.05 a year from now would be worth the same as $1.00 today. In other words, the $1.05 would be discounted by a rate which would bring it back to the present value of $1.00.

In a recent article in *Managerial Planning,* James Paulos and Fred Kirby wrote an article on the theory of discounted cash flow. The usefulness of the article is in the elementary concepts presented in the beginning which are comprehensible and follow easily into the balance of the explanation of the technique. One of the essences of the points presented is that problem dealing with a hypothetical situation in which an individual has $621 which he thinks might better be spent in the future instead of spending it now. As a result, the individual saves the money for five years and after that time, expects to have it available for whatever business purpose he desires. The individual invests the money in the bank and at the same time, investigates all of the varying investment opportunities which might be available to him. One of the opportunities he looks at requires him to invest $621 today with the understanding that he will receive $1,000 five years from now. The $621 invested at time zero is expected to grow to $1,000 at the end of the fifth year. In the same way, it can be stated that $1,000 five years from now is worth $621 today. The point is made then, that money, future money, has a present value in today's terms. The present value concept in turn is very much related to the reverse of the compound interest sequence. In this particular example, $621 today, invested today at 10%, will total to $1,000 between principal and interest at the end of five years. Using converse logic, $1,000 five years from now, multiplied by an appropriate discount factor will equate to $621 today if the factor is based upon a 10% rate.

The descriptive terms *cash inflow* and *cash outflow* are largely the combined inputs to the more popularly used expression *cash flow.* Cash flow in turn is related to the cash effect of operations resulting from the fact that not all of the expenses which appear on an operating statement are cash items. One of the easier ways in which to visualize the cash flow concept is to relate it to the computation of savings for evaluating investment proposals.

The objective in evaluating investment proposals is to determine how much money—if any—the firm will save by buying the proposed equipment. In drawing cost comparisons between present equipment and proposed equipment, include all pertinent costs, such as initial cost, operating cost, salvage value, interest, depreciation, maintenance, space, power, taxes, insurance, and labor. Below is explained one method for determining these costs.

Operating Costs

Determine the annual savings in operating costs by comparing those costs that differ from the present and the proposed equipment. If overhead, for example, is the same for both pieces of equipment, exclude it as a factor in determining annual cost savings. However, if the new machinery would produce the required number of items faster, this fact would have a bearing on labor, maintenance, and power.

The comparison of different operating costs might yield a list such as this:

	Present	Proposed
Direct labor	$ 6,000	$4,000
Indirect labor	3,000	2,000
Set-up time	500	250
Maintenance	1,600	400
Power	400	1,600
Taxes and insurance	200	1,200
Total Annual Operating Expenses	$11,700	$9,450

The comparison shows an annual operating saving of $2,250 for the proposed investment over the existing facility. This appears to indicate that the proposed investment is sound. However, before giving the "go-ahead," the finance officer must consider certain other costs, such as interest and depreciation.

THE CASH FLOW CONCEPT

Once operating savings are determined, the interest associated with different financing arrangements appears to be the other cost to consider. If, however, a few assumptions are made, the value of the project can be kept separate from the method of financing. The merit of the project, particularly small and medium-sized ones, should not be confused with the financial arrangements which have been offered. For example, if a company requires a 10% return after taxes, an 8% before-tax interest rate on a chattel mortgage would make a particular project look even more profitable than the operating savings indicate. The mathematics of the return on investment computations are such that the difference between 10% return and 8% times ½ for taxes (or 4%) are credited to the project as added income. When the time comes to purchase the equipment, the cash required may come from a 5¾% bond issue which is being issued. Thus the question 8% vs. 5¾% is an arbitrary one. It is better to assume cash payment and concentrate on the dollar savings from operations. There is an important side effect of this method. Leasing is a method of not paying cash for an asset, but instead, paying for it over a period of time plus interest charges. Thus lease proposals cannot be considered in the same way as explained above. Since tax implications may be present, a different type of evaluation is needed.

Depreciation

Another cost element that the finance officer must compare for alternative investment proposals is depreciation. The Internal Revenue Service approves several methods of determining allowable depreciation. The most common are the straight-line method, the double-declining-balance method, and the sum-of-the-year's-digits method.

If the useful life of the proposed equipment is ten years, and the estimated salvage value is 10%, a sample calculation can be shown as follows. In using the straight-line method, financial accounting depreciates the cost of the asset, less its estimated salvage value, in equal annual installments over the asset's estimated useful life. The annual allowable depreciation of a $10,-000 piece of equipment would be $900, determined this way:

$$\frac{\$10,000 - \$1,000}{10 \text{ years}} = \$900 \text{ per year}$$

The finance officer is also concerned with the depreciation charges on present equipment to determine how they compare with charges on proposed equipment. The depreciation charges on present equipment come from depreciation and fixed asset records. For illustration, suppose that the existing asset had an eight year useful life, with a purchase price of $6,500 and a salvage value of $500. This means that the annual rate of depreciation is $750 ($6,000 divided by 8 years), yielding this comparison:

	Present	Proposed
Annual Operating Expenses	$11,700	$ 9,450
Depreciation	750	900
	$12,450	$10,350

The proposed investment offers a potential annual cost saving on the books of $2,000 over the present facility. The saving may not be enough to justify making the capital expenditure. The decision for or against the investment proposal may be decisively influenced by answers to these questions:

1. What are the chances of improved equipment coming into the market before the investment pays for itself?

2. What is the advantage of acquiring equipment with a greater capacity than the business now requires?
3. Will new products likely require new machines or processes?
4. What effect will each of the alternatives have on employment levels?
5. Which of the alternatives is more flexible, more adaptable to different types of work?
6. How do alternatives compare from the standpoint of reliability and safety?

Depreciation Under the Cash Flow Concept

The difference in depreciation between before buying and after buying is a noncash expense. Every year after the purchase the added depreciation shows an additional expense on the tax return and will reduce taxes by one-half the difference. This assumes an income tax rate of 50%. This cash reduction of income taxes is a direct benefit of investing in the new asset. To arrive at the total after-tax cash return per year, the example shown above would appear as follows:

	Before Taxes	Cash Flow After Taxes
Operating Savings	$2,250	$1,125
Depreciation Increase	150	75
Total Annual Cash Benefit		$1,200

THE PAYBACK METHOD OF INVESTMENT EVALUATION

The payback method compares the amount of the investment with annual cost savings. Finance divides the annual cost savings into the total investment to find the payoff for investment recovery period. For example, if the annual cost saving is $5,000 and the investment is $10,000, the payback period is two years. The payback period test is not especially valid except for firms with a policy of investing only in assets with a relatively short investment recovery period. Even then, the payback test is not a wholly accurate indicator of investment merit. Finance can figure annual cost savings in many ways other than the method just discussed and because finance can also look at the total investment in a number of ways, payback often runs a poor second. Some firms consider the total investment while others consider only the equity portion in evaluating capital expenditure proposals. Some firms consider the entire annual cost savings and others consider the annual cost savings after taxes, after taxes and depreciation, or after taxes, depreciation, and interest. Some companies, instead of taking only *initial* operating advantage, project an average cost savings over the total life of the asset. But, as a rule of thumb device, the payback test is reasonably accurate. It enables financial management to evaluate the probable investment recovery period against the desired investment recovery period.

Deficiencies of the Method

To the academicians the deficiencies associated with this method are very openly known and the method has been decried in financial literature for years. Basically they are:

   a. Payback calculations ignore cash flows which may come in from a project after the end of the evaluation period for payback purposes. It almost assumes that the life of the project will cease once payback has been achieved.
   b. The pattern of cash flows coming in is immaterial in the payback calculation. If heavier cash flows come in, in initial years, payback treats those cash flows in much the same manner as it would treat cash flows which come in heavier in later periods of time. Obviously, under the present value concept, cash flows which come in earlier are worth more to an investment evaluation since money will be initially available for alternative investment opportunities.
   c. Payback seems to place unwarranted importance on the liquid values generated by a project and tends to bypass somewhat the aspect of profitability of an individual project. This particular point will be discussed immediately following and I do not agree that the emphasis on liquidity is necessarily a bad thing.

Relevance of the Method

In a recent article, Alexander Robichek wrote about capital budgeting and said that the practicing financial executive will find payback of little value when attempting to relate financial decisions directly to corporate objectives. I do not necessarily agree with this contention since I feel that the emphasis in his observations relies heavily on disparaging the element of liquidity in payback operations. The fact that two-thirds of American companies that use quantitative investment evaluation techniques still use payback, to me, indicates that there is relevance to this type of approach. In fact, payback itself does not really ignore the profitability of a project since, as we will discuss later, the reciprocal of the payback expressed in terms of a percentage will roughly approximate the return on investment for any given project. Liquidity is an all-important aspect of investment evaluation. In this day and age, it is even more important than it had been during the boom period of the decade of the late sixties. In some instances it is even more important than the element of profitability or return on investment. In a sense, if one accepts the dictum that "time is money," then more time means more risk. The risk that we speak of is the risk of depreciation of money over a longer period of time. Therefore, the shorter period of time in which the funds for a given investment project are outstanding, the more the risk exists that such monies may, in fact, bring worthless returns into the company. Therefore, I feel that it is only pragmatic to use a rule of reason and accept payback as a valid method for practicing professionals to evaluate investment criteria.

RETURN ON INVESTMENT CALCULATION

Many companies still use the regular return on investment method for evaluating investment alternatives. In past times this method has used calculations which might take any one of two forms:

    a. The return on the original investment
    b. The return on an average investment

In (b) above, the investment itself incurs regular depreciation over its life and therefore, the average investment is considered to be one-half of the total amount of the outlay. The actual calculation itself takes either of the following forms: for (a) above, the formula reads as follows:

$$\text{(a)} \quad \text{Return} = \frac{\text{Annual Earnings} - \dfrac{\text{Investment}}{\text{the Estimated Life}}}{\text{Investment}}$$

for (b), above:

$$\text{(b)} \quad \text{Return} = \frac{\text{Annual Income} - \dfrac{\text{Investment}}{\text{Estimated Life}}}{\dfrac{\text{Investment}}{2}}$$

The only basic difference between answers given by the formulas for either (a) or (b) is that the return on investment calculated under the average investment would be exactly double that of the return on original investment which is contained in (a) above. Some large companies still use this method to evaluate capital projects.

An example of the pitfalls of using this type of method can be seen in the following example where three projects each have the same basic features, but where the cash flows differ in terms of timing.

	Project A	Project B	Project C
Investment	$100,000	$100,000	$100,000
Life	10 yrs.	10 yrs.	10 yrs.
Income:			
Years 1 to 3	30,000	20,000	10,000
4 to 7	20,000	20,000	20,000
8 to 10	10,000	20,000	30,000
Total	200,000	200,000	200,000
Return on original investment	10%	10%	10%
Return on average investment	20%	20%	20%

The Prudent Investor

Under the present value system, the prudent investor would chose project (a), since the cash flows coming in from the project are heavier in earlier years and, therefore, are available for reinvestment in alternative opportunities. Using the average method, though, if one is not attuned to using the present value approach, each of the three alternative projects produces the same return on investment calculations and can lead to a faulty decision. The return on investment, if it is not weighted by time value of money, does not recognize the differing patterns of cash flows and consequently ignores the worth of current dollars. It is, however, a technique which can be easily understood within the context of the generally difficult to comprehend concepts of return on investment. Further, a cash-rich company or one which is not constantly subjected to the pressures of outside financing for investment decisions, might be more prone to utilize the return on investment technique not using the present value concepts since they would be less affected by the apparent concern for alternative investment opportunities. The great virtue of the technique is that the reported income, synonymous with the description of "return," is an accounting oriented concept and can be readily understood by operating executives who are used to viewing an operating statement. There is, however, a basic flaw, in that it can result in an incorrect decision if alternative investment opportunities are available and capital rationing is present. The simple fact that it ignores the time value of money and the pattern of cash flows can in many instances be a fatal flaw.

THE CONCEPT OF PRESENT VALUE

It is a truism that the more distant cash inflows are, the lower the present value of that same income. The two techniques described earlier have the same common defect that they compare cash flow in the future with a current investment without regard to the fact of the timing of the cash flows. There is no question, as it was alluded to earlier, that $621 today which could be invested at 10% is worth $100 more than $900 five years from now. In a nutshell, future cash flows are only comparable with current investments if the cash flows are discounted to their present value. Normally, the actual calculation of the present value need not be an extremely complex problem of calculation. Literally, only one part of the equation usually requires discounting, that of the cash flows. The only time that the investment side of the calculation might require discounting occurs when the investment might be spread over a period of future years. In those more common instances where the investment is a current one and largely will be made throughout the course of the initial year, it need not be necessary to apply any discounting factors since the effect, if any, of a discount factor covering the average over the period of the year would be negligible when compared to a discount factor covering only the end of the year.

Future Inflows of Cash

Future inflows of cash, however, should be discounted to the year in which the *first* investment is made, so that all payments and receipts will have a comparable value date referred to in the tables usually as year zero.

This concept can be developed a little further if one were to consider a series of future payments which would be spread over a ten-year period. Assume that $1,000 will be received annually over the next ten years. The present value of that $1,000 at 4% would calculate as follows:

After	1 year	$ 962
	2 years	925
	3 years	889
	4 years	855
	5 years	822
	6 years	790
	7 years	760
	8 years	731
	9 years	703
	10 years	676
		$8,113

The implication in the above calculation is that, if $1,000 were deposited annually, it would be equivalent to $8,113 deposited now and earning 4%. The discounted cash flow calculation will be doing the reverse of this particular calculation and taking the series of future cash flows and discounting them back to present value. Assume the same numbers as above, but transpose the input so that it reflects an operating problem. If, as a result of a capital project, for example, annual costs savings of $1,000 were generated over the next ten years, the future inflow would be equivalent to $8,113 today. The logic of this type of calculation would permit the $8,113 to be compared to the investment outlay for the project. In other words, if the project costs $9,000, one might say that the investment might not be worth the cost, since the future cash flows are worth less than the current outlay. Conversely, if that same investment could be accomplished for $5,000, then there is obviously an excess of present value resulting from future cash flows over the current outlay for the project. In the above example, the investment costing $8,113 earns an annual income of $1,000 for ten years. The rate of return, therefore, for that project is 4%. This implies that the future cash flows will be sufficient to repay the original investment and in addition, to provide a 4% return on the capital outstanding during the estimated life.

In a simplistic fashion, note the following input for a simplified problem:

Cost of investment		$1,000
Estimated life of project		3 years
Estimated income:		
Year 1	$400	
Year 2	500	
Year 3	600	$1,500

Determining the Rate of Return

The nub of the problem is to determine the rate of interest which will equate the present value of future income with the current cost of the investment and this basic calculation is at the heart of all discounted cash flow calculations. Essentially the rate will be obtained by a trial and error method. However, there are mathematical formulas available which will shorten the probing required to determine the rough parameters of percentages. Just as a howitzer expert will attempt to bracket a target, the analyst will apply much the same technique in order to establish the rate of return. In this particular case, the rate of return lies between 20% and 22%, using the following tables:

Income		20%		22%	
		Present Value	Dollars	Present Value	Dollars
Year 1	$400	.833	333	.820	328
Year 2	$500	.694	347	.672	336
Year 3	$600	.597	347	.551	330
			1,027		994

Simple interpolation between the percentages will show that the true answer to the problem is 21.6%. 21.6% represents the rate of return for the project. The calculation above shows that interest, which is equivalent to the rate of return (21.6%) is the interest earned on the outstanding balance of the investment. It diminishes to zero at the end of the life of the project and is not based on the original investment throughout the life of the project.

This technique permits a simple ranking of projects by their elemental profitability and avoids the difficulty of setting or justifying an external discount rate such as the cost of borrowing money. In practice, there is only one valid academic argument against the use of this type of approach to evaluating investment proposals. Under *very rare* circumstances utilizing a discounted cash flow type of calculation can result in a situation where either of two rates of return will give the correct answer for any one problem. This rare type of situation develops when there may be a sequence of positive cash flows followed by negative cash flows, followed by positive cash flows, etc. Under this rare type of statistical circumstance, two answers may be correct for the one problem. At best though, this type of argument is a very weak point at which to probe any softness in the technique. The advantages of this type of financial method for calculating the return on investment are formidable and can be summed as follows:

a. The rates of return which are calculated, are based on the capital which is actually invested throughout the life of the project. The earlier mentioned techniques (payback and average return) only give an approximation of the return.

b. Allowances are made for the differing patterns of timing or cash flow. In other words, using this technique distinguishes between investments which have high initial cash flows or low initial cash flows, or uniform cash flows. It gives the greatest emphasis on those projects earning initially higher cash flows.

c. The results of the calculation are readily comparable with calculations of the cost of capital. For those readers interested in the subject of the cost of capital, I would refer them to another booklet in the series, *Practical Use of the Cost of Capital Method*. However, direct comparisons can be made between the project to be evaluated and the costs of borrowing money or the cost of capital, or whatever acceptability criterion exists for the company.

d. The technique used to effect the calculation forces planners to comprehensively study the details of a project in order to provide the differing elements which are required to complete the input.

EVALUATING RETURN ON CAPITAL INVESTMENTS

The ability to achieve an adequate return on capital investments substantially determines management success. Financial management must never commit funds for plant or equipment before conducting tests for profitability. Here are several useful tests for assessing the investment merits of capital projects.

Production Savings Method

The production savings method reveals how many years it will take for a project to earn enough to return the original investment. In using this method, the financial analyst must know the amount of time the equipment is in use, the time savings per production operation, and the cost of operating the equipment. This information enables him to learn how long it will take a new asset to pay for itself through increased efficiency and lower operating costs, as this example illustrates:

Time per operation with present equipment	30 minutes
Time per operation with proposed equipment	12 minutes
Potential time savings per operation	18 minutes
Potential percentage of time savings	60 percent
Approximate usage rate of equipment	30 percent
Daily operating cost (255 days per year)	$55.00
Cost of proposed investment	$10,000

60 percent savings × 30 percent use × $55.00 × 255 days = $2,524.
$10,000 (cost of machine) divided by $2,524 = 3.96 years.

The proposed investment—if made—will pay for itself in slightly less than four years.

Without considering the usage rate, the asset would pay for itself in about one year. But when an asset is idle, it is theoretically not returning any of the investment. The production savings method does not take taxes and depreciation into account. It is valid only in determining actual production savings as a return on the capital required to purchase the asset.

Discounted Cash Flow Computation

The profitability index method—also known as the *discounted cash flow method* and the *present worth method*—shows the rate of return on the investment. This is the rate at which a firm would have to invest the capital required to purchase an asset to equal the rate of return on the proposed investment.

To use the profitability index (PI) you must know these facts:

1. Total investment expenditure and its time shedule
2. Annual cost savings
3. The asset's useful life
4. Annual depreciation allowance
5. Anticipated income tax rates on profits

Applying the Profitability Index

Assume that a firm plans to invest $1,000 in a new piece of equipment that is expected to provide savings of $400 per year. The asset's useful life is five years, after which it will be scrapped with no salvage value. To simplify the example, assume that taxes will take 50 percent of the annual profits, and that savings represent profits.

Using this data, you can figure the rate of return, or profitability index, with the help of the PI worksheet in Figure 1, by taking these steps:

1. Compute net profit (receipts less taxes but before depreciation).

Savings	Depreciation Deduction (20%) Straight-Line Method	Net Taxable Income	50% Income Tax	Net Profit
$400	$200	$200	$100	$300

Net profits for the $1,000 machine providing annual savings of $400 amount to $300. (Savings of $400 minus income tax of $100.) Enter this figure for each year of the machine's useful life on the PI worksheet.

2. At "zero time" in column 1 of the worksheet, enter the figure $1,000, the capital outlay required. (Zero time represents the time of the purchase.)
3. Using the worksheet, now find the total of disbursements in column 1 ($1,000) and net profit ($1,500), and calculate the ratio of net profits to disbursements (1.5).
4. Repeat the steps for disbursements and net profit in columns 2, 3, 4, and 5, multiplying the figures in column 1 by the discount factor for each year. This procedure gives "present value."
5. Using the graph in Figure 1, plot the ratios against the trial interest rates and connect the points with a smooth curve. The PI is the point where the

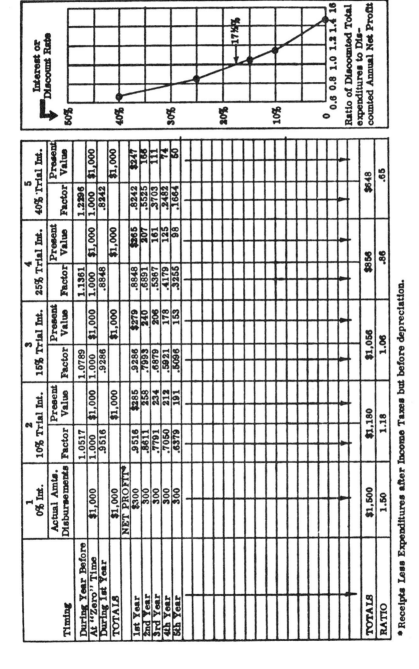

Timing	1 0% Int. Actual Amts. Disbursements	2 10% Trial Int. Factor	Present Value	3 15% Trial Int. Factor	Present Value	4 25% Trial Int. Factor	Present Value	5 40% Trial Int. Factor	Present Value
During Year Before		1.0517		1.0789		1.1361		1.2296	
At "Zero" Time	$1,000	1.000	$1,000	1.000	$1,000	1.000	$1,000	1.000	$1,000
During 1st Year		.9516		.9286		.8848		.8242	
TOTALS	$1,000		$1,000		$1,000		$1,000		$1,000
NET PROFIT*									
1st Year	$300	.9516	$285	.9286	$279	.8848	$265	.8242	$247
2nd Year	300	.8611	258	.7993	240	.6891	207	.5525	166
3rd Year	300	.7791	234	.6879	206	.5367	161	.3703	111
4th Year	300	.7050	212	.5921	178	.4179	125	.2482	74
5th Year	300	.6379	191	.5096	153	.3255	98	.1664	50
TOTALS	$1,500		$1,180		$1,056		$856		$648
RATIO	1.50		1.18		1.06		.86		.65

*Receipts Less Expenditures after Income Taxes but before depreciation.

Figure 1
Profitability Index Worksheet

263

curve intersects the heavy 1.0 ratio line. For this particular investment, the PI is 17.5 percent.

Significance of the Profitability Index Findings

The PI of 17.5 percent indicates that the proposed investment would be worth as much as investing $1,000 at 17.5 percent compound interest for five years. Given the opportunity to invest $1,000 in such a way, *it is presently worth more than $1,000*. To find the present worth of the $1,000 to be invested in the new asset, use this formula:

$$S = P(1 \times i)^n$$

Where: S = sum of money in the future
   i = interest rate
   n = number of years
   P = present amount of money

Completing the formula we show that $1,000 invested at 17.5 percent compound interest is worth $2,336 five years later. Stated differently, $2,336 five years from now has a present worth of $1,000. All the finance officer does is to figure the future value of a certain amount of today's money invested in a certain way. In our example, $1 today will be worth $2.336 in five years. In other words, that dollar actually has a potential worth of $2.336. If not invested, of course, the dollar will still be worth $1.00 five years from now.

Figure 2 shows a tabulation of discount factors for $1 received once in some future year. The year is shown in the vertical column on the far left. For each discount rate the "value now of $1 then" is shown. For example, $1.00 received in ten years has a present value of $.82 if a 2% discount rate is used. That same dollar has a value of $.191 if an 18% rate is applied. Figure 3 has to do with a dollar received *every* year for a certain number of years. This a is stream of dollars in contrast to a single dollar in Figure 2. The factors shown are the "present value of one dollar received every year for a certain number of years." For example, one dollar received for two years at a 2% rate is now worth $1.94. At an 18% rate those same two dollars are now worth $1.566.

Figures 4 through 7 are examples of a worksheet for discounted cash flow calculations created for a large oil company. Note that the investment includes a provision for working capital requirements, a frequently overlooked aspect of cash outflows.

Figure 2
Present Value of $1

Years hence	1%	2%	4%	6%	8%	10%	12%	14%	15%	16%	18%	20%	22%	24%	25%	26%	28%	30%	35%	40%	45%	50%
1	.990	.980	.962	.943	.926	.909	.893	.877	.870	.862	.847	.833	.820	.806	.800	.794	.781	.769	.741	.714	.690	.667
2	.980	.961	.925	.890	.857	.826	.797	.769	.756	.743	.718	.694	.672	.650	.640	.630	.610	.592	.549	.510	.476	.444
3	.971	.942	.889	.840	.794	.751	.712	.675	.658	.641	.609	.579	.551	.524	.512	.500	.477	.455	.406	.364	.328	.296
4	.961	.924	.855	.792	.735	.683	.636	.592	.572	.552	.516	.482	.451	.423	.410	.397	.373	.350	.301	.260	.226	.198
5	.951	.906	.822	.747	.681	.621	.567	.519	.497	.476	.437	.402	.370	.341	.328	.315	.291	.269	.223	.186	.156	.132
6	.942	.888	.790	.705	.630	.564	.507	.456	.432	.410	.370	.335	.303	.275	.262	.250	.227	.207	.165	.133	.108	.088
7	.933	.871	.760	.665	.583	.513	.452	.400	.376	.354	.314	.279	.249	.222	.210	.198	.178	.159	.122	.095	.074	.059
8	.923	.853	.731	.627	.540	.467	.404	.351	.327	.305	.266	.233	.204	.179	.168	.157	.139	.123	.091	.068	.051	.039
9	.914	.837	.703	.592	.500	.424	.361	.308	.284	.263	.225	.194	.167	.144	.134	.125	.108	.094	.067	.048	.035	.026
10	.905	.820	.676	.558	.463	.386	.322	.270	.247	.227	.191	.162	.137	.116	.107	.099	.085	.073	.050	.035	.024	.017
11	.896	.804	.650	.527	.429	.350	.287	.237	.215	.195	.162	.135	.112	.094	.086	.079	.066	.056	.037	.025	.017	.012
12	.887	.788	.625	.497	.397	.319	.257	.208	.187	.168	.137	.112	.092	.076	.069	.062	.052	.043	.027	.018	.012	.008
13	.879	.773	.601	.469	.368	.290	.229	.182	.163	.145	.116	.093	.075	.061	.055	.050	.040	.033	.020	.013	.008	.005
14	.870	.758	.577	.442	.340	.263	.205	.160	.141	.125	.099	.078	.062	.049	.044	.039	.032	.025	.015	.009	.006	.003
15	.861	.743	.555	.417	.315	.239	.183	.140	.123	.108	.084	.065	.051	.040	.035	.031	.025	.020	.011	.006	.004	.002
16	.853	.728	.534	.394	.292	.218	.163	.123	.107	.093	.071	.054	.042	.032	.028	.025	.019	.015	.008	.005	.003	.002
17	.844	.714	.513	.371	.270	.198	.146	.108	.093	.080	.060	.045	.034	.026	.023	.020	.015	.012	.006	.003	.002	.001
18	.836	.700	.494	.350	.250	.180	.130	.095	.081	.069	.051	.038	.028	.021	.018	.016	.012	.009	.005	.002	.001	.001
19	.828	.686	.475	.331	.232	.164	.116	.083	.070	.060	.043	.031	.023	.017	.014	.012	.009	.007	.003	.002	.001	
20	.820	.673	.456	.312	.215	.149	.104	.073	.061	.051	.037	.026	.019	.014	.012	.010	.007	.005	.002	.001	.001	
21	.811	.660	.439	.294	.199	.135	.093	.064	.053	.044	.031	.022	.015	.011	.009	.008	.006	.004	.002	.001		
22	.803	.647	.422	.278	.184	.123	.083	.056	.046	.038	.026	.018	.013	.009	.007	.006	.004	.003	.001	.001		
23	.795	.634	.406	.262	.170	.112	.074	.049	.040	.033	.022	.015	.010	.007	.006	.005	.003	.002	.001			
24	.788	.622	.390	.247	.158	.102	.066	.043	.035	.028	.019	.013	.008	.006	.005	.004	.003	.002	.001			
25	.780	.610	.375	.233	.146	.092	.059	.038	.030	.024	.016	.010	.007	.005	.004	.003	.002	.001	.001			
26	.772	.598	.361	.220	.135	.084	.053	.033	.026	.021	.014	.009	.006	.004	.003	.002	.002	.001				
27	.764	.586	.347	.207	.125	.076	.047	.029	.023	.018	.011	.007	.005	.003	.002	.002	.001	.001				
28	.757	.574	.333	.196	.116	.069	.042	.026	.020	.016	.010	.006	.004	.002	.002	.001	.001	.001				
29	.749	.563	.321	.185	.107	.063	.037	.022	.017	.014	.008	.005	.003	.002	.002	.001	.001	.001				
30	.742	.552	.308	.174	.099	.057	.033	.020	.015	.012	.007	.004	.003	.002	.001	.001	.001					
40	.672	.453	.208	.097	.046	.022	.011	.005	.004	.003	.001	.001										
50	.608	.372	.141	.054	.021	.009	.003	.001	.001	.001												

265

Years (N)	1%	2%	4%	6%	8%	10%	12%	14%	15%	16%	18%	20%	22%	24%	25%	26%	28%	30%	35%	40%	45%	50%
1	.990	.980	.962	.943	.926	.909	.893	.877	.870	.862	.847	.833	.820	.806	.800	.794	.781	.769	.741	.714	.690	.667
2	1.970	1.942	1.886	1.833	1.783	1.736	1.690	1.647	1.626	1.605	1.566	1.528	1.492	1.457	1.440	1.424	1.392	1.361	1.289	1.224	1.165	1.111
3	2.941	2.884	2.775	2.673	2.577	2.487	2.402	2.322	2.283	2.246	2.174	2.106	2.042	1.981	1.952	1.923	1.868	1.816	1.696	1.589	1.493	1.407
4	3.902	3.808	3.630	3.465	3.312	3.170	3.037	2.914	2.855	2.798	2.690	2.589	2.494	2.404	2.362	2.320	2.241	2.166	1.997	1.849	1.720	1.605
5	4.853	4.713	4.452	4.212	3.993	3.791	3.605	3.433	3.353	3.274	3.127	2.991	2.864	2.745	2.689	2.635	2.532	2.436	2.220	2.035	1.876	1.737
6	5.795	5.601	5.242	4.917	4.623	4.355	4.111	3.889	3.784	3.685	3.498	3.326	3.167	3.020	2.951	2.885	2.759	2.643	2.385	2.168	1.983	1.824
7	6.728	6.472	6.002	5.582	5.206	4.868	4.564	4.288	4.160	4.039	3.812	3.605	3.416	3.242	3.161	3.083	2.937	2.802	2.508	2.263	2.057	1.883
8	7.652	7.325	6.733	6.210	5.747	5.335	4.968	4.639	4.487	4.344	4.078	3.837	3.619	3.421	3.329	3.241	3.076	2.925	2.598	2.331	2.108	1.922
9	8.566	8.162	7.435	6.802	6.247	5.759	5.328	4.946	4.772	4.607	4.303	4.031	3.786	3.566	3.463	3.366	3.184	3.019	2.665	2.379	2.144	1.948
10	9.471	8.983	8.111	7.360	6.710	6.145	5.650	5.216	5.019	4.833	4.494	4.192	3.923	3.682	3.571	3.465	3.269	3.092	2.715	2.414	2.168	1.965
11	10.368	9.787	8.760	7.887	7.139	6.495	5.938	5.453	5.234	5.029	4.656	4.327	4.035	3.776	3.656	3.544	3.335	3.147	2.752	2.438	2.185	1.977
12	11.255	10.575	9.385	8.384	7.536	6.814	6.194	5.660	5.421	5.197	4.793	4.439	4.127	3.851	3.725	3.606	3.387	3.190	2.779	2.456	2.196	1.985
13	12.134	11.348	9.986	8.853	7.904	7.103	6.424	5.842	5.583	5.342	4.910	4.533	4.203	3.912	3.780	3.656	3.427	3.223	2.799	2.468	2.204	1.990
14	13.004	12.106	10.563	9.295	8.244	7.367	6.628	6.002	5.724	5.468	5.008	4.611	4.265	3.962	3.824	3.695	3.459	3.249	2.814	2.477	2.210	1.993
15	13.865	12.849	11.118	9.712	8.559	7.606	6.811	6.142	5.847	5.575	5.092	4.675	4.315	4.001	3.859	3.726	3.483	3.268	2.825	2.484	2.214	1.995
16	14.718	13.578	11.652	10.106	8.851	7.824	6.974	6.265	5.954	5.669	5.162	4.730	4.357	4.033	3.887	3.751	3.503	3.283	2.834	2.489	2.216	1.997
17	15.562	14.292	12.166	10.477	9.122	8.022	7.120	6.373	6.047	5.749	5.222	4.775	4.391	4.059	3.910	3.771	3.518	3.295	2.840	2.492	2.218	1.998
18	16.398	14.992	12.659	10.828	9.372	8.201	7.250	6.467	6.128	5.818	5.273	4.812	4.419	4.080	3.928	3.786	3.529	3.304	2.844	2.494	2.219	1.999
19	17.226	15.678	13.134	11.158	9.604	8.365	7.366	6.550	6.198	5.877	5.316	4.844	4.442	4.097	3.942	3.799	3.539	3.311	2.848	2.496	2.220	1.999
20	18.046	16.351	13.590	11.470	9.818	8.514	7.469	6.623	6.259	5.929	5.353	4.870	4.460	4.110	3.954	3.808	3.546	3.316	2.850	2.497	2.221	1.999
21	18.857	17.011	14.029	11.764	10.017	8.649	7.562	6.687	6.312	5.973	5.384	4.891	4.476	4.121	3.963	3.816	3.551	3.320	2.852	2.498	2.221	2.000
22	19.660	17.658	14.451	12.042	10.201	8.772	7.645	6.743	6.359	6.011	5.410	4.909	4.488	4.130	3.970	3.822	3.556	3.323	2.853	2.498	2.222	2.000
23	20.456	18.292	14.857	12.303	10.371	8.883	7.718	6.792	6.399	6.044	5.432	4.925	4.499	4.137	3.976	3.827	3.559	3.325	2.854	2.499	2.222	2.000
24	21.243	18.914	15.247	12.550	10.529	8.985	7.784	6.835	6.434	6.073	5.451	4.937	4.507	4.143	3.981	3.831	3.562	3.327	2.855	2.499	2.222	2.000
25	22.023	19.523	15.622	12.783	10.675	9.077	7.843	6.873	6.464	6.097	5.467	4.948	4.514	4.147	3.985	3.834	3.564	3.329	2.856	2.499	2.222	2.000
26	22.795	20.121	15.983	13.003	10.810	9.161	7.896	6.906	6.491	6.118	5.480	4.956	4.520	4.151	3.988	3.837	3.566	3.330	2.856	2.500	2.222	2.000
27	23.560	20.707	16.330	13.211	10.935	9.237	7.943	6.935	6.514	6.136	5.492	4.964	4.524	4.154	3.990	3.839	3.567	3.331	2.856	2.500	2.222	2.000
28	24.316	21.281	16.663	13.406	11.051	9.307	7.984	6.961	6.534	6.152	5.502	4.970	4.528	4.157	3.992	3.840	3.568	3.331	2.857	2.500	2.222	2.000
29	25.066	21.844	16.984	13.591	11.158	9.370	8.022	6.983	6.551	6.166	5.510	4.975	4.531	4.159	3.994	3.841	3.569	3.332	2.857	2.500	2.222	2.000
30	25.808	22.396	17.292	13.765	11.258	9.427	8.055	7.003	6.566	6.177	5.517	4.979	4.534	4.160	3.995	3.842	3.569	3.332	2.857	2.500	2.222	2.000
40	32.835	27.355	19.793	15.046	11.925	9.779	8.244	7.105	6.642	6.234	5.548	4.997	4.544	4.166	3.999	3.846	3.571	3.333	2.857	2.500	2.222	2.000
50	39.196	31.424	21.482	15.762	12.234	9.915	8.304	7.133	6.661	6.246	5.554	4.999	4.545	4.167	4.000	3.846	3.571	3.333	2.857	2.500	2.222	2.000

Figure 3

Present Value of $1 Received Annually for N Years

Illustrative Problem

   Assume that $10 million is available for investment purposes and that it is desirable to achieve a 15 percent rate of return on any investment made with the funds. An opportunity is found to invest the funds over a 20-year period. It is further probable that at the end of that period, the investment will have a residual value of $2 million. Using discounted cash flow techniques, the solution to the problem would be as follows:

Solution

Present Value Calculation
(000's)

		Present Value
Investment	$10,000	$10,000

Year	Uniform Cash Flow	15% Factor	$ Amount
1	$1,578	.870	$ 1,373
2		.756	1,193
3		.658	1,038
4		.572	903
5		.497	784
6		.432	682
7		.376	593
8		.327	516
9		.284	448
10		.247	390
11		.215	339
12		.187	295
13		.163	257
14		.141	223
15		.123	194
16		.107	169
17		.093	147
18		.081	128
19		.070	110
20	1,578	.061	96
20% Salvage Value 20	2,000	.061	122
		Total Present Value	$10,000

   Note that the residual value of $2 million though recovered in the twentieth year is a cash flow so far into the future that in terms of present value at 15%, it is worth a mere $122 thousand today. The converse logic says that if the investor had available today $122 thousand to invest at 15%, it would total to $2 million twenty years from now.

ESTIMATED CASH EXPENDITURES* (IN THOUSANDS OF DOLLARS)

WORKSHEET I

(RE: ON STREAM)	INITIAL EXPENDITURES** 19__ -3	19__ -2	19__ -1	19__ 1	TOTAL	FUTURE EXPENDITURES** 19__	19__	TOTAL
CAPITAL COST								
1. Process Units								
2. Utilities								
3. Auxiliaries								
4. Buildings & Other								
5. Land								
6. Base Estimate								
7. Contingency								
8. SUB-TOTAL CAPITAL COST								
EXPENSE:								
9. Site Preparation								
10. Plant Change								
11. Other								
12. SUB-TOTAL EXPENSE								
WORKING CAPITAL:								
13. Cash on Hand and in Banks								
14. Accounts Receivable								
15. Stores Materials & Supplies								
16. Raw Materials Inventory								
17. W.I.P. Inventory								
18. Finished Material Inventory								
19. Other								
20. SUB-TOTAL WORKING CAPITAL								
21. GRAND TOTAL								

*Supported by detailed engineering estimates.
**Timing of expenditures is based on actual outlay; assumes dollars of constant purchasing (i.e., no inflation).

Figure 4

WORKSHEET II

DEPRECIATION FOR TAX PURPOSES (IN THOUSANDS OF DOLLARS)

CALENDAR YEAR	ANNUAL PERIOD (RE: ON STREAM)	Expense 100%	Process Units —— Yr. Life	Utilities —— Yr. Life	Auxiliaries —— Yr. Life	Buildings & Other —— Yr. Life	—— Yr. Life	FUTURE REQUIREMENTS —— Yr. Life	—— Yr. Life	TOTAL INCOME TAX DEDUCTION
			DEPRECIATION OF INDIVIDUAL ASSET GROUPS BY					METHOD		
19__	-3	$	$	$	$	$	$	$	$	$
19__	-2									
19__	-1									
19__	1									
19__	2									
19__	3									
19__	4									
19__	5									
19__	6									
19__	7									
19__	8									
19__	9									
19__	10									
19__	11									
19__	12									
19__	13									
19__	14									
19__	15									
19__	16									
19__	17									
19__	18									
19__	19									
19__	20									
19__	21									
19__	22									
19__	23									
19__	24									
19__	25									
19__	26									
19__	27									
19__	28									
19__	29									
19__	30									
	TOTAL									

Figure 5

WORKSHEET III

TIME SCHEDULE OF CASH EXPENDITURES AND CASH INCOME (IN THOUSANDS OF DOLLARS)

			EXPENDITURES				
CAL. YEAR	ANNUAL PERIOD (RE: ON STREAM)		CAPITAL COST		EXPENSE	WORKING CAPITAL	TOTAL
			Land	Facilities			
19___	-3	AT START					
		DURING					
19___	-2	AT START					
		DURING					
19___	-1	AT START					
		DURING					
FUTURE 19___		AT START					
		DURING					
19___		AT START					
		DURING					
TOTAL							

				INCOME				
CAL. YEAR	ANNUAL PERIOD	GROSS INCOME	DIRECT EXP. & OVERHEADS	CASH INCOME BEFORE TAX	DEPRECIATION (WORKSHEET II)	INCOME TAXES	NET INCOME AFTER TAX	CASH INCOME AFTER TAX
19___	-3							
19___	-2							
19___	-1							
19___	1							
19___	2							
19___	3							
19___	4							
19___	5							
19___	6							
19___	7							
19___	8							
19___	9							
19___	10							
19___	11							
19___	12							
19___	13							
19___	14							
19___	15							
19___	16							
19___	17							
19___	18							
19___	19							
19___	20							
19___	21							
19___	22							
19___	23							
19___	24							
19___	25							
TOTAL								

Figure 6

270

WORKSHEET IV
TRIAL CALCULATIONS OF RATE OF RETURN (EFFECTIVE RATE)
(TIME ZERO ASSUMED TO BE POINT AT WHICH EXPENDITURES ARE FIRST MADE)

TIMING			UNDISCOUNTED (WORKSHEET III)		TRAIL 10% RATE			TRIAL 15% RATE		
CAL. YEAR	ANNUAL PERIOD		CASH-OUT	CASH-IN	FACTOR	PRESENT VALUE		FACTOR	PRESENT VALUE	
						CASH-OUT	CASH-IN		CASH-OUT	CASH-IN
19__	1	AT START DURING			1.000 .954			1.000 .933		
19__	2	AT START DURING			.909 .867			.870 .812		
19__	3	AT START DURING			.826 .788			.756 .706		
19__	4	AT START DURING			.751 .717			.658 .614		
19__	5	AT START DURING			.683 .651			.572 .534		
19__	6	DURING			.592			.464		
19__	7	DURING			.538			.403		
19__	8	DURING			.489			.351		
19__	9	DURING			.445			.305		
19__	10	DURING			.405			.265		
19	11	DURING			.368			.231		
19__	12	DURING			.334			.201		
19__	13	DURING			.304			.174		
19__	14	DURING			.276			.152		
19__	15	DURING			.251			.132		
19__	16	DURING			.228			.115		
19__	17	DURING			.208			.100		
19__	18	DURING			.189			.087		
19__	19	DURING			.172			.075		
19__	20	DURING			.156			.066		
19__	21	DURING			.142			.057		
19__	22	DURING			.129			.050		
19__	23	DURING			.117			.043		
19__	24	DURING			.107			.037		
19__	25	DURING			.097			.033		
19__	26	DURING			.088			.028		
19__	27	DURING			.080			.025		
19__	28	DURING			.073			.021		
19__	29	DURING			.066			.019		
19__	30	DURING			.060			.016		
19__	31	DURING			.055			.014		
19__	32	DURING			.050			.012		
19__	33	DURING			.045			.011		
19__	34	DURING			.041			.009		
19__	35	DURING			.037			.008		
		TOTAL								

RATIO: CASH-OUT ÷ CASH-IN

Figure 7

TRIAL 20% RATE			TRIAL 30% RATE			TRIAL 50% RATE		
	PRESENT VALUE			PRESENT VALUE			PRESENT VALUE	
FACTOR	CASH-OUT	CASH-IN	FACTOR	CASH-OUT	CASH-IN	FACTOR	CASH-OUT	CASH-IN
1.000			1.000			1.000		
.914			.880			.822		
.833			.769			.667		
.762			.677			.548		
.694			.592			.444		
.635			.520			.365		
.579			.455			.296		
.529			.400			.244		
.482			.350			.198		
.441			.308			.162		
.367			.237			.108		
.306			.182			.072		
.255			.140			.048		
.213			.108			.032		
.177			.083			.021		
.148			.064			.014		
.123			.049			.010		
.103			.038			.006		
.085			.029			.004		
.071			.022			.003		
.059			.017			.002		
.049			.013			.001		
.041			.010			.001		
.034			.008			.001		
.029			.006			−		
.024			.005			−		
.020			.004			−		
.017			.003			−		
.014			.002			−		
.012			.002			−		
.010			.001			−		
.008			.001			−		
.007			.001			−		
.006			.001			−		
.005			−			−		
.004			−			−		
.003			−			−		
.003			−			−		
.002			−			−		
.002			−			−		

Figure 7—Continued

272

8

NEW EFFECTIVENESS FOR CONTROLLERS: RELEVANT COSTS AND MARKETING ANALYSIS

INTRODUCTION

The profession of finance is in danger of being drowned by its own rigidities. The profession has made a point of concentrating its efforts on the reporting function. However, in interpreting the problems of reporting, the profession seems to give the heaviest weight to those problems which deal with how best to report yesterday's results. The most prestigious accounting firms are now engaged in a searching effort to look at themselves inwardly and to discern those accounting practices which have given rise to the tremor of discontent on the part of the investing public and professional securities advisors. Inevitably then, the efforts are directed toward the proper element of corporate reporting to stockholders. Questions such as the proper reporting of investment tax credits, long-term leases, goodwill, mergers and acquisitions have occupied the minds of the professional financial people. What has been lost in the shuffle and continues to be lost is the completely overlooked area of *internal* corporate reporting which is designed to assist the management of companies in making interim, impact decisions. These decisions are those which are vital to the daily conduct of business and reflect deeply on the ability of the decision maker to influence the daily course of operations through his understanding of the variables which are contained within the framework of the problem. Regretfully, finance has almost always ignored this aspect of reporting.

THE MARKETING CONTROLLER CONCEPT

It is the rare marketing decision that does not result somehow in a financial equation. In turn, that decision will ultimately lead to a dollar sign. Marketing is the area to focus upon for decision making because in reality it is the reason for existence of any company. No company can truly claim to be in business for the purpose of making products; rather they are in business for the purpose of selling products. Marketing is the total purpose of a business enterprise. As such, it transcends its usual status as a functional discipline and in the larger picture becomes the totality of all efforts of a company. The chances are probable that when you next see an accountant walking into a room, you'll note that he is going to walk in backwards. The reason for this is that, for the most part, he is much more concerned with where he has been. In reality, the professional discipline of accounting has been weaned on that type of perspective. From birth all of us are instilled with different types of disciplines and moralities. In our lifetimes our parents try to teach us many things. The discipline and morality in the lifetime of a professional accountant, however, means that the individual must be geared to having an end fulfillment of creating a profit and loss statement and a balance sheet. In the interim, between preparation of these statements, the financial executive must, of course, regularly report to the stockholders of a company, internally, and to other externally interested parties.

Controllership Duties

This essentially means that the financial man is oriented toward reporting what happened yesterday. To the contrary the marketing executive, the decision maker, must pursue a policy which is much more concerned with the probability of what is going to happen tomorrow. Compounding the above by what I consider to be a reluctance on the part of the financial area to enter into this sphere of marketing, I think that it will be easily discernible to realize the magnitude of the gulf which exists between the two areas. An example of the orientation of the financial executive toward reporting what happened yesterday can be seen in the formally defined controllership duties put forth by the Financial Executives Institute. These duties are reproduced below:

> *Planning for Control:* To establish, coordinate and administer as an integral part of management an adequate plan for the control of operations.

> *Reporting and Interpreting:* To compare performance with operating plans and standards, and to report and interpret the results of operations to all levels of management and to the owners of the business.

> *Evaluating and Consulting:* To consult with all segments of management responsible for policy or action, concerning any phase of the operation of the business as it relates to the attainment of objectives and the effectiveness of policies, organizational structure and procedures.

> *Tax Administration:* To establish and administer tax policies and procedures.

Government Reporting: To supervise or coordinate the preparation of reports to government agencies.

Protection of Assets: To assure protection for the assets of a business through internal control and internal auditing.

Economic Appraisal: To continuously appraise economic and social forces and government influences, and to interpret their effect upon the business.

Recently a revision to the above list by the Financial Executives Institute has given recognition to the shortcomings of the definition by including in the list the responsible assignments in the area of management information systems. What perhaps should be added to the delineation of duties by the Financial Executives Institute would be the following added definition of controllership:

Utilization of Creativity: To establish alternative reporting and analytical methods designed to measure the effectiveness of performance responsibility under the marketing concept by measuring the fiscal implications of media and promotion policy and profit responsibility under the product manager system.

I have alluded to what I perceive as a reluctance on the part of the financial man to enter into the sphere of marketing. The reluctance that I perceive exists for a number of reasons. Frankly, the variables of consumer behavior and marketing techniques are simply too complex for the average financial man to comprehend. In addition to that, the disciplined financial man runs up against the undisciplined marketing man who always claims he cannot be measured because he is creative.

THE NEED FOR FINANCIAL EVOLUTION

The profession has not had very much to boast about lately. Inevitably, when asked for its innovative recent developments, the professional group answers that it has developed direct costing and that it has perfected the return on investment concept. In reality, each of these techniques is quite dated. Direct costing was first invented about thirty-seven years ago and the return on investment concept can be traced back as far back as 1893. This type of innovation hardly bespeaks a progressive type of professional group.

As a consequence, I think there is something of a new evolution that is required of the profession. I am also not at all convinced that the evolution will come about through self-motivation. I think it may be forced upon the group by decision makers who will pull, urge, and demand. Essentially, financial people have been reluctant to change because everything they have done has been in the "comfortable" vein. Most practice in financial reporting has been oriented toward manufacturing. The chances are probable that each of you as readers have within your own company some variant of standard costing, absorption costing or direct costing. All of these types of analytical techniques measure the performance of a company in the environment of a factory. The greater problem, however, is what happens to the merchandise once it leaves the factory door.

When the factory door is closed and the finished good is moved out, the world of marketing opens up with a vengeance and one need not be dense to reason that it was only twenty years ago that the 20th Century Fund commissioned a study attempting to estimate the cost of distribution. At that time, twenty years ago, approximately 60¢ out of every revenue dollar was consumed in distribution. Of course, in defining distribution for that study, advertising, sales promotion, freight, warehousing, etc., were included. Nevertheless, the major impact of expenditures lay beyond the factory door. If we were to bring that study forward in terms of time in an attempt to update it, I would intuitively suspect that such an amount would easily be increased by 10¢. In those terms then, it is logical that over two-thirds of all expenses are consumed in some type of distribution effort.

The Financial Mentality

This is the precise area in which the financial people have been reluctant to intrude. In order to appreciate this, one must understand the financial mentality. There is a comfort in being able to walk into a manufacturing plant and see a machine turn over 100 times a minute. With each turnover, the accountant can observe that a widget is produced. It is easy for him then to stand up and say, "I can create a system—look what I've done. I have been able to calculate the cost of a widget." That same man, however, placed into the area of sales promotion would be extremely uncomfortable because once he would be questioned and asked to evaluate the profitability of a given sales promotion, he would probably be at a loss as to how to proceed. This would occur because he is now entering into a different type of world where there is a multiplicity of variables.

First there is the subject of measurement which is implicit in evaluating the profitability of something. Against what base is the effectiveness of a sales promotion measured? What motivates the consumer to react to the sales promotion? What were the objectives of the sales program? Were the qualitative objectives met as well as the quantitative?

As individuals, we are all imponderable variables. As consumers, we don't know what we are going to do tomorrow with any degree of certainty. We may have an idea of probable plans; however, is that idea a sufficient base upon which someone else can plan? We do not know, tomorrow, how much money we will have in our pockets at a precise moment in time. If we use this logic and project it into the reasoning process of the financial man we can understand his fright. He doesn't want to be a part of this type of world because everything he touches becomes like a grain of sand. I think then that this is one of the large reasons why marketing has not been served very well by the financial area. Nevertheless, I think there are concrete things which the financial area can do to assist the marketing area.

The Schism Between Marketing and Finance

Part of the fault which has lead to the present schism between marketing and finance lies within the function of marketing itself. Marketing men have always had a great deal of trouble trying to define their own profession. Even though it is an academic approach to a pragmatic problem, a definition of "marketing" is required if we are to help solve the problem. One such definition was proposed about seven years ago by the American Marketing Association. It says that marketing is the "performance of business activities which directs the flow of goods and services from consumer to user." As a definition of marketing, I think it is a superb explanation of physical distribution. Some time after that, in 1967, Remus Harris wrote an article in *Advertising Age* and said that "marketing is the total process of creating consumers efficiently." This latter definition I think is a giant step forward because included in the definition are three essential elements. He has recognized that marketing is a total process. He has further recognized that a consumer must be created, and lastly, he gives homage to the fact that it must be an efficient process. Even with the improvements in this latter definition, it is still not complete enough for use by the new breed of financial man.

Easily the finest definition that I have heard of marketing was written by Clarence Eldridge in the year following that espoused by Mr. Harris. In 1968, Eldridge wrote a series of pure pragmatic essays for the Association of National Advertisers. In one of these statements he said that "Marketing is ascertaining, creating and satisfying the wants of a consumer; *and doing it at a profit.*' This is the first blessed time that anyone has ever defined marketing in terms of making a profit. Suddenly we are taken out of the sphere of being magnanimous; out of the sphere of being the type of individuals who say, "I am creative, you cannot measure me." Suddenly all, encompassed by the marketing concept, are going to be concerned with profit responsibility, profit awareness, profit consciousness. It will no longer be possible for the marketing man to go to the sales manager and simply give him a goal of volume attainment for salesmen's quotas. What can be done now is to make the sales manager responsible for the profitability of the product mix being sold. The definition encourages selling on the basis of the mix of profitability. We need no longer listen to the sales manager tell the salesman, "Sell, sell and get rewards for selling." In fact, he may be encouraging the salesmen to sell what is easiest for him to sell; and what is easiest for him to sell may be the least profitable item for the company.

What I am suggesting in the above is only one example that might stem from a redefined marketing function. Another example is the concept of how to create a realistic incentive plan for salesmen. Why must it be like an old medieval castle with a moat around it? Why must the only people who can raise and lower the drawbridge be the sales managers? Why not have the sales managers sit down with the financially-oriented marketing man or conversely, a marketing-oriented financial man and together create an incentive plan based upon a product mix and further, calculate that the product mix in turn will be that mix which will optimize the profitability of the line, or the division, or the company. It is no longer practical to simply have an incentive plan based upon volume attainment. It is rapidly becoming obsolete.

Another facet of the redefined marketing function is involved with the product manager concept. Ostensibly, product managers are held responsible for the profits of their products. Although this is not true in every company, by and large the vast majority of companies in the United States hold managers responsible for profits. Yet, if we realistically look at the product manager, we must ask ourselves how he can exercise his responsibility. He cannot, in fact, purchase the raw materials for his products, he cannot go into the factory and tell the plant manager to increase his output by ten percent (the union shop steward would be highly unnerved by this type of affrontry). He cannot unilaterally accomplish a price change for a major product, and sometimes he cannot even create his own media program, especially in cases where companies now have staff directors for media. Nevertheless, we attempt to continue the charade that the product manager is responsible for profit. There is a tremendous anomaly here.

Effecting the Evolution

When we attempt to measure the performance of people under profit responsibility, we are measuring people on the wrong base. We are firstly concerned with the word "profit" and profit is a misleading word. In all honesty, profit is what is left over. What we should be concerned about is the semantic distinction of *profitability*. Profitability is far different from profit in that it is a *new rate* of profit. It is an incremental rate of profit that is derived from every transaction. That then, is the key to the precise measure which we can apply to individual performance.

The remaining point then is, how can we establish these concepts? The first step to accomplish this is to be willing to look the controller squarely in the eye and ask, "Are you willing to take a different type of look at your system? For all these years, you have been telling me that the magic things to look at are gross profit and net profit and you have been so accomplished in your craft that you have even broken this down to a product level. Well, standing up here as a heretic, I can say that there isn't any such thing as a net profit for a product. Products don't pay taxes; companies pay taxes."

In addition, speaking with a financial hat, I can realistically state that I, as a controller, can influence the magnitude and the direction of corporate profit. Within legally and morally accepted accounting principles, I can accomplish this type of change. Sooner or later if I do choose to exercise this power, I can distribute that effect to your product. I would reasonably have to ask whether any marketing man should be willing to be judged by the controller's changes to the profit measure. Should careers be judged by a financial man's ability to change numbers? It is hardly a fair type of measure. There is another way of accomplishing fair measurement and it is contained within the elements of relevant costing, of product life cycle analysis and of the return on investment technique. All of these, of course, are exciting, innovative financial tools and can best be implemented through the vehicle of creating the position of a marketing controller.

Relevant Costing

Relevant costing is neither standard costing, nor direct costing, nor absorption costing. It is a completely different type of costing analysis. It is an analytical tool which recognizes the concept of value. Value is what is inherent in every decision that must be made about factors which will affect tomorrow. The financial profession is disturbed about the concept of value because there is nothing in the entire theory of accounting that recognizes value. Looking at a profit and loss statement is the same as looking at cost. Looking at the balance sheet is the same as looking at cost. For example, the value of assets on the balance sheet is based on the cost at which the items were purchased, less the depreciation which has been accumulated against the assets. Nothing in those statements has to do with the value of an asset.

I am suggesting that the following be considered: scrap the traditional profit and loss statement; it is probably oriented toward reporting for another reason. It is oriented toward custodial reporting. In fact, custodial responsibility for control and reporting is nowadays becoming less and less important, not more so. Besides that, there is really not too much of a challenge left for solving reporting problems. Even if your controller cannot do it correctly, there is always the independent outside auditor to correct him. So, therefore, this is not the nub of the relationship problem which exists within the corporate organization. The challenge is to create the system which is going to orient itself toward decision making.

The essence, then, of relevant costing is to begin by separating *all* types of costs. In saying this, I am referring not only to manufacturing costs, but marketing costs, functional distribution costs, administrative costs, etc. Under relevant costing they are first separated into a classification of *direct* or *indirect* costs. For the sake of simplicity, let's assume that the definition of direct or indirect refers to whether the costs are directly attributable to the existence of the item being measured. This type of procedure is necessary. It is the classification procedure I am referring to. Accounting is preoccupied with the classification of costs and has rarely been concerned with the behavior of costs. The distinction in practice between classification and behavior is immense.

Classification does not consider variable or marginal elements of profitability. In essence, relevant costing is concerned much more with the behavior of costs than it is with the classification of costs. Once the above split between direct and indirect has been accomplished, costs are further separated into two other classifications, variable and nonvariable. The essence of the distinction is, "Does the cost vary with volume or not?" Examples of different types of costs that might vary directly with volume are commissions, manufacturing costs, spoilage, obsolescence, etc. Freight, in addition, may vary directly with volume. Advertising, on the other hand, is a direct cost, but it is nonvariable. It exists because the product exists, but does not vary directly with volume. The nature of this type of cost is that it is akin to a period cost. Advertising, over the period of the planning horizon, is generally a fixed, planned amount. If a successful campaign is launched, the unit rate of advertising based upon the number of units sold will decrease compared to the planned unit rate. If the campaign is not successful, the per unit rate will be far more expensive because fewer units will be sold. This is essentially the type of distinction that we are looking for when we separate variable from nonvariable costs. In a purely variable cost, the unit rate remains the same, while aggregate dollars change following volume. In a nonvariable cost, the aggregate dollars remain the same, but the unit rates change in response to volume changes.

Levels of Profit

Out of all of this come two new decision-making levels of profit. We will be scrapping the traditionaĺ gross profit and net profit measurements because they are not realistic for making a decision. The levels of profit which are created through relevant costing are *variable profit* and *direct profit*.

Variable Profit answers all questions of change. "What happens if I drop my selling price by 10¢ a ton?" "What happens if I increase my volume by 500 thousand pounds?" "What happens if I increase the output of my plant from eighty percent to ninety percent of utilized capacity?" The foregoing are questions of change which are asked every day. This type of system will give an almost instantaneous reply to the question which deals with the effect of such changes on corporate profits. In addition to that, it will provide *instantaneous break-even analysis*. No longer will the decision maker have to suffer with the old statistical break-even charts showing horizontal lines and forty-five degree lines representing fixed costs and sales revenues. That type of construction took hours because before the chart could be drawn, fixed and variable costs first had to be separated. Under Relevant Costing, this has already become a built-in part of the system.

Direct Profit, which is the second decision-making level of profit, answers another type of question. It responds to a question regarding economic impact of operations. Direct prőfit is a profit that exists because a product exists. Correspondingly, if a product is done away with, that amount of direct profit will also be eliminated. In this vein, it answers such questions as: "Should I close plant (a) and leave plant (b) open? What would the effect be?" "What would the effect on profits be if I discontinued the operations of division (c)?" "Should I keep product (d) in the line or should I discontinue the product?" "Should I go ahead with the marketing of new product (e) or not?"

Relevant Costing is only one of the techniques which can be used to help the financial area assist the marketing area. Another vehicle is the decision-making applications of return on investment.

THE RETURN ON INVESTMENT PROBLEM

Return on investment is an old war horse that has been trotted out quite a bit lately. It is most commonly used for purposes of stockholder reporting in annual reports. Usually the numbers that are used will be for purposes of divisional return on investment or aggregate return on investment measures. The sad truth is that there are so many other uses for the concept which can be applied to decision making but which are almost totally ignored by the financial profession.

Why not use the return on investment for a geographic selling area? Compare the profitability of district #1 versus district #2. Certainly there is no technical problem involved. All of the data input is there in any system which is available. The hang-up which is encountered by most financial people is that of the base which should properly be used for the denominator of the equation, investment. The financial people question how they can apportion the stockholder's equity to achieve geographic district profitability. The obvious answer is that you don't distribute the stockholder's equity to achieve measurements of geographic profitability. In effect, one should render unto Caesar what is Caesar's; the investment in the geographic area may only be in accounts receivable or in inventory. That, therefore, will become the common investment base for all of the geographic areas. The return on investment equation on a geographic basis would measure the profitability of the product sold in the geographic area against the incremental investment base of accounts receivable and inventories. The return on investment concept can also be applied to measuring the efficiency of the sales force. An individual salesman can be evaluated in terms of his return on investment. In effect, the equation can evaluate the profitability of adding salesmen to the sales force, for example. The concept can be used for product pricing; there is a fine formula which was developed by Wayne Keller some years ago which is not highly complex and is valid, especially for the pricing of unique products. It helps to establish the selling price of a product to the return on investment objective of a company. It will not give the marketing man the exact price that he should charge; rather, it will tell him how low he can price his product and still maintain his target return on investment. In the above sense, the marketing man may have his cake and eat it, too. He knows how low he can price the product but he does not know how high he can price the product. Obviously, the answer to that question is that he should price the product as high as he economically can and still maintain his basic demand for the product. It is, of course, an excellent vehicle for determining a "ball park" pricing structure for unique products which do not have the conventional parameters of an established market or a built-in customer demand for the product.

The concept is also highly applicable for the evaluation of new products and capital expenditures relative to the new products. If we assume that we have a fine new product but do not have the factory to make it, the options which arise from that type of situation are manifold. One can build a factory to make the new product in order to sell it, or one can build a new plant, then in turn sell the plant to a third party and lease it back from him. This type of situation is a perfect example for an application of return on investment techniques. These pitifully few examples among many should demonstrate that one must demand, or at least convince the financial people to expand their horizon to include other applications of financial techniques, so that marketing will be in a position to make the best decision for the company. There is another problem which has largely been ignored by the financial area and, in fact, has largely been ignored by the marketing area. The subject I am referring to is that of product life cycles.

Product Life Cycles

It was in 1968 that the A. C. Nielsen Company published the first definitively realistic study of product life cycles. They studied 250 major products for Lever Brothers. The products were household products covering the period from 1960 to 1965. The startling conclusion of that study was that the average life span of a new product is *2.9 years.* The 2.9 year measure covers the product from conception to prototype; from test market to national distribution; from maturity to obsolescence; to death—and in addition, the marketer also has to make a profit.

The marketing world has been inundated by the demise of what once were highly touted new product introductions. Literally, the consumer's mind has been ingrained with the names of prominent new products which, in fact, are on the downturn of their own quick, untimely down spiral. Has anyone heard of Reef Mouth Wash lately? or Hidden Magic Hair Spray? Or the F-111? Or Three Layered Jell-O? Right now there are products in development on the drawing board which are going to obsolesce many existing products today. For example, Xerox is working on a copier innovation which could obsolete everything that is currently on the market. Their development will not come into fruition until four or five years from now. However, even then it will have a profound effect upon its market. When was the last time you had breakfast cereal with freeze-dried fruit in it?

Profit Planning for Marketing

The point of all of this is, that when doing profit planning for marketing, the conventional method of profit planning encourages *planning in a vacuum.* Profit planning always assumes that the product is going to last forever. When was the last time you took your products, segregated them into the stages of the life cycle of the products, and then looked at the *quality* of profit? If the attribute of quality to profit strikes one as being odd, consider that it is an entirely normal reaction. I would assume that we are all American capitalists. We open up the stock pages of the *Wall Street Journal* each day and say, "The stock is going up," or "The stock is going down." Usually, the correlation for stocks going up or down is with the earnings per share. What I am submitting to you is that a company whose earnings per share is increasing may be a very sick company. No one questions *how long* the sources of those earnings are going to continue.

For example, the coffee market in the United States is declining about one percent a year. The leading companies that make coffee, though, have managed to increase earnings. Somewhere, in some future time, a curve will intercept those earnings. The curve that will intercept the earnings will occur because the per capita consumption of coffee has been going down from about 3 cups a day in 1963 to 2.6 cups a day at present. At that point in time, the companies will be in for a rude awakening. It is prudent at this point to ask yourself, "What is the quality of the dollar of profit attributable to coffee, compared to the quality of profit of a good, new product which is expanding its market?" Further, ask whether there is a difference in the quality of profit. Why not then take this innovation in profit planning and view your situation in the light of the stages of the life cycle in which your products are located?

IMPLEMENTING THE MARKETING CONTROLLER CONCEPT

It is reasonable, of course, to ask how all of this can be accomplished, especially if one has a conventional controller. I think that the accomplishment of this type of concept leads us to a discussion in detail of the marketing controller concept. The only excuse for not having a marketing controller is if you happen to have a conventional controller who appears to have a single head, but in reality has two heads.

A marketing controller really is a man with two heads. Ostensibly, one can make a search and in your job specification, specify that this man must be more powerful than a speeding locomotive; he must be able to leap tall buildings in a single bound; and must be able to be faster than a speeding bullet. Obviously, there aren't too many of these types of fellows around. In a pragmatic sense, I think one must create them. Further, I think they can be created by taking a financial analyst and simply immersing him thoroughly and completely in the marketing sphere—even to the extent of having him participate in sales force activities and in product management activities for a period of time, concurrent with the financial training. It has been my experience that after about a two-year period, one *might* develop a marketing controller. The key to the position is that the man has to report to two people; I think that this is the only way that it will work. I am speaking about a marketing controller who will be a staff member of the marketing function and who will primarily report to the marketing head. He will secondarily report to the financial controller. It will obviously take an extremely mature individual to undertake this type of relationship. I think to do otherwise, having him report to the financial controller first and then the marketing head, would tend to brand the man as a misfit from out-of-town, or as a controller's spy. It would defeat the very essence of the program. It is almost akin to the problem raised in the manuscript of the "Territorial Imperative." If the man will report to the financial controller first and have a primary loyalty to that man, then the "Territorial Imperative" of marketing will raise its head and he will be eventually excluded.

Many of the problems about which I am writing stem from the common conception of corporate organization charts.

The Faults of Organograms

There are two basic faults with an organization chart. The first fault is that there are a lot of little boxes in it, and one box has a tendency to say to the other box, "This is my job; keep your dirty hands off of it." There is an additional problem. Most often the big boxes have little boxes which hang down and which denote assistants. One assistant will quite often look at the other assistant and say, "Why is his box higher than my box?" When hard put for an answer, one can obviously see that the other box is making more money or his boss is more important. In essence then, conventional organizational charts breed insularism.

A better concept of an organization is in the shape of a good old fashioned wagon wheel. The wagon wheel which I envision has an axle, and a hub and spokes. The hub of the wheel is marketing because that is what the company is in busines for. As indicated earlier, the company is in business to sell products; not just to make them. If the reader can accept the logic stated above, then perhaps this logic can be stretched so that the reader will accept the fact that the rim of the wheel is composed of service areas which will augment that function. One of the service areas may be finance, one may be purchasing, one may be manufacturing and so forth. The spokes, in turn, are simply lines of communication between these elements of the corporate organization. This would then produce a modern, functional, pragmatic, organization chart. If this is acceptable to the reader, then I ask that you further accept the concept of the marketing controller. He is there as a service function to marketing and he is there only to help someone make a decision. He is not there to make debits or credits; he is not there to do any routine assignments. He is there to be a quantitative financial advisor, a financial conscience, or what have you. There is no proper name to call this type of individual; for better or for worse, in this writing he has been called a marketing controller. Further, such individuals really do exist.

In 1965, The Nestlé Company innovated the concept of a marketing controller. Marketing controllers are stationed in each of the major marketing divisions and figuratively they sleep in bed with the people of the division. It has been an eminently successful program. In fact, it has been so successful that last August as an offshoot of that program, the position of a manufacturing controller was created. Only recently, a further position which is a step in the evolution of the marketing controller was created. The position is that of a physical distribution controller. In the future, this concept might be expanded further to include the functional decision-making areas of purchasing and administration.

FINANCE: A MULTI-RESPONSIBILITY

The evolution of medicine has brought about profound changes in our perception of doctors. When we have problems with our throat we no longer go to a general practitioner; we would rather see an ear/nose/and throat doctor because he has the special skills required in that area. If we have problems with our eyes we will go to an opthalmologist. In this sense, finance is no different. The kinds of decisions which have to made in each of the functions are simply too complex to permit the corporate staff man to assist a functional area. In addition, the corporate staff financial man is usually isolated in his ivory tower. Besides that, there is always the spectre behind his shoulder of generally accepted accounting principles and the obligation to report what happened yesterday. Therefore, one must recognize that finance has not one responsibility but many. Obviously and essentially, one of those responsibilities is a reporting function for yesterday. More importantly though, the mission in life of the financial executive should be to help make someone create a sound decision.

In the context of a marketing controller, I am going to list in the following examples of types of assignments which this type of individual would ordinarily perform. Essentially their jobs revolve about closely controlling media expenses; they advise on the optimum timing for different strategies; they measure the efficiency of promotional spending; they analyze media production cost; they evaluate the profitability of an individual customer; they evaluate geographic profitability; they monitor the production efficiency of operations scheduling for the manufacturing area.

The role of the marketing controller is and will be different depending upon the type of company. Quite often they will present sales-oriented financial reports and by that I do not mean to imply sales by district, by territory, or other such types of reports. I am inferring sales by customer, compared to how much of an inducement was paid to a customer to perform certain services.

In that manner the marketing-oriented financial man will be able to determine the profitability of our selling efforts to an individual customer. The customer is frequently paid performance payments, especially in the consumer products industry, or he gets some other type of sales promotion incentive. These things can be measured against the *performance* of the customer, not just the amount of items which he purchased. In addition to that, one can measure the purchase performance of the customer against his own neighboring competition for a company's products. In a sense, the marketing controller can custom tailor a market measure which competes with a particular customer to whom the company sells. When that is concluded, one can then give the salesman a tool to say to the customer, "You increased your purchases almost ten percent a year for product (a); in addition to that we gave you $60 thousand in incentives for purchasing our product. But you know, your own bed fellows, your competition, who also buy from us in this area, increased their purchases by fifteen percent; we only paid them $50 thousand." This is the type of warning flag which a marketing-oriented sales report can raise so that the salesman covering a customer can have a viable sales tool with which to confront him.

Incentive Plans Based Upon Profitability Attainment

Marketing controllers in other companies quite often design incentive plans based upon profitability attainment. Further, they assist direct accounts to optimize their purchasing and inventory policies. If necessary, some marketing controllers have gone on loan to various major customers. In that respect, what better good will device can be employed than attempting to assist one of your major customers by sending him a qualified man to help?

Companies now are beginning to recognize the worth of the marketing controller concept and are fondly embracing it. In fact, Johnson & Johnson has really reorganized their financial area to employ this concept. In addition, it is currently being actively explored by Bristol-Myers and Crown Zellerbach.

Change is not going to come if one does not display a curiosity sufficient to cause the change. In order to accomplish the transition to a marketing controller concept, you, the reader, are going to have to ask for it; you will have to demand it, because I don't think the change will come from within.

Moreover, when the change comes, I think it will be through evolution, certainly not revolution. Revolution makes people defensive, and there is no place for that type of atmosphere within any company. Thus far, the experience of major corporations with the marketing controller concept has proven that it is an eminently successful tool to achieve better decision making. What more could a company ask for?

SAMPLE SITUATIONS
USING RELEVANT COSTING

Situation 1

Product Manager Jim Jones has been informed that the manufacturing cost of Product A has increased ten percent. What are his alternatives to maintain present profit levels?

(a) Raise the selling price
(b) Reduce marketing expenses
(c) Reformulate the product

. . . If the selling price is increased to cover the additional cost, two major points must be considered: (1) will the shelf price be competitive and (2) will the volume decrease to a level not conducive to the profit structure of the company?

. . . If he reduces marketing expenses this may have the same effect as a selling price increase. For example, Product A sells for $5.00 a case to the retailer and we allow a $1.00 off-invoice promotional allowance. The net price to the retailer is $4.00 per case. If we reduce the allowance to $.50 per case, the net price to the retailer is now $4.50 per case. The retailer, if he agrees to buy the product, will in all probability increase the shelf price. The increased shelf price may lead to reduced sales.

. . . Reformulation of a product is probably the last alternative. If major ingredient changes are made, this may affect the quality of the product, thereby causing drastic volume reductions.

Situation 2

Examine the profit and loss statements under the following conditions:

(a) Change in volume
(b) Increase in selling price
(c) Increased manufacturing cost; maintain same profit margin

. . . When a variation in volume occurs, the following expenses would change: sales proceeds, cost of sales, freight, warehousing, and discounts. The preceding expenses are known as variable expenses because they vary with volume. Expenses which are established by marketing personnel are known as direct product costs. Advertising, market research and promotions are examples of these expenses. The preceding expenses do not vary with volume, the exception is certain types of promotions, i.e., off-invoice allowances and free goods allowances.

. . . When a change in selling price occurs the following expenses would vary: sales proceeds and discounts. Off-invoice promotional allowances may have to be increased to offset the higher cost of the retailer. Cost of goods, freight, warehousing, spoiled goods and advertising expenses would remain constant, assuming the volume did not change.

. . . Assume we make twenty percent direct profit on Product A. The cost of manufacturing is increased five percent. What are the alternatives to maintain the 20 percent margin?

(a) Increase the selling price
(b) Reduce marketing expenses
(c) Combination of both

Situation 3

Exhibit I shows the plan for Product A for the years 1971 and 1972 and actual results for 1970.

. . . In comparing 1970 actual results versus latest estimate 1971 plan it is apparent that certain changes have occurred:

(1) The selling price has increased $.050 per pound. What caused this increase? In 1970 we sold 50% of Item A and 50% of Item B. Item A sells for $4.00 per pound and Item B sells for $2.00 per pound. When we calculate the average selling price of the product we arrive at a selling price of $3.00 per pound as follows:

Item	% Mix	Selling Price
A	50%	$4.00
B	50%	2.00
Total	100%	$3.00

. . . In computing the selling price for the latest estimate 1971 plan, we realize that we are not selling more of the higher priced Item A than we had anticipated. In the calculations the following become obvious:

Item	% Mix	Selling Price
A	52.5%	$4.00
B	47.5%	2.00
Total	100.0%	$3.05

Form No. 5485
7/70

PRODUCT PLAN – PROFIT AND LOSS ACCOUNT   Product PRODUCT A

	Revision I 19			Original 1972			Latest Est. 1971			Actual 1970		
				625,000			550,000			500,000		
	PER LB.	AMOUNT	%	PER LB.	AMOUNT	%	PER LB.	AMOUNT	%	PER LB.	AMOUNT	%
Plan Sales Units - Pounds												
Bonus Goods - Pounds												
TOTAL					625,000			550,000			500,000	
Net Proceeds from Sales				3150	1968800	10000	3050	1677800	10000	3000	1500000	10000
Variable Cost of Goods Sold				1600	1000000	5079	1500	826000	4983	1500	750000	5000
Freight and Charges				029	18100	91	027	14900	88	025	12500	83
Warehouse Expenses				017	10600	53	016	8800	52	015	7500	50
Spoiled Goods				002	1300	06	010	5500	32	002	1000	06
Cash Discount				063	39400	200	061	33600	200	060	30000	200
Distributors' Discount												
Commissions				157	98400	500	153	83900	500	150	75000	500
TOTAL VAR. EXP.				268	167800	850	267	146700	872	252	626000	839
VARIABLE PROFIT				1282	801000	4071	1263	694800	4145	1248	624000	4161
Advertising - Media				080	50000	253	091	50000	298	200	100000	664
Promotions				480	300000	1523	455	250000	1490	400	200000	1334
Promotions												
SUB-TOTAL				560	350000	1776	546	300000	1788	600	300000	2000
Extraordinary Promotions												
Prior Years Adv./Promotion												
Market Research				080	50000	253	045	25000	149	050	25000	166
Other												
TOTAL DIRECT PRODUCT COST				640	400000	2029	591	325000	1937	650	325000	2166
DIRECT PROFIT				643	401000	2042	672	369800	2208	598	299000	1995
Less-Provision for Contingency												
NET DIRECT PROFIT				643	401000	2042	672	369800	2208	598	299000	1995
Period Factory Expenses												
Direct Divisional Expenses												
Other Period Expenses												
NET PROFIT (LOSS)												

Exhibit I

. . . Reviewing the preceding tables shows that the increase in selling price is due to "mix"—selling more of one item than another lower priced item.

(2) The cost of sales increase of $.02 per pound is attributable to the sale of the higher priced item. In a great majority of the cases, the higher priced item's cost of manufacturing is higher.

(3) Freight and warehousing expenses are raised to reflect anticipated increases for physical distribution costs.

(4) Spoiled goods in the latest estimate plan is increased to cover unusual spoilage problems in certain areas. In constructing the original 1972 plan, prior years' actual spoilage rates are considered to arrive at a more equitable rate. The latest estimate, 1971 rate, is disregarded since it represents an unusual spoilage problem and hopefully will not recur in the future.

(5) Discounts and commissions are based on prior years' history, unless there is a change in the method of sale of a product. For example, in 1971 the product is sold solely through brokers, as reflected in the 5% shown in Exhibit I. If, in 1972, we plan on selling through a distributor, we would have to build in an additional expense since distributors are usually paid a 20% commission.

(6) In latest estimate 1971, the advertising expenditure was reduced $50 thousand and the promotions increased $50 thousand. The product manager of Product A feels that the additional monies concentrated on increased off-invoice allowances will result in additional volume of 50,000 pounds. He also feels that his advertising expense of $100 thousand in 1970 was excessive in obtaining the resulting poundage. In concentrating his advertising to certain key areas, he hopes to reduce his expense and also increase volume.

Situation 4

We plan on introducing a new product into the Syracuse area in the fall. How many units do we have to sell to reach a break-even point? Assume the following data:

(a) Selling price of $3.00 per unit
(b) Cost of sales of $1.75 per unit (includes freight, warehouse and discounts)
(c) Direct promotional expense ($.75 per unit)
(d) Fixed expenses of $10,000 (heat, light, water, depreciation, taxes, advertising)

> Note: Advertising is considered a fixed expense since it is purchased in advance of sales and does not vary directly with volume.

	Per Unit
Net Proceeds from Sales	$3.00
Cost of Sales	1.50
Variable Expenses	.25
Variable Profit	$1.25
Direct Promotional Expense	.75
Direct Profit	$ .50

. . . In reviewing the following chart we see that 20,000 units will have to be sold in the Syracuse area to break even. This figure can be quickly calculated by dividing the fixed costs ($10,000) by the Direct Profit per unit ($.50). (See Exhibit II.)

Situation 5

Region I sells 20,000 units of Product B at $3.00 per unit. To obtain this volume, Region Manager, Mr. Jones, spends $1.25 per unit on advertising and promotions. The selling expenses applicable to Region I amount to $15,000. What profit or loss is Region I returning? (Use same variable profit data as in Situation 4.)

Units Sold	20,000
Sales @ $3.00	$ 60,000
Cost of Sales @ $1.50	30,000
Variable Expenses @ $.25	5,000
Variable Profit	$ 25,000
Advertising/Promotions @ $1.25	25,000
Direct Profit	$ -0-
Selling Expenses—Direct	15,000
Loss in Region I	$(15,000)

. . . In analyzing the above P&L, it can be seen that Mr. Jones is "buying" the 20,000 unit volume. Although Region I shows a variable profit of $25,-000, the profit after deducting advertising, promotions and selling expenses amounts to a *loss* of $15,000. His variable profit is spent entirely on advertising and promotions. Is this justified? What will happen to the volume if marketing expenses are cut to $.75 per unit? Assume we will lose 5,000 units in sales if we make the reduction. How will this increase or decrease our loss in Region I?

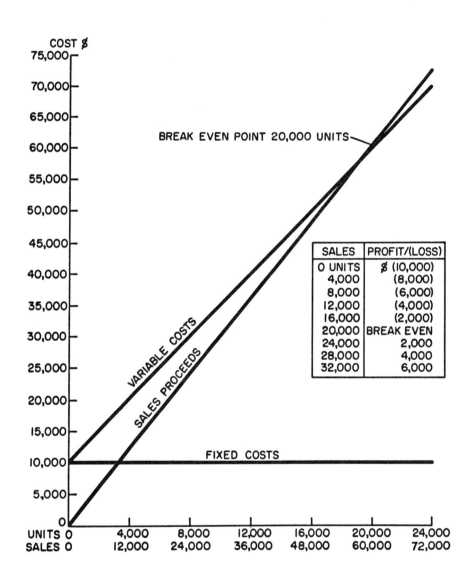

Exhibit II
Product B—Break-Even Chart

Units Sold	15,000
Sales	$45,000
Cost of Sales	22,500
Variable Expenses	3,750
Variable Profit	$18,750
Advertising/Promotion ($.75 per unit)	11,250
Direct Profit	$ 7,500
Selling Expenses—Direct	15,000
Loss in Region I	$(7,500)

. . . In reducing marketing expenses $.50 per unit, we anticipate a decrease in volume of 5,000 units. Although the volume is down 25 percent, the loss in Region I is cut in half ($15,000 versus $7,500).

The above illustrates the point that there are times where lower volume means more profit.

Situation 6

If we analyze Exhibit I we arrive at the following conclusions:

(1) Sales proceeds are up $291,300
   (Original 1972 versus latest estimate 1971)
(2) Volume is up 75,000 pounds

Questions:

(a) How much of the increase in proceeds is due to volume?
(b) How much is due to mix?

Due to Volume:

75,000 lbs.	(additional volume)
×$3.05	(old selling price)
$228,800	Due to additional volume
62,500 *	Due to mix between packs or price increases
$291,300	*Total Increase in Sales*

* In 1972 we plan on selling the following:

Item A	359.4 lbs.	57.5%
Item B	265.6 lbs.	42.5%
Total	625.0 lbs.	100.0%

Due to Mix:

The 10¢ per pound increase in the sales proceeds rate is due to mix as follows:

| | Sales Breakdown | | |
	Original '72 %	Latest Estimate '71 %	Selling Price
Item A	57.5	52.5	$4.00
Item B	42.5	47.5	2.00
	100.0%	100.0%	

Original '72 Plan

$$57.5\% \times \$4.00 = \$2.300$$
$$42.5\% \times \$2.00 = .850$$

Selling Price $3.150

Latest Estimate '71 Plan

$$52.5\% \times \$4.00 = \$2.100$$
$$47.5\% \times \$2.00 = .950$$

Selling Price	$3.050	
1972 Selling Price		$3.150
1971 Selling Price		3.050
Due to Mix		$ .100

From the above analysis it can be seen that the total selling price rate variance is due to mix, with price increases playing no part.

Situation 7

Refer to Exhibit I and assume (contrary to Situation 6) that 1972's volume of 625 thousand pounds came all from one size. What would happen if we came out with an economy size version of this product with a variable profit of $1.00 per pound? It would be promoted at the same rate (48¢ per pound) as the existing item. If we introduce the new item, it is expected that instead of our present forecast of 625 thousand pounds, our volume estimates would look like this:

Present Size	400,000 pounds
Economy Size	300,000 pounds
Total Product A	700,000 pounds

What profit effect would this new size introduction have?

Solution: If we sell the estimated 625 thousand pounds of our existing product, our variable profit, less promotions, would be:

Total Units	Per Unit	Total Dollars
Variable Profit	$1.282	$801,000
Promotions	.480	300,000
Variable Profit Less Promotions	$ .802	$501,000

If we introduce the new size, our profit statement would look like this:

	Present Size		Economy Size		Total	
Units	400,000		300,000		700,000	
	Per Unit	Dollars	Per Unit	Dollars	Per Unit	Dollars
Variable Profit	$1.282	$512,800	$1.000	$300,000	$1.161	$812,800
Promotions	.480	192,000	.480	144,000	.480	336,000
Variable Profit Less Promotions	$ .802	$320,800	$ .520	$156,000	$ .681	$476,800

As you can see from the above data, introduction of the economy size would accomplish the following:

(1) Volume would rise from 625 thousand to 700 thousand pounds.
(2) Profits would drop $25 thousand to $476,800. Stated in other terms, the additional 75 thousand pounds would actually cost $25 thousand in profits.

9

COST-SAVING TECHNIQUES
IN DATA PROCESSING

INTRODUCTION

Is data processing equipment for your company? The answer today, as always, requires a minute and exhaustive analysis, by experts, of the many facets of your business. More and more, however, the question is becoming not so much whether data processing equipment is applicable to your company, but *how much* data processing is correct for your company. It is commonly agreed that sooner or later, and with few exceptions, all companies will have to use data processing equipment in some phase of their operations if they are to remain competitive. More and more improved equipment; more ideas; lower costs; and the growing availability of service bureaus are bringing the advantages of EDP to more and more smaller companies. The substance of the following remarks will: (1) give you help in your approach to the consideration of EDP (Electronic Data Processing) as a means of cutting costs and getting better, quicker information; (2) discuss the question of cost of the equipment—purchase, lease, or other methods; and (3) show how many smaller companies are profiting from the use of EDP.

EVALUATING YOUR COMPANY'S NEEDS

There are some fundamental questions companies should ask themselves in deciding whether or not it would be profitable to install data processing equipment at this time. The questions are interdependent. A "yes" or "no" to one or several questions will not necessarily bring about a decision one way or another. All must be considered as part of the picture. Thus, the "yes" and "no" answers of two companies might match closely, yet one will be ready and the other not.

The Rate of Growth

Are your sales growing and/or continuing to grow appreciably? Are you expanding or going to expand your products?

The ultimate growth of two equal-sized companies might be about the same, but their *rate* of growth could be sharply dissimilar. For example, Companies A and B are competitors and each has sales of $700,000. Company A is developing several new products and expects to boost its sales to $1.5 million in three years. Company B is proceeding at a slower pace, and expects to reach $1.5 million in sales in five years. In all probability, Company A is ready for data processing equipment now; Company B will have to wait a while.

Another point: rate of growth can play an important part in another way. The greater number of units handled by EDP, the less cost per unit. Regardless of other considerations, Company A, in the example above, could figure on a faster drop in costs for the use of EDP than could Company B. This one factor could be decisive.

The Type of Products That Warrant Use of EDP

If you make, sell, or distribute few numbers of large and expensive products, the need for EDP is small, or nonexistent. On the other hand, if you make, sell, or distribute large numbers of a product, or products, regardless of price, the need for EDP grows as the numbers increase. The production or handling of large numbers of a product requires repeated processes in various phases of operations. Repetition might be termed the handmaiden of data processing.

In many instances, the amount of money involved is small in comparison with the numbers themselves. Hence, a company doing $10 million in sales might not need EDP, while another firm doing $1 million in sales could not function properly without it in some phase of operations.

The Number of Customers and Paperwork

Sheer numbers, once again, could be a primary factor in making a decision. Number of customers and paperwork usually go hand in hand. However, there are exceptions: some types of businesses sell to relatively few customers, but the paperwork involved is enormous, necessitating EDP. The interdependency of these questions might be further illustrated here. Manufacturer A makes large, expensive machinery, has few customers, and has no need for EDP. Manufacturer B makes the same kind of machinery and has fifty times the customers as does Manufacturer A. B's decision is as obvious as A's.

Considering Cost Reductions in Given Areas

Companies contemplate use of EDP in critical areas, i.e., those operations that, by their very nature, are most important to the successful operation of the business. They range from inventory control and accounts receivable to sales analysis and job scheduling. The point is (a) could data processing do the job as well or better, and (b) would it do it at a lower cost? There's no sense in investing time and money in a system unless it's going to do an equal job at lower cost, or a better job at equal cost.

Does EDP Offer Extra Benefits?

Can EDP give you information that isn't feasible to compile now because of manpower costs? Information in given areas may be important, yet not be possible to produce because of the high cost. In addition, the extra benefit often is purely a by-product of EDP—produced at no extra cost.

Going Beyond Cost Comparison

While it is true that every company cannot cut costs by the use of electronic data processing, you, as a financial executive, should take the broad approach when you consider EDP. Simply, it means this: you should go far beyond a mere comparison of the costs of a computer system and the costs of your present system, whatever it is. In addition to the necessary direct comparison, you should also consider the following factors:

1. What savings might follow in other areas of the business if I process the related paperwork on computers? What does it mean to me to be able to shorten inventory holdings to half their previous size because I can take readings (and action) on stocks in one-fourth to one-fifth of the time it used to take?
2. What additional jobs could a computer handle—once we've started it on its main job—that might yield added profits or benefits? If I get a computer to handle payroll, and the payoff may take two to three years, I may hesitate. But if I know payroll will take fifteen to twenty hours a week, it won't take long to work up other legitimate uses which will speed up my payoff.
3. To what extent will the computer be useful to me as a link to other automated developments—in my firm, industry, or the economy generally? Which ties will be established to possible automation progress in the warehouse or assembly line? Does the fact that I can send tax reports to the government on magnetic tape—or that "coded" machine media are slowly becoming a means of communication between businesses—affect my needs?
4. Possibly most important, can I use a computer for statistical and mathematical analysis of different phases of the business, to give me an edge on competition? Is long-range planning for me? Is more searching market analysis possible with my facilities and personnel? Is operations research needed?

THE QUESTION OF COMPANY SIZE

All of what has been said should be weighed in deciding whether or not a computer is for you. Probably the most frequent doubt raised is the question of company size: are you too small for a computer? Just how important, however, is size as a criterion? Some management consultants suggest a stated number of office employees (such as 100) as a minimum size to justify computer installation. But while figures such as these merit careful study, no arbitrary figures should be set. More and more, smaller companies are enjoying the benefits of data processing equipment, many through the use of service bureaus, pooled use of equipment, and the like.

For example, suppose you use a computer for extensive calculations of alternatives—setting up different sales quotas, alternative budgets, varied long-range plans, or general economic forecasts—on your own. You run into an area where it's hard to measure with any accuracy the specific benefits or actual cash gain for your firm, and you might engage in extensive work along those lines even if you have twenty employees in your office. In fact, this type of analytical use may be the best growth insurance for your firm.

Should You Wait for the Dust to Settle?

Even today, many companies are still waiting for the dust to settle down, to weigh others' experiences more carefully and, above all, are waiting for the price of machines to come down. They're also fearful of obsolescence because of rapid changes in the field. All of these reasons for caution are valid up to a point—particularly the price factor. There's little doubt that some would do better to wait until machines come down in price. Don't overlook the fact that machines are available in a variety of price ranges right now—including some at extremely low prices. You might want to look up special-purpose computers, set up to do one specific job for you—like controlling airline flight reservations, or performing a set routine for handling bank checks.

Then, too, don't forget there are other ways around the cost problem: service bureaus, pooled usage, and so on. In any case, neither the price nor the hope that better machines will soon be available should be sufficient to deter you from at least looking into the possibilities.

If you can get financial or other benefits from these machines now, there's little reason to wait. Profits realized now—invested in other improvements now—may yield returns through improving your competitive position that you might never equal or replace at a later date. The fear of obsolescence is a bit exaggerated. If current systems can pay off for you in two to three years, the danger of later obsolescence offers no legitimate obstacle. Usually, while many design changes have taken place, the basic computer principles have been relatively unchanged since they were discovered.

Impact of Computer Installation

Perhaps the biggest problem of all is the impact of a computer installation on your total company structure. In practice, most firms will put in a computer to handle one major operation, and the only immediate changes will be in a given department. But computers will, sooner or later, begin to be the center of more and more data-processing activities. And this may lead to lots of unnecessary improvisation and rejuggling at a later date.

It may not be necessary—or even possible—to say right off that a computer will have such-and-such precise effects on your total company structure. However, the more closely you study this total interrelation from the start, and the more you weigh all possible implications of a computer installation—even if you start it off on just one job—the more easily you can control changes needed later on.

Two Steps in Considering Cost Cutting by Computer

A completely successful study of the economies available to your company by the use of EDP calls for a total systems study. To do this properly, two steps should be taken:

1. *Set up a formal study group in the company,* consisting of you, your controller or chief accountant, the head of any machine accounting unit now in existence, the systems head or office manager (if you have one), and the department heads most affected by any major changes. It might also be well to have another top company official, as well as yourself, in the group.
2. *Use outside management consultants to conduct the formal study, working with your internal group. Why?*
   - They bring a more objective approach—in place of the pretty strong subjective feelings and fears some of your study group will have. Of course, the consultants must be sensitive to the feelings of all personnel, which is why they need the close cooperation of a substantial company group.
   - They're more familiar with the different equipment—in a field where it gets harder to keep tabs on new developments with each passing day.
   - They usually have experience in dealing with actual installations—and this is priceless.
   - Their skill in basic systems analysis and work measurements can be approached only by a few of the nation's giant corporations.

Be careful not to underestimate the time and cost requirements of a study. Also allow for extra time for delivery, for getting your system to run smoothly (debugging), and to train your personnel to attain real proficiency. Leave plenty of margin for error in planning all of the above. Don't throw away old records until the installation is running smoothly. Don't set up such tight schedules for use of the computer that adequate allowance isn't made for breakdowns, interruptions, and errors.

BUYING, LEASING, OR USING A SERVICE BUREAU

Your company may be sold on the idea of automation, but there are still several alternatives for it to consider. You may find it practical to proceed along any of the following lines:

1. Purchase the entire EDP system equipment from a manufacturer.
2. Lease the equipment from a manufacturer on a straight lease basis with either the option to renew or the option to purchase.
3. Lease the equipment from a leasing company in a "lease-back" arrangement.
4. Purchase the main frame or the computer and lease all the additional peripheral equipment from a manufacturer.
5. Use a service center to have your tapes or cards serviced.
6. Use another firm that has spare computer time and rent time from them.

Making the Right Decision

In making a decision, you must do what is best suited to your own needs. What others are doing is not necessarily valid for you. Some points to consider follow.

In the long run, purchasing is cheaper than leasing, but purchasing involves much greater investment and much greater risk. Consider the number of years required to recover the purchase investment—this will give you some inkling of the risk. The annual dollar saving after the investment has been recovered will help establish the profit.

You may prefer to lease because you do not have the capital to purchase and because you are worried about obsolescence. However, obsolescence is not as formidable a problem as it may seem—the basic computer is not changing as radically as you might suspect; the peripheral equipment, which is changing, is not so expensive to replace. Perhaps it would be cheaper to borrow the capital than to lease.

When you lease from a manufacturer, the equipment is likely to be kept in better condition (since the manufacturer owns it), but this is usually the most expensive way to lease. This may be counteracted by the fact that you are generally only committed for a short term—a ninety-day cancellation clause is usual.

If you are not concerned about a long-term commitment, a "lease-back" arrangement with a leasing firm may be the answer. Here is how it works:

a. You lease a computer from a manufacturer.
b. A leasing company advances you the purchase of the computer and you purchase it and sell it to them.
c. The leasing company leases it back to you for a longer term and at a lower leasing rate than you could have procured from the manufacturer.

You may lick the obsolescence risk by buying the main frame or computer and leasing the peripheral units. This will also enable you to keep up with your changing needs without the expense of buying entirely new equipment.

As to the choice between leasing equipment and using a service center—it rests on simple arithmetic. Figure the cost of service center time per hour and the leasing cost per month. Consider also the cost of using your own operators, and the allowance for the amortization of starting costs. For example, if the cost of leasing machines is $10,000, and it costs you $100 an hour to rent service center time, without taking other factors into consideration, the break-even point would be 100 hours per month of service time.

Purchase of Used Equipment: A Case History

In deciding whether to rent or buy equipment, the application of the facts to your particular business, and yours alone, is essential. For example, James B. Orr, Treasurer, reports that the decision of Owens-Richards Company, Inc., Birmingham, Alabama, to buy, rather than rent, equipment resulted in a saving of over $450 a month for sixty-three months. This result, however, is based upon the facts applicable to Owens-Richards:

• The system uses mechanical punched-card equipment: sorter, tabulator, printing keypunch, reproducer, and collator.
• A basic comparison of purchase and rental prices revealed that twenty-four months' rental would equal the purchase price, and the company had no plans for changing the system for a number of years. Note that the bank loaned the money for purchase, with repayment at approximately the same amount as the rental price.
• Maintenance was on a "per call" basis with no contract, and ran relatively low: less than one month's rental per year. (After sixty-three months, the equipment performed excellently.)
• Since used equipment was purchased, depreciation was set at ten years. Most of the equipment will last much longer than that. (This, according to Mr. Orr, makes out a good case for the purchase of used, mechanical, punched card equipment.) There is reason to believe that electronic equip-

ment might outlive mechanical equipment with lower maintenance costs. Thus, size and long-term requirements of the company are important considerations.

Service Centers or Bureaus

Probably the most practical introduction to computers for most average firms is through the service bureau or service center—just as it is with punched cards. In fact, those now using punched cards can have these same cards processed more rapidly in computer service centers. Some computers will work on the same cards. Others require card-to-tape converters, which the centers can provide.

Here again, the very smallest offices can gain gradual entrance into the computer field in this manner. What's more, they can probably arrange, for a nominal fee, to work with some service centers to train some of their own personnel in the computer arts. You can also make arrangements to experiment with various possible applications of mechanization.

What Is a Computer Service Bureau?

Basically, the computer service bureau is a complete data processing operation. You can rent as much—or as little—of its facilities as you need. Each bureau maintains:

1. Extensive computer equipment.
2. A trained staff of programmers (people who plan how the computer will use the information you supply to the bureau).
3. Systems analysts (people who help you decide what information your business needs and how you can secure it).
4. Other specialists.

Bureaus are maintained in many cities by most of the major computer equipment makers—General Electric, National Cash Register, Honeywell, Univac and others. The largest chain of computer service bureaus is probably that maintained by the Service Bureau Corporation, a subsidiary of IBM. In addition, there are a number of independent computer service bureaus across the country.

Most computer service bureaus tailor their services to your particular problem and operation. In addition, a number of bureaus now offer packaged programs for such common business operations as payroll and accounts receivable. These packages are standard ways to do the job through EDP—from the initial invoice or other record, through the computer operation, to the final reports. Generally, these packaged programs cost less to install than the specially tailored programs.

How to Get Started

At first, the man from the computer service bureau may seem a little nosey. He'll want to know why you want them to do the particular job you're discussing and what you expect them to help you accomplish with it. Along with one of their systems analysts, the bureau representative will dig deeply into your present way of doing the job. They'll check with your workers as to what they do and why they do it. They'll also check on what happens to every piece of paper involved in the operation. Then, together with other specialists at the service bureau, they'll develop an EDP method for doing the job.

Finally, you'll get a detailed report on your present methods and operating costs, together with an equally detailed explanation of a possible EDP solution to your problem—including costs and a suggested way of doing the job. At the same time, the bureau representative will outline what responsibilities the bureau will assume for accuracy of work done, for delivery of work to you on time, etc. (Normally, up to this point, the bureau's services won't cost you a dime.) Then, it's up to you to decide if you'll go ahead and work with the service bureau in solving your problem.

How to Judge the Quality of the Service Bureau

Obviously, your decision will be helped by knowledge of the quality of the work being done by the service bureau you are considering. Check these things:

Training of systems analysts: These men should have a thorough knowledge of business practices and computer operations. Their job is to decide what information your business needs and how EDP can secure it better and faster. Ask them about their experience in business and their educational background. Find out how long they've been in systems work.

Bureau operation: Ask to see a customer job being processed (preferably one similar to yours). This will let you see the actual working situation. Is it free from loose papers and other clutter? Is a *current* book of operating procedures available? Are machines pretested for accurate adjustment before the job is run?

Quality control: Does the bureau have a man responsible for the accuracy of work done for customers?

Experience of other users: Ask the bureau for names of other customers. Find out from them if the bureau meets its deadlines with accurate data. See that it does not bill for charges not in the contract.

How Small Companies Use Service Bureaus

The biggest single group of service bureau customer includes companies with gross annual sales under $500,000. Here are some of the money-saving uses to which companies have put EDP through a service bureau:

Eliminating order-handling bottleneck. First-year salary savings: almost $25,000. Inventory volume reduction: eighteen percent. Inventory investment slashed: over thirty-seven percent. That's the way a computer service bureau paid off for a Texas electronic parts distributor.

Concerned because order handling was slowed down by a mass of paperwork, and well aware that he could not afford to invest in the special equipment he'd need to do the EDP job himself, the president of the firm turned to the computer service bureau in a nearby community for help. The system developed for him by the bureau cut order processing time from four days to one, and tightened up his control on his salesmen and his inventory.

One girl now handles a job that six used to do. The customer order, received by mail or telephone, is typed on a combination warehouse shipping order/packing slip form. An attachment to the typewriter automatically produces a special punched paper tape as the order is typed.

Much of the order typing is done automatically by special cards with a code similar to that on the tape, punched along one edge. Two types of cards are used. The customer card (maintained for regular buyers), when inserted into the typewriter attachment, automatically writes customer name, address, shipping and routing instructions, credit terms, and other information. The item card describes each part, including stock number, stock bin location, and price. Use of edge-punched cards for standardized information speeds typing time and eliminates almost all errors from the order processing operation.

Paper tape is mailed daily to the computer service bureau. The service bureau uses the paper tape to feed order information into the computer. The computer prepares the invoice, making extensions and figuring approximate discounts. Invoices are mailed by the bureau direct to the customer. (One copy is returned to the distributor to be matched for their files with a copy of the original shipping order.)

Weekly, the president of the distributor receives these reports from the service bureau:

- sales by item for the week, for the month, and for the year
- sales by salesman for the week, the month and the year

Control of inventory costs. Sales up nearly twenty percent. Inventory investment down over thirty percent. What did the trick? A simple ten-key adding machine. Lloyd Sunderland, president of Sunderland Motor Company, Jerseyville, Illinois, told us the story. He employs twenty people and had gross sales of about $1 million last year.

The man at his parts desk uses a ten-key adding machine to record sales and receipts of parts. The first three figures on the tape list the number of parts, and the remaining seven figures indicate the part number. "It would have been simpler to use a punched paper tape machine," Mr. Sunderland said, "but using the adding machine keeps our equipment investment down." The paper tape is sent regularly to a nearby Service Bureau Corporation office. Every two weeks, they send Mr. Sunderland a report on parts sales and receipts and replacement parts orders, prepared by the service bureau computer.

At first, Mr. Sunderland reduced his parts inventory investment. "Now it's back up almost to the original figure," Mr. Sunderland reports. "But we now have a better coverage of parts. The reports I got from the computer showed me where there were gaps in our parts list. We've plugged them and are able to keep our operating costs down by having the right part available at the right time."

A Colorado packaging equipment manufacturer uses computer service bureau facilities to control inventory of over 850 parts on thirty-five different production models. The firm employs sixty-five people and hopes to push its gross sales to over $2 and a half million this year.

Copies of parts issue forms for the week are sent each Friday afternoon to the service bureau. The following Monday morning, the company receives a report showing the number and dollar value of each part used—for the week, the month, and the year to date. The report also indicates the balance-on-hand for each part, and the amount of each which must be ordered to replenish stock. Reports are ready for use three to four days earlier than was possible under the old manual system, and the reports are more complete and accurate. But, even more important, the company has cut its parts inventory investment by almost forty-two percent and is saving the salary of three clerical workers.

Sales Planning and Control

An outlay of only $100 per month means tighter controls on sales and inventory, and more time for sales people to work at selling, for a medium-sized clothing concern. The store records all sales by listing sales tickets on a punched-tape-producing adding machine. (The punched tape is similar to that used by the Texas electronic parts distributor.) At the end of each month the punched paper tape is sent to a nearby National Cash Register Company computer service bureau for analysis.

Forty-eight hours later, the bureau delivers to the clothing company a complete breakdown of sales by department number, price-line, and sales person. Total of the monthly bill from NCR: $100.

The computer-produced sales analysis:

1. Spots slow-moving merchandise items early, to permit prompt action that will speed up inventory turnover and increase profits.
2. Eliminates several bookkeeping and sales analysis jobs, cutting the cost of each sale made.

3. Catches clerical errors made on the selling floor.
4. Simplifies sales recordkeeping and gives sales people more time to actually sell.

Punched-Tape Adding Machine and a Service Bureau

Donald A. Schwartz, Executive Vice President of Integrated Data Processing, Inc., a service bureau, points out that with the punched-tape adding machine and an EDP service bureau, the economies of automatic data processing are within reach of the smallest business.

What economies? There is an elimination of manual card punching and repunching for verification, and a reduction of the time required to reconcile differences. (The punched tape is in balance before it goes to the service bureau, so there is little likelihood that the processed report will be out of balance.)

How does it work? You can use an inexpensive tape input device such as the Synchro-Monroe adding machine. The operator places identification codes into the adding machine keyboard by using the non-add key followed by quantities with the plus or minus bar. These figures are translated into electrical impulses, activating a tape punching unit which converts them into combinations of holes punched in paper tape. The perforated tape can then be processed by high-speed electronic equipment at the service bureau.

What advantages? Data is handled only once at the point of origin. There is no need to handle the same figures at different stages in the accounting routine. The Synchro-Monroe differs from an adding machine in that its adding ability is not its primary attribute. Its primary function is to enter information on a punched tape for further processing by punched card or computing equipment. The fact that it does add, however, and does provide a tape of visible printed figures of the entries with a total for proof, insures numerical accuracy. This control over accuracy in the initial stage is a key factor in the success of a data processing system.

With this system, the company's activities are recorded on a punched tape adding machine and the tape is sent to an EDP service bureau. In a short time the company gets back from the bureau printed journals, a general ledger, a balance sheet, and an income statement. The need for handwritten journals, debiting and crediting, posting and balancing the general ledger, and drafting and typing financial statements is eliminated.

THE CUSTOMER USAGE PLAN

Another way for a small company to translate its own know-how into computer usage is through a "customer usage" plan. It paid off for T. Y. Lin and Associates, Van Nuys, California. The company is a structural engineering firm that specializes in prestressed concrete work. The firm employs forty-five people and has a gross annual business of almost $1 million. Under a plan that the service bureau calls "customer usage," T. Y. Lin and Associates does its own data processing work but doesn't own the computer. Customer usage means that your workers actually operate the computer equipment themselves. You are responsible for the full use of the equipment and the quality of the work done. You save costs by using computer service bureau personnel, but your work takes low priority in the bureau operating schedule—meaning that your people have to do the job in off hours "on available time."

The problem at T. Y. Lin was designing a prestressed concrete beam, taking an experienced engineer about one and a half days. Most of this time was spent on routine calculation and checking of results. T. Y. Lin president, Edward Rice, told us: "As our volume increased, our entire staff was engaged in the routine of plugging numbers into formulas. It was becoming doubtful that we could acquire and train personnel fast enough to keep up." Yet Mr. Rice found that his men were solving problems that were quite similar in nature and answer. Conclusion: "It should be possible to program a computer to give us the solutions we wanted."

Learning Computer Language and Operating Methods

Complications set in. Mr. Rice talked with a number of computer experts, and found that his engineers and the computer programmers and systems men just didn't speak the same language; it looked as though this communication barrier would be impossible to vault. The solution was to train T. Y. Lin people to run the computer. Mr. Rice sent one of his men to a nearby independent service bureau run by Computer-Mat, Inc., Los Angeles, to study computer language and operating methods. Then, using this man's know-how, Mr. Rice set up a computer program to run on Computer-Mat equipment. As a result, answer time was cut from twelve hours to six minutes and costs were slashed over eighty-five percent.

The next step: Mr. Rice soon found that his firm's needs had outgrown the capacity of Computer-Mat equipment. So he started renting time on the computer belonging to nearby North American Aviation, to supplement the work he was doing with Computer-Mat. As a result, there was a strong improvement in staff morale, as his men realized they were free of the drudgery of routine calculations. For the firm, it meant being able to take on vital new business, since it made the best possible use of the abilities of its technically trained workers.

THE COOPERATIVE DATA PROCESSING CENTER

In many of the examples of the application of EDP to the smaller organization, the use of the service bureau is a part of the success of the operation. There's still another approach for those who have been frightened by the price of an electronic giant: the cooperative data processing center, organized and operated by companies in like fields—or neighbors, even if not in the same field. It is possible that some companies that are looking at smaller special or general-purpose computers might do better to team up with other companies to get one of the giants.

A Case in Point

Four large companies in one field, in the same city, have set up a major cooperative center which has met with great success. They established a totally new company, releasing people from all four payrolls to be part of this new setup.

Each of the companies conducts a nationwide operation. Their branches are standardized on punched cards. The center works on a careful schedule: cards from all branches of any one company arrive at the center on the same day, regardless of branch location. Each company has three such coordinated days during the month—none of them conflicting, of course. It's interesting to note that the major initiator of this project took the step because the machine it felt it could afford—and justify in terms of specific jobs the machine could do—was undesirable because "we needed a complete system, not simply a series of speedier job routines." The machine that would provide the complete system was one the company could not afford alone, but it would not settle for a smaller job.

Keys to the success of the project were that the preliminary steps to discuss the system involved the top officers of the company, and the stress was on a full partnership rather than on one firm running the show with the others coming in on a second-shift or part-user basis.

Among the steps new partners had to take was to standardize terminology used in processing, which varied considerably even though the firms did the same work. They have striven for unanimity in operating decisions, despite the very unequal sizes of the businesses involved. They got all personnel from within the parent companies by training and upgrading.

To get started, they spent one month on a parallel run—duplicating on their computer work that was first run off and verified on tabs—to check the accuracy of the new equipment. This type of direct approach is adaptable to many different areas. In addition, there are ways of getting a cooperative unit other than by setting up a completely new center. These are:

1. You might get together with some other firms and approach an established independent punched card service center to consider making the center the core of a cooperative group. The firms involved might be those already using the service agency's punched card facilities. They'd then all have confidence in the ability and discretion of the center's owner.
2. You could approach a university—one with or without a punched card service center. Together, a new computing facility can be established—with sharing of all expenses or benefits as above.

The particular attraction of this type of arrangement is that colleges and universities have the pools of skilled mathematicians and statisticians who can help participants use some of the advanced research techniques the average concern is all too ill-equipped to handle.

Either of the above approaches can provide training and experience which will enable a firm to go into a solo operation at a later date. The cooperative data processing method need in no way be limited to joint computer centers. Why not arrange—with or without a separate physical center—to share with related firms or next-door neighbors any of the more expensive office machines? This includes punched card systems, better photocopying, microfilming, duplicating equipment, or advanced billing or mailing machines, etc.

Data Processing Equipment for Small Companies

Data processing equipment (including computers) is no longer reserved for the giants. Smaller companies should make an appraisal now on whether it is feasible or not for them. A number of factors make this evaluation advisable:

1. Technology (greater speed) has been developed over the past two years. As these faster machines replace older equipment, the price of this older equipment comes more within reach of smaller companies (both buying and leasing).
2. Equipment for retrieving information is more flexible, opening up a variety of uses heretofore unobtainable.
3. New, small machines can now perform a variety of functions which were formerly attainable only on costly equipment.
4. In many cases, new data processing equipment can replace conventional punched card tabulating equipment, and rent at about the equivalent of existing tabulating machines. (The cost for buying or renting tabulating machines has come down accordingly.)

5. New, half-speed systems, developed some time ago, open the way for use of EDP by many companies that couldn't do so before (the machines are cheaper by fifty percent to lease and buy.) The following list, compiled by Electronic Computer Programming Institute, shows illustrations of the use of data processing equipment in smaller companies.

Sales Volume	No. of Customers	Product or Service	Application
$1,000,000	700	Manufacturer—fabricated metal products, shelving bins, lockers	Production control, labor payroll accounting
$2,000,000	75	Engineering firm	Critical path technique of scheduling and control
$3,000,000	800	Manufacturer—power transmission equipment	Job scheduling, production control, attendance recording, inventory control
$4,500,000	750	Manufacturer—furniture	Production planning, sales analysis, order processing, billing, inventory control
$5,000,000	1,100	Distributor—resistors, capacitors, switches, transformers	Inventory control, order writing, billing, purchasing, printing price lists for parts catalog
$5,000,000	1,500	Manufacturer—carpets	Order processing, billing, accounts receivable, freight accounting, production planning, inventory control
$6,000,000	2,500	Manufacturer—pants	Order writing, billing, sales analysis, traffic control
$6,000,000	550	Manufacturer—labeling machines	Inventory control, work in process, job costing, machine shop loading, job shop simulation, accounting control
$7,000,000	4,000	Manufacturer—shirts	Billing, accounts receivable, inventory control, sales analysis, commissions
$9,000,000	4,500	Manufacturer—shoes	Inventory control, billing, accounts receivable, cost control, budgeting, accounts payable, general ledger accounting

Keeping Correct Concept in Mind

Typical of what can be done with EDP in the small company with the right approach and a common-sense viewpoint is illustrated at Carbon Limestone Company, Lowellville, Ohio. John A. Bannach, Treasurer, points out that it is well to keep in mind that not all computers and electronic data processing machines are "brains," but high-speed processing and storing machines.

After a survey, Carbon Limestone installed an NCR Compu-tronic machine to replace two older accounting machines. Three functions were put into the computer system:

- *Payroll:* Computation of wages (200 employees), expense distribution, individual earnings records, paychecks, payroll journals, quarterly payroll tax returns, and withholding statements.
- *Sales accounting:* Customers' invoices, maintenance of accounts receivable ledgers, sales distribution, and cash receipts.
- *General accounting:* Accounts payable with preparation of voucher register, distribution, voucher check, and check register.

Results: Equipment-wise, the cost was a stand-off. The computer cost the same as two new models of the machines in use. However, these are the definite benefits:

- Records are neater, more accurate, and prepared faster.
- Elimination of a high-priced technician used on the old system.
- Equipment will permit general ledger bookkeeping on the machine in the future.

Bannach points out that there's more to it than buying a machine and watching the results come in. Patience is necessary. Carbon Limestone scheduled the installation of its program over a period of one year, and even with the most careful planning of the most minute details in advance, bugs developed, and unworkable programs were encountered. Vital to the success of your installation is the assignment of a person qualified in office procedures to the job, and to get the continued cooperation of the equipment manufacturer.

MAKING THE TOTAL SYSTEM WORK

In discussing the pros and cons of a total electronic data processing system, there are many who will cite the disadvantages of a total system for the smaller company. This has not been the experience of the General Dental Supply Company, Inc., in New York. This $2 million, seventy-five-employee business successfully installed a total system, the first in its industry. According to Leopold Lapidus, Treasurer, the smaller company can benefit greatly, if certain simple rules are followed. They are as follows:

Prerequisites

The project, of course, must have firm support from top management from the start; this support must recognize that the planning and implementation will take a number of years. And, of course, throughout the entire process, the company must be guided by a competent and experienced systems planner —with particular knowledge of small businesses and their problems.

Initial Steps

The employees come first; they must be convinced of the importance of a smooth-running, well-coordinated business, with particular emphasis on the the fact that the project is *not* a cost-cutting, job-elimination plan. If new methods are installed, employees will be trained at management expense for the new methods. The systems planner should then make a detailed survey of the business and how it is carried on, with emphasis on the strengths and weaknesses of its personnel. The environment in which the business operates should be a part of the survey, encompassing political, social, and competitive factors, and the prospects for growth.

Based on the survey, a Master Plan should be set up, which would include:
- A detailed "chart of functions."
- An organization chart based on the chart of functions.
- A comprehensive chart of cycles.

This would be the cycle of processing a customer order: (a) Sales Department—obtains order and forwards to: (b) Credit Department—accepts or rejects. Rejected order returned to Sales Department. Accepted order forwarded to: (c) Warehouse—fills order and sets back order processes, if any, in motion; filled order forwarded to: (d) Billing Department—bills order, sends packing copy to Shipping, customer's invoice copy to Data Processing, and so on.

If graphically presented, the charts will show that there are a few major cycles which encompass all the operations necessary to carry on the business, and that these cycles are interrelated.

The Master Plan must be reviewed with top management in every detail so that management's knowledge of the business can be put to best advantage to modify and improve the plan. It goes without saying, of course, that top management must approve the concepts of the Master Plan.

Implementation

It is necessary, of course, to work out with management a program and timetable for implementing the plan. These basic principles should be observed:

- The Master Plan, in most cases, will have to be separated into "modules," or subsystems, which can be installed into the framework of the business to both improve operations and cause the least disturbance.
- Relations between company and suppliers and customers must either remain the same or be improved. No temporary letdown can be permitted.
- The "profit impact" of the installation of each subsystem must be budgeted in advance.
- Affected personnel must be informed and trained; wherever possible, "pilot projects" should be used to test planning and personnel.
- Supervision and evaluation of performance should be very thorough immediately after the installation of each subsystem and may be withdrawn as performance warrants.

Management can assure the success of the program through the exercise of two responsibilities: (1) at all times use the system by working through its channels, and (2) to engage outside professionals (preferably those who had a hand in the installation) on a periodic basis to review the system and suggest improvements.

Profitability Determination for the Small Distributor

EDP provided the means for determining the profitability of some 30,000 to 40,000 items stocked at four branch warehouses of the Mine and Smelter Supply Company, Denver, Colorado. The company is engaged in the wholesale distribution of industrial supplies, and the existing accounting system permitted determination of both gross and net profit operating results at each warehouse.

According to V. C. Barnhart, Secretary-Treasurer, an adverse trend in both gross and net profits at each branch pointed up the necessity of a deeper study into the profitability of the various commodities stocked. On a manual basis, the study was both physically and economically impossible, since only a net profitability factor would provide the necessary analytical data for a judgment. This was the problem: which commodities, which customers, and which sales territories were producing a *net* operating loss while appearing to carry a satisfactory *gross* profit.

Studies of the situation revealed two things:

- The existing accounting procedure could produce, manually, all of the information needed for data processing, but at prohibitive cost.
- With EDP, sales information about transactions could be related to operating expenses and divided into "fixed and variable" classifications in such a manner as to produce vital *net* profitability rates on each commodity, customer, and territory.

Business consultants were called in, and after going through the almost inevitable frustrations of switching from one system to another, EDP became the key tool in attaining the ultimate objective of net profitability determination.

EDP plays a part in two closely related functional activities in achieving the goal:

1. The development of basic sales statistical information on a commodity category level, broken down by out-of-stock and by factory-to-customer classifications.
2. A system of allocating operating expenses (overhead) to each classification of sale on a basis which permits costing of each segment of the sale (commodity, customer or territory) to produce a net profit for each.

Objective No. 1. Here EDP is proving itself. A by-product, (automated) punch tape, produced as a billing to the customer is prepared. Through a system of coding, the merchandise is classified as a major or minor category, the transaction as an "out-of-stock" or "direct transaction," and the sales territory credited with the sale is tabulated. The punched tapes are then sent to an independent service bureau, where all the pertinent information is punched on cards. The cards may then be sorted, collated, read, and printed to furnish any type of sales report desired, and in whatever detail is felt needed.

Objective No. 2. The gross profit percentage is determined for each commodity, and this percentage follows the commodity in whatever segment of sales the commodity is classified or used. Furthermore, each commodity is measured by the "lines of billing" involved in each transaction for a given period. Operating expenses are then reduced to a "cost per line of billing" which becomes a common denominator for the allocation of overhead expenses to each and every segment of sales, regardless of how classified in the final reporting. The result was that gross profits, determined at the commodity, customer, and territory level, produced through allocation of operating expenses according to the number of lines of billing involved, become the "net profitability" factor through which a commodity line, customer, or territory can be tested. The above method of overhead application, of course, is "Simplified Operating System Cost Analysis" (SOSCA) and is advocated by the National Industrial Distributors' Association.

Punch Card Inventory Control for the Small Company

Punch-card inventory control for a small company can be successful, according to O. B. McConathy, Secretary-Treasurer of Arnold Pipe Rental Co., Corpus Christi, Texas, which rents oil field equipment on a daily fee basis. The system for his small company costs the same as the manual system it replaced, and in addition provides: (1) much more diversified reports in a shorter time, and (2) more time for the material control department to expand and improve its area of operation.

The equipment rented consists of small-diameter drill pipe and handling tools. The mechanized inventory control system revolves around these conditions:

- Each piece of equipment individually identified.
- Equipment transferred as needed between five geographical locations in two states.
- Material control department must visually inspect equipment once each year.
- Approximately 9,000 pieces of equipment separated into 66 groups.
- Income analysis needed on each piece of equipment.
- Disposal of all equipment that is not revenue-producing.

With this in mind, the following data is placed on each card:

1. A code number for each of the 66 classifications.
2. A four-digit subcode number is assigned to each code group. (Example: The code and subcode number for the first-numbered Adapter is 1-0001. Thus, the system allows for the numbering of 9,999 Adapters.)
3. Description of the equipment.
4. Date of purchase.
5. Voucher number supplied by the Accounting Department.
6. Cost of the equipment.
7. A designation of whether the equipment was purchased new or used, which permits easy analysis of equipment subject to depreciation rate limitations and investment credits.

In addition, space is provided on the card for Material Control to indicate the date of inventory or visual inspection, the location of the equipment at the time of inspection, miscellaneous remarks, and space for recording biannual income.

The system provides these benefits:

- A means of income analysis of equipment in detail and by groups.
- A comprehensive analysis of the age of the inventory at a minimum cost.
- A mechanical footing of all inventory cards allows a monthly comparison of the inventory value with the General Ledger Controls.
- A print-out of the complete inventory by geographic locations is available. Material control can use the print-out to expedite verification of the inven-

tory. (This procedure alone cuts by seventy-five percent the inventory time required to verify and write a description in longhand.)

HOW TO CONSOLIDATE SMALL OPERATIONS
FOR EFFECTIVE USE OF EDP

If the accounting operations of small subsidiaries cannot be mechanized, you may find the experience of Geo. F. Brown & Sons, Inc., of Chicago, to be of interest. The accounting function of the company involves the maintenance of records and accounts for thirteen separate corporations; eight of these are wholly-owned subsidiaries, and four are insurance companies managed by Geo. F. Brown. Maurice L. Wooden, Treasurer, reports that effective EDP operations have resulted from a number of steps taken by the company.

Among these steps are:

1. All employees are employed by the parent company, and there is thus just one payroll—even though there are normal parent-subsidiary relationships and company-managed operations.
2. The parent company owns all fixed assets and equipment, and pays all operating expenses of its subsidiaries or managed companies. The latter pays the parent a fee for the services. In the company's operation, the subsidiaries (not the managed companies) are not intended as separate entities for profit determination. Thus the fee allocated to the subsidiary is not viewed as an estimate or allocation of the actual expenses of that subsidiary for accounting purposes.
3. Since the basis of the system is uniformity, the first rule is the elimination of duplication. For example, formerly there were two to ten banks for each corporation; now one bank may handle several corporations. This has eliminated printing and storing an inventory of check forms, the reconciliation of many bank statements, and the need for minimum balances. In some cases, business develops a high volume of actual cash and check receipts which require local deposit. Local depositories are utilized, but all accounts in excess of a modest balance are forwarded daily by depository transfer system to the central account.

A transaction will illustrate the system. When payment is received, a receipt voucher is prepared (the same for all companies). The funds are identified only as being (a) premium or general operating funds, or (b) belonging to the managed or subsidiary company.

- General receipts are identified by general ledger number as in any system, except that they are segregated only into two groups.
- Premium receipts are grouped, but no coding to the general ledger account is done on the deposit slip.

Vouchers representing the day's deposits are rushed to the accounts receivable section in batches throughout the day, so cash is being applied within a few minutes after it has been put into process.

An open file of punched cards represents accounts receivable, each premium billing or credit on a separate card. Within the grouping of the subsidiary and managed companies all receivable cards are combined. For each payment received, cards are withdrawn or created. Although sorted together, each card is punched with a code for the company involved. When the day's remittances are balanced, the cards pulled and created are listed by EDP and totals by company provided. This provides the credit to the accounts receivable general ledger control.

The same breakdown is developed for disbursements. Disbursements are drawn against the common fund, but are charged specifically against the several companies' interest in the total fund by company code entered on the account breakdown of the charge. For example, we may issue a credit refund to a producer and deduct a smaller balance owed a second company; by coding the credit to accounts receivable in one company, less a charge in the second, and issuing a check for the net, the EDP adjusts our records to reflect the revised interest of all companies in the fund, and to adjust our receivable balances in both companies.

All disbursements are coded with indicative information to make it possible to print an EDP voucher register, and check register. Departmental codes are punched, making analysis of income and expenses by departments possible. Though some handling and control batching of this is done by the companies manually, the cards, once punched, are sorted and processed as one job. Only as one last pass are they finally separated by company.

USING MICROFILMING FOR SAVINGS

Microfilming is now big business. The growth of different industries normally is triggered by innovation and, in that respect, the growth of the microfilming business from an estimated $500 million at present to an expected $1 billion by 1975 is no exception. A good part of the current growth and the anticipated growth in the next half decade will have come about because of the adaptability of microfilming to computer output. The marriage of the computer and microfilming has been called by the industry Computer Output Microfilming (C.O.M.). The industry has grown at such a pace that there is now a National Microfilm Association (NMA) which represents the industry as a spokesman. C.O.M. operates directly from the computer and prints at the computer speed. Normally this is almost thirty times faster than conventional recording methods. It saves incredible space because a small cassette can hold 2,300 pages of information and has the ability to fit in the palm of an individual's hand. More than twenty-five companies today are now developing or producing C.O.M. equipment, and the response to it has been extremely exciting. Robert Asleson, who is President of University Microfilms in Ann Arbor, Michigan, noted that C.O.M. can reduce mailing costs by close to ninety percent and "reduce catalog revision cycles and updating times to a fraction of the previous requirements." It is possible through the use of microfilm to reproduce catalogs and other bulky material on a six- to eight-inch microfilm which might contain up to 200 pages of information. It is the contention of some experts that even further reduction of size is possible by using higher-reduction microfilm equipment together with a computer. When that time comes, books will be printed only on demand, eliminating inventory and transportation problems. The technique has proved a boon to hospitals and doctors who have been and will be able to store many more records within the confines of limited administrative space. A leading business magazine recently reported that a Manchester, New Hampshire department store lost $1 and a half million of inventory in a disastrous fire and had $1 and a half million of customer charge accounts destroyed. The inventory itself was covered by insurance and the customer records are re-established because the credit manager had a regular policy of microfilming the records and stored them safely off the premises. That same magazine also reported that the microfilming of engineering documents places films on the factory floor.

The Boeing 747 was built more efficiently because the blueprints for production were all microfilmed. This had the effect of easing the handling of the documents and the speed of referencing various phases of the documents. Planes and submarines, it is expected, will be carrying their own blueprints for maintenance and repair on a microfilmed operations sheet. The reason for this is that weight and space are prime considerations in these types of vessels.

A Profit-Improvement Device

Robert Miningham, a systems consultant with Wright Data Systems Incorporated, recently reviewed the use of microfilms as a profit-improvement device. It must be remembered that in viewing the cost savings available through the use of microfilming, the key is the speed of the microfilm reproduction. Ordinary output printers for computers are much slower than the speed of the computer itself. This is not the case with microfilming equipment. One month's output of an IBM 360/30 line printer can be produced in approximately one day by a computer microfilm recorder. The printer itself is capable of printing at the rate of only 2,500 characters per second. In contrast, the microfilm recorder attached to the computer can print the equivalent of 120,000 characters per second. Mr. Miningham reports that the printing of a 1,000-page report on an IBM 360/30 will cost about an hour of computer time, or approximately $65 based upon service bureau charges. In contrast, he contends that a service employing C.O.M. could print the same report on microfilm for about $15, in effect creating a savings of approximately $50 per computer running hour. Another facet of cost savings possible through the use of microfilm has to do with the reduction in the cost of materials for reports. Reports which are copied on microfilm cost about one-tenth the cost of reports produced in a conventional fashion on paper. The savings manifest themselves most when reports are produced which are to be delivered to more than one user. Considerable savings are possible by printing only the original and first copy of a report and microfilming all additional copies. It would be only logical, then, for corporations to use preprinted forms for many of their reports enabling them to save an even greater amount of money, since the C.O.M. system can photograph a form design at the same time it photographs information coming from the computer tape. Preprinted forms are therefore unnecessary. Mr. Miningham reports that one company, having a 3,000-page weekly report distributed to few locations, can save over $4 thousand a year through the use of microfilm.

Savings in Handling Costs

Concurrent with the cost savings in the physical cost of materials are savings in handling costs, since large quantities of paper are eliminated through the use of microfilm. It has been estimated that in one month's time a computer can turn out approximately two tons of paper. The attendant computer-type operations of bursting and decollating for reports are eliminated through the use of film, and Mr. Miningham estimates that one man operating a C.O.M. system can handle over a million pages a month. In addition to the bursting and decollating time savings, binding costs are also eliminated. Approximately 3,000 pages of information can be packed in a cartridge for less than a dollar. Paper binding costs for the same type of operation are approximately $10.00 for the same number of pages.

Reduction of Distribution Costs

Distribution costs are prone to being reduced through the use of microfilming. A 3,000-page equivalent report placed on microfilm can be sent almost across the country by airmail for approximately thirty-six cents. That same report sent by fourth class mail, if it were on paper form, would cost approximately $6.00. In fact, if telecommunication devices were used, it would be even more unwieldy for transmitting a 3,000-page report. It would require at least seventeen days and nights, and a high-speed data transmissional terminal would require at least eight hours to send the same report; each would be at a very high cost.

Another aspect of cost savings reported by Mr. Miningham is that microfilm systems tend to fill a large gap between batch processing and real-time systems. If it is required to update a file not more than once a day and the actual power of the computer is therefore not needed to manipulate data, the large computer system may, in fact, not be needed, and the cost associated with such a system can be eliminated if a microfilm system can be designed which will provide for the updating of files and the preparation and distribution of information in less than six hours.

Increased Individual Worker Productivity

One of the beauties, of course, of storing information on microfilm is the rapid retrieval of such data which is possible. When a microfilm system replaces a tub file or other manual techniques which may be employed, there are more benefits than the obvious which are derived because of the increased speed of retrieval. Individual worker productivity can be vastly increased, thereby reducing the unit cost for such operations.

Thus far we have talked about the computer-oriented aspects of microfilm savings. The growing surge toward microfilm was instigated not because of the C.O.M. system, but because of the dollar effect of space savings. At today's building rates, any system which can free space occupied by file cabinets or machines can be a tremendously effective vehicle for cost reduction. In New York City, for example, space costs may range between $5.00 and $25.00 per square foot, depending upon the location and the facilities. Using that square footage for the employment of filing cabinets is an economic waste. Any microfilm system which will permit the elimination of such cabinets in favor of floor space for employees can affect profits significantly. It must be remembered that under conventional systems, if such cabinets are not eliminated, the provision for space for any additional employees usually involves the knocking down of walls, the changing of air-conditioning ducts in ceilings, lighting, etc.

As a rule of thumb, it is possible to achieve a reduction of more than fifty percent in the cost of printing and distributing computer reports through the use of the C.O.M. system, rather than using paper as the output of the computer.

10

SUCCESSFUL USE OF
NEW MATHEMATICAL MODELS

THE ESSENCE OF FINANCIAL MODELS

Total information is not a virtue. In fact, it can be an eroding vice (vise?). In fact, so many misconceptions have arisen around the theme of mathematical models for financial planning that many companies have now seen fit to disband this area of computer applications and have reverted back to utilizing the two basic resources of the efficient executive—his brain and his hand. In fact, during the economic downturn which took place in 1970, many corporate and computer operations research executives for the first time had something in common with their advertising and research and development counterparts; they were the first to have their jobs cut out from under them during times of employment retrenchment. Even a man such as David Hertz, a computer expert, has said, "It hasn't been clearly demonstrated yet that computers are helpful to the top management process."

Some years ago, Merle Crawford wrote an article called "The Shotgun Marriage Between Mathematics and Marketing" in which he expressed the opinion that exotic marketing models were largely a failure because of the inability of the model-oriented man to communicate to the individual who is not necessarily so oriented. He complained that in many respects the technically-oriented people had developed a jargon of their own and, in fact, had built a castle with a moat around it into which only those who are privy to the jargon could enter. In a large sense, the jargon problem has a great deal to do with the effectiveness of corporate model-building for financial planning. At the outset, let me state my opinion that I do believe that there are effective corporate models for financial planning, but they are pitifully few. I also believe that it is an evolutionary way of the future which will become more effective and more widespread as the limitations of such models are more widely understood. The challenge, after all, in a simulation program which is the essence of a model, is to capture the essence of a total organization. Even before the model is created, it is created with an impossible objective. No one can ever be sure that any plan has accounted for all of the alternatives among the choices which can be made, nor can we be sure that all of the relevant inputs have been included. This, though, need not be a constraining criterion for limiting the effective use of corporate models. An analogy might be drawn to the automobile which may be driven despite the fact that the carburetor may not be in the best shape nor the brake linings completely perfect. The essence of the argument is that the automobile nevertheless does take you from one destination to the other.

A Simulation Program

A simulation program, the essence of the model, is in reality a mixture of determinable facts, certain assumptions regarding the future, judgments as to the sensitivities of variables, calculations which are intrinsic to the business, and, above all, human intuition—guesses, if you will. And largely, this combination of characteristics takes the physical form of an iceberg because the model in the final analysis is reduced to a workable combination of mathematical formulae. The formulae, however, take on the profile of a piece of matter. Because in order to construct the visible portion of the model which is the end product, the input data which is used for the model has undergone a series of massages which have taken on the appearance of atoms, nuclei and subparticles of matter. In other words, it is a process of reducing complex systems which in turn have subsystems, which in turn have subsystems feeding them. The model, therefore, is an extremely complex piece of achievement which is constantly changing and constantly growing. Any model in order to be effective must be a flexible model and capable of producing its output in a manner which is understandable to the user and, moreover, it must be a model which is oriented toward pragmatic decision-making.

THE PEOPLE INVOLVED IN THE MODEL PROCESS

The computer has already had a major effect on the financial profession as it serves private companies. In using the term "financial profession," I am alluding to the accounting staffs for the most part, along with financial planning personnel if they are separate. Regretfully, however, many in the financial profession, including practicing public accountants, view the application of financial planning more in terms of budgeting than they do in true simulation.

There is a distinct difference between a plan and a budget and unfortunately the public accounting restrictive view of budgeting hinders true financial planning whether through the application of model-building or not. A financial plan is a true guide, a road map. The plan has an objective, the road map shows the various routes, the side streets, the crossroads, the alternative choices as to how to reach the destination. It is easy to trace that road which can bring the driver most easily to his destination in the shortest and safest time.

The budget on the other hand, is very much like a two-lane highway. There is a right side to the road and a left side to the road and the driver must stay somewhere in between the right side and the left side if he is to stay within the budget. The end objective, of course, may still be the same.

However, in terms of practicing business problems, I have too often seen situations where close to the end of the year individuals have discovered that they have not made expenditures in the amount of the budget and therefore they have turned around and said, "By golly, I've still got $300 thousand to spend and I'll find a way to spend it before the end of the year." Planning models do not deal with this latter type of situation. They are much more concerned with the former. This type of orientation, which stems from the rigidity of financial disciplines which are inherent in the training of most financial individuals, leads me to suspect that the burden of construction for financial planning models will ultimately, if it has not already done so, fall into the specialized area of operations research.

John Dearden, in an article, once indicated that one of the difficulties facing practicing operations research personnel is that unlike other professionals, such as lawyers, doctors or accountants, the cross which the operations researchers had to bear is that they continuously have to explain what their discipline is. That by itself creates terrible difficulties in trying to reach the practical, pragmatic business executive.

Operations Research

Operations research is a wide area of activity. It certainly is not a new or mysterious profession which has sprung up in response to the fact that a computer exists. This is not a question of Parkinson's Law as it applies to the creation of new professions. In fact, operations research involves an extension of many of the techniques, ideas and principles which have been used by business for many years. What has happened, though, is that all of this body has been compressed into a formal and recognized discipline which now has a proper name. In its essence, though, it is an attitude. The American Management Association in one of its papers, says that the operations research approach to a business problem involves the following basic steps:

1. Observation and general study of the problem area
2. Definition of the problem
3. Fact-finding
4. Analysis of the data and construction of a model or hypothesis
5. Comparison of the model with observed data
6. Repetition of each step, if the model proves not in agreement with observed data, until a satisfactory model is constructed

Dearden adds in one of his papers that a descriptive type of definition is also needed to assist the understanding of the technical definition. He cites the following elements of operations research as being characteristics of the operation:

a. There is a team approach to problem solving
b. The members of the team represent different areas of expertise of scientific background
c. There is a mathematical model
d. There is interaction and involvement with the decision makers

Each of the foregoing citations begins to lower the level of the water around the iceberg by fractions of an inch so that underneath the top we are now beginning to expose the layer of complexity involved in model-building. At this juncture, though, it is probably appropriate to add that these caveats which are being offered regarding the complexities of model-building are not intended to frighten off the reader from either considering or utilizing these techniques. Many facilities are available which are relatively inexpensive to use and which still incorporate the essence of model-building.

It is still a truism that there are not many companies doing very extensive operations research work. However, there are a number of companies which are finding interesting uses for variants of operations research techniques. William Vatter in his most interesting study, published in *The Accounting Review* demonstrated very clearly that the search for effective uses of mathematical models continues, however, in areas which are alien to simulation and model-building. Companies interviewed in his questionnaire overwhelmingly applied the greater part of their operations research techniques to studies involving factor analysis, queuing models, linear programming models and various regression analyses.

Dearden indicates that he feels that there are four general categories of tools for formal operations research methods. He cites these as, financial models, statistical models, mathematical programming and simulations. He is correct in observing that financial models have been with us for some time. He observes that, in fact, business would be lost without them. He makes the important observation, though, that because simulation techniques did not appear until the decade of the sixties, it is clear why operations research has become so closely identified with mathematical programming, especially linear programming. Of course, the operations research which we are discussing in the context of this paper goes far beyond linear programming techniques and, indeed, we will progress in short order to the financial model in particular.

It is probable that if planning models are to become effective, changes in basic corporate organization will also have to be created. One of the reasons for the essential failure of operations research as a functioning management group has been the fact that operations research personnel, for the most part, do not have access to the highest levels of management where decisions are made. As a result, they have frequently been derided and their profession misunderstood. Nevertheless, it should not detract from the value of the operation.

It would appear to me that the soundest approach to an effective organizational concept for decision-making is to establish a separate functioning area for management sciences. This separate area should be independent of the data processing system. For too long management science techniques have been associated with the computer and more often, operations research and systems groups have found themselves reporting to the head of data processing. In essence, this is an anomaly because the two fields can be very alien to each other. Just as physical distribution should be an independent reporting function, so should operations research.

Artists and Models

One of the first things that is necessary to accomplish in order to continue the discussion of model-building and proceed toward its application in financial planning is to define the precise nature of a model. A model purports to be a representation of the real world. It is a computer program which has as its basis input mathematical equations. These in turn are designed to simulate realistic business situations and reflect the operating nature of the business.

Generally the model is completely mathematical. The challenge in the creation of models is to build one which will react and produce results which are likely to mirror actual operations. Clark Sloat indicates that he felt it was possible to identify different relationships with well-known scientific theories and as a result, include the data in a form which has been proven by scientific experiments. He says that the use of mathematical expressions is scientifically determinable and can be relied upon for probabilities and further that product demands can be identified with known types of distribution curves, so that he felt that, over a period of time, there was a correlation of actual results with predictive results.

George Gershefski wrote a fine paper for the Planning Executives Institute recently dealing with the development and applications of a corporate financial model. In the course of writing that paper, he cited some of the work done for the Sun Oil Company. One of the more valuable aspects of that paper was a question and answer session which he used as a base for expanding on the concept of the Sun model. Because of the relevance of his observations to the subject being discussed, it is appropriate here to review some of Mr. Gershefski's feelings about different aspects of model building, especially as it concerns financial planning:

. . . Once developed, a model provides accurate projections rapidly and inexpensively; it is comprehensive and follows a precise documented procedure. In short, management can be quickly provided with meaningful decision-oriented information.

. . . Models are extremely valuable for comparing and evaluating alternative courses of action that might be followed; by compiling the results of feasible alternative plans, they can provide management with information which is helpful in determining realistic objectives for the corporation. Models are also useful in short-term profit planning by providing an independent estimate of net income for gauging how well current operations meet management targets for profitability, growth and stability. Finally, models are an efficient means for developing a revised estimate of income when originally planned circumstances are expected to change. It is important to note that models neither create plans nor make decisions; they do, however, provide structured information to aid in these processes. Models will be most effective when employed in a company which plans on a formal basis and which follows a style of management by objectives.

. . . A chess game can provide another view of the concept of a model. If, in addition to the board on which the game is being played, one of the players has another chessboard set up beside him with the pieces in identical positions as in the real game he could move the pieces to determine the outcome of various strategies in advance of his actual move. The chess set at his side would serve as a model of the real game.

Examples of Functional Model Applications

At this point, it should be somewhat obvious to the reader that a model can be many things and that there are various applications within corporate life for models. The applications extend into various fields. Some of the better known examples of functional model applications are for:

- warehousing and distribution
- inventory control
- sales forecasting
- production scheduling
- large volume of processing
- distribution costs
- decision simulations
- labor negotiation models
- capital budgeting

- product pricing
- portfolio analysis
- risk analysis for product innovations

No function within a business or no element of the business is an island unto itself. If I were to paraphrase John Donne, each function is, "A piece of the continent; a part of the main." For example, Exhibit 1 shows the conceptual view of a new product model which is currently in use by Detroit Diesel Allyson, which is a division of General Motors in Indiana. Looking at the concept of the new product model, it is obvious to the viewer that many elements of the "marketing" new product model involve relevant inputs which are related to financial planning. Even within this somewhat simplified view of the model, the following are various inputs required from financial planning:

Capital investment

Production expenses

Fixed manufacturing costs

All of the relevant accounting data involving:
  working capital
  depreciation
  unit prices, etc.

The output for the model is expressed in terms of return on investment with a stockholders' eyeview of the result. In addition, the following are decision outputs stemming from the model:

Annual cash flows

Annual profits before and after taxes

Annual dollar sales

Present value

Annual lost sales

Sensitivity analysis

This latter phrase, sensitivity analysis, is an interesting newcomer to the jargon of model-building. In reality, sensitivity analysis is nothing more than the consideration of possible changes in the basic data input for a given problem. The consideration of the changes measures the effect of such changes on the final result. It is also an examination of the magnitude of change required in basic data before the entrance of new data is applied to the final basic solution.

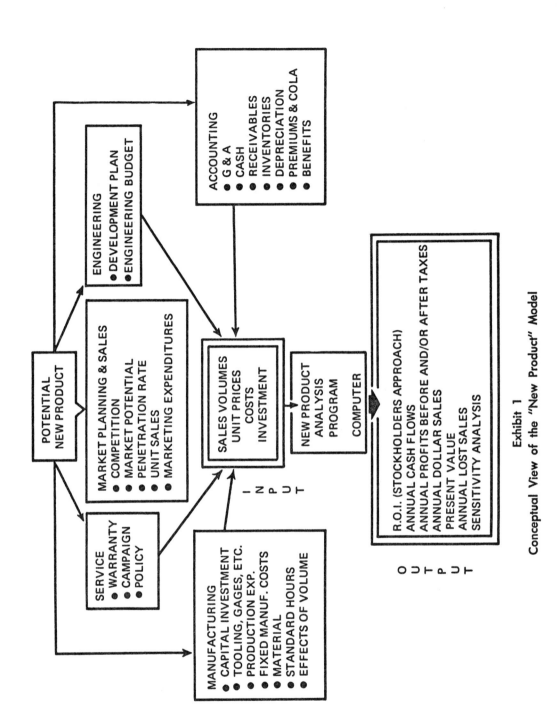

Exhibit 1
Conceptual View of the "New Product" Model

338

THE DESIGN OF THE MODEL

Michael Tyran wrote recently that, in order to develop an effective and appropriate projection model, certain common considerations are inherent in most design systems. He cites the following:

1. Data requirements
2. Manual procedures
3. Participating organizations
4. Level of sophistication
5. Level of process
6. Organization structure composition
7. Assessment of historical data
8. Specific flow and data interface

A predecessor even to these steps is the formulation of a corporate objective or goal to be integrated into the model. George Gershefski in his paper cites the following as the sequence to help management achieve that very first step:

> The first step in all planning is collecting pertinent information from each department of the company. Complete data on operations and costs are not required at this stage; only those forecasts or assumptions necessary to make a projection with the model are needed. Generally, this is less than that required to make a full-scale budget projection because of the equation and relationship within the model.
>
> There is also a change in emphasis. As an example, the investment and the sales volume for a typical marketing outlet are requested. The total sales volume is *not* to be estimated at this point since it depends on the total amount of capital allocated to the sales effort and the investment and volume per outlet. The capital allocation, in turn, depends on management's profitability and growth targets which are being determined as a result of this process.
>
> After having collected the required forecasts, the next step is to develop and to evaluate various planning alternatives. As an illustration, consider a company which has two areas competing for capital: the marketing segment and the raw material supply, or production, segment. To determine the consequences of investing in one area versus the other,

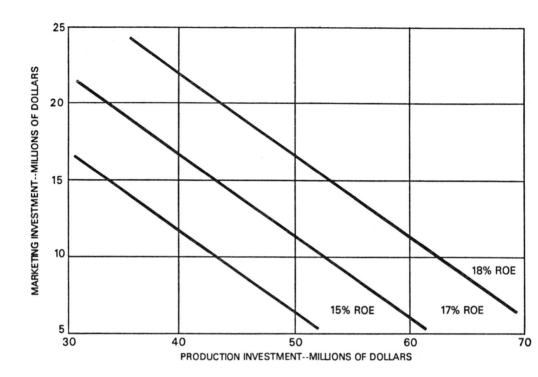

Illustration 1

the financial model projects profitability assuming different investment allocations between the two. The results of a number of allocations are summarized in Illustration 1. The chart shows the amount of money invested in production along the horizontal axis and the amount of money invested in marketing along the vertical axis. To construct the diagram, the return on equity for each case is plotted versus the amount of money allocated to each area. Points with the same return on equity are connected to form a line of equal value. Illustration 1 is based on hypothetical data and implies that cases of equal value formed a straight line. One line, for example, is labeled 18 percent return on stockholders' equity. This means that any combination of investment mix that falls on this line will earn 18 percent return on stockholders' equity. A production investment of $40 million along with a marketing investment of $22 million would result in an 18 percent return, as would a $60 million production investment along with a $12 million marketing investment.

When an approach of this type is taken, problems evolve outside of the model which must be analyzed and resolved. For example, in a particular case there may be inadequate manufacturing capacity to handle the market share considered. If so, it is necessary to determine the manufacturing facilities required, submit the appropriate changes to the model, and re-examine the investment allocations.

Once realistic forecasts have been made, executive management selects that investment allocation or combination of alternative plans which will meet the corporate goals as they define them. Return on equity is the management goal in this illustration. However, management may also be interested in such items as earnings per share, percent debt in the capital structure and earnings stability. Thus, they may choose an investment of $50 million in production and $16.5 million in marketing since it yields an 18 percent return and provides the most satisfactory level of achievement relative to other management aims.

A model projects the anticipated performance for each department of the company to determine the total corporate outlook. Thus, choosing a corporate target also implies an operating plan and investment level for each area. In the case of marketing, for example, the amount of money to be invested would be determined directly; this can be translated into a specific sales objective. If each department accomplished the designated tasks, then the company as a whole will attain the desired goals.

At this point in the process, detailed plans and budgets are prepared by each department to meet the desired objectives. A consolidation of the individual plans results in an overall profit plan for the coming period. This step is followed by the usual ones of comparing actual with planned results and of determining reasons for any variations. If the economic outlook changes substantially, it may be necessary to repeat the process since revised goals may be appropriate.

All models begin with the initial input of data. An example of the data flow for an organizational financial plan is shown in Exhibit 2. Based upon this type of organization for requiring data flow, models can be created for the various areas which were cited earlier.

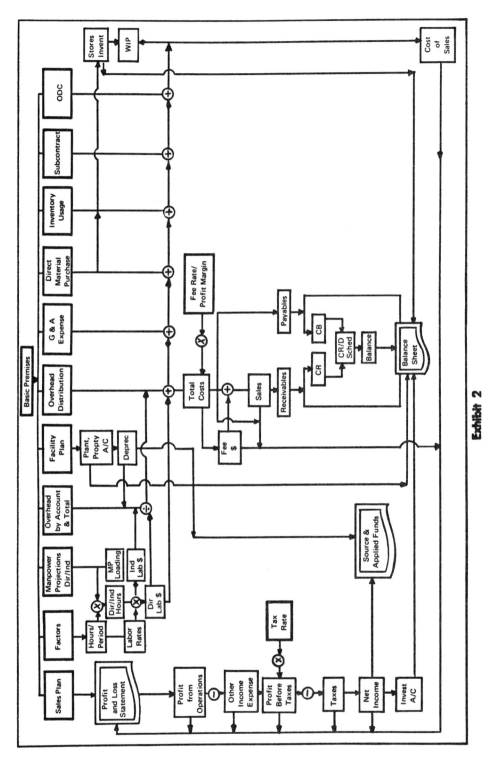

Exhibit 2

Organization Financial Plan—Data Flow

(Michael R. Tyran, "A Computerized Decision-Simulator
Model," *Management Accounting,* March 1971, p. 21)

342

INVENTORY CONTROL MODELS

The Vatter study referred to earlier indicated that one of the most popular fields for the application of modeling techniques is in inventory control. Inventory control lends itself to modeling techniques because, generally speaking, the variables inherent in inventory levels are not nearly so susceptible to change as they are in, for instance, marketing problems.

Most practicing executives are familiar with the expression EOQ. The initials stand for the expression "Economic Order Quantity." This is a statistical procedure whereby inventories are theoretically optimized by automatic repurchase patterns. The essence of inventory management involves a problem of a delicate balance of costs. These costs necessarily are opportunity costs; they are the costs of alternative actions.

Certainly the penalty for carrying excess inventory involves severe charges and the inflation of working capital requirements. The risks that are inherent in a poor inventory policy include those of obsolescence and damage to materials. In addition, space costs, inventories, taxes, and imputed interests are real considerations in the level of inventory maintenance. The word "optimized" was used previously for a specific purpose.

There is absolutely no virtue in attempting to achieve an inventory policy which will assure that all distribution points have sufficient stock to make all orders to customers at the time that all orders are requested. Any system that will attempt to achieve 100 percent coverage of requirements is a costly system and can be proven statistically unprofitable. A far better minimization program involves that of balancing the costs of carrying the inventories sufficient for 100 percent deliveries against the cost of being out-of-stock. The cost for being out of stock is an opportunity cost which is inherent in the risk that a consumer may not come back to purchase an item if it is not found to be immediately available.

It is, of course, possible to live on a day-to-day basis and frequently have stock-outs. No company with any operating intelligence could afford this type of program since it would inevitably be detrimental to its commercial policy. The basic question then arises, as was stated by Clark Sloat, as to "How much inventory we should carry and when we should reorder the various items we are required to use so that we can maintain a reasonable balance between the costs of carrying inventories, the costs of running out-of-stock and the costs of purchasing materials."

It is a truism that the importance of inventory largely depends on the nature of the individual industry. Obviously, service industries do not suffer the same inventory penalties as do purely commercial industries.

The problem can be looked at really only in one way. William Parks wrote that only one goal is really appropriate for any inventory system. But in his view it can be expressed in either of two ways—to minimize the total cost or alternatively, to maximize the profit within a specified time, considering the various resource requirements. Further, when opportunity costs are included in the total cost, it is his view that the aims are identical. Total costs in this sense can be defined as a combination of *order costs*. This is a cost which is incurred when ordering merchandise or establishing the mechanics of making the material available.

Carrying Costs

Carrying costs are expenses which are generally associated with the cost of capital, insurance, storage costs, obsolescence, spoilage costs and the cost of not having the alternative investment opportunities because inventories are in stock.

Shortage Costs

Shortage costs were referred to earlier as the cost of being out-of-stock when the merchandise is requested by a customer. In this sense, this type of cost includes the actual penalty of being deprived of the profit margin and, in an opportunity sense, the cost of never regaining the customer.

Most statistical texts teach that the EOQ formula is the best inventory control system in the traditional sense. Mr. Parks indicates that in his view it is inadequate for practical commercial use for the following reasons:

1. The formula assumes that the costs of being out-of-stock are relatively insignificant and thus can be ignored for the most part. In this sense, it is his contention that it fails to recognize one of the three earlier cited main costs of carrying inventory.
2. It fails to allow for comparisons of low points on several curves simultaneously, thereby rendering itself useless when quantity discounts are available. In other words, the EOQ formula is adequate only when no quantity discounts for purchasing are involved in the sales policy of the company.
3. It fails to provide an estimation of variation, thereby necessitating an arbitrary safety stock, an item not provided for in computing the *best order quantity*.

Traditional Definitions

Traditional EOQ quantities are found by minimizing the total cost when that cost is defined as including only carrying costs and the basic order costs as well as the initial basic material costs. The following traditional definitions are given for inclusion in the formula for economic order quantities. They are, following Parks, as follows:

$$TC = \text{Total cost}$$
$$Q = \text{Order quantity}$$
$$O = \text{Order cost}$$
$$T = \text{Material cost}$$
$$C = \text{Carrying cost}$$
$$K = \text{Annual demand}$$

The derivation of the formula, although necessary, is not particularly significant to the discussion, therefore, based upon calculus, the final formula for EOQ is determined as follows:

$$EOQ = \sqrt{\frac{2KO}{CT}}$$

One of the difficulties in the EOQ equation is the cost of determining the penalty for being out-of-stock. Even if the answer cannot be explicitly calculated, an attempt should be made to make an approximate estimate for the cost of being out-of-stock based upon the probabilities of repurchase. This is necessary because the only realistic method of determining an inventory reorder point must consider the interplay between the factors of cost.

In other words, at the best level, carrying costs and shortage costs are equal. In that respect, it is somewhat analogous to the discounted cash flow calculation in which an interest rate is sought that will equalize both inflow and outgo. Parks points out that the reorder point should be increased until the carrying cost of adding one more unit to the inventory just balances the expected costs of being out-of-stock.

Certainly the techniques for inventory models are derived from statistically complex formulas, some involving the Poisson distribution, which is a method of describing a series of independent events. In some instances, management service areas of major accounting firms who have tackled the inventory control problem have been able to achieve a reduction of at least fifteen to twenty percent in inventory levels while still maintaining adequate customer service as defined by the respective managements of the companies. It is expected naturally that not every company can afford either the management services area of major accounting firms or their own operations research staffs. At the very least, however, the IMPACT program, which is a "canned" program for inventory control offered by IBM, is available for purchase and has proven to be a highly effective instrument for inventory control.

Warehouse	Market Requirements	Unit Transportation Costs From Plants				
		1	2	3	4	5
A	50 M	$.250	$.375	$.375	$.500	$.175
B	250	.175	.250	.325	.450	.140
C	75	.100	.225	.275	.425	.175
D	25	.140	.220	.225	.425	.190
E	30	.195	.190	.150	.400	.220
F	40	.325	.210	.175	.235	.315
G	50	.350	.190	.150	.210	.325
H	200	.290	.190	.220	.125	.240
I	60	.295	.175	.190	.110	.250
J	40	.220	.090	.210	.150	.215
K	20	.450	.200	.175	.175	.340
L	150	.175	.350	.275	.325	.175
M	70	.200	.350	.300	.325	.200
N	10	.225	.375	.325	.350	.225
	1,070 M					
Productive Capacity	1,300 M	250 M	300 M	250 M	300 M	200 M
Unit Production Cost		$4.00	$3.50	$2.50	$4.00	$3.50

Exhibit 3

MODEL USES IN PHYSICAL DISTRIBUTION

The problems inherent in the physical distribution function include some of the problems already cited in inventories. However, because of the diversity of the function and its place as an arbitrator between production capacity and sales requirements, the questions of physical distribution often find themselves placed in an allied but distinctly different pattern from those of inventory control. For example, practical business questions often arise which ask:

a. What is the optimum location for our warehouses?
b. Which manufacturing plant is best located to service the various warehouses?
c. What type of transportation should be utilized to deliver merchandise into the warehouses?
d. What level of customer service was needed to stay ahead of competition?
e. How much time is needed for order processing, packing, etc.?
f. Were the added costs for improvements in customer service resultant in an ultimate increment to profits or not?

In his writings on the subject, Clark Sloat cited a simple problem which was easily solved by the use of mathematical programming methods. The problem is shown in Exhibit 3. Notice that the following data is shown in the problem:

Geographic warehouse requirements

Geographic plant manufacturing capacity

Unit production costs by plant

Freight costs per unit from each plant to market

In his simplified problems, Sloat asks two basic questions regarding the problem:

1. How much should each plant produce?
2. Which warehouse should be supplied from which plant?

When the statement of the problem is transcribed in terms of a formal mathematical formula, it can be placed into a preprogrammed computer and the solution evolved in a matter of minutes. The solution to the problem just shown is in Exhibit 4. Sloat, a member of Price Waterhouse & Company, has indicated that use of this type of mathematical technique can produce savings of five to ten percent of the cost of the services, provided that the services have previously been very carefully established. It is his opinion that savings of five to ten percent are fairly representative of achievements.

		Plants				
Warehouse	*Requirements*	1	2	3	4	5
ALTERNATIVE I:						
A	50,000					50,000
B	250,000	30,000	70,000			150,000
C	75,000	75,000				
D	25,000			25,000		
E	30,000			30,000		
F	40,000			40,000		
G	50,000			50,000		
H	200,000				200,000	
I	60,000				60,000	
J	40,000		40,000			
K	20,000			20,000		
L	150,000	145,000		5,000		
M	70,000			70,000		
N	10,000			10,000		
Production		250,000	110,000	250,000	260,000	200,000
Plant capacities		250,000	300,000	250,000	300,000	200,000
Unused plant capacity		0	190,000	0	40,000	0
Unit production cost		$4.00	$3.50	$2.50	$4.00	$3.50
ALTERNATIVE II:						
L		(70,000)		70,000		
M		70,000		(70,000)		
ALTERNATIVE III:						
L		(10,000)		10,000		
N		10,000		(10,000)		

Exhibit 4
Optimum (Minimum Cost) Solution

Avoiding Costly Mistakes

Writing recently in the *Financial Executive,* J. H. Hennessy, Jr. indicated that much faster response times are being achieved both in filling custom orders and in replenishing stocks of real time computer systems and a wide variety of operations research techniques involving advanced inventory and probability theories. As a result, he says that physical distribution has been surprisingly underrated because of the overshadowing preoccupation with computer control for inventory. In those companies which have attempted to remodel the physical distribution systems, some costly mistakes have occurred because the companies did not understand the following:

. . . Did not clearly understand the level of customer service needed in terms of lead time and percent order filling.

. . . Did not realize that the time increments for order processing, picking, and packing quite often make up for large segments of overall required lead time for the distribution of products.

. . . Failed to recognize that small increments of time are involved when shipping distances between source points and customers are extended; nor, on the other hand, how premium shipping modes and faster handling methods can reduce lead times from distant points —approaching the lead time for regular local delivery.

. . . Companies failed to visualize how the variability in demand for regional stocks would increase relative to the increase in number of regional stocking points. This, in turn, requires larger safety allowances and a larger overall inventory carrying penalty for the corporation.

. . . Had misconceptions as to the importance or need for fast delivery on the part of most customers.

. . . Failed to realize that increases in the number of regional stocking points results in increases in the number of back orders within the system.

. . . Did not evaluate the financial tradeoff between improved customer service and added costs.

In order to develop competitive service parameters for the creation of a viable distribution system, Mr. Hennessy created a discussion guide which serves as the basis for developing the distribution model. It is reproduced below. It should be remembered that physical distribution is consuming an increasingly larger part of the revenue dollar.

DISTRIBUTION SYSTEM DISCUSSION GUIDE

(Reprinted by permission from *Financial Executive*, April 1969, J. H. Hennessy.)

Competitive Customer Service

What is competitive service in terms of:
- Delivery cycle time?
- Percent order fill?

What is competitive importance of delivery relative to other competitive influences such as:
- Features or quality of product?
- Price?
- After-market service (i.e., replacement parts for mechanical products)?

What competitive advantages in terms of lower delivered cost of products can be achieved by field inventories:
- Shipping in bulk to major markets?
- Final assembly of products close to major markets?
- Other?

Our Present Customer Service

What is the estimate of present lost orders:
- In dollars?
- As a percent of sales?

What would happen to lost orders if:
- More or fewer items were stocked?
- More or fewer stock locations were employed?
- Higher or lower inventory levels of items presently stocked were carried at present distribution points?

Do lost orders also produce lost customers:
- Does poor delivery merely lose the order on which the delivery is late?
- Does poor delivery not only lose the order in question but cause the customer to go elsewhere on a continuing basis?

Is present customer service competitive:
- Delivery time?
- Line-item fill percentage?
- Order-fill percentage?

- Can we reduce the present inventory investment without other offsetting increases in costs and still meet competition?
- Could we increase the present inventory investment and thereby make a larger percentage return on this investment?

Inventory Profile

Are the items we stock consistent as to physical characteristics such as:

- Size and weight?
- Packaging and shipping characteristics?
- Substance (i.e., metal, fabric, etc.)?
- Storage characteristics (inside, outside, perishable, nonperishable, etc.)?
- Value-density relationships?

If not consistent in what significant classes do they group?
Are items stocked consistent as to markets:

- End use?
- Types of customers (producer, distributor, consumer, etc.)?
- Industrial user classifications?

If not consistent, in what significant classes do they group?
Are items stocked consistent as to demand characteristics:

- Demand consistency?
- Seasonal characteristics?
- Customer service?

Is not consistent, in what significant classes do they group?
What is the number of items in each of the above classes of inventory?
What dollars and percentage of total annual dollar demand do the items in each class represent?

Items Constituting

Class	Top 75% of Sales $	Next 15% of Sales $	Lowest 10% of Sales $	Class Totals
Number of Items				
% of All Items	%	%	%	100%
Sales	$	$	$	$
Average Inventory	$	$	$	$
Sales to Inventory				
% of Class Inventory	%	%	%	100%

Distribution System Profile

How many stocking activities are in existence:

- Factory?
- Regional?
- Territorial?
- Specific products?

How many warehouse facilities are in each type of activity and what is the approximate number of square feet in each:

- Factory?
- Regional?
- Territorial?
- Specific products?

What is the rationale behind the present number and location of stocking points in each distribution plan?

What is the mission of each level or type of distribution activity and how does it relate to the other levels?

What are the total number of items and average inventory investment in each distribution level or type of stock and for the largest and smallest outlets within each level or type?

What is the average inventory turnover in each level of distribution and high-low turnover of outlets at each level and for each product category?

What modes of transportation are in use and under what criteria?

- Common rail carrier?
- Common motor carrier?
- Common air carrier?
- Owned carrier?
- Private carrier?

Do transportation modes and policies differ between master and regional warehouses and territorial depots and/or between stocking points within each of these classes of stocking facilities? If so, how?

Inventory Policies

What products are stored in the plants at which manufactured?

What products are also stored in regional or national master warehouses serving territorial depots and why?

What items are stored in area or local warehouses and why?

What is the criteria for master warehouse stocking?

What is the criteria for regional warehouse stocking?

What is the criteria for local warehouse stocking?

Do the criteria which govern the replenishment of stocks in each of these stocking levels differ and if so how?

Do the criteria differ as to product classes and if so, how?

Are safety stock criteria common for master, regional, and territorial depots, and are they computed on the basis of national, regional, or territorial factors?

Do stocking criteria create pyramiding of stocks between levels?

How are products classified as to movement:

- What are criteria for a fast-moving port?
- What are criteria for other classes—slow-moving, medium, others?

Are criteria predicated on:

- National sales movement?
- Regional or territorial sales movement?
- Combination?

What criteria are used in determining order size and frequency for replenishing inventories in each stocking level:

- Economic lot formula?
- Fixed number of orders divided into annual forecast?
- Fixed order size divided into annual forecast?
- Other?

What criteria are used in establishing order points:

- Fixed order cycle time with provision for a specified percentage variation but uniform demand?
- Fixed order cycle time with provision for demand variations?
- Fixed order cycle time with provision for:
    Variation in cycle time?
    Variation in demand rate?
    Seasonal variations?

How is demand variation measured:

- From forecast sales?
- From historical sales?

If safety stocks are established how is this done:

- Guess of interaction of demand and lead-time factors on stock-out frequency and estimated safety stock required to keep stock-out frequency livable?
- Analysis of demand variations from forecast and application of a factor to the standard deviation to produce a specific frequency of stock-out (i.e., 5% or 1%)?
- Formulation relating demand variation and order quantity to produce:

Minimum recovery period when stock-out occurs?
Minimum pieces on back order between time of stock-out until replenishment takes place?

- Formulation which balances cost of carrying safety stock to lost order cost?

Inventory Practices

What practices are observed with respect to the following:

ORDER PROCESSING

Order Profile:

What are the typical number of line items and shipping and weight characteristics of specific classes of orders, such as:

- Seasonal?
- Product class?
- Customer class?
- Special sales?
- Special handling—i.e., emergency, overseas?
- Other?

What is number of orders received each month in total and for each class?

What are the average, mode, and upper and lower quartiles of line items per order, each month; in total and for each class?

What are the back-order percentages for each of the above classes of orders in terms of number of orders and line items per order?

What differences exist in the uniformity of demand rate for each of the above classes of items?

Order Entry:

Is order entry a centralized function or are orders entered at local warehouses?

What is the order processing sequence and functions and the elapsed time and manhour values for each:

- Mail and registry?
- Edit?
- Credit and special terms?
- Warehouse documents and controls?
- Back-order procedure?

Are items out of stock at one location ordered against stocks in other locations? If so, under what controls?

What is the order time cycle for each class of order such as:

- Large seasonal orders?
- Specific product classes?
- Specific customer type?
- Special handling—i.e., emergency; overseas?
- Other?

Methods and Equipment:

What basic order processing methods are in use:

- Manual?
- Manual—mechanical?
- Unit record (tabulating)?
- Computer:
    Sequential processing?
    Random processing?
- Combination?

What is the number and make of each class of equipment in use in the order entry system?
If rented, what is the annual rental cost?
What is percent utilization of this equipment for the inventory function?

PICKING, PACKING AND SHIPPING

What picking plan is observed—line, zone, or other?
How has the warehouse been laid out?

- Bin trip activity?
- Bin trip density?
- Other?

Where are reserve stocks placed in relation to ready stocks?
How frequently are locations of items in the warehouse established to reflect activity status?
Are individual picking tickets received from order entry?
Are picking tickets presorted into picking sequence to insure optimum picking time?
Are picking tickets for items on back order prescreened to prevent pickers from walking to empty bins?
Are partially filled orders held for complete filling or shipped partial? What factors govern?
Do items requiring emergency handling bypass the normal order entry procedure for expedited picking?
What equipment is used to expedite the order-fill cycle:

- Conveyors?
- Automated pickers?
- Others?

What is the packing procedure:

- Pickers do own checking and packing?
- Separate checkers and/or packers do checking and packing?

What is the average pick-pack time cycle for specific class of orders and products?

What provisions exist for maintaining control over status of orders in process, and for communicating advice to customers on delayed or back-order items?

With respect to specific classes of orders and products what are the manhour requirements per order and per line item for:

- Picking?
- Packing?
- Shipping (loading)?

STOCK STATUS AND REPLENISHMENT

What procedures exist for communicating that a reorder point has been reached at a bin location to the stock control and procurement organizations?

What are the average time requirements for:

- Recognizing that a reorder situation exists?
- Instituting a replenishment order on the vendor or other source?
- Upon receipt of items ordered, communicating the availability of the items received to the inventory control organization?
- Updating of stock status records upon notification of receipt of items by the inventory control organization?

What procedures exist for short-cutting replenishment procedures where items go on back order?

What reports and records exist in connection with stock status, and are these suitable as to format, content, and timeliness?

Are stock status, purchase order, and accounts payable procedures integrated? If not, what advantages are served thereby?

What systems and equipment are used for stock control:

- Manual?
- Manual—mechanical?
- Unit record (tabulating)?
- Computer:

  Sequential processing?
  Random processing?

What are the costs for these activities?

Are the capabilities of the system in terms of stock status reporting appropriately related to the capabilities of the organization to respond to information made available and are they consistent with competitive requirements?

Cost Factors

What is the cost for storing product at the various stocking levels and by types of product:

- Master?
- Regional?
- Territorial?
- Product?

How have, or how should, such costs be developed so that they can be applied to products with different weight-cube-and-value relationships?

What is the cost for handling an order:

- Order processing?
- Picking?
- Packing?
- Shipping?

How are replenishment order sizes determined and what cost factors are applied and how have they been developed?

How have, or how should, such factors be applied to products with different weight-cube-value relationships?

In evaluating different stocking configurations and warehouse operating concepts, how can or should changes in the following factors be reflected by changes in the appropriate cost factors?

- Bin cube utilization?
- Warehouse cube utilization?
- Concentration of stocking closer to packing operations?
- Mechanization and conveyorization?
- Number of items stocked?
- Lead-time periods?
- Stock-out frequency criteria?
- Number and location of stocking points?

How have, or can, freight costs be developed for each mode of transportation to reflect:

- Differences in the weight-cube-value relationships of products?
- Differences in routings?
- Differences in distances shipped?

What changes occur in inventory holding and handling costs with changes in the number of regional or area warehouses, or with changes in their mission, and how are these changes reflected by changes in transportation costs and costs for lost orders?

In a study done approximately twenty years ago, it had been concluded then that distribution costs as defined in the study consumed approximately 60¢ out of every revenue dollar. Although modern valid statistics are not available for the sake of comparison, it is probable that that number has increased certainly to about the 70¢ level. This makes all the more important the acceleration of a program to remodel a physical distribution system based upon the most efficient design which can be produced by the interaction of statistical and probability theory along with plain old commercial horse sense.

MODELS FOR PORTFOLIO MANAGEMENT

Contemporary market analysts are more aware than ever that there are many variables in securities markets and that indeed the variety of these variables has increased in the more recent past. Every technique that is available, including sticking a wet finger to the wind, can and probably should be used for portfolio selection. However, whereas in the past, much portfolio selection was based upon manually and mentally generated subjective evaluations of price earnings ratios, new techniques involving linear programming and quadratic programming have evolved which, at worst, can offer the manager an alternative course of action and an evaluation of the risk that is faced in choosing a portfolio configuration.

Linear Programming

Linear programming is one of the most appropriate techniques for computing the best composition of an investment portfolio. Obviously, the use of such a technique is dependent upon specified investment objectives, constrained by natural and imposed parameters. The two main considerations involved when evaluating any investment are the potential risk involved and the amount of potential return that can be expected within a given time period. Obviously these two factors are mutually independent of each other and vary inversely with each other. In other words, a safe investment carries a lower return than a riskier investment. Using linear programming techniques, it may be possible for a medium risk portfolio, for example, to represent a ninety percent probability of a seven percent return annually. Thus, through the use of this type of logic, a portfolio manager can determine whether it is better to have the ninety percent probability of a seven percent return or a ninety-five percent probability of a six and one-half percent return. Applying the linear programming technique to such problems enables the manager to make this type of decision. The constraints that might be built into a linear programming portfolio problem could involve such typical considerations as:

1. The price earnings ratio cannot exceed sixteen
2. The earnings growth rate must exceed twelve percent
3. Price appreciation must be greater than eighteen percent
4. Yield cannot be less than three percent
5. The range of the yield must be less than one-half percent

Based upon the objectives and the constraints, a linear programming matrix is constructed and as a result of that matrix, a number of solutions may be possible. Without going into specific statistical techniques or complicated examples of sample portfolio problems, it is better said that linear programming is an ideal technique for optimizing portfolio analysis. It does have certain advantages over quadratic programming because it provides greater flexibility and utility.

Quadratic programming deals with constraints, but the constraints are of a secondary nature as compared to the linear programming technique in which these are "first-degree functions." In essence, the linear formulation is better suited for portfolio analysis since any return function may be accommodated and it tends to offer a more realistic approximation of actual conditions.

In addition, many "canned" linear programming computer programs are readily available and are offered for service either by service bureaus or the larger computer concerns. Bond portfolio analysis is a logical extension of securities portfolio analysis with the exception that generally speaking the objective in bond portfolios is to maximize the bond yield, whereas in the securities portfolios analysis, probabilities of appreciation and yields tend to be more important. For those interested in the particular subject, I would commend an article for reading which appeared in the *Financial Executive* in February of 1967 by Alan Bean called "Portfolio Analysis and Stock Selection by Computer."

RISK ANALYSIS MODELS FOR NEW PRODUCTS

An extremely interesting working paper by H. Paul Root at the University of Michigan was recently published dealing with the subject of risk analysis for product innovations. In the context of this working paper, which is an overall document, the computer simulation model developed by Professor Root includes the following components:

The marketing plan

The manufacturing plan
    Capital investment plan
    Manufacturing cost estimates
    Unit variable costs

The financial plan
    Cost estimates for the financial plan
    Other financial estimates

        Financial summary information

    The computer analysis cost

The importance of this working paper is that the model presented in the paper has been used successfully in real life situations. One corporation which has successfully pioneered in introducing risk analysis models for overall planning has been CPC, International. That company has found that in-house training seminars acquainting personnel with the objectives and techniques employed in the model were the most effective way to achieve the understanding in successful implementation for the model. One of the key factors in their success has been the fact that they made the model more easily accessible to line managers. And the model was explained in depth to selected corporate officers.

Major Types of Plans

The inputs required for each of the major types of plans are as follows:

Marketing Plan
        Unit price
        Promotional expenditures
        Unit sales
        Marketing cost as a percentage of sales

Manufacturing Plan
        Capital investments
        Fixed manufacturing costs
        Capacity limitations
        Variable costs

Financial Plan
        Depreciation
        Other fixed costs
        Costs as a percent of sales
        Working capital requirements
        Tax rate
        Present value discount rate
        Return on investment calculation options
        Terminal year options

The above mass of required input data is specified as required annually or otherwise for products or product types and, most importantly, is expressed in terms of probability of attainment and best estimate.

The computer program was originally written in Fortran IV and has been adopted for a variety of computers ranging up to the new third generation computers currently in use at the University of Michigan. In philosophizing on the results of the sensitivity analysis program, Professor Root made an interesting observation when he said that the implementation of this type of technique has shown that the use of this model can change the behavior of the user in the analysis process. This is an extremely interesting deviant from rationalization that the process often follows the other way around and the tail wags the dog. In any event, the paper is a significant contribution to actual corporate business practice and new product development as it applies to finance.

CONCLUSION

The world of mathematical models for financial planning is growing more sophisticated and is expanding in concept at a frightening rate. One planning model called PROPHIT is in existence and uses a modeling concept which will permit the user to prepare alternative solutions to a problem and consequently increase the probability of making a correct business decision. Its virtue is that several possible courses of action can be charted in a very short period of time and, through the use of a terminal, a model can be defined which fits a particular business situation.

Once the model has been defined, a report of projected data and its probable results is available. A typewriter-type terminal is used which is connected to a large service bureau corporation computer center by ordinary telephone service which is installed in the facility of the user. The user is charged for the computer time and the storage which is used. The process is so simple that the data is typewritten at the terminal keyboard; the computer then processes the data and transmits the forecast back to the terminal where it is printed in output form. Not too many years ago this type of procedure would have been considered part of an Alice in Wonderland tradition and would have been much more suitable for a James Bond type of novel than the prosaic environment of the average business executive.

There is no question in my mind that modeling is beneficial and that it is here to stay. What must be carefully evaluated by the potential user is the ability of the user to fully understand and comprehend the limitations of any mathematical formula. Outside of the physical laws of nature, it is the rare event which can be mathematically programmed to behave in a precise manner. No model is the end-all of a decision. It is merely an adjunct to the finger-in-the-wind tradition.

11

NEWER, MORE PRODUCTIVE
BUSINESS RESULTS ANALYSIS

FINANCIAL RATIOS

Financial facts and data cannot be used in their raw form. There must be interpretation and analysis of these data—and this interpretation and analysis is an important function of the financial department. By analyzing data, the financial officer can assist management in:

1. Understanding historical results
2. Highlighting current trends
3. Forecasting the financial future

Since the data are not usable in their raw form, there must be some basis for comparison. Basically, these comparisons can take two forms. The first, and most general of these comparisons, is a comparison of the company's operations with industry generally, or with specific competitors. These are external comparisons. The second type of comparison is a comparison with goals and objectives which the company set for itself; these are internal comparisons.

External comparisons can be made with specific companies (e.g., competitors), or with statistics for entire industries or groups of companies. Particularly in the latter case these comparisons can be made by means of financial ratios.

The ratio is one quantity (a numerator) divided by another (the denominator). The ratios fall into several categories as shown in Figure 1.

The ratio is an indicator which is used to test the strength of the financial structure. To use this indicator norms must be available to measure against. For example, to say that the ratio of debt to equity is .650 is meaningless unless some means of evaluating .650 is available. Dun & Bradstreet annually publishes complete tables of ratios for 72 types of businesses. Figure 2 shows a sample of these ratios. Many trade associations publish financial ratios for their particular industries. These reports are produced on a cooperative basis and are generally available only to companies who submit their financial

365

Type	Name of Ratio	Numerator	Denominator	Notes
Liquidity	Current Ratio	Current Assets	Current Liabilities	
	Acid Test Ratio	Cash & Securities & Receivables	Current Liabilities	
	Collection Period	Average Receivables	Annual Sales Divided by 365	Number of days of sales outstanding as receivables
	Inventory Turnover	Annual Cost of Goods Sold	Average Inventory	
Effectiveness of Assets	Asset Turnover	Annual Sales	Total Assets	
	Fixed Asset to Sales	Fixed Assets Net of Depreciation	Annual Sales	
Profitability	Return on Sales	Profit After Taxes	Annual Sales	
	Return on Assets	Profit After Taxes	Total Assets	
	Return on Net Worth	Profit After Taxes	Net Worth	
	Debt to Equity	Total Debt	Total Equity	Dollars of debt per dollar of equity funds
Borrowing Capacity	Cash Flow to Sales	Profit After Taxes plus Depreciation	Annual Sales	Rate of cash profit per sales dollar
	Time Interest Earned	Profit Before Interest & Taxes	Interest	
	Cash Flow to Debt Service	Profit After Taxes plus Depreciation	Annual Rate of Debit Repayment	Rate of cash profit to cash obligations

Figure 1

366

MANUFACTURING: FOOD AND KINDRED PRODUCTS:
Canned and frozen foods

Item Description (for accounting period 7/68 through 6/69)	A Total	B Under 50	C 50 to 100	D 100 to 250	E 250 to 500	F 500 to 1,000	G 1,000 to 5,000	H 5,000 10,000	I 10,000 to 25,000	J 25,000 to 50,000	K 50,000 to 100,000	L 100,000 and over
				SIZE OF ASSETS IN THOUSANDS OF DOLLARS (000 OMITTED)								
1. Number of establishments	1588	357	208	133	177	311	246	96	38	9	4	9
2. Number without net income	457	141	65	58	64	33	69	9	12	2	2	2
3. Total receipts (in millions of dollars)	8071.3	68.6	56.2	46.8	203.5	520.2	992.4	1187.9	817.6	596.3	331.7	3249.5
Selected Operating Factors in percent of net sales												
4. Cost of operations	76.1	71.1	68.5	75.6	86.1	79.5	82.6	90.0	76.6	82.9	78.1	66.6
5. Compensation of officers	.7	2.3	3.6	3.2	2.3	2.1	1.1	.5	.8	-	-	-
6. Repairs	1.0	1.6	.5	2.4	.5	.8	.8	.5	1.3	.8	-	1.2
7. Bad debts	-	.5	-	-	-	-	-	-	-	-	-	-
8. Rent on business property	.7	.5	-	1.1	.9	-	.5	.6	.8	1.3	1.8	.8
9. Taxes (excl Federal tax)	1.9	2.3	2.2	1.5	1.3	2.4	1.7	1.5	1.8	1.3	1.8	2.1
10. Interest	1.4	1.3	1.1	1.1	.8	1.0	1.3	.7	1.5	1.4	2.5	1.7
11. Depre/Deplet/Amort†	2.1	2.8	2.0	2.5	1.5	1.9	1.9	1.4	2.5	1.6	3.4	2.4
12. Advertising	2.3	2.3	-	-	-	-	.7	.8	1.1	1.6	2.4	4.3
13. Pensions & other benef plans	.6	-	-	-	-	.5	-	-	.6	-	-	1.1
14. Other expenses	10.8	12.6	12.1	11.4	5.6	9.3	8.7	5.3	10.3	7.2	11.0	14.8
15. Net profit before Tax	2.3	2.9	9.0	-	.6	1.6	-	*	2.6	2.1	*	4.6
Selected Financial Ratios (number of times ratio is to one)												
16. Current ratio	1.6	3.2	1.8	.9	1.2	1.4	1.4	1.2	1.5	1.6	1.2	2.2
17. Quick ratio	.5	2.5	1.1	-	.5	.5	-	-	-	.6	-	.7
18. Net sls to net wkg capital	6.4	24.5	10.4	-	21.4	10.9	8.6	12.0	6.9	8.1	12.0	4.3
19. Net sales to net worth	3.3	21.2	7.0	5.7	6.8	5.5	4.9	5.9	3.0	4.1	5.3	2.2
20. Inventory turnover	-	-	-	-	-	-	-	-	-	-	-	-
21. Total liab to net worth	1.1	1.3	1.1	1.7	1.2	1.3	1.5	2.3	1.1	1.1	3.3	.7
Selected Financial Factors in percentages												
22. Current liab to net worth	75.0	39.3	79.9	145.5	107.9	105.2	118.7	195.8	85.2	79.5	157.1	42.9
23. Inventory to curr assets	64.3	19.3	35.8	39.7	56.1	62.2	64.3	77.8	66.7	55.7	56.1	61.7
24. Net income to net worth	8.6	98.1	51.4	13.7	7.3	10.8	8.1	7.8	7.4	8.3	3.6	8.7
25. Retained earn to net inc	60.4	83.5	100.0	82.6	85.4	94.9	87.7	92.4	88.4	84.7	100.0	39.9

†Depreciation largest factor

Figure 2

Illustrative Chart of Ratios for Industries available in
Almanac of Business and Industrial Financial Ratios,
Prentice-Hall, Inc., Englewood Cliffs, N.J.

data. Collection Period—This ratio states the number of days required to collect the average accounts receivable dollar. The formula for computing it is:

$$\text{Collection Period} = \frac{\text{Average Accounts Receivable *}}{\text{Annual Sales}} \times 365$$

* Average Accounts Receivable is the average of the balance at the beginning and at the end of the year.

The collection period gives a good indication of the delinquency of customer payments. If, for example, sales are on a Net 30 basis and the collection period is 45 days, one can see that the average bill is paid 15 days late. Another important use to be made of this ratio is for predicting changes in the level of receivable with changes in sales volume. In the 454 day example, receivables can be estimated as 1½ months sales ($\frac{45}{30} = 1\frac{1}{2}$). When it is used this way, care should be taken to investigate seasonal shifts in collection period. Some companies have a 90 day collection period at Christmas time and a 45 day the remainder of the year. For companies with a seasonal trend, the chart shown in Figure 3 will instantly compare the receivable picture to previous years.

| | | Collection Period | |
Month	2 Years Ago	Last Year	This Year
Jan.	42	39	46
Feb.	44	45	48
Mar.	40	46	52
Apr.	48	49	55
May	51	54	
June	50	50	
July	54	52	
Aug.	46	49	
Sept.	42	47	
Oct.	41	44	
Nov.	40	45	
Dec.	38	43	

Figure 3

TECHNIQUES FOR SPEEDING COLLECTIONS

To improve the collection period means more cash on hand. Several moves can be made to speed up collections. Tighter credit rules and tougher collection procedures are major steps and run the risk of lowering sales. Offering cash discounts will, if anything, attract new sales. The drawback is the cost of offering a cash discount. The cost to go from Net 30 to 1%, 10 days would be computed as follows:

1. With $100,000 outstanding and a 50 day collection period, the sales per day would be $100,000 ÷ 50 or $2,000 per day.
2. If, 1%, 10 days were offered, and the collection period became 20 days, the receivables then become 20 × $2,000 or $40,000. This means increased cash of $100,000 − $40,000 or $60,000.
3. The cost per year, if all sales were discounted, would be 365 × 2,000 × .01 or $7,300.
4. The percentage cost of the $60,000 would be $7,300 ÷ 60,000 or 12.2%.

At first glance a financial manager might discard the idea as too expensive. First he must consider—

a. He has increased his cash on hand which could immediately be used to pay off a 6% loan and, thereby, further improve his current ratio (explained below) and acid test ratio.
b. The improved current ratio and lower debt may allow him to get new long-term debt to finance capital projects which would otherwise have been turned down.
c. The discount terms may attract more customers and offset the financial cost with greater sales.

Lock Boxes

Companies whose operations cover a wide geographic area have found the use of bank lock boxes to be a very efficient means of receiving collections from sales to customers. Lock box arrangements are relatively simple.

In their high sales volume areas companies will rent post office boxes. The mailing address shown on its invoices to customers in these areas will contain the post office box number. The billing company then enters into an agreement with a bank in the area, whereby the bank becomes the company's agent with respect to picking up its mail. The bank at frequent intervals throughout each day cleans out the contents of the post office box. The overall result of this arrangement is that customer's checks, which are usually drawn on local banks, are immediately processed for payment by the firm's bank. Copies of these checks and other data contained in the customer's mailing are forwarded to an accounts receivable area according to the company's directions.

This procedure is to be compared to the former practice of having customers mail all of their payments to a central point, usually corporate headquarters. In the case of customers located far from corporate headquarters this meant checks coming cross-country only to be returned through the banking system for payment at their point of origin.

Use of lock box systems have provided companies with collections as much as three to five days earlier than systems in effect prior to their adoption.

Important "Borrowing Capacity" Ratios

The amount of debt which a company can employ without incurring excess risk or higher cost depends on the firm's financial condition. The most important ratios to measure ability to borrow are Current Ratio and Debt to Equity Ratio. The Current Ratio is the amount of assets which will be converted to cash within a year divided by the liabilities due within one year. It is, therefore, the ratio of potential cash within one year to known demands on cash within a year. A one to one ratio would mean no liquidity or safety margin. A two to one ratio would mean one dollar in reserve for every dollar obligated for payment.

So long as the ratio exceeds one to one, the current ratio can be improved by more efficient use of current assets as follows:

1. Lowering cash balances and using the extra cash to retire current liabilities.
2. Lowering the collection period and using the cash generated to reduce current liabilities.
3. Improving inventory turnover and applying the cash to current liabilities.

If the ratio is less than one to one, the above measures will actually worsen the ratio. However, in these circumstances, the financial manager is faced with the need to ration his cash resources in relation to the maturities of current liabilities, and any additional efficiency which he is able to achieve in the use of cash will assist in that effort.

The debt to equity ratio assesses a very fundamental fact—what part of the funds comes from outsiders and what part comes from stockholders. A lender is vitally interested in this ratio since a sure sign of financial trouble is excessive borrowing. To decide how much borrowing is excessive requires comparative data from similar companies, and an assessment of the relative risk involved in the cash flow of the companies.

Data necessary to make comparisons must be obtained from a variety of sources. The U. S. Department of Commerce publishes a pamphlet which lists many of these sources ("Guides for Business Analysis and Profit Evaluation," published by the U. S. Government Printing Office). If a precise comparison with a particular competitor is required, it will be necessary to calculate the relevant information from the competitor's published statement, or other available information.

HOW MUCH DOES MONEY COST

When additional capital is to be invested in new products, two questions must be answered. First—What return will there be on the invested money? Second—What will the additional capital cost the company?

If $100,000 were to be added to inventory for a new product line, what is the financial cost of carrying that inventory? If banks would lend the $100,000 at 6%, the temptation is to say that the inventory costs 6% per year. However, the borrowing of the $100,000 has increased the debt to equity ratio and decreased the current ratio. This means additional borrowing will be harder to get. Eventually a company which borrowed for all its needs would reach its debt limit. At this point banks would say "No more loans until more equity funds are put in the company." New equity funds have a cost since new stockholders would want a 10% after-tax return. Thus borrowing the $100,000 at 6% before taxes will lead to a need for other money at a 10% after-tax cost. Beyond this, of course, are the additional costs of carrying inventory such as taxes, additional warehousing charges, spoilage, insurance, and so on.

Computing the Cost of Capital

The procedure for computing the cost of capital is as follows:

1. Recognize the difference between before-tax and after-tax cost. For example, a company paying a bank 6% interest has a $.06 \times .5$ or 3% after-tax cost assuming a 50% tax bracket.
2. List all major sources of capital on a balance sheet as shown in Figure 4.
3. Compute the before-tax cost of tax-deductible types of funds (See Figure 4).
    a. For loans use the annual interest rates.
    b. For secured loans use the interest rate plus service charges.

    EXAMPLE: If receivable financing costs 1% of invoices used as security plus 7% interest, the computation would be

$$\text{Total Cost} = (\text{Svc. Charge}) \times \frac{\text{Sales}}{\text{Receivables}} + \text{Loan Interest}$$

$$= 1\% \times \frac{1,000,000}{200,000} + 7\%$$

$$= 12\%$$

An alternative method of computing the cost is from past records. The total of the bank's service and interest charges for the past year is divided by the average loan balance. The average loan balance is obtained by totalling the twelve month balances and dividing by 12.

Type of Funds	Computed Cost Before Taxes	Tax Multiplier	After Tax Cost
1. Trade Credit (lost discounts)	.09	.50	.045
2. Bank Loan	.06	.50	.030
3. Secured Loans	.120	.50	.060
4. Bonds	.064	.50	.032
5. Accruals	.000	.50	.000
6. Preferred	.600	1.00	.600
7. Common Stock	.100	1.00	.100

Figure 4
Source of Capital-Cost Computation

c. The cost of trade credit on which discounts were missed is a possible cost to be considered. If the discount period is shown as D.P. and the actual pay period as P.P., the cost in percent per annum is

$$\% \text{ cost} = \frac{\text{Discount } \% \times 365}{(\text{P.P.} - \text{D.P.})}$$

$$= \frac{.01 \times 365}{50 - 10} = .09$$

d. The cost of term loans, mortgages and bonds is computed by adding the interest rate to the amortized expenses of obtaining the debt. A 20 year 6% bond issue for a million dollars which had a $50,000 underwriting expense would be computed as:

$$\text{Cost } \% = .06 + \frac{(\quad 50{,}000 \times 1 \quad)}{(1{,}000{,}000 \times 20)}$$
$$= .064$$

    e. Other liabilities such as accrued payroll, accrued taxes and trade credit on which discounts are taken have no tangible cost.

4. Equity Funds have a cost which must be *imputed*. When a stockholder invests in a company, he expects a return on his money. How much he expects depends on the risk involved which in turn depends on the type of company. A utility stockholder will be happy if his money earns 7% while in an electronics company the figure might be 15%. The management's task is to earn this expected return. Thus the cost to the management is the 7%, 15% or whatever the stockholders expect of them. Preferred stockholders clearly state their expected return on the stock certificate. Common stockholders do not spell out their expectations. It is up to the financial manager to estimate them.

    a. *How to Compute the Cost of Preferred Stock*

      Since the dividend is paid out of after-tax funds, the tax multiplier is 1.00 as shown in Figure 4. The cost is simply the coupon rate. The exception would be preferred stock with a redemption date (similar to a bond). In this case, the underwriting costs can be amortized as was explained for bonds above.

    b. *How to Estimate the Cost of Common Stock*

      The stock market offers the best means of measuring what percent return stockholders require. This is done by computing the

Type of Capital	Dollar Amt.	(A) Fraction of Total Capital	(B) After Tax Cost	(A) Times (B)
Trade Credit	75,000	.15	.045	.0067
Bank Loan	25,000	.05	.030	.0015
Secured Loans	50,000	.10	.060	.0060
Accruals	25,000	.05	.000	.0000
Bonds	50,000	.10	.032	.0032
Preferred Stock	50,000	.10	.060	.0060
Common Stock	225,000	.45	.100	.0450
	500,000			.0684

Figure 5

price/earnings ratio for all publicly held stocks in the same business and of the same relative size. If ten times earnings were chosen, the cost of capital is 10%. For 12 times earnings, the cost would be 8.3.%

The weighted average is computed in Figure 5 by multiplying the fraction of total capital (A) by the after-tax cost (B) of each kind of funds found on the balance sheet. The sum of the products is the cost of capital.

How to Use the Cost of Capital

The average after-tax cost per dollar of capital can be put to several uses such as—

1. Use in determining satisfactory percentages of return on investment required for new capital investment.
2. Checking trends of the cost of money compared to the total economy.
3. Analyzing cost trends of the component types of capital.

To put the cost of capital in perspective one must think of the balance sheet in terms of capital. The asset side represents the uses of capital and the liability side represents the source of capital. Therefore, profit is the return on assets or uses of capital. Interest, dividends and retained earnings represent the distribution of the profit to the sources of capital. In this context cost of capital takes on a very definite meaning.

Comparing the Cost of Capital to the Return on Capital

Figure 5 explains how to derive a Cost of Capital figure—specifically 6.84%. To what figure should this 6.84% be compared? The proper ratio is the Return on Capital. This is the after-tax profits excluding interest from expenses.

The formula for computing it is—

$$\text{Return on Capital} = \frac{\text{Profit After Tax} + [(1\text{-Tax Rate}) \times \text{Interest}]}{\text{Total Assets}}$$

What does it mean when the Return on Capital is greater than, or less than, the Cost of Capital? The meaning is dependent on the circumstances in each case. First, it should be emphasized that the Cost of Capital is based on a calculation of historical relationships; it is a calculation of the cost of the amount of capital which has actually been utilized in the business. Thus, in Figure 5, the total capital of $500,000 is the amount actually employed in the business, without regard to the value of the assets which may have been acquired with that capital. It may be that this capital has been used in part to acquire a very valuable piece of property at a very favorable price; that value is not reflected in the Cost of Capital. Yet the cost of the common stock portion of the capital is a reflection, at least in part, of stockholders' expectations for the industry in which we operate. This expectation may well comprehend the earning power of valuable assets acquired in the past at low cost. In this case, the fact that the company was showing a Return on Capital substantially above its Cost of Capital may not be any basis for assuming that the stockholders are satisfied with the company's performance. It may merely reflect the stock market assessment of the true value of the capital being employed in the business. The converse can also be true, where a business has high cost assets on the books.

The above discussion points up a difficulty in using the historical Cost of Capital as a guideline in making future investment decisions. Particularly if a very significant move is made by a company (e.g., a major expansion, an acquisition, or a retrenchment), there may be a reaction in the price/earnings ratio of its stock, so that its cost of Capital for that decision is different than would have been calculated based on the formula given above. Thus, in the example given in Figure 5, if the company is only selling at eight times earnings, the common stock portion of its capital is costing 12.5% after tax, and the composite cost of capital would be nearly 8%. Conversely, if the company makes a move which is favorably interpreted on the stock market, and its stock moves permanently to 15 times earnings, the composite Cost of Capital would fall to 5.3%. Obviously, management is interested in knowing what will be the cost of adding new capital, rather than merely what is the cost of the capital already employed. As we have already indicated, this new capital cannot all be assumed to be borrowed capital—at some point there will be the need for new equity capital. It may be that the mix of new capital will approximate the existing mix between borrowed and equity capital. If that is the case, we must still decide whether our company can attract new equity money in competition with other companies with similar risks. Only if the company's future prospects compare favorably with others of similar size (particularly in the same industry) can we rely on the cost of capital which we have assigned to the common stock segment of the total capital.

The Effect on Cash Reserve Policy

A financial manager who knows what his cost of capital is can improve the company's return on investment by careful control over the use of cash resources.

A. *Status with Excess Cash*

1.
Balance Sheet

Cash	50,000		
Marketable Securities	200,000	Debt	400,000
All Other Assets	750,000	Equity	600,000

2.
P & L Statement & Return on Capital

Return on Operations excluding Interest	$76,000
Return on Marketable Securities (2%)	4,000
Total Return on Capital	$80,000

$$\% \text{ Return on Capital} = \frac{80,000}{1,000,000} = 8\%$$

3. *Cost of Capital*

Type of Capital	(A) After Tax Cost	(B) % of Total Capital	A × B
Debt	.03	.40	.012
Equity	.10	.60	.060
		Cost of Capital	.072

B. *Status Without Excess Cash*

1.
Balance Sheet

Cash	50,000	Debt	400,000
All Other Assets	750,000	Equity	400,000

2.
P & L Statement & Return on Capital

Return on Operations excluding Interest	76,000
Return on Marketable Securities	
Total Return on Capital	76,000

$$\% \text{ Return on Capital} = \frac{76,000}{800,000} = 9.5\%$$

3. *Cost of Capital*

Type of Capital	(A) After Tax Cost	(B) % of Total Capital	A × B
Debt	.03	.50	.015
Equity	.10	.50	.050
		Cost of Capital	.065

C. *Comparison*

	With Excess Cash	Without Excess Cash
Cost of Capital	7.2%	6.5%
Return on Capital	8.0%	9.5%

Figure 6
How Excess Cash Holds Down the
Return on Capital and Increases the Cost of Capital

Example: A company which holds large cash reserves in low interest treasury bills can improve its return on investment quite easily. If there is no use for the funds in the business, they can over a period of time be turned back to the stockholders as dividends. If the cash returns 2% after tax, and the overall cost of capital is 6%, the return on assets will improve if the cash is removed from the balance sheet. An example of this is shown in Figure 6.

Use of Cost of Capital to Make Capital Investment Decisions

The calculation of the cost of capital can play a role in capital investment decisions. In reviewing alternative proposals showing various rates of return, the minimum acceptable rate must be spelled out. To set this "hurdle rate" the cost of capital must be known, although a somewhat higher rate may be set, in order to cover such expenditures as corporate overhead, which may not be included in rate of return calculations.

Moreover, the "hurdle rate" must be set at a level which will permit the company to meet its goals for earnings growth, and profitability in relation to shareholder equity. These considerations may keep the "hurdle rate" considerably above the cost of capital.

POST-COMPLETION AUDITS OF CAPITAL PROJECTS

Once a proposed project has met or surpassed the "hurdle rate," and has therefore qualified for a commitment of funds, it is often forgotten in terms of analyzing its actual financial performance. The concept of post-completion audits has been introduced in an attempt to overcome this generally acknowledged deficiency.

Post-completion audits involve periodic reviews which attempt to compare actual cash flows with the estimated cash flows which were used in justifying the project originally.

These comparisons have several useful purposes. If the personnel responsible for supplying estimates to be used in evaluating proposed capital projects are aware that their estimates will subsequently be reviewed in the process of verifying estimated rate of return calculations, then the best possible estimates will probably be supplied at the time of the original study. These estimates would include, for example, sales data, estimated selling prices, estimated product life cycle, any savings to be generated by the investment, and so on.

If the "estimators" have actual data fed back to them, variances can be highlighted in a manner which will provide assistance in the preparation of future estimates. A third and very important use of post-completion audit data is that in many cases the need for alternative courses of action is highlighted. This can range from developing new marketing strategies to simply getting out of the business.

With all their usefulness, post-completion audits are not without certain limitations. Unfortunately these limitations are frequently overlooked when this relatively new approach to analyzing financial performance is being recommended.

Somewhat ironically, the very advantage offered to management by rate of return calculations can present a problem in doing post-completion audits. Rate of return calculations, as a tool for assisting management in making capital investment decisions, have become popular because they offer a simple yardstick. In ROI calculations all the variables; all the estimates; all the assumptions which are related to a proposed project, are quantified and reduced to a single figure, viz., the percentage rate of return.

This rate of return answer reflects the earning power of the proposed project over its entire life and can be readily measured against the earning power of alternative opportunities for investing capital.

Discounted Cash Flow Technique

The most popular and the most meaningful approach to computing rate of return is use of the discounted cash flow technique. This technique gives full recognition to the time value of money (i.e., a dollar *possessed* today is of more value than a dollar *promised* some time in the future). Under the discounted cash flow approach the rate of return for a particular project is that rate at which the present worth of the investment is equal to the present worth of the cash flow generated by said investment over its life. The discounted cash flow approach is given full treatment in another booklet in this series, *Simplified Use of the Discounted Cash Flow Method of Evaluation*.

Cash flow can occur on a levelized basis, i.e., the same amount each year (see Exhibit A) or, as is more likely, on an irregular basis (see Exhibit B).

Let us now assume that the $1,000,000 project referred to in Exhibits A and B was justified on the basis of its estimated 15% rate of return and that it is to be the object of a post-completion audit. Now what are the limitations of such an audit which were previously referred to?

As was noted above, the 15% rate of return reflects the earning power of this project over its entire estimated life of ten years.

The basic limitation of a post-completion audit is perhaps best indicated by the question, "Can a project be properly audited before its estimated life has run out since its original evaluation was based on its performance over its entire estimated life?" The difficulties inherent in this question are portrayed in Exhibits D and C. These exhibits differ from Exhibits A and B in that they reflect the actual cash flows which were recorded as opposed to the estimated cash flows contained in Exhibits A and B.

Let us further assume that the investment decision was made on the basis of the data shown in Exhibit A and that it was decided to "track" the financial performance of the $1,000,000 investment on an annual basis. The "tracking" will be performed using the actual cash flow data contained in Exhibit C. Using this approach we see it is not until the fifth year of this project (halfway through its estimated life) that the cash flow generated by the investment reaches the level originally predicted. But we can also note that during the second half of the project's life, cash flows are far in excess of originally predicted levels. What has obviously happened is that the nature of this project's life cycle, or put another way, the time-shape of its earning power, was inaccurately predicted.

Exhibit C, of course, assumes that this particular project was never abandoned by management and that over its ten year life it earned precisely the 15% originally estimated. What would have happened in real life? Is it not possible that based on the early years' performance, as indicated by the post-completion audit process, this project would have been abandoned? The point being made here is that post-completion audits can be misleading if not handled properly and can result in the making of bad decisions.

A comparison of cash flow data shown in Exhibits B and D further highlights this point. In years two, three and four the actual cash flow recorded in Exhibit D are far in excess of the estimates shown in Exhibit B. However, over the remaining life of the project, just the opposite is true. Through the improper use of the post-completion audit technique, management might well have been encouraged to commit additional capital to an area which has passed its peak and is heading toward the end of its life cycle.

An additional limitation of post-completion audits is reflected in Exhibit E. This limitation also relates to the difficulty encountered in attempting to evaluate a project at a particular point in time whereas the original evaluation was made on estimated performance over the project's entire life.

What often occurs is a confusion over the methods of financial evaluation. Projects which are justified using the discounted cash flow technique are subsequently evaluated in post-completion audits using the so-called accountant's method of computing rate of return. This is highlighted in Exhibit E. The cash flows in this Exhibit are identical to those in Exhibit A which using discounted cash flow gave a rate of return of 15%. Yet a post-completion audit using the accountant's method provides annual rates of return which begin at 10% and through annual progressions end up at 99% in the tenth year.

What we have attempted to point out in the use of these Exhibits is that post-completion audits, as with other management tools for analyzing financial performance, must be used with care. One thing that is clear from the above is that in post-completion audits no attempt should be made to compute a rate of return for the particular period under review which will then be compared to the overall project's rate of return as originally computed.

What is to be recommended in post-completion audits is a periodic review of the assumptions upon which the original study was based and the resulting cash flows which were used in justifying the project.

EXHIBIT A

RATE OF RETURN COMPUTATION
USING DISCOUNTED CASH FLOW TECHNIQUE

(EVEN CASH FLOWS)

Year	Investment	Cash Flow Generated by Investment	Present Worth 15% Factor	Present Worth Amount
0	$1,000,000			
1	—	$ 199,250	.8696	$ 173,269
2	—	199,250	.7561	150,654
3	—	199,250	.6575	131,008
4	—	199,250	.5718	113,931
5	—	199,250	.4972	99,067
6	—	199,250	.4323	86,136
7	—	199,250	.3759	74,898
8	—	199,250	.3269	65,135
9	—	199,250	.2843	56,647
10	—	199,250	.2472	49,225
Total	$1,000,000	$1,992,500		$1,000,000

Equal at 15%

EXHIBIT B
RATE OF RETURN CALCULATION
USING DISCOUNTED CASH FLOW TECHNIQUE
(UNEVEN CASH FLOWS)

Year	Investment	Cash Flow Generated by Investment	Present Worth 15% Factor	Amount
0	$1,000,000			
1	—	$ 50,000	.8696	$ 43,480
2	—	109,000	.7561	82,415
3	—	200,000	.6575	131,500
4	—	300,000	.5718	171,539
5	—	350,000	.4972	174,019
6	—	350,000	.4323	151,304
7	—	300,000	.3759	112,770
8	—	201,000	.3269	65,707
9	—	150,000	.2843	42,645
10	—	99,600	.2472	24,621
Total	$1,000,000	$2,109,600		$1,000,000

Equal at 15%

EXHIBIT C
RATE OF RETURN COMPUTATION
USING DISCOUNTED CASH FLOW TECHNIQUE
(UNEVEN CASH FLOWS)

Year	Investment	Cash Flow Generated by Investment	Present Worth 15% Factor	Amount
0	$1,000,000			
1	—	$ 25,000	.8696	$ 21,740
2	—	35,000	.7561	26,463
3	—	60,000	.6575	39,450
4	—	150,000	.5718	85,770
5	—	200,000	.4972	99,440
6	—	300,000	.4323	129,690
7	—	600,000	.3759	225,540
8	—	800,000	.3269	261,520
9	—	300,000	.2843	85,290
10	—	101,525	.2472	25,097
Total	$1,000,000	$2,571,525		$1,000,000

Equal at 15%

EXHIBIT D
RATE OF RETURN CALCULATION
USING DISCOUNTED CASH FLOW TECHNIQUE
(UNEVEN CASH FLOWS)

Year	Investment	Cash Flow Generated by Investment	Present Worth	
			15% Factor	Amount
0	$1,000,000			
1	—	$ 50,000	.8696	$ 43,480
2	—	200,000	.7561	151,220
3	—	400,000	.6575	263,000
4	—	500,000	.5718	285,900
5	—	300,000	.4972	149,160
6	—	100,000	.4323	43,230
7	—	56,100	.3759	21,090
8	—	50,000	.3269	16,345
9	—	50,000	.2843	14,215
10	—	50,000	.2472	12,360
Total	$1,000,000	$1,756,100		$1,000,000

Equal at 15%

EXHIBIT E
RATE OF RETURN CALCULATION
USING ACCOUNTANT'S METHOD

Year	Investment	Cash Flow Generated by Investment			Rate of Return
		Return of Capital (Depreciation)	Return on Capital	Total	
0	$1,000,000				
1	1,000,000	$100,000	$99,250	$199,250	10%
2	900,000	100,000	99,250	199,250	11%
3	800,000	100,000	99,250	199,250	12%
4	700,000	100,000	99,250	199,250	14%
5	600,000	100,000	99,250	199,250	17%
6	500,000	100,000	99,250	199,250	20%
7	400,000	100,000	99,250	199,250	25%
8	300,000	100,000	99,250	199,250	33%
9	200,000	100,000	99,250	199,250	49%
10	100,000	100,000	99,250	199,250	99%

SOURCES AND USES OF FUNDS

A periodic review of changes in capital structure is an important duty of the financial manager. This is done by making a Statement of Sources and Applications of Funds. It is generally done yearly as a part of a general financial review. The balance sheet is consolidated into not more than twenty asset and twenty liability accounts. The titles used are those commonly seen on simplified balance sheets such as the example in Figure 7. Last year's balance in each account is subtracted from this year's balance. If the account carried a debit balance, the difference is put in the debit column. The proper sign is also derived via this rule. If this year's balance is larger than last year's, the sign is plus, if less, the sign is minus. The converted difference is used to eliminate minus signs. Any negative debit is changed to a positive credit. Any negative credit is changed to a positive debit. Once this has been done, the dollar amounts in the credit column are moved to the sources column. The debit amounts go to the uses column.

A few examples of the meaning of the statement shown as Figure 8 are as follows:

1. To increase the accounts receivable is a use of funds since there will be that much less cash available.
2. To increase bank loans is a source of funds since there will be that much more cash available.
3. To increase the depreciation reserve on the buildings is to change profit and loss with a noncash expense and thereby increase the cash. This is, therefore, a source.
4. To increase Retained Earnings is a source of funds since cash will increase.
5. To decrease Accounts Payable is a use of funds since cash will decrease.

The S & A Statement Tells the Financial Story

The financial manager seeks to make good use of the funds available to the company. The S & A Statement delineates all the sources of funds. These sources may be thought of as all the cash generated in the past year. The applications represent all the cash consumed in the past year. Figure 8 is an example of a five-year spread of sources and applications of funds.

Inventory climbed each year and is shown as an application. Money was reinvested in fixed assets each year. This was another major application. Major sources were depreciation and retained earnings. The five-year spread quickly points out important balance sheet changes and trends.

	Balance This Year	Balance Last Year	Difference Dr.	Difference Cr.	Converted Difference Dr.	Converted Difference Cr.	Uses	Sources
Cash	50,000 Dr	30,000 Dr	+20,000		20,000		20,000	
Acct. Rec.	200,000 Dr	245,000 Dr	−45,000			45,000		45,000
Invent.	300,000 Dr	270,000 Dr	+30,000		30,000		30,000	
Other Curr.	30,000 Dr	27,000 Dr	− 3,000		3,000		3,000	
Invest. in Subid.	80,000 Dr	80,000 Dr						
Land	40,000 Dr	40,000 Dr						
Bldg	180,000 Dr	160,000 Dr	+20,000		20,000		20,000	
Deprec. Res.	30,000 Cr	21,000 Cr		+ 9,000		9,000		9,000
Equipment	290,000 Dr	257,000 Dr	+33,000		33,000		33,000	
Deprec. Res.	80,000 Cr	57,000 Cr		+ 23,000		23,000		23,000
Automobiles	44,000 Dr	44,000 Dr						
Deprec. Res.	24,000 Cr	17,000 Cr		+ 7,000		7,000		7,000
Other Assets	12,000 Dr	12,000 Dr						
Accounts Payable	150,000 Cr	172,000 Cr		− 22,000	22,000		22,000	
Taxes Payable	48,000 Cr	49,000 Cr		− 1,000	1,000		1,000	
Notes Payable	80,000 Cr	112,000 Cr		− 32,000	32,000		32,000	
Accruals	74,000 Cr	62,000 Cr		+ 12,000		12,000		12,000
Other Liabilities	37,000 Cr	12,000 Cr		+ 25,000		25,000		25,000
Mortgages	121,000 Cr	132,000 Cr		− 11,000	11,000		11,000	
Term Loan		137,000 Cr		−137,000	137,000		137,000	
Preferred Stock	120,000 Cr			+120,000		120,000		120,000
Common Stock	194,000 Cr	188,000 Cr		+ 6,000		6,000		6,000
Retained Earnings	268,000 Cr	206,000 Cr		+ 62,000		62,000		62,000

Figure 7

All figures in thousands of dollars

	Sources					Applications					5 Year Recap	
	Year 1	Year 2	Year 3	Year 4	Year 5	Year 1	Year 2	Year 3	Year 4	Year 5	Sources	Applications
Cash	10.3				11.0		5.4	7.6	8.1		0.2	
Receivables	4.1	12.1	6.2	48.1						44.4	26.1	
Inventory						24.8	41.1	7.7	17.2	10.6		101.4
Fixed Assets						57.4	44.8	58.0	68.9	32.1		261.2
Depreciation	38.6	44.2	32.8	29.7	28.8						174.1	
Other Assets	2.0			2.0	7.1		16.0	4.0				8.9
Payables	18.7	19.1			27.4			1.2	39.1		24.9	
Accruals	6.5	3.5		4.8				2.0		4.1	8.7	
Bank Loans		6.8	12.8		6.8	23.8			41.1			385
Preferred Stock				50.0							50.0	
Common Stock												
Retained Earnings	25.8	21.6	28.7	19.8	30.1						126.0	
Totals	106.0	107.3	80.5	154.4	112.2	106.0	107.3	80.5	154.4	112.2	410.0	410.0

Figure 8

Important Checkpoints in S & A Statements

Listed below are several methods of using an S & A Statement as a financial barometer.

1. Add up all the sources which come from current assets and liabilities. Subtract all the uses which come from current assets and liabilities. If the balance is a positive number, it is the net addition to working capital. If it is negative, it is the net loss of working capital.
2. Compare all fixed asset accounts to all depreciation accounts. Did depreciation cover the cash required for new acquisitions?
3. Check the long-term trend of the inventory account. If it is a major use, what is the ratio of the change in inventory to the change of sales? This ratio should not exceed the cost of sales percentage.

PRO FORMA BALANCE SHEETS

The liquidity of the company shall be projected forward for several years advance to assure sound planning. Over longer periods of time receipts and disbursements become more difficult to estimate. The formulas become complicated and the assumptions more and more vague. A better method for long-term projection is the Pro Forma Balance Sheet.

The Pro Forma Balance Sheet is completed in the following three steps:

1. Estimate sales, production, purchase activity for future periods.
2. Based on these estimates predict the amounts of all major asset and liability accounts at the end of each future period except cash.
3. Subtract total assets other than cash from total liabilities to get the cash balance.

STEP 1—ESTIMATING SALES, PRODUCTION AND PURCHASES

Many firms require the marketing division to make sales forecasts which can be used for budget purposes. Such an estimate would be ideal for this purpose. If no such estimate is available, the financial manager can make one as follows:

1. For each major sales type or product line determine an annual growth rate.
2. Multiply each growth factor (1.06 for 6%) by current annual sales to determine next year's annual sales. Repeat again for each additional year.
3. Based on historical data break the annual figure into monthly or quarterly estimates. For example: 1st quarter 30%, 2nd quarter 20%, 3rd quarter 18%, and 4th quarter 32%. The choice of quarterly vs. monthly depends on whether a pro forma balance sheet will be generated for the end of each quarter or each month.

To obtain production and purchases per quarter or per month, the sales level, plant capacity, manpower needs and other factors must be taken into account. An estimate of production takes the form of 60% of the next quarter's sales but not to exceed $120,000 which is plant capacity. The 60% is the inventory cost factor per sales dollar. Purchase requirements can be based on production estimates. An estimate of purchases takes the form of 48% of the next quarter's production.

STEP 2—ESTIMATING THE BALANCE SHEET ITEMS

Estimating procedures are applied to only certain balance sheet accounts. Those not estimated are assumed to be fixed. The criteria for deciding which accounts are to be treated as fixed are:

1. Relatively small dollar balances in the account.
2. No simple connection between the balance and sales or production levels.
3. No known pattern to variations in the account balance.
4. The account is known to carry a fixed balance.

Examples of accounts which should be treated as fixed are Investment in Subsidiaries, Deposits and Prepaid Items, Land, Preferred Stock, Common Stock, Exchanges Payable.

Estimating Receivables

The historical data on the collection period is used to determine receivables levels; three situations are possible:

1. The collection period may be steadily rising or falling.
2. The collection period may show a major seasonal pattern.
3. The collection period may be constant.

Use of these assumptions and the current collection period allows the estimation of the future collection periods. A sample worksheet is shown in Figure 9. Note that the Notes Column is used to write down the assumptions made. These notes are valuable for review of assumptions and techniques at a later date.

Computation of Receivables

From the sales forecast the quarterly sales figures are entered on the worksheet. These are then converted into sales per day by dividing by 91. Multiplying sales per day by the collection period gives the receivables balance.

	1st Quarter	2nd Quarter	3rd Quarter	4th Quarter	1st Quarter	2nd Quarter	3rd Quarter	4th Quarter
Collection Period Last Year Average 39 days Assume-Constant except 4th Quarter which is +20% or 47 days	39	39	39	47	39	39	39	47
Sales in Current Quarter	$600M	$470M	$520M	$840M	$660M	$517M	$572M	$924M
Sales Per Day Current Quarter Quarterly Sales 91	6.59	5.16	5.71	9.23	7.25	5.68	6.28	10.15
Accounts Receivable Collection Period X Sales/Day	257.0	201.2	222.7	433.8	282.8	221.5	244.9	434.3

Figure 9
Pro Forma Worksheet

Techniques to Improve the Accuracy

Depending on the accuracy desired and time available any of the following sophistications can be added:

1. Estimate the collection period by product lines or sales groups which match the sales forecast. A worksheet is filled out for each one and figures added to obtain total receivables.
2. Assume a compound variation in collection period. An example would be —Collection period steadily rising and also showing seasonal variation.
3. Allow for price level increases or decreases.

Estimating Inventory Levels

The most difficult item to estimate for manufacturing concerns is inventory. Several approaches are possible. Estimates can be based on man hours of labor, units produced, pounds throughout, or some other physical index. If physical indexes are used, they are generally first estimated in the production and purchase figures. Retail concerns can generally base inventory estimates on percent of sales. Both methods are explained below. Physical index of man hours is used in Figure 10 and percent of sales in Figure 11.

Estimating Inventory on Physical Index Basis

Based on nonfinancial factors such as level of employment policy and equipment capacity, a production schedule is made out. The man hours in the example in Figure 10 show a plant which adds an extra shift during the fourth quarter. These man hours are converted into dollars by using a company-wide labor and overhead rate. This is computed on Line 3 and is added to raw material purchases to get total addition to inventory. The subtractions from inventory are calculated as a percentage of sales on Line 6. The additions netted against the subtractions give the net change in inventory on Line 7. This added or subtracted from the beginning inventory gives the new inventory balance on Line 9.

Estimating Inventory Based on Percent of Sales

The technique is similar to the previous example except that additions to inventory are based on sales. In Figure 11 the current sales are used to compute 30% of the addition to inventory on Line 2. The next quarter's sales are used to compute 70% of the addition to inventory. In both cases the

Item	Line	Notes	1st Year				2nd Year			
			1st Quarter	2nd Quarter	3rd Quarter	4th Quarter	1st Quarter	2nd Quarter	3rd Quarter	4th Quarter
Sales Current Quarter			600	470	520	840	660	517	572	924
Raw Material Purchases		From Purchase Schedule	94	104	168	132	103	114	185	112
Factory Man Hours		Level Production except 4th Quarter which is +33%	30.0	30.0	30.0	40.0	33.0	33.0	33.0	44.0
Labor & Overhead Added to Inventory		Labor Rate 3.25 Overhead Rate 6.35 Addition to Inventory (3.25 6.35) × Manhours	286.5	286.5	286.5	382.0	315.2	315.2	315.2	420.2
Total Added to Inventory		Add Raw Matl. to Labor and Overhead	380.5	390.5	454.5	514.0	418.5	429.5	500.2	532.2
Total Depletions of Inventory		68.9% of Current Sales	413.5	323.8	358.3	578.8	454.7	356.2	394.1	636.6
Change of Inventory		Additions less Depletions	-32.9	76.7	96.2	-64.8	-36.2	73.3	106.1	-104.4
Old Inventory		Inventory Prior Quarter	184.4	151.5	228.2	324.4	259.6	223.4	296.7	402.8
New Inventory		Old ± Change	151.5	228.2	324.4	259.6	223.4	296.7	402.8	298.4

Figure 10
Inventory Estimate Based on Physical Index
(All figures in thousands)

Line		1st Year				2nd Year			
		1st	2nd	3rd	4th	1st	2nd	3rd	4th
Sales	1	600	470	520	840	660	517	572	924
Inventory Addition for Current Quarter	2	.30 X .62 X Current Sales	112	87	97	156	123	96	106	172
Inventory Addition for Next Quarter	3	.70 X .62 X Next Quarter Sales	204	226	364	286	224	248	401	315
Total Additions to Inventory	4	Line 2 plus Line 3	316	313	461	442	347	344	507	487
Total Deletions from Inventory	5	Current Sales times .62	372	291	322	521	409	320	355	573
Old Balance Inventory	6		488	432	454	593	514	452	476	628
New Inventory	7	Old balance plus additions minus deletions	432	454	593	514	452	476	628	542

Figure 11

Estimating Inventory on Percent of Sales

(All figures in thousands)

inventory value to sales ratio of 62% is used. This means that each dollar of sales is valued at $.62 when it is put in inventory. The deletions from inventory are computed using the same 62% factor times the current quarter's sales. The net change is calculated and added or subtracted from the opening balance as in Figure 10.

How to Make Inventory Projections Even More Accurate

More involved computations will add to the accuracy. The choice of exact method will depend on the availability of detailed data, time available, and other factors which the financial manager may wish to take into account. Some alternatives are:

1. A breakdown of sales, production, and purchase schedules by product line with a worksheet for each.
2. Estimate minimum and maximum inventory levels for each product line. Minimums are based on protection against out-of-stock and maximums are based on physical limits of storage areas. Review all balances to make sure no minimums or maximums have been violated. If they have, schedules must be revised.
3. Allow for change in cost levels of labor, overhead and materials in future periods.

Control of inventories requires continuous attention if we are to avoid tying up unnecessary resources in this form. Naturally, the inventory forecasts developed in the fashion outlined above will only be a rough tool in judging the adequacy of the inventory control procedures. Where inventories represent a large investment, it will be necessary to make more detailed analyses.

One type of analysis is provided through the construction of an inventory control system which weighs the cost of a "run-out" (in terms of lost profit on a sale) against the cost of carrying enough inventory to lower the probability of run-out. In order to be reliable, this system will require data on experience with sales frequency, as well as cost data for the cost of carrying inventory, and the cost and profitability of sales. The data must be adjusted whenever major changes in them occur. Also, the results (the recommended inventory levels) must be modified when there is a major sales promotion. Such a system as this requires computer-assisted calculations in most instances, and can be utilized profitably only where the potential saving from lower inventory levels will justify the cost. This potential saving is measured by the cost of carrying the extra inventory.

A more general method of analyzing the adequacy of inventory levels is to compare levels (in relation to sales or cost of sales), with the relative levels of similar inventories maintained by competitors. While some competitors will have different sales mix or cost trends, the comparison will nonetheless serve as a goad to operating management to achieve reduction in relative inventory levels.

Estimating Other Current Assets and Miscellaneous Current Liabilities

Minor accounts which are not treated as fixed can be treated as varying with sales. Figure 12 shows a simple worksheet where each is treated as a percentage of sales of the current quarter.

Estimating Fixed Assets and Allowance for Depreciation

Future plans for capital spending must be forecast carefully. The forecast of fixed asset balances involves more than a listing of those projects which management can now foresee. It also includes an estimate of those other expenditures which cannot now be foreseen precisely, as well as an estimate of retirements and sales that will take place during the forecast period.

For the next one or two years, it may be that the known new projects will provide a relatively complete list of likely additions to the fixed asset accounts. Longer term forecasts will require estimates of additions that cannot now be foreseen.

Retirements and sales of fixed assets are particularly difficult to forecast, unless they are occasioned by new capital investment which replaces an existing asset. Nevertheless, even in the absence of a capital replacement, there will be a certain level of retirements and sales associated with any large fixed asset balance.

Once the fixed asset balances have been forecast, it is well to assess the reasonableness of the totals. Will the forecast additions result in productive capacity throughout the period at a level consistent with the forecast growth in sales, after considering products which may be purchased for resale? What is happening to fixed asset balances in relation to earnings after taxes? Are large fixed asset costs being added with no apparent increase in profits? If the answers to these questions suggest unfavorable trends, the assumptions used in the forecast must be reexamined.

Depreciation Estimates

To obtain the accuracy required an estimate of depreciation must be made. The depreciation is subtracted from the sum of new purchases and the old balance in net fixed assets to get the new net fixed assets. The following eight steps should be used to schedule the depreciation:

Item	Notes	1st Year				2nd Year			
		1st	2nd	3rd	4th	1st	2nd	3rd	4th
Sales per Quarter	From Sales Estimate	600	470	520	840	660	517	572	924
Other Current Assets	3.1% of Quarterly Sales	18.6	14.6	16.1	26.0	20.5	14.6	17.7	28.6
Accruals	2.7% of Quarterly Sales	16.2	12.7	14.0	22.7	17.8	14.0	15.4	25.0
Taxes Payable	1.8% of Quarterly Sales	10.8	8.6	9.4	15.1	11.9	9.3	10.3	16.6

Figure 12
Worksheets for Other Current Assets,
Accruals and Taxes Payable

Item	Line	Old Balance	1	2	3	4	5
Annual Purchase	1		104	118	148	170	205
Depreciation on Old Balance	2		60	50	40	30	20
1st Years	3		12	24	24	24	24
2nd Years	4			15	30	30	30
3rd Years	5				16	32	32
4th Years	6					17	34
5th Years	7						14
Total Annual Deprec.	8		72	89	110	133	154
Gross Fixed Asset Balance	9	480	594	712	860	1030	1235
Depreciation Reserve Balance	10	180	252	341	451	584	738
Net Fixed Assets	11	300	342	371	409	446	497

Figure 13
Five-Year Projection of Fixed Assets Balance

1. A schedule of depreciation of fixed asset already being depreciated is made. This will show a declining dollar value as depreciable value of the oldest assets reaches zero. See Line 2, Figure 13.
2. A depreciation formula for new assets is chosen—straight line, declining balance, or sum-of-the-digits. The straight line has been used in Figure 13 since it simplifies the computation.
3. An average life of assets purchased is chosen. If purchases contain large amounts of automotive and building items, separate schedules should be made for these. Their life estimates (4 years and 30 years) would distort the average estimate.
4. Depreciation is assumed to start in mid-year of the year of purchase. Thus the depreciation in the year of purchase is one-half the following year.
5. A separate line is used for the depreciation on assets of each future year.
6. Total depreciation (Line 8) for the year is the sum of the depreciation on Old Balance and the five future years.
7. The Gross Assets are computed as the sum of Net Fixed Assets of previous year (Line 11) plus this year's purchases (Line 1).
8. The new Net Fixed Assets (Line 11) is the Gross Assets (Line 9) less Total Depreciation (Line 8).

Estimating Accounts Payable

The dollar amount in this account depends on the following factors:

1. The terms of sale of suppliers.
2. The payment policy of the company. Three alternatives are payment within the discount period, payment on net terms, payment after an extended period past the due date.
3. The daily dollar rate of purchases.

A two-year projection of accounts payable is shown in Figure 14. The procedure used to produce the estimate is as follows:

1. From Figure 10 show the purchases per quarter.
2. Divide quarterly purchases by 90 to obtain daily rate of purchases as shown on Line 2.
3. Determine the payment policy and convert it to days of payable outstanding. Allow a percentage for processing delay. Typically a company paying within 10 days shows an average of 13 days' payables actually outstanding. The three days represent invoices in transit, checks in process, and checks in transit.
4. Multiply the purchases per day (Line 2) by the days of payables unpaid (Line 3) to get the total variable payables outstanding.
5. Determine the amount of Basic Miscellaneous Payables by estimate or analysis. An accurate analytical method is shown in Figure 15. The total payables is plotted against purchases. A straight line is drawn through the area where the points cluster and projected back to the vertical axis.

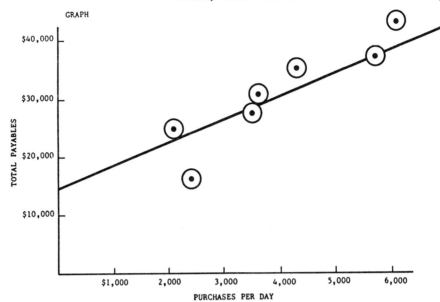

DATA - Compiled from past records

Monthly Purchases	Purchases Per Day	Payables (End of Month)
$ 69,000	$ 2,300	$15,000
105,000	3,500	27,000
126,000	4,200	35,000
174,000	5,800	36,000
60,000	2,000	24,000
102,000	3,400	31,000
180,000	6,000	43,000

Figure 15

Estimating Basic Miscellaneous Payables

This vertical height represents the fixed basic amount of payables. This basic or fixed amount represents the continual purchase of operating supplies and overhead items. The amount of these purchases bears no relation to volume.

6. Total is determined by adding the basic amount to the variable amount (Line 5 to Line 4).

Estimating Bank Loans

Bank credit can take several forms and each would be handled in a separate way. The most important form is line of credit borrowing. These funds are used for "cash fill-in" to offset periods of heavy inventory or receivables. Since the pro forma balance sheet serves to predict the cash balance, the amount of line of credit borrowing has a direct effect on the cash balance itself. The proper approach is to assume that half of the line of credit will be outstanding. This leaves one half as a contingency reserve. Once the pro

Figure 14
Estimating Accounts Payable

Item	Line	Notes	1st Year				2nd Year			
			1st	2nd	3rd	4th	1st	2nd	3rd	4th
Purchases	1		212	180	284	410	219	195	300	444
Purchases per Day	2	Purchases divided by 90	2.35	2.00	3.15	4.55	2.43	2.16	3.33	4.93
Days of Payables Unpaid	3		13	13	13	13	13	13	13	13
Variable Payables	4	Days times Purchases per day	30.0	26.0	41.0	59.1	31.6	28.1	43.3	64.1
Basic Miscellaneous Payables	5		14.0	14.0	14.0	14.0	14.0	14.0	14.0	14.0
Total Payables	6		44.0	40.0	55.0	73.1	45.6	42.1	57.3	78.1

Figure 16
Estimated Retained Earnings
(All figures in thousands)

Item	Line	Notes	1st Year				2nd Year			
			1st	2nd	3rd	4th	1st	2nd	3rd	4th
Sales	1	From Operating Budget	600	470	520	840	660	517	572	924
Variable Costs	2		402	310	347	514	447	330	358	567
Fixed Costs	3		183	183	183	183	192	192	192	192
Profit Before Taxes	4		+15	−23	−10	143	+21	−5	+12	+165
Profit After Taxes	5		+8	−12	−5	+72	+11	−3	+6	+83
Payout Ratio	6		.60	.60	.60	.60	.60	.60	.60	.60
Annual Rate of Earnings	7	Total Earnings for Year	63	63	63	63	97	97	97	97
Quarterly Dividend	8		9.5	9.5	9.5	9.5	14.5	14.5	14.5	14.5
Previous Retained Earnings	9	Line 9 ÷ Line 5 − Line 8	742.0	740.5	719.0	704.5	767.0	763.5	746.0	737.5
New Retained Earnings			740.5	719.0	704.5	767.0	763.5	746.0	737.5	806.0

397

forma statement is complete, and cash balances predicted, the amount of bank loan can be revised upward or downward as required. If an annual cleanup is required by the bank, in the quarter when activity is the lowest the bank loan should be assumed to be zero. Choice of the quarter when the line of credit is cleaned up is critical. The cash shortage may occur in the cleanup period instead of in the period of peak sales and inventory.

A bank loan requiring installment or periodic payments can be estimated precisely. A bank loan which is secured by inventory or receivables can be estimated based on the inventory or receivable estimate. Banks or other lending institutions generally apply a reserve ratio to such loans. If 80% of the secured receivables can be borrowed, the loan balance would be set at .80 times receivables. Two important exceptions must be allowed for in cash estimates as follows:

1. If certain accounts are disallowed as security in a receivable loan, the amount must be adjusted downward to allow for this.
2. There may be periods when all the borrowing capacity will not be used. This is determined after the pro forma statement is complete and the statement adjusted accordingly.

Estimating Other Current Liabilities

Taxes Payable, Accrued Payroll, and other such accounts can be treated as either fixed or variable. If treated as variable, the formula would be—

$$\text{Taxes Payable (Estimated)} = \frac{\text{Taxes Payable (Base Period)}}{\text{Sales (Base Period)}} \times \text{Sales (Estimated)}$$

A representative base period is chosen to obtain the ratio Taxes Payable to Sales per Quarter.

Estimating Long-Term Debt

Unless a specific new loan is planned or a specific type of debt set for retirement, the normal retirement rate should be used. If the purpose of the pro forma statement is to plan for long-term debt, different plans and methods can be explored once the basic estimated balance sheet is completed.

Thus the first pro forma balance sheet should represent the status quo and variations introduced afterwards.

Estimating Preferred and Common Stock

As explained under Long-Term Debt the status quo is the basic assumption. Thus no substantial changes would be projected. If employee stock purchase plans or stock options are in effect, an allowance can be made for an increase in Common Stock. Stock dividends have the effect of increasing common stock by the exact dollar amount that the Retained Earnings decrease. Since the total effect is simply to transfer dollars from one equity account to another, the stock dividend can be ignored.

The same reasoning would apply to a stock split.

Estimating Retained Earnings

The balance in Retained Earnings is effected by two variables—profits and dividends. The profits are estimated as part of the budgeting process. By applying the sales estimate to the operating budget, a profit figure can be generated for each future quarter. See Figure 16, Lines 1 to 5. To establish the amount of earnings to be paid out as dividends, a dividend plan must be chosen. The alternatives are as follows:

1. Pay out a fixed percentage of after-tax earnings.
2. Pay out a fixed amount per year.
3. Pay no dividends.
4. Distribute more than is earned.

Figure 16 has been computed based on a 60% payout ratio. First the annual rate of earnings is computed on Line 7. This quantity is divided by 4 and multiplied by .60 to obtain the quarterly dividend. The previous balance in retained earnings is shown on Line 9. The old balance plus profits after taxes minus dividends gives the new balance shown on Line 10.

PREPARING THE PRO FORMA BALANCE SHEET

With all the component figures available, the final sheet lays out the entire balance sheet except cash. Figure 17 shows how in Step 1 the total liabilities are computed by totalling the various estimated balances. In Step 2 the estimated balances in all asset accounts is subtracted from total liabilities to arrive at cash. Depreciation reserves are negative asset accounts and are added not subtracted. Step 3 involves all revisions of the first set of estimates required to bring the cash balance to optimum levels. As shown in Figure 17 the line of credit balance is lowered in the 1st quarter of the 1st year to reduce the cash balance to the optimum level. The loan balance is increased in the 3rd quarter of the 1st year to compensate for the low cash balance.

Item	Line	Note	1st Year				2nd Year			
			1st	2nd	3rd	4th	1st	2nd	3rd	4th
Step 1										
Payables			44.0	40.0	55.0	73.1	45.6	42.1	57.3	78.1
Accruals			16.2	12.7	14.0	22.7	17.8	14.0	15.4	25.0
Misc. C.L.			82.0	82.0	82.0	82.0	82.0	82.0	82.0	82.0
Bank Loan (Line of Credit)			150.0	150.0	150.0	150.0	150.0	150.0	150.0	150.0
Common Stock			240.0	240.0	240.0	240.0	240.0	240.0	240.0	240.0
Retained Earnings			740.5	719.0	704.5	767.0	763.5	746.0	737.5	806.0
TOTAL LIABILITIES			1,272.7	1,243.7	1,245.5	1,334.8	1,298.9	1,274.1	1,282.2	1,381.1
Step 2										
Inventory			432.0	454.0	593.0	514.0	452.0	476.0	628.0	542.0
Accounts Rec.			257.0	201.2	222.7	433.8	282.8	221.5	244.9	434.3
Fixed Assets			380.0	385.0	390.0	395.0	400.0	405.0	410.0	415.0
Other Current			18.6	14.6	16.1	26.0	20.5	14.6	17.7	28.6
Other Assets			37.0	37.0	37.0	37.0	37.0	37.0	37.0	37.0
TOTAL ASSETS LESS CASH			1,124.6	1,191.8	1,258.8	1,405.8	1,192.3	1,154.1	1,337.6	1,456.9
Step 3										
Unadjusted Cash			148.1	51.9	−13.3	−71.0	106.6	120.0	−55.6	−75.8
Revised Bank Loan			100.0	same	220.0	280.0	same	same	260.0	270.0
Revised Cash			98.1	same	56.7	59.0	same	same	54.4	44.2

Figure 17
Pro Forma Balance Sheet

400

12

SCIENTIFIC ACQUISITION
ANALYSIS AND EVALUATION

TRENDS IN MERGER ACTIVITY

The urge to merge certainly is not dead; it is not even dying. In the first quarter of 1971, the number of merger announcements was close to 1,200. This was a decline of approximately 200 from the period a year earlier.

In the first quarter of 1971, approximately 45 percent of all transactions were acquisitions for stock, whereas in earlier periods of time that relationship had been higher. At the same time, transactions for cash and debt increased to 35 percent, a ratio higher than a year earlier. This is probably in belated recognition of the fact that cash, too, may offer a substantial premium in value over equity securities. It is cash which can be invested now, whereas securities are at the mercy of the stock market price earnings multiple. Even if the cash were invested in the stock market at random, many studies from the University of Chicago have shown that over a long period of time the average annual increase in value of stock portfolios, including capital gains and dividends, averages a little bit over 9 percent per year; a handsome return by any stretch of the imagination, and an excellent inducement for selling for cash. It is true that stock-for-stock transactions are tax free at the time of the transaction; but sooner or later that tax must be paid.

PATTERNS OF MERGER ACTIVITY

Another interesting facet of merger and acquisition activity is the spin-off of portions of companies. It is almost as if someone reversed the usual logic and said that, "the sum of the parts is equal to more than the whole." One example of this is the spin-off of L.C.A. Lighting by Walter Kidde. By terms of the spin-off, L.C.A. issued its own stock to be sold publicly; the multiple of the stock sale being significantly higher than the multiple of Kidde itself. Using this type of transaction, Kidde pocketed approximately $25 million from the sale of its less than majority interest in L.C.A. Kidde still retains a majority interest in the firm. According to Robert Healy who is an expert in mergers and acquisitions with Price Waterhouse & Company, the partial spin-off has almost given rise to a new strategy for corporate organization. He observes that some analysts have even gone so far as to label it an emerging form of conglomeration. The flexibility given the conglomerate company by partially spinning off its subsidiaries may enable it to survive far better than the so-called classic and more rigid type of conglomerates. This technique has enabled the traditional conglomerate to become much more flexible in its approach to survival.

Spin-offs have many benefits for cash-poor companies. Bob Healy notes that Brunswick Corporation made a public offering of Sherwood Medical Industries, one of its subsidiaries, selling off approximately 15 percent of the company at $29.00 a share. Brunswick thereby raised $30 million dollars. Armour & Company spun off Armour-Dial to its own shareholders at the equivalent of $18.50 a share and thereby gained some $33 million for the treasury.

Looking for a Marriage Partner

There are approximately a quarter of a million corporations in the United States with more than 25 employees, and further, a little over 10 percent of these companies are publicly held. Therefore, the odds are overwhelmingly probable that acquirors will be looking at privately held companies to acquire. Frank Butrick cites what he considers to be eight signs indicating that a firm wants to be bought out:

> 1. Mr. Butrick suggests that a study of the credit ratings and reports on small to medium/large firms can give a clue as to whether a company might be ripe for acquisition. He suggests that those firms whose sales are under $500 thousand for founder-managed firms and up to $5 million for firms managed by the first generation beyond the founder, may be on the lookout for marriage if their payments of monies which they owe tend to be slow. This, of course, would be indicative that they are short of capital. In addition to that, Mr. Butrick suggests that firms which are heavily in debt may also be ripe candidates to take over.
>
> He correctly observes that one should not fall too heavily in love with a favorable financial picture. An overinsistence on the takeover of a profitable company can lead to a very high acquisition price. Acquisitions, as will be subsequently noted, should be bought based upon future performance. Furthermore, that future performance should be as it would appear under the ownership of the acquiring company. In fact, the essence of the calculated purchase price should be the *present value of discounted future earnings* under the new acquiring company.

2. Another clue, according to Mr. Butrick, is that any firm which is doing less than $3 million of sales volume annually and concurrently having an elderly president who is substantially the sole owner, may well be a candidate for takeover since the owner at that age may well be thinking of retiring. Mr. Butrick does make the observation that, if any of the heirs apparent to the throne of the elder sole owner appear as functionalists on the board, the acquiring company should shelve the prospect until the heirs apparent actually inherit the firm.

3. Mr. Butrick further makes the suggestion that, in a firm of any size, one should look for a firm with a female president. It is his contention that if she is the founder's widow, sister, or daughter, her attorney runs the place. A clue which he discerns is the meaningful key as to whether the woman is, in fact, an operating president or a delegator, is whether she heads up her own labor negotiating team and maintains company contacts with major customers. If, however, she has delegated these vital phases of small company management, then, in his opinion, the firm will be for sale.

4. Mr. Butrick somewhat cynically indicates that any firm whose sales volume is up to $20 million or so may be for sale if the majority of stock is held by the founder's survivors who are not necessarily active in the firm's management. He feels that the operating officer is more likely to be a "loyal retainer" who has been with the company for a number of years and who has worked himself up through the ranks; being in such a position he may not be in sympathy with a prospective takeover. In this type of situation, it is the author's suggestion that the acquiror identify the company's attorney and in a somewhat tactful manner ask him to search out firms which might be for sale. The obvious intent of this ploy is that the firm by whom the attorney is being retained will be mentioned as a possible candidate.

5. It is regretfully a truism that many sons never live up to the reputation or the expertise of their fathers. In this vein, Mr. Butrick's suggestion is that one look for a family-owned corporation of any size where the current president is the son of the founder and where the characteristic iron hand of the father rules. I believe that Mr. Butrick is playing the psychological odds that the sons are faced with an almost insurmountable burden in the beginning, trying to live up to a task for which they were improperly prepared. Although I do not necessarily agree with Mr. Butrick, he contends that the normal historical pattern is for the founder to build the corporation, the second generation to run it down, and the third generation to salvage it.

6. He next suggests that wholly-owned subsidiaries of any firm in which the parent and the subsidiary are of widely divergent sizes, may

be a candidate for examination. If the original owner of the subsidiary remains as a general manager, Mr. Butrick feels that the potential merger may be a valid one. If, however, the original owner has retired or has left, the observation is that the parent has probably not trained the replacement for that owner. In his estimation, Mr. Butrick implies that this is a classic way for an acquisition-minded company to lose money—to buy a small firm with one-man management and then have no replacement for the man at the time he leaves.

7. The suggestion here is that the acquiring company should look for any other company or division of a company whose present owners have held it between the period of six months or three years. Mr. Butrick's logic here is that this is a just long enough time to discover all the things that have gone wrong but it is not necessarily a long enough lapse in time to have taken care of the problems.

8. Using a bit of Machiavellian philosophy, he suggests that one should watch for a family-controlled company where the bulk of the stock of the company is owned by its employees. The theory here is that because the vast holding of stock is by the employees, this type of ownership becomes a device used to eliminate the possibility of an outsider buying in. The sequence to the logic suggests that the acquiring company entice the family ownership portion of the capital into selling the firm. The hypothesis then is that the employees owning the balance of the stock will immediately cave in and make it easier for the acquiror to take over the company.

Mr. Butrick's reputation has preceded him and although I cannot accept all of his suggestions, his roadmarkers or his psychology, it is not enough simply to reject them out-of-hand, because many of them have merit on their faces. The broad facts of life are that in many instances these *are* the types of companies that are ripening on the vine, waiting for a marriage partner. It is to these companies that one must immediately address himself to make the initial contact and to keep following up that initial contract periodically in the event that the initial overture is rebuffed. The above is a somewhat cynical look at the business world, to be sure. Nevertheless, this is the way that the ball bounces.

Accounting Under a Pooling of Interest Plan

The Accounting Principles Board clearly restricts those combinations which can be booked on the basis of a "pooling of interests," as well as requiring an amortization of goodwill, the excess of the acquired company's purchase price over its adjusted book value.

Accounting on a "pooling" basis assumes that (A) and (B) when merged will add up to a new entity called (A) + (B). The two companies which have been married not only can combine current results, but in addition, historical results can be recapped to show the combination in the form as if it had been on a pooled basis in earlier periods. The surviving acquiror carries its new assets at the value given on the books of the acquired company, regardless of the amount of money actually paid for the acquired company. In addition, the new company is not required to amortize goodwill either at all, or over any stated period of time. In terms of economics, this is a profoundly logical end-product of a merger. Two + two in arithmetic always equals four; the logic of The Accounting Principles Board is that two + two may equal five if one of the units of two were really worth three. It was precisely the pooling of interest technique that made such a profound change in the level of acquisition activity in the decade of the sixties. In one year alone, between 1966 and 1967, almost all of the mergers were treated as poolings.

In order to qualify as a candidate for a pooling of interest treatment, neither the seller nor the buyer can have been a division or subsidiary of another corporation for a period of at least two years prior to the new combination. In addition, the combination can be carried out only through the exchange of common stock, and must be tendered for "substantially all" of the voting common stocks of the seller. Another requirement under the APB Opinion is that there can be no contingent payouts or commitments for future additional payments. The surviving company cannot plan or intend to sell off any "significant part" of its assets that it acquires other than to eliminate the duplicate facilities or excess capacity. Properly so, restrictions made difficult the use of a pooling technique in order to camouflage poor operating results. If a company acquires another firm after its own fiscal period has closed, but before its report has been published, it can no longer account for the new firm's results as its own for the prior year. It must show in footnotes what the results would have been had the two firms been combined during that period.

In an article in *Business Horizon,* Richard Hillman summarized the six requirements for pooling treatment:

1. *Purchase Amount*—At least 90 percent of the selling company's voting common stock equity ownership must be purchased—and within a one-year period.
2. *Purchase Instrument*—Common stock must be paid for at least 90 percent

of the common stock of the selling company. Generally, the buyer may also exchange preferred and debt securities with the seller as long as the common for common portion meets the 90 percent requirement.

3. *Independence*—Neither the selling nor buying company can be a division or subsidiary of another corporation (and this independent status must have been maintained for 2 years prior to the acquisition).

4. *Contingent Payments*—No commitment for future additional acquisition payments may exist (no earn outs or contracts to retire the stock in the future).

5. *Future Transactions*—There can be no planned or intended disposal of a significant part of the assets of the selling company within 2 years after the combination except to eliminate duplicate facilities or excess capacity.

6. *Combining Results*—A pooling combination taking place after the end of a fiscal year but before financial statements are released must *not* replace the normal statement of one year's earnings to reflect a favorable acquisition. The statements must show in footnotes, however, what the results would have been had the two firms been counted as one.

THE FACT-FINDING PROCESS

Ralph Waldo Emerson once wrote in an essay on friendship that there is no such thing as a true friend in nature; that it is a paradox. He was implying in his definition of friendship that there was no human being on earth who had never held a mask before another human being; that in all cases, none of us are ourselves. It is much the same in the process of a marriage contract. In many instances there are assumptions by the uninformed that the information which is presented by the selling parties is completely accurate and trustworthy on its face. This assumption, essentially naive, runs completely counter to the expression of *caveat emptor*. Often the pressures of time will also cause faulty fact-finding. One of the dangers in negotiating a marriage is attempting to rush the process through so that a closing date can be held at the earliest possible time. It is this type of artificial deadline which often leads to conclusions at the beginning that there is simply not enough time to gather all of the facts in evidence. Therefore, the entire careful screening process becomes laid aside in favor of a haphazard fact-finding exposition. Another empty gesture on the part of senior managements of companies is the ego factor whereby the chief executive, or some other high officer, feels that they alone must be privy to acquisition negotiations. Even though they may have acquisition teams or specialists in the areas of taxation, financial analysis, corporate legal affairs, etc., they are ignored, in the final analysis, in favor of the egoism of the senior executive who feels that he must carry through the mystique of merger negotiations by himself.

Many Booz Allen studies have given truth to the fact that slightly less than half of all acquisitions are failures if judged by the objectives of the acquiring company.

Often, the time required for gathering the pertinent facts about a selling company is not nearly as long as is first supposed. Certainly an acquisition investigation should not be considered as an audit in a true accounting sense. It therefore is not the same type of audit as is normally made for purposes of certifying accounting statements. Instead, one may term it as a "management audit," and may exclude many steps which would be considered a necessary part of an annual audit. Informational requirements can be made much easier by specifying in the terms of the purchase contract that the seller deliver a certified statement for its most recent fiscal period. The purpose of the "management audit" then, is to bring the status of the company up to date from the time of the last certification. To that end, much less stringent informational requirements are in order.

Acquisition investigations should never be the work of an individual. There should be some type of an investigative team who can bring to the investigation a spectrum of skills. The company in question should be audited in a management sense but not in an accounting sense, in the fields of marketing, engineering, industrial relations, manufacturing processes and employee relations. A tailored check list of required facts should be developed and an outline prepared so that the investigating team can merely go through a countdown for completion much in the same manner as an airline pilot does before he is ready for takeoff. One such check list, developed by Willard Rockwell, is reproduced below:

Diversification Check List

The following is a check list developed by the Rockwell Manufacturing Company, Pittsburgh, Pennsylvania, to be used as a guide and reminder when investigating companies for possible purchase. Rockwell cautions that neither this nor any other check list can replace the sound judgment that comes from experience, but that it has proven practical and valuable as a working tool and as a reminder to check points which might sometimes be overlooked in an investigation.

A. General
1. Statement of proposed transaction and objectives.
2. History of business and general description.
3. List of officers and directors; affiliation. *Poor's Register.*
4. Stock distribution—number, principal holders, etc.
5. Organization chart.
6. Policy manual.

B. Financial
1. Latest audited financial statements. *Who are the outside auditors?*
2. Last available financial statements.
3. Ten-year summary financial statements.
4. Projected operating and financial statements.
5. Full description of securities, indebtedness, investments, and other assets and liabilities other than normal day-to-day accounts.
6. Chart of accounts and/or description of accounting practices relative to inventories, fixed assets, etc.
7. List of bank accounts, average balances.
8. Credit reports from banks and Dun and Bradstreet.
9. Federal income tax status; i.e., excess-profits-tax credit, any loss or unused EPT credit carry-forwards, latest year audited, any deficiency claims, etc.
10. Summary of state and local tax situation; i.e., applicable taxes, un-

employment tax rate, any deficiency claims, etc.

11. Tax status of proposed transaction; recommendation for best method of acquisition.

12. Complete list of insurance policies, including description of coverage and cost: workmen's compensation rate.

13. Statement of responsible officer of business as to unrecorded or contingent liabilities.

14. Nature of inventory.

C. Sales

1. A brief description and history (if any) of the product line.

2. A 10-year record of product sales performance.

3. A long-range forecast of growth or contraction trends for the industry of which the product line is a part.

4. A three-to-five-year forecast of anticipated demand for the product.

5. An estimate of the industry's ability to supply present and anticipated demand.

6. A three-to-five-year forecast of sales expectations for this company (share of the market).

7. An analysis of the effect of anticipated increased volume and/or cost reduction on:
   a. Product demand and share of the market.
   b. Market saturation and overcapacity.

8. An analysis of the effect of the geographic location of the new facility on:
   a. Product demand and share of the market.
   b. Distribution costs (freight savings, warehousing, etc.)
   c. Competitive position.

9. A review of present sales management, selling force, advertising and sales promotion policies for adaptability and adequacy in relation to new facility.

10. A review of present competitors and competitive practices including:
    a. Description of competitive products.
    b. Location.
    c. Estimated share of market.
    d. Pricing policies.
    e. Methods of distribution.

11. An analysis of present and/or probable pricing policies for the product line considering:
    a. Competitive position.
    b. Cost pricing.

12. An analysis of present and potential domestic and export customers:
    a. Major types of customers and percent of sales to each.
    b. Geographical location.
    c. Buying habits.

D. Manufacturing
  1. Description and layout of plant and property.
  2. List of principal machine tools—age and condition.
  3. Opinion re maintenance and "housekeeping."
  4. Utilities—availability, usage, rates.
  5. Estimated total annual fixed cost.
  6. Organization, departmentalization.
  7. Transportation facilities.
  8. Description of area, including climate, hazards from flood, etc.
  9. Opinion re adequacy of auxiliary equipment—tools, patterns, material handling equipment, etc.
  10. Detailed expense schedule.
  11. Building codes, zoning laws, and restrictions.

E. Purchasing
  1. Principal materials used.
  2. Relation of material costs to sales.
  3. Purchasing methods.
  4. List of principal suppliers, items, location.
  5. Inbound freight costs.
  6. Workload—last 12 months:
     a. Number of purchase orders issued.
     b. Value of purchase orders issued.
     c. Value of outstanding commitments.

F. Research and Engineering
  1. Description and condition of facilities:
     a. Drafting room and office.
     b. Experimental room.
     c. Laboratory.
     d. Special test equipment.
  2. Engineering personnel—quality and quantity of technical talents . . . employed . . . unemployed.
  3. Product designs—evaluation: condition of drawings.
  4. Patents and trade-marks—coverage, existing applications, litigation.

G. Labor
  1. Number, sex, age, and color—present employees.
  2. Direct, indirect, administrative: number and cost.
  3. Number of potential job applicants from surveys or census.
  4. Determination of types of skills available in the area from state employment service and other sources.
  5. Location and availability of students from high schools and technical schools.
  6. Union—copy of contract.
  7. Labor relations history.

8. Appraisal of working conditions. *Vacations; medical program.*
9. Statistics on turnover: reasons.
10. Description of incentive system: average rates incentive and hourly.
11. Employment and personnel policies.
12. Accident frequency.
13. Ratio of total labor cost to sales.
14. Pension and welfare plans. *Implications of discontinuance of former plans.*
15. Appraisal of transportation, community recreation facilities, housing.
16. Evaluation of labor situation in area.

H. *Legal*
1. *Anti-trust*
2. *Trade-marks*
3. *Litigations*
4. *Pending contractual obligations*

I. *Insurance*
1. *On buildings*
2. *On vehicles*
3. *Prepaid?*
4. *Liability*
5. *Business interruption*

Items in italics above are additions by this author.

The Acquiror's Reasoning for an Acquisition

One of the most difficult decisions that can ever face a management group within a company is to decide whether to merge or combine the company with another. The risks inherent in such a possible move are formidable on the face. One need only look at the recent history of L.T.V. to realize that acquisition policy is not the panacea for profitability. Conversely, one can look at the well-structured organization of companies such as Textron who have successfully integrated most of their acquisitions. This type of policy for a well-planned company has the potential of opening up new product areas and has proven to be the catalyst which creates the base for a profit takeoff.

There are a number of important reasons, both financial and operating, which dictate why corporations may choose to acquire going concerns.

A. *Financial Reasons*
1. Exploit an opportunity
2. Avoid the risk of internal development programs

3. Use idle capital
4. Take advantage of tax losses
5. Increase market value of stock
6. Effect more rapid growth
7. Improve on profit level or trend in present business
8. Secure a source of capital
9. Spread business risk
10. Provide a market for stock

B. *Operating Reasons*
  1. Offset seasonal or cyclical fluctuations in the company's product mix
  2. Improve on volume level or trend in present business
  3. Reduce dependence on a single product
  4. Satisfy customer's demands for additional services
  5. Broaden the customer base
  6. Acquire new customers and new markets
  7. Obscure the details of the primary area of activity from competitors through diversification and the publication of the consolidated report
  8. Take advantage of an existing reputation
  9. Obtain business in a new territory
  10. Obtain a research and development group
  11. Strengthen the management
  12. Acquire a particular product
  13. Increase the utilization of present resources
  14. Enhance power and prestige of the owner, president, or management of the company
  15. Provide an outlet for frustrated interests or excess management capacity
  16. Add glamour and greater interest to the company.[1]

In scanning the financial and operating reasons for acquisitions, I believe we can summarize them all under one heading. The long range objective behind all acquisitions must be the increased market value of the stock of the existing corporation.

One disturbing fact concerning acquisitions is the relatively poor track record regarding the actual versus anticipated success of such ventures. All too often, two or three years after the acquisition has been completed, the acquiring organization cannot forecast long range results anywhere near as optimistically as it could have done at the time of the negotiations. Any in-

---

[1] C. Drayton, C. Emerson, and John Griswold, *Mergers and Acquisitions: Planning and Action,* a research study and report prepared for the Financial Executives Research Foundation, p. 40.

vestment decision is concerned with a choice among available alternatives and it is always subject to an unknown future environment. Actual future costs, markets and prices will invariably differ from any single set of assumptions used as a framework for weighing proposals.[2] Furthermore, when the decisions are made, frequently they seem to be based on politics or on feelings about certain companies, rather than on sound logical consideration of the key or determinant variables involved.

A variety of criteria, such as payback, average annual return, net present value and the internal rate of return (DCF), among the most prevalent, are used to varying degrees in an attempt to justify potential acquisitions. Most theoreticians today speak up for either the net present value or the discounted cash flow approach as opposed to the previously popular average return and payback methods. Indeed, most practitioners, I believe, favor the discounted cash flow approach. However, it should be noted that none of these evaluation techniques are capable of handling all of the facts surrounding the quantitative evaluation of an acquisition. A number of writers have expressed themselves in favor of raising the rate by which cash flow streams should be discounted in order to compensate for the risks involved in an acquisition. In other words, normally the (DCF) calculation will yield a percentage answer which should be compared to the cost of capital. What is suggested here is that the cost of capital minimum criteria should be a multiple of the true cost of capital, depending upon the risk involved in the acquisition. This inflated rate penalizes projects whose cash flows are heaviest in later rather than early years.

In the following section an evaluation technique is presented which will allow the decision-makers in a company to most efficiently place the proper price tag on a potential acquisition. The objective here is not only to assess what is the fair market value of a potential acquisition, but also to determine whether the expected returns are high enough to surpass the minimium rate of return established by the policies of the company.

THE EVALUATION TECHNIQUES FOR AN ACQUISITION

The major problem in completing a merger or acquisition is to establish a value for the cash purchase or an exchange ratio if payment is to be made in stock or other securities. In almost all cases, the potential future earnings are determinative. These earnings are, in one way or another, translated into

---

[2] David B. Hertz, "Investment Policies That Pay Off," *Harvard Business Review*, January–February, 1968, p. 97.

a going concern value. This value is never absolute, but a best judgment appraisal, and the best that can be hoped for is to establish a range of negotiation within which a transaction can be consummated. The highest price in the buyer's range, which he may choose to call his evaluation peak, becomes the sum total of his optimism for the future earning power of the combined enterprise which he envisions will result. As mentioned previously, there are various yardsticks for evaluation, all of which must be tempered by the degree of competition which exists for the particular business enterprise.[3]

Methods for Determining Value

Generally, going concern value is of most interest both to the buyer and seller. The methods of evaluating going concern value can vary significantly. One basis uses historical earnings directly in the computation and attempts to weight the later earnings more than the earlier ones. The security analyst's approach will be utilized. Past earnings will be reviewed but only insofar as they reflect the future prospects. We will attempt to assess the value of a firm strictly on its future potential. In addition to the above approaches, many organizations examine book value and appraisal value as indicators of the value of a going concern.

Book Value

The book value is not a significant measure of the value of a company because its basic function is to provide a means of establishing asset values for accounting purposes. These costs are basically the original cost of the assets which may bear small relation to the present costs or to the ability of the assets to produce earnings. Book value is important to many stockholders as a measure of participation in the net worth of a company and for this reason, becomes a factor in measuring the reasonableness of exchange of stock. Traditionally, the pre-merger book value of a share is compared with the post-merger book value to determine if any dilution has occurred. Since it is obvious that increased per share earnings should be the true measure and because book value is not connected to earnings or earnings potential as is the market value of stock, it would not appear reasonable to make decisions based on evaluation of book value. It should be noted, however, that a number of corporate managements have shelved potential mergers because of a per share decrease in book values of combined companies.

---

[3] Drayton, Emerson, Griswold, *Mergers and Acquisitions*, p. 73.

Appraisal of Assets

This method simply attempts to place a replacement or market value on each asset. It is an inadequate decision tool simply because the appraisal value of the assets may have small relation to their ability to produce earnings. The important consideration in acquiring a company is the expectation of earnings as a going concern and an appraisal does not accomplish this.

Going Concern Value

Where two companies entering a business combination are in the same industry, their financial statements may be compared without much difficulty. In the absence of any unusual conditions affecting future profits of either company, agreement may be reached readily as to the period or periods for which earnings should be averaged as a valuation factor.

A five-year historical period is most common for this purpose. It has been recommended that where expansion of profits is demonstrated in the five-year economics that some sort of weighting should be devised to give a higher value to later earnings.[4]

There are several methods of using past earnings to measure the future. One of the most popular is the "Capitalization of Earnings." Average the earnings for a period of time, say five years, and then capitalize this average at an appropriate rate. The assignment of a capitalization rate is ordinarily not an easy task. The best initial source is usually the price-earnings ratio accepted by the market for similar companies in similar businesses. Whether the acquiring company is willing to accept the market's view on the subject is likely to depend upon the purposes of the acquisition. In a diversification situation the acquiring company may very well be willing to accept a high price-earnings ratio and thus a relatively low return on investment in order to participate in a growing field. If, however, the acquiring company's objective is to strengthen itself in its present line of business, it may be reluctant to dilute its earnings and its return on investment by purchasing a company that will produce a low yield in relation to the price paid for it.

---

[4] George D. McCarthy, "Premeditated Merger," *Harvard Business Review,* January–February, 1961, p. 75.

Exhibit 1

Year	Earnings Company A	Earnings Company B
1	$ 50,000	$100,000
2	50,000	100,000
3	100,000	100,000
4	100,000	50,000
5	100,000	50,000
	$400,000	$400,000
Average Earnings ÷ 5	$ 80,000	$ 80,000
Capitalized (10x)	800,000	800,000

The above demonstration shows earnings over a five-year period for two potential acquisitions. You can see from the above that both companies would be evaluated the same. From a logical standpoint, you would be inclined to choose Company A because of its better earnings record in the later years. Hence, a more accurate result can be obtained by weighting the earnings to give more consideration to the more recent earnings. The following method gives at least partial consideration to the different patterns of earnings:

Exhibit 2

Year	(1) Weight Factor	(2) Earnings Company A	(3) Weighted Earnings (1) × (2)	(4) Earnings Company B	(5) Weighted Earnings (1) × (4)
1	1	$ 50,000	$ 50,000	$100,000	$ 100,000
2	2	50,000	100,000	100,000	200,000
3	3	100,000	300,000	100,000	300,000
4	4	100,000	400,000	50,000	200,000
5	5	100,000	500,000	50,000	250,000
Total 15		$400,000	$1,350,000	$400,000	$1,050,000
Average Earnings ÷ 5		80,000		80,000	
Average Earnings ÷ 15			90,000		70,000
Capitalized (10 times)			900,000		700,000

Exhibit 2 illustrates the importance of weighting. Company A now clearly appears the better choice. There are two major concerns in any comparison of this sort:

1. Do the arbitrary weights assigned give adequate consideration to the future potential earnings for both corporations?
2. What assets were required to produce the earnings for both companies? Asset efficiency can be as critical to a decision as earnings pattern. Hence, we must view the asset side of both these companies. The next procedure is to compute the average rate of earnings produced by the specific assets applied and then project the earnings by multiplying the assets applied at the end of the period by the average rate.

Company A

Year	Net Worth Beginning of Year	Earnings	Weight Factor	Weighted Net Worth	Weighted Earnings
1	$ 600,000	$ 50,000	1	$ 600,000	$ 50,000
2	615,000	50,000	2	1,230,000	100,000
3	625,000	100,000	3	1,875,000	300,000
4	675,000	100,000	4	2,700,000	400,000
5	750,000	100,000	5	3,750,000	500,000
	$3,265,000	$400,000	15	$10,155,000	$1,350,000

Average ÷ 5   653,000   80,000

Average Weighted ÷ 15	677,000	90,000
Average Rate of Return (Unweighted) (80,000 ÷ 653,000)		12.3%
Average Rate of Return (Weighted) (90,000 ÷ 677,000)		13.3%
Projected Earnings (Unweighted) (800,000 * × 12.3%)		98,400
Projected Earnings (Weighted) (800,000 × 13.3%)		106,400

* Represents net worth at end of period.

If the capitalization rate of ten times earnings is used, Company A would have a value of $984,000 or $1,064,000 depending on whether a simple or weighted average is used. The same analysis can be used on Company B and a comparison of the results for the two companies can be made.[5]

The method depicted above is not without merit. It does give us a rather good picture of the earning power and efficiency of the assets in the past. The rationale is that over a period of years the net assets applied have been

---

[5] Drayton, Emerson, Griswold, *Mergers and Acquisitions*, p. 84.

producing at a certain rate and unless something is indicated to the contrary should continue to do so, and should do so on the latest amount of assets applied.

It can perhaps be seen where this method would be very helpful under certain specific conditions, namely with:

1. Companies in the same industry.
2. Relatively the same size.
3. Same price-earnings ratio.
4. Mature market where past history is a good indicator of future profitability.

Also, it can be seen that in too many cases we cannot assume all of the above-mentioned conditions. We are often faced with the acquisition of a company which is much smaller in scope than ours, or one that is in a growing market. This method is also biased in favor of either the buyer or seller, dependent on what conditions prevail. For example, it is biased in favor of the buyer when earnings are growing at a rapid rate and in favor of the seller when the earnings are declining. While this method has usefulness, a method is required which will explicitly concern itself with the future flows expected. An economic evaluation of the future potential and not a rule of thumb approach to the future is needed. Further, we require an evaluation technique which will enable us to determine the maximum we can afford to pay for a particular acquisition and still yield a satisfactory return. The method must consider the timing of our future flows as well as the risks involved.

In trying to determine the maximum amount we can invest, I recommend the present value approach. For example, a selected rate of interest, such as cost of capital or a subjectively assigned target rate of return, can be used to calculate a present value and this value can be used as the purchase price for a business. When we have determined the maximum to be paid for a business, the investment base to ascertain what expected rate of return (DCF) will result by lowering the price can be varied. We are then often able to compare what we would expect to pay with what the seller is asking. An important reason for trying to estimate future flows rather than concentrating on past history is that often a very large corporation with its technical and sales know-how can realize a much better yield than the smaller company. Further, with this as a consideration, the amount that a large company can afford to pay a smaller one is often in excess of what the smaller company is asking.

The key objectives of this approach are:

- Provide a quantitative technique for evaluating acquisitions in spite of their uncertain nature.

- Require the organization to deliberate seriously and objectively regarding product life, product pricing, costs, and so forth, which discipline is a proper function of management.
- Provide a reference point from which an acquisition program can be evaluated on a continuing basis.

Procedure

The mechanics of this evaluation are as follows:

- An acquisition price is selected. This selection can be made at random. (For simplicity sake, we shall assume that the depreciation base is equivalent to the acquisition price.) This amount represents our initial cash outflow.
- Other cash outflows, such as working capital, are put down in the proper years.
- Cash inflows are estimated
  —Net Profit
  —Plus depreciation
  —Plus any other incomes such as recovery of working capital at the end of the product life, plant salvage value, tax credits on expenses, and so forth. If the economic life is less than ten years, recovery of working capital in particular should be included.
- Net Cash Flows are calculated by combining for each year the cash inflows with the cash outflows.
- The Net Cash Flows are discounted at the desired minimum rate of return using "Present Value" tables.
- If a positive return results, we know that a higher acquisition price can be considered. Conversely, when a negative return results we know that the price is too high. Therefore, by a tedious process of trial and error, we are finally able to arrive at that acquisition price which when combined with the other cash flow streams gives us a yield equal to zero when discounted at the cost of capital or other minimum acceptable rate of return.

Example

	($000's)
Estimated Acquisition Price (Selected at random)	$10,000
Product Life	10 years
Net Profit—years 1 through 10	$1,200
Depreciation—straight line—10 years	$1,000
Working Capital	$1,000
Minimum Rate of Return	10%
Tax Rate	50%

Year	Cash Outflow	Cash Inflow	Net Cash Flow	DCF at 10%
0	$10,000		$(10,000)	$(10,000)
1	1,000	$2,200	1,200	1,091
2		2,200	2,200	1,817
3		2,200	2,200	1,652
4		2,200	2,200	1,503
5		2,200	2,200	1,366
6		2,200	2,200	1,241
7		2,200	2,200	1,129
8		2,200	2,200	1,027
9		2,200	2,200	933
10		3,200	3,200	1,235
				$ 2,994

The above calculations indicate that an acquisition price somewhat in excess of $10,000,000 can be afforded and still yield at least a 10% return.

To continue with the trial and error process, I have selected an estimated acquisition price of $14,000,000.

Revised Example	($000's)
Estimated Aquisition Price	$14,000
Product Life	10 years
Net Profit—years 1 through 10	$1,000
Depreciation—straight line	$1,400
Working capital	$1,000
Minimum Rate of Return	10%
Tax Rate	50%

Year	Cash Outflow	Cash Inflow	Net Cash Flow	DCF at 10%
0	$14,000		$(14,000)	$(14,000)
1	1,000	$2,400	1,400	1,273
2		2,400	2,400	1,982
3		2,400	2,400	1,802
4		2,400	2,400	1,639
5		2,400	2,400	1,490
6		2,400	2,400	1,354
7		2,400	2,400	1,231
8		2,400	2,400	1,121
9		2,400	2,400	1,018
10		3,400	3,400	1,312
				$ 222

The preceding indicates that a $14,000,000 acquisition price comes very close to the price limit. If we were to carry this process one step further, we would find by interpolation that $14,500,000 is the maximum price we could afford to pay and still yield a 10% rate of return.

This method is consistent with the thinking of Ezra Solomon who in *The Theory of Financial Management* makes mention of this approach in his chapter on the cost of retained earnings. In this chapter, he discusses the *external yield criterion*. He contends that in any reasonable market, external investments (acquisitions) should be available which offer an earnings yield equal to and having the same degree of certainty as those offered by the company's existing assets. The return available on such external investments is appropriately measured by K_e and this represents the minimum rate of earnings required from internal investment.[6]

There are many factors which will have a bearing on deciding what the actual acquisition price should be. For one, competitive conditions may require bidding for a potential acquisition. Too conservative an approach to bidding and the acquisition would be lost to a competitor. The conditions which dictate what the actual bid price is are too numerous to evaluate quantitatively. It is my belief that once a maximum bid is determined, a highly selective study must be made which could include an evaluation of possible maximum prices which competitors can afford.

INTEGRATING THE ACQUISITION

One of the major pitfalls is the conceptual thought that once the company has been purchased, the process of amalgamating the company into the existing parent organization is completed. Acquisition failures occur when executives fail to think through a conceptual planning scheme for the complete integration of an acquired company. Functional integration of the acquired company generally falls into the realm of finance, marketing and manufacturing.

In the area of *finance*, integration is usually accomplished quite quickly but sometimes on different levels. One of the most important ways in which a company can be integrated into the financial area is to take apart the required company's operation and determine which parts of the operation are similar and compatible with the acquiring company. For example, some of the immediate thoughts which lend themselves to compatibility are the process

---

[6] Ezra Solomon, *The Theory of Financial Management,* Columbia University Press, 1963, p. 53.

of billing customers, the process of inventory control and the process of accounts payable. For the most part, unless there are widely divergent sizes between the acquiring and acquired company, such a combination can result in compatible integration into the existing financial structure. One of the things that a financial man is always aware of is the factor of economies of scale resulting from centralization of certain vital financial functions such as cash management. This can manifest itself in the reduction of the number of banking relationships as a result of the acquisition. By accomplishing this, a number of compensating balances can be cut substantially, thereby reducing outstanding cash requirements. Reducing the level of cash balances throughout the corporate environment should be one of the major objectives of the corporate integration of the acquired company. It is quite possible also in the area of fringe benefits to either directly lower rates or insurance or pension plans or at least add the new employees to the plans at minimal costs.

It may also be during the integration phase of an acquisition that by phasing the newly acquired company into the already existing data processing system of the parent that peripheral EDP equipment formerly owned by the acquired company may be phased out and absorbed by the existing larger equipment of the parent. This too can serve the economies of scale since it is probable that the larger equipment owned by the parent has a much higher capacity for output than the generally smaller equipment owned by the acquired company. The assumption here, of course, is that there is a divergence in size between the buyer and the seller in the transaction. Another factor to be reckoned with is the capacity factor in data processing operation. It is the rare company that operates its central computer control for more than 30 percent of its theoretical time. Utilizing the newly acquired company and absorbing it into the centralized console can effectively increase the payoff on data processing equipment.

In the area of *marketing,* one of the approaches of integration is to create a program which will place the products of a new company under the umbrella of the surviving parent. This can have the great benefit of identifying the smaller, newly acquired company with the image and reputation of the parent through the use of promotions and coordinated sales. Another method in marketing of integrating the new with the old is to make full use of existing channels of market distribution. For example, if the larger surviving parent has established lines of distribution through its sales force, wholesalers, brokers and distributors, it may well be that the newly acquired company can simply be considered as an addition to an already existing line and in effect, better utilize the capacity of these distribution channels. It certainly would not make sense to operate the existing distribution of the acquired company on a basis parallel with the existing distribution of the surviving company if there are points of similarity in their methods. The last marketing area in which meaningful integration can take place is in the administrative side of the marketing function. Here it may be that an existing group product manager can merely add another new product to his umbrella of already existing products. It certainly does not necessarily mean that a new vice presidential or other type of decision-making overhead expense need be created.

Integration of an acquisition in the *manufacturing* function is different in most respects from that of the integration into the financial and marketing function. One of the ever-present objectives of the manufacturing function is to find products which are compatible with and countercyclical to existing products manufactured in existing plants. In this respect there may be major opportunities for integration along manufacturing lines. Certainly from the purchasing side there may be economies of scale in the area of purchasing, in the area of economic order quantities, in the area of level production, utilization of existing capacity and utilization of labor force.

Within the framework of integrating an acquisition, whether it be along the lines of the financial, marketing or manufacturing function, the essential point to be kept in mind is that there is such a delicate balance between maintaining the identity of the old company which is always a worthwhile objective to pursue and the submergence of the acquired company in the maze of the existing parent's bureaucracy. If the latter course is effected, then it is the personal opinion of the writer that a successful acquisition integration will be a very difficult result to obtain.

THE EVENTUAL PROFITABILITY OF ACQUISITIONS

There is a great deal of interest in the after-results of corporate mergers; however, very little evidence dealing with the profitability of corporate mergers has been gathered to date. Even so, the evidence that has been presented has given rise to mixed conclusions. As an example, two recent studies were concluded and one reported that actively merging firms were very markedly unprofitable while the other suggested that actively acquiring firms were neither more nor less profitable than comparable firms in a similar industry which did not pursue such aggressive acquisition policies. One of the problems in dealing with this type of conflicting data lies in the definition of how to measure the profitability of a merger. Certainly one of the obvious ways of measuring profitability is by looking at the merger in terms of its objectives. One must assume in the capitalistic society in which we live that corporations have as a merger objective the eventual increase in profits (maximization) and the subsequent increase in the equity of the stockholder.

Thomas Fogherty recently pursued this line of investigation in an article which appeared in *The Journal of Business*. He concluded that the investment performance of actively merging firms is generally worse than the average investment performance of other firms not actively pursuing acquisitions but nevertheless, in the respective industries of the acquiring firms. In fact, one of his conclusions suggested that mergers even have a neutral impact on profitability. Mr. Fogherty also suggested that the stock price performance of active acquirors was even worse than the performance of their earnings per share and in that respect, he concluded that mergers are a risky form of investment. In any event, one of the more obvious conclusions which must be drawn in any discussion on merger activity is that those companies, be they conglomerate or otherwise, having a determined, carefully thought out plan for acquisition procedures, will inevitably produce a better final resultant corporation. Textron is one such example of a company with a unity of purpose in the area of acquisitions. There is no doubt that growth companies falter because the strains of growth create management problems that are sometimes too great for the available resources within the firm. These types of problems have a way of aggravating the weaknesses which are already apparent within the management of the parent company. In a more stable and slower moving situation, these weaknesses may never become apparent. In a great many of the growth situations, however, four major weaknesses are always potentially present:

1. An increase in executive work load which becomes unmanageable as a result of a lack of careful planning for integrating the acquisition.
2. An inability on the part of the surviving management to cope with the complexity which is brought about by newly revised organizational relationships.
3. Lines of communication become longer and longer and sometimes more remote. This has the inevitable penalty of manifesting itself in a loss of control.
4. The process of placing unqualified men in key jobs as a result of the reorganization may ultimately have a deleterious affect on the careers of the men and the efficiency of their work. The men may not be fully qualified in their new role and this type of weakness will be highlighted in any company in which an accelerated pattern of growth is making itself felt.

I would suspect that in the decade of the seventies, the main thrust of corporate acquisition activity will be on the capabilities of the managers themselves. As David Linowes said, "The management capability approach first identifies the acquiring company's own unique attributes; then organizes itself to handle problems that may arise later; and finally sets up a structure which provides for a full-time executive, flexible procedures, and strategic planning."

13

EFFECTIVE COST REDUCTION
IN MATERIALS HANDLING

INVENTORY CONTROL

It's surprising how many companies fail to realize the great importance of building inventory with an eye toward proper balance among types of items. These firms also are often lax in controlling the supply of goods to square with their projected sales. Another point: these companies do not take a proper physical inventory, with the result that their profits are distorted and they may be overpaying on their taxes.

The suggestions outlined below should help clear up such practices and solidify the financial stability of those companies that are not following these ground rules.

Your Inventory Checklist

Because of the ceaseless attention to inventories by business publications and because the inventory investment is probably the largest single current asset in many balance sheets, most companies are aware of the cost-cutting effect of reducing the inventories they carry. However, inventory reduction still remains a fertile ground for cost reductions. Poor sales forecasting and production planning are probably the basic causes of inventory losses. To cut your inventory costs, ask yourself the questions below:

- Are we effectively using the inventory controls we are supposed to have? Have we violated our original concepts by short-cutting and trying to out-guess our suppliers?
- How current is our inventory? When did we last "age" it and what did it show? Should we sell some of the slow-moving items?
- What is the turnover time on various items we produce? Can we concentrate on those that tie up the least capital? A product produced in two weeks (and sold) obviously ties up less cash in inventory, per dollar of sales, than a product that takes six months to produce and sell.

- What is the materials content in our various inventory items? An item with a high materials content per dollar of sales ties up more cash in inventory than an item with a low materials content. In a seasonal business, it is far better to stockpile labor than material.
- Can orders be rescheduled so that deliveries coincide with needs, instead of anticipating them? Many items, in the course of production, require purchased parts. If lead time can be shortened, less money will be tied up in inventory.
- Can more high material content components be subcontracted? Items of high materials content tie up cash in inventory.
- Do we know, with respect to each item of inventory, the percent of labor and material to value? Shouldn't this show on the stock cards?

Concentration on High-Value Items

Does it cost you as much to keep track of pencils as it does electric motors? The expense was the same for one company until it put controls on an inventory value basis. The Treasurer reports: "We found that we were spending quarters to count pennies. Now we watch the dollars and let the pennies look after themselves."

The moral for many companies: concentrate control where it pays off—on high-value items; exert less control over low-value items. Here are some illustrations:

1. *Saving with simple control:* A survey showed one company that seventy-three percent of its inventory represented only 4.5 percent of inventory investment. To reduce the cost of controlling these low-cost items, they were placed in a fenced-off, self-service area. Clearly marked gravity-feed shelves and wide aisles were designed to make selection easy, just as in a supermarket. Employees now "shop" for needed supplies and take their selections to a "cashier" who adds up their "purchases" and bills the appropriate department. As a result, this supermarket procedure cut inventory control costs thirty-four percent.

2. *Cut time spent on inexpensive items:* The company had been applying the same controls to diesel engines and sealed-beam lamps. The company then coordinated engine purchases with production schedules so that engines came in and were installed on the same day. Previously a number of them had to be kept on hand. Result: overall inventory investment was reduced twenty percent, and the space used to store the engines was available for other uses.

3. *Cutting control costs on low-value items:* Some other ideas for cutting inventory control costs on low-value items:

- Review inventories of small items only at set times; the interval should be as great as practical without risk of running out. This, combined with a simplified issuing system, will reduce control costs.

- Keep a simplified stock record card (bin tag) right where the material is stored. Record additions and withdrawals on the spot as they occur. This provides an easy way to keep a running count and cuts additional accounting costs.
- Establish a reserve quantity and separate it physically from the rest of the supply; package it separately; insert a divider to indicate when the reserve is reached or even attach a reorder slip at the beginning of the reserve quantity. When the supply is reduced to this point—reorder. That's all there is to it. No recording, no reviewing, no counting.

How to Choose Items to Control

Here is a method of picking out low-value items to control:

1. Compute your total inventory control cost.
2. Divide this by the number of items in inventory to determine the *unit control cost.*
3. Determine the cost to purchase or make each inventory item.
4. Arrange the prices of all inventory items in descending order of value.
5. Analyze this list to determine the value distribution of your inventory items. Then ask: How many warrant the control cost?

The value of some inexpensive parts will be much greater than their price indicates. The production of an important assembly may be held up for want of a five-cent part. Therefore, in your analysis—after determining unit control cost—single out critical items for special treatment.

Operations Research

By turning the attention of the company's Operations Research Steering Committee to inventories, Arthur M. Wittman, Treasurer of Standard Register Co., Dayton, Ohio, reports that his company achieved a twenty-one percent reduction of investment in inventory. In addition, other advantages resulted:

- Reduced cost of possession
- Improved service to production and customers
- Improved inventory balance
- Improved inventory turnover

The approach included the use of the simulation process, which can be used when a mathematical solution to many interacting variables present in the overall inventory problem become too complex for an absolute practical solution.

The premise is not new; management is continually confronted with problems which offer several alternate solutions and must decide on the best. The choice, of course, is made by comparing the alternatives, using some appropriate measure of evaluation—usually profit, cost, or service. During the process, management attempts to visualize what will happen to profit, cost, or service under each of the alternatives. As the variables become more complex, mental simulation becomes more difficult, and in some cases impossible.

Here is where electronic data processing can help. It helps simulation by accelerating the occurrence of events in a given functional area so that several years' activities can be simulated in a matter of minutes. By examining the results of alternate policies, management can evaluate the results, select the policies and procedures to be incorporated into the operation of a given functional area, and thereby determine the most desirable course before it is taken.

Raw Materials Inventories

In applying simulation to raw materials inventories, Standard Register used an IBM 1401 Inventory Management Simulator Program. Through the program, these things were measured:

- Method of forecasting demand
- Setting order points
- Establishing order quantities
- Lead times
- Safety stocks
- Review frequency

The results of varying these factors were measured in terms of: (1) Amount of investment (average investor); (2) level of service provided; (3) number of replacement orders; and (4) inventory range.

Thus, by subjecting the actual demand for, or usage of, various raw materials to the effects of varying policies and procedures, the company determined the investment required to provide varying levels of service to customers. From this information, management could evaluate and select the service level, with its associated required investment, which would most nearly meet its objectives.

Finished Goods Inventories

In this area, the company used the Economic Ordering Quantity theory of equating costs that increase with the number of orders handled and the costs that decrease with the number of orders handled. This permits the computation of an ordering or producing quantity that will keep total costs at a minimum.

The use of this theory requires the development of the following basic data:

- Annual usage
- Cost of possession
- Ordering cost or step-up cost

In addition to the development of these basic data, it was necessary for Standard Register to create mathematical expressions of the total variable costs involved in the handling of various classes of finished goods inventory items.

The actual means of computing the Economic Ordering Quantity for any given situation is derived mathematically from these expressions of total variable cost. The methods to be used in deriving the Economic Ordering Quantity formula for any specific condition are to be found in almost all of the literature dealing with scientific inventory management.

By substituting cost and usage data in the formula for Economic Ordering Quantity, and in other formulas developed from it, the following may be computed:

- Economic Ordering Quantity in dollars and/or units
- Number of times to purchase or produce per year
- Total cost of possession
- Total annual ordering or set-up cost
- Total annual variable cost

Since the arithmetic involved in making these computations for a number of items is laborious, Standard Register developed, through the medium of the Fortran programming language, a computer program to accomplish the output.

Advantages of Monthly Inventory

In a complex stock situation, a monthly inventory has many advantages. A case in point is a business like the Al Semtner Drug Depot, Dallas, Texas, a public warehouse specializing in drugs, drug sundries, and cosmetics. The company handles broken case shipments down to individual items. In a situation like this, O. B. Hamilton, Treasurer, reports these advantages of a monthly inventory:

- It helps get older stock out first.
- It reveals slow-moving items that take up space.
- It helps eliminate out-of-stock conditions—resulting in more revenue for the the company's principals.
- It eliminates possible refurbishment by master shippers due to shabbiness or soiled condition.

In addition, the monthly physical inventory program provides an excellent reconciliation between the actual physical inventory and the theoretical inventory on IBM cards. The latter is arrived at as follows: Semtner invoices for most of its principals, and ships from a copy of the invoice. Errors, however, can be made in picking and checking an order (for example, #6019 picked for #6109; #528 picked for #528M, etc.). In addition to upsetting the physical inventory, it gives the customer material he did not order; only part of these may ever be called to the company's attention (if the customer received a better item). The monthly reconciliation also helps spot errors on the other side of the fence: machine tabulation. This can happen with a corroded point or weak rheostat—or an error by the key punch operator.

Monthly Verification

The monthly inventory, and verification, is a simple process:

1. Physical inventory is taken on an IBM card, with stub, consecutively numbered.
2. The actual count is written on both the stub and tab card.
3. The stub is attached to the inventorized item.
4. The card is sent to key punch, and quantity and description are punched in.
5. Inventory cards are merged with the theoretical inventory cards.
6. The reprint shows the actual and theoretical inventories, reflecting inbalance, over, and short items.
7. Differences are checked out and proper adjustments made on the theoretical inventory cards.

This procedure also permits processed cards to be stored in a minimum of space. One month after reconciliation, the cards are junked and sold as used paper—the proceeds going to the employees' recreational fund.

Coordinating Inventory with Customer

A plan, based on the concept of *service-selling,* that provides both rigid control of inventory and increased sales has worked successfully for a Cleveland distributor of several lines of small machinery, construction items, and automobile parts. The plan embodies one of the strongest selling points you can offer your customers: assurance that they will never suffer loss through understocking, overstocking, stockouts, or parts obsolescence of your products.

In essence, the company coordinates its own inventory very closely with those of its customers. In so doing, the company not only cuts its expenses by maintaining proper levels of its own inventory, but it is in a position to boost its sales to customers.

The following basic factors on which the program is based are adaptable to many firms' inventory control:

1. The company salesmen stock, count, and replenish supplies in customers' bins.
2. The salesmen send in reports on inventory of key items to the main office. These are processed promptly to insure both the company and its customers against overstocks or stockouts.

3. The company uses four regional warehouses to insure prompt local deliveries. (Due to tight control under (2), regional warehouses are always properly stocked.)

How the Salesmen Operate

Company salesmen, distributing over 7,000 products, make about 2,000 calls a day servicing more than 40,000 customers—each of whom is contacted at least once a month.

Each salesman organizes the customer's stock bins and cabinets (which are installed and supplied by the company), checks the inventory, and writes orders to bring stocks up to the proper level. The company gets added mileage out of its program. During his service calls, the salesman tries to evoke criticism and suggestions from his customers on company products. If successful, he passes the information on to the company's product research analysts. This group and the engineering department then may possibly develop new or improved products.

The bin-stocking and order-writing activities of the salesmen at customer locations tie directly back to inventory operations through the receipt at headquarters of the replenishment orders. This activity has been one of the strongest selling points for the distributor.

How to Set Up a Simple, Fast and Accurate Inventory Count

Knowing the way to handle an inventory count is knowing the way to big savings. Taking physical inventory is usually a long and complicated job—taking up your time plus the time of your work force—often at premium rates. And all too often, you wind up with an inaccurate count. *Result:* Overpayment or underpayment of taxes—as well as trouble with distorted budgets and production schedules. *What can you do about it?* Make your inventory count a step-by-step operation that leaves no room for mistakes.

Get Ready Properly

Set up an inventory task force—two or three of your best men—to lay the groundwork for the actual counting. Have them prepare written instructions for workers. Have them outline the methods they're going to use when taking the inventory. Then work together with them to:

1. Get *all* inventory arranged for easier counting. Have workers clean up each department, and make sure of the location of all products. Separate your inventory into three main classes: raw materials, work in progress, and finished goods.
2. Segregate all rejects, and all obsolete or salvage material.

3. Tag all materials for easy identification. Three types of perforated tags are needed—one for each class of inventory.
4. Check mechanical counting, weighing, and measuring equipment. Be sure it's in good working order—and be certain it's accurate.
5. List all materials on hand that won't be considered as inventory. This includes supplies, construction materials, consignment-in, and all goods sold but not yet shipped.
6. List all items owned by you—*but which aren't on hand*—that must be included in inventory. Examples: Inventories out on consignment, in public warehouses, at contractors, or in sales offices or branches.
7. See that all sales and purchase invoices are consecutively numbered, and assign a definite cut-off point for inventory taking. This way you'll know exactly what goods are to be counted as part of your current inventory—even though they may be in transit.
8. If possible, set a deadline for halting production. This will speed up your count—and cut down on duplication.

How to Take a Count

Divide your workforce into counters and writers. The actual count should be supervised in each area. If production can't be stopped, double check to see that the inventory count is not duplicated.

How to be systematic: As a member of the inventory team passes down the aisle, he tags each section or bin—if this hasn't already been done. He then fills out whatever information is required on the tag. Next, he tears off the portions of the tags giving the descriptions and quantities, and counts them. The tags should be signed by the workers responsible for the count.

The supervisor's main function: He must verify the physical counts and *compare* them with the available records. Any difference between the physical count and the records should be reported immediately.

How to Insure Accuracy

An inventory count that isn't accurate defeats its own purpose. You're in no better shape than you were when you started—and you might even be in worse shape.

To be sure your count is accurate, use the following tested principles according to how they fit your type and method of operation.

Don't use abbreviations. They can be a big stumbling block for any inventory counter. All too often, the abbreviations have been coined by one person. No one else knows what they mean. Whenever possible, write out full descriptions.

Checking grade and quality. Only experts should take inventory of products which are difficult to judge according to grade and quality. Guesswork—by workers who really don't know—is a giant step toward an inaccurate count.

Use of detail. A detailed breakdown of items may help—or it may hurt. Make the amount of detail specific—be sure everyone knows it. Otherwise, you'll wind up with far too much or far too little.

Valuing of work in progress. Many companies go way off base because they can't set the value of the components in partly finished products or sub-assemblies. Keep accurate process-cost records so that the cost of all components can be clearly identified. Then, once you determine the manufacturing stage, you know your true labor and material costs at that particular stage.

Keep things up to date. Process-cost records should be kept up to date, since standards keep changing. Changes in material and labor cost must be constantly recorded—and applied—or costs will often turn out to be unrealistic, perhaps by wide margins. If these records aren't current in your company, now's the time to get them up-to-date—before the inventory count starts.

Tips to Speed Up the Count

You don't have to sacrifice time in order to get accuracy. You may even be able to cut down on your inventory time—and your worker's overtime payments—by using one, or all, of the following methods:

1. *Use a portable tape recorder.* This cuts down on the need for *both* a counter and a writer to make the physical check. If you intend to use this procedure, however, remember these points:

- Number each spool of tape consecutively.
- Mark the location of the inventoried material on the spool.
- Make random checks on accuracy.

2. *Use ratio scales.* When a product is made up of many small component parts, counting by weight can save you lots of time. You can get a quick count just by balancing the predetermined multiple against the one component.

You may want to consider using a two-way radio to speed up your inventory taking. If you have hard-to-get-at places in your plant—such as narrow aisles or high shelves—the counter can relay his figures to the writer sitting at a desk some distance away. Make it a point to inventory every piece, no matter how low the price or insignificant its use. Lack of even a small component, due to an inefficient inventory count, can cause expense and time-wasting delays in your production.

STORAGE OF INVENTORY

For most companies, storage of inventory presents two major problems: (1) cost, and (2) space. The problems become multiplied when a company operates in more than its local environs. For example, the firm that ships and has to store goods in widely separate areas can save or spend a substantial amount of money by making the right or wrong choice or choices on which method (or methods) it uses for storing its inventory (i.e., its own facilities, public warehousing, or contract warehousing).

In the final analysis, the method of storing goods depends upon the type and scope of operations of a particular company. What is best for one might be the worst for another. This section points out the various advantages and disadvantages involved in storing goods in your own warehouse or using a public warehouse. After weighing the pros and cons, you'll be able to make the choice that will work out best for your company.

A key decision in controlling your distribution costs is whether to maintain your own warehouse or warehouses, or use public warehousing. There is no pat formula; you have to evaluate your company's operations as a whole. The points below will help you come to the right decision. If your business is a small one, the use of public warehousing can help you overcome the "quick-delivery" advantage bigger companies have because of their multiple inventory locations.

Arguments for Public Warehousing

1. *It conserves working capital.* You avoid outlay for "bricks and mortar" and other capital expenditures (plus the headaches and costs of insurance, employee problems, payroll and real estate taxes, traffic operations, and property maintenance). So you have more working capital for your business. You can, of course, conserve capital by leasing your own warehouse instead of building or buying it.

2. *It provides flexibility.* Facilities and costs match your needs of the moment. If your volume requirements vary or your products change, or if a change in the location of your warehouse is indicated, you are not committed to full-time, long-term costs. You pay only for the space actually used on a per-package, per-hundredweight, or other unit basis per month.

3. *It tightens inventory-billings.* You can have the warehouse bill your customers for what they get from your inventory. Your customers will remit directly to you. The billing will be tied to the perpetual inventory of your stock

that the warehouse keeps for you. The result is a cut in the billing lag and maintenance of a proper inventory level.

4. *It allows ready determination of unit costs.* Warehouse receipts permit ready prediction and budgeting of cost for each unit of merchandise; this is more difficult to ascertain when you use your own warehouse.

5. *It offers special services.* Public warehouses have come a long way from the time when they served only as storage depots. Now they perform, with know-how, many special services in materials handling, office and paperwork, and financing services that your own warehouse operation may not be equipped to handle. Some examples:

- Handle and consolidate pooled carloads
- Consolidate shipments
- Break down bulk shipments into individual orders
- Can, bottle, sample and inspect bulk goods
- Mark, stencil, wrap, and tag goods
- Maintain lists of accredited customers and make regular deliveries to them
- Obtain credit information
- Offer delivery services
- Install appliances and other equipment you sell

Public warehouses say they render these services at prices manufacturers can't duplicate on their own.

6. *It integrates distribution.* Warehouses are developing into distribution centers from which operations are integrated forward and backward, expediting goods all the way from factory to customer.

"Integrating the separate functions into one continuous-flow operation develops maximum efficiency at lowest cost," says C. William Drake, President, Lehigh Warehouse & Transportation Co., Newark, N.J. "There is no breakpoint in the handling operation from shipper to customer. Unnecessary putting down and picking up are eliminated. Peaks and valleys in the use of labor and equipment are largely smoothed out. There is one management, one office, one overhead, one profit."

Lehigh Warehouse & Transportation Company worked out an example of integrated distribution with Dow Chemical Co. Dow used to ship drums of chemicals from its plants across the country to Lehigh Warehouse. This incurred the expense of shipping the empty drums back to Dow plants. Costly tank cars were tied up in long, cross-country hauls. Now, Dow ships by tanker and barges to Lehigh's bulk-liquid tank. Dow gets the advantage of the low cost of bulk shipment by water, and avoids the high cost of shipping drums and tying up tank cars on long hauls. Customers who buy by the drum get better service at lower cost. Customers served by tank car or by tank trailer get service two or three days later.

Originally, a substantial volume of Dow's product went from Lehigh's tank to a public canner. After canning, the product was returned to Lehigh for storage and distributed to customers as needed. This, too, was changed. Lehigh itself now does it all—mixing ingredients, canning, labeling, packaging, storing, and delivering—resulting in additional service improvements at lower cost.

7. *It furnishes high-grade loan collateral.* Warehouse receipts that may be used as collateral for bank loans—frequently up to seventy percent of the value of the stored goods—can be issued only by public warehouses. This financing benefits companies of all sizes and is particularly helpful to the capital needs of the small and growing business.

8. *It provides desirable locations that a company itself sometimes couldn't buy.* Public warehouses are usually strategically located and immediately available. Other space suitable for warehousing with such features often is not available.

9. *It permits warehousing of small volumes in locations that would not support company warehouses.* Small companies can enjoy warehousing facilities that they couldn't afford to set up themselves. Larger companies, furthermore, can use public warehouses to package smaller lines of goods that otherwise would not be economically feasible. Lower costs in areas in which warehouses are located often makes these smaller operations worthwhile.

Arguments for Private Warehousing

These advantages of private warehousing are frequently cited:

1. *It affords better control over products.* A company has intimate knowledge of its own products and they are handled only by its own employees. So it is in a better position than public warehouses to promote cost cutting in handling, packaging, prevention of damage, workloads, quality control, and other elements of warehouse operation.

2. *It proves more economical in special situations.* A nationwide manufacturer with heavy production and marketing may find privately owned warehouses quite economical. If there is sufficient volume to maintain an even load, the cost may compare favorably with that of public warehousing.

3. *It may reduce handling costs.* A company may be able to design warehousing facilities for automatic handling, which would not be possible in a public warehouse.

Combining Methods

After considering the advantages of both types, you may find that the best solution for your company is to take advantage of the good points in both and combine your warehousing operations. Your own warehouse is probably a vital part of your distribution operation, and you can't therefore get rid of it entirely. But many companies warehouse a good part of their inventory themselves and store the rest in public warehouses. A combination can insure uninterrupted flow of goods, while allowing for fluctuations in inventory without disruption of unit warehouse costs.

How to Keep Down Warehouse Expenses

Since you may not be able, or want, to get rid of your own warehouse entirely, here are some simple ways to keep down its operating costs:

- Store big and heavy objects at or near floor level so they can be easily moved from carts to storage space.
- Arrange small items such as washers or bolts at waist level, for easy inspection or pickup in order-filling.
- Put the most commonly used items near your outgoing transfer point. Place infrequently used items in the rear, up high.
- Be sure the light is strong enough for easy reading of labels and order forms.
- Develop a simple and easy-to-use letter and number code for controlling the location of particular items in your storage area. This will also help control theft of inventory.

1. Maintain tight inventory controls as part of your accounting system, and make actual inventory counts at irregular intervals.
2. Screen carefully all prospective warehouse employees.
3. Employ sufficient guards to at least act as a deterrent.
4. Provide identification badges for all warehouse employees, and issue special passes for visitors.
5. Either lock or permanently cover all unused exits.
6. Have members of management make frequent unannounced visits to the warehouse.

Contract Warehousing

Contract warehousing, as distinguished from public warehousing, may be a way for you to trim your distribution costs. To be profitable, a public warehouse must handle many accounts; this necessarily means standardization. A contract warehouse, however, gives specialized service, tailored for each customer; you may find the rates lower than those of public warehouses. Typically, when a company wants to warehouse and distribute all or a specific part of its product through a contract warehouse, the warehousing firm handles the warehousing and distribution for a trial period. After this period, the contract warehouseman may obtain a written agreement to handle all, or a certain part, of the company's merchandise.

Here are the services and advantages of a typical contract warehouse. While many of the operations overlap those of the public warehouse, they are given *in toto* to provide a complete picture of the contract warehouse.

Typical Services Performed

In the regular course of operations, the contract warehouse company may provide the following services for its customers:

1. *Warehousing.* In a metropolitan area, maintain a number of warehouses adjacent to leading railroad, truck, air, and port facilities, for domestic and export shipment.

2. *Trucking.* Make deliveries in the metropolitan area.

3. *Packaging.* If the contract warehouse offers packaging service, many customers may find that it can be done more cheaply than they can do it themselves.

4. *Perpetual inventory.* The customer can determine his exact inventory on a daily basis.

5. *Insurance.* Coverage protects all merchandise from loss or damage and includes:

- Burglary
- Theft
- Mysterious disappearance
- Workmen's compensation
- Public liability
- Property damage
- Fidelity bond

In addition, a contract warehouseman carries the required *warehouseman's legal liability* against fire, sprinkler leakage, water damage, explosion, vandalism, riots, strikes, and civil commotion.

6. *Shipping information.* Although the customer pays for shipping his merchandise to the warehouse, the contract warehouseman will advise on the best and cheapest way to ship.

7. *Billing.* If necessary, the contract warehouseman will bill for you, and ask that remittances be made directly to you. Most companies, however, prefer to do their own billing.

Some Collateral Advantages

Those who use and recommend contract warehousing say that it can:

- Do the job at less than it would cost the customer to do it himself.
- Do the job more efficiently.

Here are specific benefits that customers realize through lower cost and increased efficiency:

1. *Elimination of warehouse facilities.* This permits more of your own space to be used for manufacturing or selling. Eliminating warehouses is even more important in peak seasons. Then, space needs become critical and keeping up with deliveries is a real problem.

2. *More time for manufacturing and selling.* For many companies, distribution is a headache that uses up a lot of time. If an outside source absorbs the headache, the company can focus on manufacturing and marketing.

3. *Reduction in personnel problems.* Elimination of warehouse employees means elimination of the time and money spent in hiring, firing, training and, if a union is involved, greater freedom from union problems.

4. *Reduction in shipping cycle.* An efficient contract warehouse is geared to ship any item within twenty-four hours of placement of the order. This reduction in the shipping cycle can mean:

- Less money invested in inventory.
- Faster servicing of customers.
- Reduced billing lag and, therefore, fewer outstanding receivables.

5. *No losses in inventory.* Since a contract warehouse exercises strict control over—and insures—all merchandise, the customer is reimbursed *for any loss in inventory,* for any cause whatsoever. You can't obtain insurance for mysterious disappearance of inventory on your own premises. Even if you carry theft and fidelity insurance, you bear the loss for inventory shortages on your premises which you can't prove were caused by theft, robbery, or larceny.

6. *Simplification of paperwork.* Duplication is eliminated and forms and shipping documents for each account are consolidated. One contract warehouse, for example, has reduced the shipping, receiving, and inventory control forms of a nationally-known retailer from seven forms to one standard form. The contract warehouse may put its customers' names, slogans, trademarks and similar matter on its trucks at no extra cost. This helps to keep the customer's products in the public eye.

What Does It Cost?

The contract warehouse tailors its costs to each customer's type of business. All costs are fixed, so that the customer's treasurer can predetermine the cost he adds on each item. These costs may be either (a) fixed on a fixed unit-price basis or (b) on a stipulated rate per hundredweight. Thus, on a hundredweight basis, a contract warehouseman might use the following price schedule:

- Stipulated amount per cwt. for handling in.
- Stipulated amount per cwt. for handling out.
- Stipulated amount per month for warehousing.

The sum of the three items represents total charges to the customer. There are no extras. *Billing* for all product lines is made on a current, operational basis, and *storage* is charged on a fiscal thirty-day period that starts from the day of arrival at the warehouseman's premises.

HOW TO KEEP SHIPPING COSTS DOWN

Using the wrong carrier to ship your merchandise is not only costly from the viewpoint of initial expense, but in many cases you run the risk of paying for lost or damaged goods because the carrier is financially unsound.

Another way to cut shipping costs is to know how to pack and classify your goods. Many firms eat up profits by packing improperly and failing to take advantage of the cheapest classification available.

By following the suggestions in this section, you'll probably be able to trim your shipping costs in one degree or other. In some cases, you may realize substantial savings.

The Proper Carrier

Mr. Stephen Tinghitella, editor-in-chief of *Traffic Management* magazine, points out the risks run by the company that does not investigate the reliability and integrity of its carrier. He also highlights the steps to take to make sure you are selecting the proper carrier.

Here are some specific risks you face if you hire the wrong carrier:

1. *Unpaid freight claims.* Naturally, all carriers are *responsible* for damage to freight in transit if it is due to the carrier's fault or neglect. Even so, in the event of extensive damage you may wind up bearing most of the loss if the carrier doesn't have sufficient insurance and is not financially responsible. Note these important points:

   a. The minimum insurance *required* by the Interstate Commerce Commission is $2,500 per vehicle and $5,000 for loss or damage at any one time or place.
   b. Contract carriers (truckers operating under a specific contract with you, rather than common carriers operating under the bill of lading) are not required by I.C.C. regulations to carry any cargo insurance at all.
   c. In almost every city in the United States, all that local carriers need is a city trucking license. They are not required to carry cargo insurance, nor are they subject to any regulations; furthermore, they're not required to report to any government agency.

If your trucker carries only minimum insurance, or is without adequate insurance, collection of the full value of damaged or destroyed cargo would depend upon the financial resources of the trucker. If damage or loss results from your own negligence (poor packing, for example), truckers that operate under I.C.C. rules must refuse to reimburse you; payment of such a claim would, in effect, be a "rebate device," which is illegal. If liability is in doubt, reliable carriers almost always require some proof of their liability before settlement is offered. On the other hand, many good carriers assume partial responsibility if rough handling of cartons is evidenced, even if it was not directly traced to them. If your carrier agrees to allow a claim, but tells you to take the amount off your freight bill, don't do it unless the shipper is a governmental agency. Such practice is forbidden by the I.C.C. and has been declared illegal by the courts. The law requires that all tariff charges must be paid in full, with no deductions or rebates.

2. *Loss of goodwill.* Most of your customers tend to view your trucker as your agent or representative. Thus, dissatisfaction with a delivery will carry over to your company. For example, a delay in delivery or the arrival of goods in a damaged condition may strain relationships with a customer; you could very easily lose a highly profitable account.

3. *Risk of criminal liability.* Watch out for the trucker that offers to perform services declared illegal by I.C.C. rulings and court decisions. Here are examples of the more common violations:

- Acceptance of freight for delivery beyond the carrier's authorized franchised limits.
- Offer of services which may not be covered in a carrier's tariffs, such as inside delivery.
- Allowance of claim deductions from freight bills.
- Payment of claims without proof of carrier liability.
- Agreement to rates other than those authorized.
- Falsification of the bill of lading for any purpose. The shipper who knowingly enters into such an illegal agreement is equally liable with the carrier to prosecution for any violation, and the penalties are severe.

Six Steps to Selecting the Right Carrier

Mr. Tinghitella suggests the following steps to make sure you select a carrier that will measure up to your standards:

1. *Obtain a trade report.* This will give you an idea as to the carrier's business integrity, and in addition is a reliable indicator as to what kind of service you can expect.

2. *Get references.* To find out whether the carrier renders reliable service and performs all other obligations (handling claims, sending tracers, etc.), contact a few of its customers and ask them about their experiences.

3. *Check its insurance policies.* Make certain your trucker not only has sufficient value coverage, but also that all risks inherent in your class of shipment are included. This is particularly important for shippers whose merchandise is subject to unusual risks, such as perishable goods or products that will be spoiled by freezing. If you ship inherently dangerous materials, make certain your shipper has adequate public liability protection. (Many chemical and petroleum firms play it safe by carrying their own public liability insurance in addition to the carrier's.)

4. *Look up its operating ratio.* If the carrier is regulated, its ratio figure is on file with the I.C.C. This is an index of operating results, obtained by dividing operating expenses by operating revenue. It gives the cost in cents of producing $1 of operating revenue, and thus indicates how well or poorly the carrier's business is functioning from the profit point of view. The carrier with an unsatisfactory average operating ratio generally may try to cut corners and resort to drastic economies. This can only lead to inferior service and loss to the shipper. As a rule of thumb, an operating ratio of 96¢ (four percent net profit) is considered good.

I.C.C. franchise is no guarantee. The mere fact that the carrier is operating under authority of the I.C.C., or under a state franchise, *does not necessarily mean he is responsible and trustworthy.* It merely means that at the time the authority to operate was granted, the carrier met all requirements. Since that time, method of operation and service could have deteriorated appreciably.

5. *Review the carrier's tariff.* Make sure that the services offered are adequate for your type of shipments and include the destination to which your shipments are made.

6. *Inspect his terminal facilities.* A quick visit may prove to be an eye-opener.

The membership roster of the National Freight Claim Council is a reliable guide to ethical carriers. Every one of the 1,500-odd carrier members has pledged itself in writing to strict observance of the Council's rules and regulations, which constitute the trucking industry's only code of high professional ethics and standards in the handling of freight claims.

Getting the Most from Your Transportation Dollar

Shipping costs, like everything else, keep rising. While you can't stop the rates from rising, you *can* cut costs by more careful record-keeping, better scheduling and routing methods, and a sharper analysis of rate policies. Here are some ideas that will help you get the most mileage out of your transportation dollar:

1. *Assign traffic responsibility.* Continuous application of cost-control techniques is the best way to cut costs. If you have an annual transportation bill of $100,000 or more, a full-time traffic manager is probably warranted. With less volume, you may want to assign one individual on a part-time basis, or retain a traffic consulting firm.

2. *Audit your freight bills.* You may fail to detect overassessments because of incorrect descriptions or classifications. It's good sense to have your freight bills audited by a reliable freight audit bureau. For some firms, rate experts have discovered refundable overcharges amounting to thousands of dollars. Most audit agencies charge fifty percent of the refunds collected, with no charge if there are no recoveries.

3. *Cut paperwork.* Consider clearinghouse methods, such as the Chase Manhattan Freight Payment Plan for Shippers. Costs can be substantially reduced under this plan, since the bank:

- consolidates all of your freight charges in one account
- eliminates processing of the carrier's statement
- eliminates check writing
- reduces postage and mailing expenses

4. *Be accurate and complete in preparing the bill of lading.* Even a small mistake may be costly. Correct weights, number of packages, complete routings, and prepaid or collect charges should be clearly shown. The documents should also indicate one shipper, consignee, and destination.

Tips on Routing and Scheduling

1. Investigate the possibilities of pooling shipment with other companies in your area to get reduced rates. In many areas, nonprofit shipper associations can reduce transportation costs by assembling and consolidating small shipments into carload or truckload lots, and routing the individual shipments to the proper destinations.

2. Consolidate small orders for the same day or week and consider using freight forwarders for less-than-carload or truckload deliveries.

3. If you can stagger your pickups and deliveries properly, you can:

- Eliminate costly idle periods for your personnel.
- Avoid demurrage charges amassed by freight cars arriving faster than they can be unloaded.

4. Proper attention to product descriptions, bulk, weight, and packaging is very important.

- If you conform to the carrier's terminology on bills of lading, you lessen the likelihood of higher classification.
- If you ship your product in an unassembled state, you may get a special low rate. Sometimes a small change in design will qualify an item to travel at a lower rate.
- If you can use new lightweight materials in your product, you may be able to effect a gross weight reduction and reduce shipping costs. A reduction in bulk may keep you from paying for empty space.
- If you can consolidate parcels into large containers, you may qualify for lower rates.

5. Consider the possible advantages of regional warehouses or even your own trucks to lower freight costs.

6. Check your carrier's schedules thoroughly. The normal schedule, rather than the speedier, more expensive service, may be entirely satisfactory.

7. Make use of the stop-off privilege. As many as three stop-offs for partial unloading are allowed by many motor carriers. Only a nominal charge is made for each intermediate stop-off. By combining shipments for a few customers who are along the same route leading to your ultimate destination, you can usually come out well ahead.

8. Install mechanical aids. You can speed up expensive loading and unloading time by utilizing more efficient materials-handling devices and equipment. An electrically-controlled tractor, for example, usually requires fewer workers and reduces damage to merchandise.

9. Consider using air freight for certain classes of merchandise.

Get the Best Break from the Rates

You can't change the rates, but you can study them for the best possible break.

1. Sort out your differently rated products. When articles with different rates are shipped in the same package, the highest rate usually applies.
2. Shop around for the best rates. Don't assume that all carriers are obligated to charge the same rates. But use common sense; the cheaper carrier may be slipshod and cost you more in the end.
3. Weigh the importance of freight costs in considering bids from various suppliers. Sometimes a lower shipping price will more than offset the additional cost of a slightly higher bid.

How to Trim Freight Costs

If your commodity classifications are not clear and complete, you may be paying higher freight costs than necessary. Proper classification is not an easy task, since carrier rates are, for the most part, a maze of technical jargon. (For example, aluminum rods and aluminum bars are in different classifications and the distinction between classifications is often hard to determine, even in companies directly concerned with such shipments.)

As a simplified guide, published I.C.C. rates could be given this breakdown:

- First class rate is a 100% rate
- Second class rate is 85% of first class
- Third class rate is 70% of first class
- Fourth class rate is 55% of first class
- "Double first class" is 200% of first class

OBTAINING CORRECT FREIGHT RATES

Despite the technical language, however, many materials can be easily classified to bring them below first-class shipping rates. The factors below are the ones which largely determine freight rates. You can't capriciously switch classifications at will. Deliberate attempts to use erroneous rates are illegal. There is a formal procedure for the obtaining of a correct freight rate. For example:

1. *The composition of the product.* Whether a product is wood, iron, steel, rubber, aluminum, brass, copper, etc., makes a difference. For example, Superior Auto Co. makes auto parts. The shipping clerk described the products as "auto parts" on the bill of lading. Without further identification, it received first-class rates. A review of the correct descriptions revealed that adding the words "iron or steel" to "auto parts" would save fifteen percent, and change the rate to second class.

The same company also shipped rubber floor mats under the category of "auto parts." When the proper description of "rubber floor mats" was used, a fourth-class rate was assessed, affording a savings of forty-five percent.

If your company pays for shipping charges, such changes in classification can lead to big savings.

2. *Packaging of the product.* The method of crating, assembling, and packaging also has a bearing on rates. For example, Prime Mfg. Co. makes office equipment, which is disassembled for shipment. The traffic manager makes sure that the bill of lading specifies "stands, metal, K.D." This means that the equipment is being shipped "knocked down" so that a cheaper rate applies.

The old practice of charging by commodity value is bowing to a trend toward rates based on volume, weight, and number of containers. Containerization can mean freight economy, since many products take lower rates if consolidated and packed in larger containers. American Standards Association, Inc., 10 East 40th Street, New York, N.Y., 10017 has adopted national standards for container sizes.

3. *Processing of the product.* Rates can be affected if your product requires additional processing, refinishing, etc. For example, Fulton Iron Foundry was shipping castings described as "finished." Fulton's customers, however, would further process the castings by machining, drilling, heating, or painting them. Fulton checked with the carriers and found it could ship its castings as "unfinished" and take advantage of a lower rate.

Here's an easy-to-apply moneysaver:

- List your products that are shipped most frequently, with descriptions and type of package.
- Consult your freight carrier for the correct technical descriptions of them.
- Have these items preprinted on bill of lading forms in sets of at least three copies (original, shipping, sales). Leave some blank lines for items shipped only occasionally.

This will cut down on errors and save time. Remember, however, your bills of lading should be complete and accurate; correct weights, number of packages, complete routings, prepaid or collect charges, and so on should be clearly shown; documents must show the shipper, consignee, and destination. Even a small mistake can be costly. Prepare and post lists of items you ship with their ratings. This can minimize time wasted on errors and inquiries.

Procedure in Getting a Reduction in Freight Rates

More dollars can be saved by having classifications changed than by any other method of freight rate reduction, according to George Olsen, an independent traffic consultant, Jersey City, N.J. In reappraising your present ratings, keep these general classification rules in mind:

- *Similar items should have similar classifications.* This is the "rule of analogy." It's particularly useful in properly rating a product that hasn't been classified previously. The trick is to find the right precedent—an item similar to yours with a low rating; this will present a strong case for lowering the rating of your product.
- *An article described as a combination of materials travels under the highest possible rating.* Check to see if the bulk of your shipments consist of one or a few components, each of which would be lower if classified alone. Thus, you could reduce your freight bills by splitting a more general listing.

Grounds for Negotiating a Lower Rate

You can negotiate for a lower freight class rating on a number of grounds:

1. *Change of materials.* A switch to a less expensive material gives you cause to ask for a lower rating. Even if you switch to a more expensive material, one that reduces your production costs, you might still win a lower rating. (See item 4.)
2. *Change in description.* Sometimes a change in description will do it. For example, one company had been shipping artists' oil paints as "artists' materials." After checking classifications, it found it could ship at a lower rate if the material were described as paint in tubes. Companies producing new products should make use of this method.
3. *Breakdown into components.* If you're now shipping an article in parts or subassemblies that previously went fully assembled, try to apply the "splitting" rule.
4. *Price changes.* If tough competition has forced you to cut your prices, it lowers the monetary value of your shipment and may entitle you to a lower classification.
5. *"Release" agreement.* A "release" agreement between you and your carrier to fix a maximum valuation on a shipment in event of loss or damage may lower the rate. The carrier's liability is limited and he can afford to reduce the rate. The I.C.C. permits this when the class of your commodity has a wide range of values and the commodity is particularly prone to loss or damage.

Obtaining a Lower Classification

The procedure is about the same whether you are dealing with a motor carrier or railroad classification committee. It's complicated, and a firm unfamiliar with lowering classification, or too small to have a traffic expert, would do well to take on an outside consultant to handle the case. They're available in most medium to large cities; consult the yellow pages of your phone directory.

The procedure involves two steps:

1. File a proposal with your regional classification committee, which will schedule it for a public hearing. The addresses of the committees:

Railroads:

Official Classification Committee
1 Park Avenue
New York, New York 10016

Southern Classification Committee
101 Marietta Street
Atlanta, Georgia 30303

Western Classification Committee
202 Union Station
Chicago, Illinois 60606

Truckers:

F. G. Freund
National Motor Freight Classification Committee.
1616 P Street, N.W.
Washington, D. C. 20006

2. Support your request at the hearing. You can do this in writing or in person. Here are some ideas:

- Document your request meticulously. It's not easy to get a more favorable classification. You have to provide clear justification.
- Cite specific entries in the tariffs to justify a lower rating. Give proof of price changes with customer order slips, or production economies with internal cost records.
- Present evidence—such as carrier invoices from common customers—of instances where other shippers have a lower classification for the same or similar products. Each regional group must agree with your proposal before it can be published. The whole procedure takes three to four months.

Saving with Air Freight

Air freight is no longer the exclusive province of luxury goods or emergency shipments. It is coming more and more within the reach of small companies, and it continues to get cheaper. Although in itself a more expensive manner of transportation, air freight may afford sizable reductions in related expenditures and in other phases of distribution. Here's how:

- Reduced in-transit time cuts your needs for inventories, plant storage facilities, and warehouse space in distribution areas. These items incur taxes and insurance costs, and tie up capital.
- Crates are moved fewer times to and from warehouses and surface transport-trimming handling charges.
- Damage and spoilage in transit is reduced.
- Packaging is simplified.

Shipping by air also offers these indirect and long-term planning advantages:

- Distribution can be more easily and centrally controlled.

- Prompt and fast service to customers can be of sufficient importance to outweigh any cost handicaps.
- Entry into new markets may not necessitate construction of farflung warehouse systems.
- Land values around airports are still low relative to real estate nearer other forms of transport—should you be considering the acquisition of land for a new plant site.
- The market for your perishables can be far wider than ever previously contemplated.

Shipping by air offers cost and time-saving advantages in production as well as in distribution. Expensive machinery downtime can be cut drastically if replacement parts or equipment for repair are sent by air.

Even if not applicable now, you should keep your eye on developments in air freight. Currently, the efforts of the airlines to break out of the "premium" traffic category and into the basic distribution market have helped, and will continue to help, cut your costs. Then, too:

- The main objective of the airlines is to offer progressively lower rates for larger shipments.
- There's a possibility you'll no longer be faced with complicated rate structures based upon the type of commodity.
- Airlines are expanding and improving their air freight service to make it fit better into your distribution operations.

Ero Manufacturing Company, producer of auto seat covers and other accessories, centralized all made-to-order operations in Chicago with the help of air freight shipments. The line of custom seat covers accounted for only a small percentage of total sales, but took a disproportionate share of production facilities in plants all over the counrty. The switch to air enabled Ero to end duplication of costly custom patterns and specialized equipment, to reduce stocks, and to shunt supervisory personnel and skilled workers into production of its standard line.

Six Ways to Hold Air Freight Costs Down

Get all the profits that are coming to you when your goods take to the air. Thousands of companies don't—and are overpaying heavily on their air shipments. To get every last air-mile for your dollar:

(1) *Ship on the right airline:* Whenever possible, use an airline which services both your location and the place the shipment is going to or coming from. The transfer of shipments from one airline to another at some midpoint, which happens when they are tendered to a nonconnecting line, skyrockets charges and adds to transit time. *Set up a guide list* of airlines serving your

location and also serving other terminal cities most frequently involved in your air shipping.

(2) *Name your commodity on the bill of lading:* It can make all the difference in your costs. For example, if your hasty and uninformed clerk had filled in "mdse." instead of "periodicals" on the airline B/L or has filled in nothing at all, you could be billed at a much higher rate on the shipment. Find out if there are "Specific Commodity" names and classifications to fit the goods you ship. See that the right ones are entered on your appropriate airline B/L's to get the lowest rates.

(3) *Send some shipments by forwarders:* Airlines generally charge a fifty-pound minimum rate. Airfreight forwarders have their own rate scales and lower minimum weight rates. They can often airlift your lighter shipments at a better price. Contrary to the implications of some advertising, there is *no one* airline or forwarder who can give you the lowest rate on all shipments to all points. Get rate sheets from airlines *and* forwarders who serve your location. Compare them (particularly in the lower weight ranges) to determine when, where, and how you'll get the best buy.

(4) *Save on multiple pickups or deliveries these four ways:* For a number of shipments at the same time, use your company vehicle for local delivery to or from the airport. Check with your carriers on possibilities of using cost-cutting "Assembly Bills," "Distribution Bills," and "Deferred Air Freight."

(5) *Call for pickup on time:* If your call to the air carrier for a pickup is placed too late in the day for the driver to get it on his route, delivery of your shipment could well be delayed for an additional twenty-four hours. This is a critical time-lag for an airfreight shipment, and could cost you goodwill and money. Get your carriers' pickup schedules for your location, and be sure your company's pickup calls are placed on time for same-day pickup.

(6) *Pay only what you owe:* Audit all air-carrier bills for these four areas of overpayment: (a) Mathematical errors on your bill. (b) Extra charges you don't owe; i.e., you are charged for a pickup when your own man actually delivered the package to the airport. (c) Wrong commodity scale: The airline biller may have overlooked the fact that your goods travel on a lower commodity rate scale. (d) Payments made on both original and duplicate invoices. (By C.A.B. regulations air carriers bill on a seven-day credit basis and their duplicate invoices come in pretty fast.)

Assign a responsible person to investigate "air" advantages and cost angles *for your own company.* He should determine where you will gain the most from air shipping on particular items, to or from specific regions, to or from special customers or vendors, under special circumstances, and through use of the right carriers.

The proper air carrier to specify on shipments of various weights and routing should be spelled out for the two people in your organization who do the actual specifying. They are:

- *Your purchasing agent:* He names the air carrier to be used for inbound shipments on his purchase orders.
- *Your shipping manager:* He calls for whatever carrier is to pick up and fly each shipment.

Provide these two key employees with lists of carriers selected to service frequently-used air routes. Indicate the weight ranges in which each is to be used. Show them how and when to specify other airfreight economies that apply.

The Best Delivery Service for Lighter Shipments

Customers are insisting on fast delivery service today, more than ever. Many hold inventories of purchased goods to *bare minimum* levels. It adds up to pressure on you to supply goods in more frequent, often small, batches—and to do at the lowest possible cost per shipment.

You'll save money by using the best single delivery service for each of your lighter shipments. There's no pat formula for choosing the right carrier in each and every case, of course. But in talking with a number of shippers, we were able to put together the following broad recommendations.

- *1 to 20 pounds, nationwide:* One good bet is to use parcel post for this weight-range—when you want steady nationwide delivery.
- *1 to 20 pounds, East-Midwest-West:* Here you'd be smart to look into United Parcel Service, which operates in many states within the East, Midwest and Far West.
- *20 to 125 pounds, nationwide:* Railway Express Agency (REA) Surface Express can give you economy in this category.
- *1 to 5 pounds, by air:* You'll probably find REA Air Express to be among the more competitive services here.
- *10 to 50 pounds, by air:* Air freight forwarders may offer good rates and speedy handling in this weight range.
- *50 pounds and up, by air:* Dealing directly with the airlines themselves might well save you money with the heaviest air shipments.
- *Small lots-short hauls:* Bus service can work out fine for deliveries of small lots 100 to 200 miles away. But in most cities it's still a terminal-to-terminal service only. You have to provide your own delivery and pick-up to and from the terminals.
- *Multiple small shipments, picked up at one place at one time:* Truckers are angling for your business in multiple small shipments now. One reason for

their new interest is the action of railroads in barring some less-than-carload lots, including those of big shippers. As a result of this action the *amount* of small shipments to be handled has gone up fast recently.

With competition for small shipments getting hotter among carriers, it'll pay you to seek out and press for the most advantageous deal—especially when it comes to long-term shipping contracts. Talk to a traffic consultant when you've got a complicated shipping problem or when you want your overall shipping procedures reviewed for efficiency. A good consultant will be up-to-date on the many local and regional variations among carriers, in service and cost advantages.

To be directed to a reliable traffic consultant in your area, write—stating your needs—to the National Freight Traffic Association, Suite 226, 919 18th Street N. W., Washington, D.C.

FILLING SMALL ORDERS PROFITABLY

In the competitive battle for business, small orders can be a problem for most companies. Certain costs of filling small orders are often as high as those incurred for large ones. Yet, with few exceptions, firms find that for one reason or another, they must fill small orders to keep customers happy.

A company can go a long way toward solving this problem by analyzing the frequency and size of its small sales, its methods of distribution, and its costs for distribution in the affected areas.

Examine Frequency and Size of Orders

Keep records of the number and average size of small-order sales according to (a) customer, (b) product, (c) salesman, and (d) sales district. You'll know where small orders are most heavily concentrated. Comparing these areas with more favorable ones may reveal the reasons for such practices and suggest remedies to rectify the situation. The following is a proven technique: (1) A shift to a more dynamic salesman might be indicated. (2) The area might hold so little potential that it would pay to notify the few customers there that no further small orders would be filled. (3) A more economical method of transportation might be discovered and thus make small accounts profitable.

Checking Sales-Expense Ratios

Recording direct sales expenses for each salesman and district reveals the relation of these expenses to total dollar sales and hence relative efficiency of the sales effort. (A variation would be to add a prorated share of general sales administrative expense.) Many small orders usually produce a high ratio of expense to sales. Making salesmen aware of this can move them to drive for larger orders.

Using the Best Distribution Methods

The cost of some phase of distribution may be the prime factor in making your small orders unprofitable. Since distribution involves a number of steps, you should consider the following questions and how they should be settled:

- Is this the best way of doing it?
- Can it be done better or cheaper some other way?
- How will a change at any given point affect other operations and relations with customers?

The cost difference in distribution costs for large and small orders is reflected in the following survey made by the American Meat Institute some time ago.

Size of Order (lbs.)		Average Distribution Cost per cwt.
Over 500	....	$ 1.53
200 to 500	....	2.06
100 to 200	....	3.03
50 to 100	....	4.51
25 to 50	....	8.42
Under 25	....	19.05

A close look at your distribution setup can lead to a reduction in cost of handling small orders by (1) simplifying order-filling, invoicing, and collection practices; (2) changing package sizes; (3) improving warehouse facilities; and (4) establishing separate small-order departments.

A food manufacturer studies his costs of handling orders direct to independent retailers and institutional trade as compared with reaching them through distributors. Direct selling involves servicing many small orders and accounts. The result: it would be more profitable to make sales through distributors.

Analyzing Distribution Costs

You can't solve a small order problem until you determine the cost of filling the order and how these costs are divided among the various phases of distribution. If a complete analysis of distribution costs isn't feasible, rough cost measurements will go a long way in solving the small-order problem.

Trade associations occasionally prepare cost surveys on an industry-wide basis with comparative data that helps solve small-order problems.

How to Compute Order-Handling Costs

In analyzing small orders, most companies use an average of handling costs that is expressed in a single figure. This figure is a composite of (1) average order cost, (2) average cost of handling (or filling an order), (3) average billing cost, and (4) order cost per invoice (the same cost average may be called by different names). Unlike conventional accounting, this method allows items of expense to be identified, isolated, and evaluated.

To illustrate order-processing costs, here is a summary of order costs prepared by a chemical company:

Origin of Cost	Average Cost per Invoice
Order and stock function, city desk	$3.56
Shipping office (bills of lading, etc.)	0.11
Billing department	0.50
Mailing, postage, etc. of invoice and cash receipts	0.07
Storage and filing of invoice copies	0.07
Accounts receivable and credit records	0.29
Divisional order departments (stock orders and specialties)	0.79
Total	$5.39

Setting Prices that Vary with Order Size

Some companies use cost data to help them establish price differentials based on estimated savings that result from handling larger orders.

Here are some examples of quantity pricing determined by cost studies.

- An apparel company discovered that the extra expense of handling an order for less than one dozen items justified a 50¢ charge.
- A producer of abrasives found that, as order quantities increased beyond one ton, it achieved measurable savings mainly in selling costs. The company now places an eight to nine percent premium charge on orders below one ton.

Saving Money on Paperwork Costs

Operating on the theory that petty sales should be segregated and filed at minimum expense, one company has set up a system that involves only one clerk for all small order paperwork.

It has cut small-order paperwork costs to $1 per order, compared to a range in most other firms of $2 to $7. Here's how it works:

The small-order clerk types a snapout form that has (1) shipping labels, (2) a packing memo in duplicate, and (3) duplicate invoices. He sends all shipping labels and memos to a shipping clerk. When shipment is made, the duplicate shipping memo is returned to the small-order clerk. The small-order clerk sends out the invoice and files the duplicate *by date only.* No ledger cards are set up or entries made on existing ledgers.

When the order clerk receives payment for the sale, he removes the appropriate invoice from the unpaid (date) file and moves it to a "paid" file. Any overdue invoices are easily spotted since the duplicate copy remains in the unpaid (date) file until payment is received. If it isn't received, the clerk sends out a reminder. The only bookkeeping necessary is the entry of daily or weekly totals of sales and payments. The customer doesn't receive any monthly statements and the paperwork should come to less than $1 per order. The composite form can be varied to fit the particular methods used by your company.

Other Expense-Saving Ideas for Small Orders

Here is what a New Jersey company does to save costs on small orders:

1. It separates its small orders from larger ones on its conveyor belt system. Thus, there is no time lost in shipping since packers have only the right-size box at hand. Also, the uniformity reduces errors in mailing charges.
2. It groups like orders of the same item in bins. This allows use of single-size cartons, thus speeding the packers' work.
3. It uses envelopes for the address label with the invoice enclosed. This saves four cents in postage and eliminates a shipping label.
4. It reduces its credit-investigation charges by eliminating credit checks on sales below a given figure.

Beat Buying Costs with a Verbal Ordering System

You may be able to cut buying costs with a verbal ordering system on small orders. Here's how one company saved money:

The Tracerlab-Keleket division of Laboratory for Electronics, Inc. initiated verbal ordering to meet its small order demand. Buyers place orders for off-the-shelf items by telephone, and the suppliers fills out Tracerlab's combination purchase order-invoice as he takes the order. One form, filled out only one time, takes care of the paperwork requirements for both the supplier and Tracerlab. The purchase order form, which Tracerlab supplied to vendors, includes copies for purchasing, receiving, accounting, the requester, and the vendor.

According to Wendell H. Benway, Tracerlab's materials manager, verbal ordering has a twofold advantage: "The ability to place a lot of orders without wasting valuable time, and a quick reaction time on deliveries."

How Verbal Ordering Works

Here is the step-by-step procedure followed by Tracerlab and its suppliers under the verbal ordering system.

1. The Tracerlab buyer gets a request for an off-the-shelf item. He calls the supplier and places an order. He records the transaction in a log book for control, and sends the requisition to file.
2. The supplier fills out Tracerlab's purchase order-invoice form as he takes the order. He gets the purchase order control number, items wanted, quantity, price, and so on. If the buyer is unsure about the price, he can get it at the time he places the order.
   The supplier keeps his copy of the invoice and forwards the original plus any other copies to Tracerlab along with the order.
4. The Tracerlab receiving clerk signs the form and keeps his copy. He then distributes copies to purchasing, accounting, and the man who wanted the order.
5. The buyer reviews his copy for price discrepancies, then files it. If there is a pricing problem, the buyer is responsible for notifying accounts payable.

When Tracerlab sends a part out for servicing by a supplier, the purchase order-invoice again cuts paperwork. Used for such "outbound purchases," the form is handwritten by the originator and sent along with the part.

The company has also successfully incorporated the form into its blanket order purchasing contracts. When material covered under the blanket contract is needed, the man who wants it simply telephones the supplier himself, following the same procedure a buyer would follow. This not only cuts the paperwork, it saves the busy buyer's time.

See if the verbal ordering system would prove to be workable in your small order setup. Talk to your suppliers about the idea. According to materials manager Benway, suppliers "really like the system once they start using it." Point out to your suppliers that they'll profit from an increased volume of business, and they'll get your orders without the necessity of having a salesman call.

SAVING PURCHASING COSTS

The Defense Department is often an innovator in purchasing techniques, and when they innovate in areas of cost-cutting, it pays to observe their actions. The following are some case histories showing how the Defense Department slashes costs to the bone in five critical areas. Your obligation to yourself is to observe these areas and establish the applicability of these questions to your own operating considerations:

Buying Piecemeal or Complete?

Bids for supplying military sleeping bags were coming in at a very high price and when one concerned employee in the Defense Department tried to establish the reason for it, he found that sleeping bags were being made by two processes. One involved washing and chemically treating feathers and down used in the bags; the second called for sewing and filling the cloth shells.

Further checking disclosed that (1) most sewing firms were not set up for processing feathers and down, and (2) most feather companies had no experience in sewing shells. As a result, only those few firms able to perform both operations bid on the bags and their bids, consequently, were quite high. One of the solutions was that future contracts were divided into two parts— one for feather and down processing, the other for sewing and filling the shells. This *lowered* the price of a sleeping bag from $9.57 to $6.96. In two years, the Defense Personnel Support Center in Philadelphia saved $1.1 million on such purchases. The employee received a cash award for his suggestion, plus extensive writeups in Defense Department publications. The applicability to nondefense-oriented operations is simply to check to see if you are paying more than necessary for purchase materials that require prior processing. If you are getting your material from one supplier, the question must be raised whether you could buy it cheaper by dealing with several sources. On the other hand, if you're buying the material from several suppliers, would it be cheaper to use one supplier? The main point here is that no purchasing agreement should stay unchallenged for long. The purchasing agent must be constantly alert for better or cheaper sources of supply, or combinations of sources.

Replace Damaged Merchandise or Repair It?

Traditionally, damaged training rifle stocks at the San Diego Marine Corps Depot were thrown away and replaced with new ones. The replacement cost was $10.57 each. Operating in this manner, it had long been taken for granted as an unavoidable consequence of damage, even though it was a high-priced arrangement. Using available shop facilities, a Marine sergeant came up with a simple method for repairing the stock with fiberglass putty. The outcome was that rifle stocks which were almost as good as new were produced at a cost of only 34¢ each. In just a three-month period, this cost-cutting step saved the Marine Corps almost $15 thousand.

The key to savings achievement like this is to know the costs in precise detail. Any company today cannot afford to be fuzzy about costs when the decision has to be made as to whether to repair or replace, to make or buy, or to lease or buy, etc. Having a good cost accounting system and a knowledgeable cost accounting group can help you make the right choice between alternatives.

Materials Handling: Complete Units—Or Subassemblies

A civilian employee of the Air Force in Texas has found a way to give the U.S. missile program a lot more value for its shipping dollars. A number of missile re-entry vehicles were being shipped to a factory for alterations. The cost of each container used in shipping the vehicle was $2,000. The cost was apparently justified by the big job the container had to do. It had to protect a complete, bulky, re-entry vehicle—including its easy-to-scratch nose cone. But on checking, the alert employee found that not all of the vehicle had to be shipped. It was necessary to send only the part which required modification. And this, he learned, did not include the delicate nose cone. Even a simple piece of observation such as this has resulted in large savings. The employee designed a lighter container that had definite advantages. It cost only $55.00. The result was the elimination of $50,000 in costs on twenty-six containers. The lighter container plus the part to be altered weighed 700 pounds compared to 2,500 pounds for the old package. As a result, the 1,800-pound weight reduction led to a shipping charge cut of an additional $14,000. The total savings, a result of the increased efficiency and the change in containers, was over $65,000.

The object lesson for today's companies is that one must not just hunt for cheaper ways of doing the same job. One must satisfy himself whether the nature of the job itself can be changed so that better results can be achieved at lower costs.

Savings Specifications

Working together, engineers of the Red River Army Depot in Texas have come up with a way to slice nearly two-thirds off the yearly cost of cleaning Army tanks. For several years the Red River Depot had been spending some $88,000 annually on iron grit, using the "shot-blast" method of cleaning tanks. Iron grit was chosen over steel grit for this job because it was about one-third cheaper. The trouble was, for a long while no one had tried to figure out how the two materials compared as to quantities required for the tank cleaning job. When engineers at the Depot turned their attention to the problem, they learned that steel grit would actually be more economical. It was discovered that "shot-blasting" used up iron grit almost five times as fast as it used up steel grit. This canceled out the price advantage of iron grit. After that, the Depot began to use steel grit exclusively at an annual savings of some $57,000.

The object lesson here is to measure out what you pay for everything in your company budget against what you can realistically expect to get in return. This is no different than the traditional financial measure for efficiency, called return on investment. Just as in this case, false economy could be costing you thousands of dollars a year—in overtime caused by equipment break-downs and lost business due to a poor location, or in low grade performance by incompetent or underpaid employees. For example, if you buy most things at twenty-five percent less than the going rate, make sure you don't get forty or fifty percent less in value.

Production Economy

When you're buying a lot of socks—or anything else—a production economy that looks tiny can lead to a huge reduction in the price you pay. Socks are a major item of clothing purchased by the military. As part of an overall cost-cutting program, experts looked into the methods that suppliers were using to manufacture socks. They discovered that one operation, closing the toes of the socks, was being done with an unnecessarily-complex looping operation by a knitting machine.

Having checked into nonmilitary sock production methods, the Defense Department men knew the toe-closing could be done in a simpler way—with a sewing machine. They asked their suppliers to make this change. As a result, the price of each pair of military socks came down by 1¼¢. On a recent overall purchase of more than ten million pairs, the total savings amounted to over $127 thousand. The object lesson here is to look behind the high prices you're paying for merchandise. Make sure your suppliers aren't guilty of "gold-plating"—giving you more than you need in either materials or processing, deliberately or otherwise. Be sure that you own operations aren't set up to give unnecessary extras. Other techniques aside from Defense Depart-ment considerations are also available which can cut purchasing costs and achieve large dollar savings. For example, with one change in your purchasing methods you can:

1. Get substantial price discounts on purchases
2. Slash paperwork costs
3. Conserve cash
4. Do it without increasing inventories or adding storage space

The technique which can be used is known as a blanket order. A blanket order is a contract for a large quantity of a given item—for long-term needs—at discount prices. The way in which it is used is to first estimate all needs for a particular item a year in advance. Once this has been done, an arrangement is made with a supplier. An agreement then follows which will commit the purchaser to buy the entire amount from the supplier. The advantage of this type of method is that the order is treated as a single purchase—qualifying it for a huge quantity discount.

In using this technique, you must specify in your order that the supplies are to be delivered to you *when and as you need them*. You may agree to have a specific amount delivered every week, month, or what have you. Or, you may prefer to set it up so that you get the delivery only after you call in for a certain amount. Instead of making out purchase orders every week or every month, one purchase order is prepared. This again is another vehicle for cost savings. In order to get the quantity discount, you do not have to pay for the entire new supply at once. Normally, blanket order contracts run for one year and provide for monthly billings. In some cases the supplier will even agree to bill only as the amounts are actually shipped. Either way, you don't have to put out a large amount of cash at one time.

Lastly, a unique cost reduction device which affects purchasing policy was placed into effect by a number of parts distributors in the Nashville, Tennessee area. They pooled orders from the factory. Shipments are made in carload lots. When a shipment arrives, the car is placed by the railroad at one warehouse, and the other firms send over crews with trucks to unload their shares. The results of this type of cooperative effort are savings amounting from the big difference between full carload shipping rates and less-than-carload shipping costs. Together with quantity discount savings, these more than offset added paperwork costs.

HOW TO CUT SHIPPING COSTS ON INCOMING FREIGHT

You can put a big dent in your company's incoming freight bills with an easy one-step cost-cutter: *you* select the routes and carriers for goods being shipped to your company.

How you save: Your suppliers are mainly concerned with getting your order out of the plant and on the road. So they're not always on the lookout for the best and least expensive way to ship your order. You can eliminate this profit drain by preselecting the most economical delivery routes and carriers.

Electronics Communications, Inc., of St. Petersburg, Florida, increased operating efficiency, and cut incoming freight bills by more than twelve percent. Here's how: on each purchase order calling for delivery of goods, ECI gives the supplier specific instructions. It spells out preselected shipping methods and routes. After the goods are delivered, ECI pays for the shipping charges covered on the purchase order—and not a cent more.

Tips on Operating Company Trucks

If you have found that operating your own trucks is more economical in many cases than using outside carriers (or if you need trucks in other phases of your business), you should take the next step and make sure that you are operating your trucks in the most economical way.

Here's a quick checklist. The questions are paraphrased from a pamphlet issued by the truck and coach division of General Motors Corporation, but have equal application to whatever make of truck you operate.

Yes	*No*	
———	———	Have we selected equipment which, though nominally more expensive, will operate economically over a longer period?
———	———	Have we specified an axle that, if necessary, can be altered without excessive expense?
———	———	Do clutches have sufficient capacity for long life with low maintenance?
———	———	Do transmissions have enough reduction in low gear for good grade ability so they won't shorten the life of drive-train parts?
———	———	Do we use larger than standard brakes for operations in heavy traffic or hilly terrain?
———	———	Do we get bulk rates by purchasing fuel at a central point?

Use Water Transportation to Save Costs

You can save from ten percent to more than fifty percent on transportation costs if you ship or receive goods on inland or intracoastal waterways. *Bonus feature:* besides cutting costs, water transport opens up brand-new profit opportunities. Markets that were uneconomical because of high shipping costs are becoming giant new profit areas for many smaller companies.

The inland and intracoastal system is a giant waterways network that includes vast sections of the United States and Canada. Of course, the waterways are a practical and low-cost means only when speed of delivery is not essential, but many companies overcome this problem by shipping far enough in advance of delivery dates. At the same time, many buyers specify that incoming orders must be shipped by water transport whenever possible.

For information on just how to get these savings, write to: American Waterways Operators Inc., 1250 Connecticut Ave., Washington, D. C.

Reducing Your Packaging Costs

You can cut down on your packaging costs by taking advantage of new techniques—and making inventive adaptations of old ones.

Here are some case histories:

1. *Why use a pail when a box will do?* A Chicago firm had always shipped its chocolate drink base to commercial users in specially coated steel pails. The pails protected the contents, a liquid, but had several cost disadvantages: steel costs kept rising, expensive washing and sterilizing facilities were needed, shipping rates were high, and the round shape wasted space.

A major canmaker supplied the company with an alternative: a 275-pound test corrugated container fitted with a presterilized polyethylene bag liner capable of holding sixty pounds. The new containers were shipped flat. The bag lines were shipped separately and glued into the inside of the box just before shipping. Only minor changes were needed to adapt the pail-filling equipment to the new containers.

Immediate cost savings of five to ten percent were realized. Furthermore, the knocked-down cartons were easier to store, and when filled took up less than seventy percent of the floor space. In addition, a testing laboratory determined that the filled containers could be stacked eight high without stress. There was some customer resistance to the change, which was easily overcome —the company passed the savings on to the customer.

The corrugated-polyethylene combination is no longer a new idea in liquid packaging, but it may be a cost-cutting approach to your products.

2. *Old material—new use.* A medium-sized East Coast firm, which boasts a modern, conveyor-equipped shipping unit, cut its material-protection costs by putting another type of material to a new use. On the suggestion of a packaging consultant, it replaced expensive honeycomb wadding with "egg flats"—the same papier-mâché-type separators used in bulk packaging of fresh eggs! The company found that this material offered full protection to its product, besides being lighter in weight, flexible, and easy to stock and store. In addition, it was much less expensive.

3. *Do not overprotect.* The shipping department was packing small, light-weight, sturdy articles in 275-pound test double-walled corrugated boxes. The practice stopped when a supervisor pointed out that the job could be equally well done with 175-pounders. The change eliminated a double loss—about twenty percent of the containers' cost, plus unnecessarily high carrier charges. Evaluate all practices (even the simplest) in your shipping room. Flexibility in changing rules, exercising originality, and learning from the experience of other firms can make a big difference in your profits.

Special Approaches

Two techiques—multi-pack cartons and plastic packaging—may lower your shipping costs, give better product protection, and improve customer service.

1. *Multi-pack cartons*. If your headache is filling less-than-case orders, developments in multi-pack cartons can help. The new cartons are designed so that the full case can be snapped apart into smaller lots merely by breaking along a perforated line. The smaller lots are ready for shipment, and require no additional gluing or taping. Users report savings of up to fifty percent in reduction of handling time and elimination of the need to stock a wide variety of carton sizes.

For example, a Louisiana company reports substantial savings since it adopted a divisible shipping container for its line of Tabasco pepper sauce. The divisible container is actually three units in one: it consists of two one-dozen bottle cartons packed inside a printed outer carton, with a perforated line dividing it in half. The construction satisfied the company's desire to encourage the purchase of the two-dozen orders. All that has to be done to get at the two "ready-to-go" packages is to cut along the dotted line.

2. *Plastic packaging*. You may be able to cut down on the volume of commodities damaged in shipment through the use of plastic protection. International Business Machines reduced its overall packaging expense by thirty percent in this way.

IBM had been shipping its colored electric typewriters in heavily-padded corrugated boxes. The bulky padding required the use of cartons much larger than would ordinarily have been needed. In order to eliminate the bulk, and improve the protective qualities of its containers, IBM turned to a die-cut box liner coated with polyethylene. The liner is bolted to a fibre pad in the bottom of the shipping container. The plastic coating protects the typewriters' color finish from abrasion—and permits IBM to use a carton half the original size. In addition, the compact carton has forty percent more stacking strength.

For details on this type of product protection, contact the Mengel Co., Corrugated Box Division, Louisville, Ky. If you're now using bulky padding and oversized containers to cradle your delicate products, start thinking about a suitable cost-saving substitute. Or, if your shipments are now so well packed that there never is any product damage, it's possible that you're spending too much on packaging quality. Try for the best balance—minimum damage and lowest packaging costs.

Packaging Plus

You can cash in on a growing trend. More and more suppliers are building *extra functions* into the packages they use for their products; look for them in your purchases. A lighting supplier offers fluorescent lamps in a carton with a top that lifts off. This top becomes a handy disposal unit for replaced bulbs. One maintenance contractor from South Bend, Indiana, reports that the package cuts bulk replacement time so much that many customers can't afford to refuse his services.

That's what Garton Toy Company does at its plant in Sheboygan, Wisconsin. The company uses waste bread-wrapping material bought nearby. This material's nonabrasive surface, plus its water-barrier properties, makes it ideal for wrapping metal parts. It's also excellent as a filler inside the package.